WITNESS TO WAR AND PEACE
Egypt, the October War, and Beyond

AHMED ABOUL GHEIT

The American University in Cairo Press
Cairo New York

This edition published in 2018 by
The American University in Cairo Press
113 Sharia Kasr el Aini, Cairo, Egypt
200 Park Ave., Suite 1700
New York, NY 10166

www.aucpress.com

Copyright © 2013 by Nahdet Misr Publishing House
First published in Arabic in 2013 by Nahdet Misr Publishing House as *Shahadati 'ala al-harb wa-l-salam*

English translation copyright ©2018 by the American University in Cairo Press

Translated by Sarah Enany

English translation supported by the Arab League Educational, Cultural and Scientific Organization (ALECSO)

Dar el Kutub No. 27482/17
ISBN 978 977 416 885 7

Dar el Kutub Cataloging-in-Publication Data

Aboul Gheit, Ahmed
        Witness to War and Peace / Ahmed Aboul Gheit.—Cairo: The American University in Cairo Press, 2018.
                p.   cm.
                ISBN 978 977 416 885 7
                1. Aboul Gheit, Ahmed
                2. Politicians
                3. Egypt—Politics and Government
                923.3

1 2 3 4 5   22 21 20 19 18

Designed by Amy Sidhom
Printed in the United States of America

CONTENTS

To the memory of my father the pilot, Major-General Ali Ahmed Aboul Gheit, who said, "My son will be foreign minister," when I was still a young man.

To my mother, Fatima Mohamed al-Messiri, who took good care of me.

To my wife and lifelong companion, Leila Kamal al-Din Salah, who stood staunchly by me in all my many struggles.

To my sons, Kamal and Ali. How sweet it is to have loving and loyal sons.

To all those under whose leadership I have worked and whose advice I have taken.

To all those who have worked with me over the years, with mutual affection and a shared passion for our country, for which we have always been willing to give our all.

Thank you.

The arrogance of power . . . deluded some of us . . . [in]to the belief that they were capable of not only writing history but also rewriting it to alter its facts and ignore its lessons.

—From Ambassador Ahmed Aboul Gheit's statement before the Fifty-Ninth Session of the United Nations General Assembly, September 24, 2004, describing Israel's positions throughout its wars and negotiations with the Arabs

FOREWORD
to the English Edition

Francis J. Ricciardone
President, The American University in Cairo

Ahmed Aboul Gheit is one of the last of the living giants of Egyptian statecraft whose lives have spanned the end of the Egyptian monarchy, the establishment of the modern Republic of Egypt through successive revolutions and elections, the establishment of the State of Israel, and the several wars and still unfolding story of the complex peace between those two modern states and their neighbors. During this period, modern successor states to the Ottoman Empire, from North Africa through the Gulf, have arisen, and some have collapsed. In several cases, most notably that of the Palestinians, people of former Ottoman lands continue to struggle to establish fully independent states or, in the case of the Kurds, more or less autonomous sub-state polities. The dynamics between Egypt and Israel have always proven pivotal and central to the fate of the entire region. The future of Palestine, in particular, certainly hangs in that balance.

The great modern drama of state genesis and failure across MENA has engendered rich scholarly documentation and study, particularly in English. Yet, firsthand memoirs by leading Egyptian players are scarce, even in Arabic. Hence, much of even the most insightful analysis of Egyptian decision-making through Egypt's succession of modern wars and crises amounts to commentary by keen observers at some distance in time and space from the Egyptian figures themselves. The past great leaders in modern Egyptian–Israeli–Palestinian and broader Arab affairs—Presidents Nasser, Sadat, and Mubarak—regrettably have left scholars no published memoirs comparable to the records published by their Israeli or American counterparts and their senior diplomatic and military advisors.

As Aboul Gheit has pointed out, other influential statesmen of the inner decision-making circle around Presidents Sadat and Mubarak, such as Osama al-Baz and Ahmed Maher al-Sayed, have each passed away without having recorded their testimonies of this dramatic period in global affairs. Such historical personal diaries or archival official documentation as the presidents and their senior advisors may have generated are not readily available even to the most reputable private scholars, as a matter of Egyptian state policy. Aboul Gheit cites the absence of published memoirs as what compelled him to record his own direct observations.

Hence, Ahmed Aboul Gheit's *Witness to War and Peace* would be of unusual importance to Arab and international scholars if only for the scarcity of other documentation, especially as published in English, by Egyptian participants in, and witnesses to, leadership decision-making in the era of war and peace, and in the genesis and failure of post-Ottoman and other foreign imperial-era states and aspirant states. But his work also stands out for its candor and authenticity, based on contemporary personal notes recording his own thinking and reactions to major historical developments.

Aboul Gheit's record of the personalities and thinking of Egypt's top decision makers in times of crisis is fascinating for its intimacy and contemporaneity. These influential figures are too little known even to the rising generation of Egyptians, much less to foreigners. But of equally compelling value to the student of modern Egyptian and regional history is Aboul Gheit's presentation of his own personality and analytical outlooks as a proudly Egyptian nationalist and statesman.

I was a young American student of foreign and regional affairs, and a very junior American diplomat, during most of the period that Aboul Gheit chronicles in *Witness to War and Peace*. Only later, as I returned to Cairo in 2005 as the U.S. ambassador, did I have the good fortune to meet and work closely with Aboul Gheit, by then several years into what later would extend to a seven-year tenure as foreign minister of Egypt. The rare privilege of observing how his deep erudition and patriotism shaped his dealings with foreign counterparts, particularly of my own country, proved profoundly illuminating.

Aboul Gheit's lifetime of continuing national service is as exceptional for its distinction as for its length—yet it authentically represents the characteristic Egyptian traits of deep faith, perspicacity, tenacity, and resilience. His close accounts certainly offer important insights for the rising generation of Egyptians and others who can access Aboul Gheit's original Arabic editions. But those insights will be of particular value to foreign diplomats, business people, scientists, and scholars, who recognize the importance of deep understanding of this unique, pivotally important, and complex country, as the fundamental requirement for successful engagement with it in any sphere of endeavor. In the service of that high purpose, the American University in Cairo Press is proud to make Ahmed Aboul Gheit's *Witness to War and Peace* available to a wider global readership through this English edition.

FOREWORD
to the Arabic Edition

Ambassador Mohamed Assem Ibrahim
Former Egyptian ambassador to Ethiopia, Kenya, Sudan, and Israel

Dear Reader,
It is a great honor to introduce you to this book, a true achievement. In writing this, I have a threefold responsibility: to the reader, to this profound and multidimensional book, and finally, to the author, a lifelong friend.

I shall start with the author. For seven years, we knew him as the foreign minister of Egypt. Preceding this were four decades of loyal service to the diplomatic corps, a steady rise through the ranks culminating in his position as the most senior ambassador and Egypt's permanent representative to the United Nations.

I met Ahmed Aboul Gheit more than half a century ago. We started secondary school together, and met regularly at the Armed Forces Officers' Club—our fathers were both officers, his in the air force and mine in the artillery corps. We shared a passion for public affairs that started in 1958. Like all of our generation in that tumultuous era, which started with the 1952 revolution, then witnessed the British withdrawal, the nationalization of the Suez Canal, followed by the Tripartite Aggression in 1956, the union with Syria, and other events that are common knowledge, we dreamed of a new dawn for Egypt's role in the world, a date, as the phrase goes, with destiny.

Ahmed Aboul Gheit was, and still is, passionate in his love for his country, confident in his abilities and in the iron will of the Egyptian people, strong as the granite out of which the statues of Ancient Egypt are carved, still standing today in the central squares of the world's greatest cities. He bears an unconcealed enthusiasm for history and riparian civilizations in

Egypt, Iraq, and China. It was Aboul Gheit who first introduced me to his-torian Arnold Toynbee, when we were no older than fifteen. We spoke of Ancient Greece, and the struggle between warlike Sparta and civilian-spir-ited Athens, and how Athens finally won a decisive victory over Sparta, even though the latter had emerged victorious in the Peloponnesian War. We spoke of the mechanisms of the rise, decline, and fall of empires, and the cycles of Egyptian history over four thousand years; we discussed the-ories of war, and the great military philosophers; we spoke of battles that changed the course of history and the reasons for them, how they were managed, and their ultimate outcomes and consequences, how peoples and armies related to the leaders of thought and literature, and the role of leadership abilities, especially in crisis.

Ever since I have known him, Ahmed Aboul Gheit has been an early riser, often before five in the morning. Never one for late nights, he is also the first to leave our company for bed. I doubt that he has ever worked less than twelve hours a day, and very frequently longer. Above all, he is loyal: to his family, to his friends, and first and foremost to his country. He has made no secret of his ambition. In every position he has held, he has been a whirlwind of intelligent activity, hard to keep up with in both quantity and quality. It was only natural that he be assigned the most important of posts. When stationed in Cairo, he was needed at the Foreign Ministry, at the office of the national security advisor, on the prime minister's staff, and even became assistant to the minister for office affairs twice in succession. In New York, he served three tours of duty, in addition to Moscow and Cyprus. He was ambassador to Rome and head of the Egyptian diplomatic mission to New York.

Step into his house and you will be overwhelmed by the sheer number of encyclopedias and reference books. He has conversed with the cultural elite in Cairo and in the world capitals where he has worked, and amassed an incomprehensibly vast number of friends and acquaintances, with an exceptional memory for detail whenever he meets any of them again.

During his university years, he was greatly influenced, in my esti-mation, by the writings of Winston Churchill. He has left no biography or memoir unread: Mao Tse-Tung, Gandhi, Lenin, Ataturk, even Hitler, Mussolini, and Stalin, and all the Second World War Allied leaders. These rivers have all flowed into Aboul Gheit's personality, which has matured with time and experience. One of our conversations that has remained etched into my memory is when President Nasser decided, in May 1967, to close the Gulf of Aqaba to Israeli maritime traffic. "I'm afraid," he said to me, "of Israel launching a raid and invading Sharm al-Sheikh before we can fully mobilize in Sinai. They'll want to secure their shipping routes to Eilat," which President Nasser had effectively closed with his blockage of Aqaba.

"If there is a confrontation between the two armies," I replied, "I'm very much afraid it will be 1956 all over again."

And so it was. Neither of us was yet older than twenty-three.

A full year before he left the Foreign Ministry, Aboul Gheit began to think of compiling his copious notes and diaries as a contribution to our national memory, a gift to the generation about to assume responsibility in the near future. He was aware that a great deal of our history, both in Egypt and in the Arab World, is being written by others. Our own views of history, our archives and record-keeping, our laws on declassification of documents, and so forth, are woefully inadequate for any state in this century. I need only mention the fiasco that occurred when we were trying to find the international treaty demarcating Egypt's borders with Palestine. We simply could not locate the thing in our files, and were reduced to getting copies from Turkey and the United Kingdom in order to refute Israel's (invalid) claim to Taba. The original copy *was* in Cairo, that much we knew; our filing system was just so outdated and unworkable that it was impossible to find.

For these reasons, and more, Aboul Gheit has decided to put pen to paper, giving today's and tomorrow's readers access to his information and eyewitness accounts. This may help bring the Egyptian point of view into the picture.

I have some observations on the book you are holding, having had the opportunity to read it before publication. The author has chosen the title, *Witness to War and Peace*; however, I believe that he was not only a witness but also an active participant, as you may note in the coming pages, over four successive eras: first, the period from the June defeat to the decision to engage in large-scale military action; second, the time of armed conflict; third, the interventions during the ceasefire between the end of war and the commencement of peace; and finally, the peace process.

The book is entertaining, although it is documentary in nature. Aboul Gheit's style is lucid and his phrases well-turned, although never too informal. This is a book that is hard to put down. It unpacks weighty secrets with literary flair and a human touch, revealing the untold story of the saga of war and peace.

Most important, Aboul Gheit has meticulously documented his experiences. He has transcribed speeches and copied documents; he has noted the names, dates, and locations of every action, with exemplary objectivity and neutrality. This professionalism stems, no doubt, from his previous readings of the greats.

One thing that is almost unique about Aboul Gheit among his peers is this: he does not pretend to know what he does not know. He has only documented what he has personally taken part in or witnessed firsthand. He has claimed far less credit for himself than is actually his due. He also affords the reader every opportunity to differ with his conclusions, as evidenced by his clear demarcation between documentary evidence and his own (or indeed others') personal opinion.

You may also notice that he tends to look at the big picture—not the star but the constellation. He analyzes Egypt not in a vacuum, but in relation to its position on the wider world stage. This by no means indicates any inattention to specifics. In other segments, when he analyzes the behavior of leaders in times of political and military crisis, or in the segment on relations with the Palestine Liberation Organization (PLO) and its gradual introduction to, and acceptance into, the world political arena, he goes into minute, almost microscopic, detail.

This may be one of the most neutral and unbiased books originally written in Arabic in its description and analysis of events, even taking into account the sometimes conflicting human emotions and reactions that accompanied them. There are two main paths in the book: first, the conviction that the process of war and peace finally led, despite all the issues and criticisms, to banishing the defeat of 1967 from Egyptians' hearts and minds. The second is his unwavering love for anything and everything related to the nation of Egypt: its people, its armed forces, and its diplomatic corps, which he highly appreciates, knowing the acumen of its leaders.

This is a central reference for any student of this period of our contemporary history. I promise you hours of edification and entertainment.

INTRODUCTION

The idea for this book was born on October 6, 2009. On that day, I wrote an article for Egypt's premier national newspaper, *al-Ahram*: it was a character study of the Egyptian national security advisor during the October War, and my personal experience of him over two years from August 1972 to February 1974. During that period, I witnessed firsthand the Egyptian national security apparatus' preparations for the war, to reclaim Egypt's honor and pride after our defeat in June 1967. Directly the article, titled "24 Sa'a jasima fi hayati ma' Mohamed Hafiz Ismail" (24 Decisive Hours in My Life with Mohamed Hafiz Ismail), was published, I received a great many encouraging comments. Many people asked me to write more about this period, a watershed in Egypt's military and political history, as, they said, we desperately need more genuine and serious documentary sources covering this critical and historic time in Egypt's national efforts.

Gradually, I acceded to their requests. I wrote more pieces on the October War and my personal experiences with the office of the national security advisor. This continued from October 2009 to October 2010. The articles, twelve in total, together formed a series entitled, "Witness to War." Their publication elicited surprise from readers. How, they asked, could a sitting foreign minister, with all the weighty responsibilities of this challenging and critical period in Egyptian history, find the time to write all these articles, including the minute details of the 1973 military conflict that he set down at the time?

It became clear that a great many people felt that these articles constituted a useful addition to histories of our armed conflict with Israel.

1

In October 2010, while still foreign minister, I began to realize the importance of writing down my eyewitness accounts of the stages of Egyptian history that spanned the October War and its aftermath.

Two factors encouraged this endeavor and compelled me to write things down for posterity. The first was the declining health of Dr. Osama al-Baz, political advisor to the Egyptian president for more than thirty years. His memory was failing and the chance had been lost for him to document his long experience with the Palestinian struggle, the Palestinian–Israeli settlement, and the Arab–Israeli conflict. The second factor, of equal importance, was the sudden death of Minister Ahmed Maher al-Sayed in September 2010. His death was a shock to us all. His friends and acquaintances had similarly wanted him to write about his experiences with the Arab–Israeli issue, especially during his tenure with National Security Advisor Hafiz Ismail during the October War, and with Egyptian Foreign Minister Mohamed Ibrahim Kamel in the period from Sadat's historic visit to Jerusalem in November 1977 to the Camp David Summit in September 1978 and Minister Kamel's resignation. During this period, Ahmed Maher did a great deal and had profound influence. We had always thought that he would write his memoirs, submitting his vast wealth of experience for publication. But this did not occur, for reasons I never fully knew. It was a great loss not only for Egypt but also for our diplomatic history. For my part, I had tried over and over to urge and encourage Osama al-Baz and Ahmed Maher al-Sayed to "write, write, set it down!" The first was struck by an illness that destroyed his memory, while the second left it till too late. We shall all strut and fret our hour upon the stage, and then be heard no more. Therefore, I have decided to write while I still can, work and duties notwithstanding. I have written what I can. There may not be time in the future, so here are my testimonies of important, even critical, moments in the history of Egyptian diplomacy.

In the final months of 2010, I wrote eight more articles, entitled "Witness to Peace," also published in *al-Ahram*. When I left my ministerial post on March 6, 2011, I decided to write about more of my experiences in the period starting with 1967 to my appointment as foreign minister on July 11, 2004, when I succeeded my dear friend and staunch supporter Ahmed Maher al-Sayed. This book covers and evaluates all the events I witnessed personally starting with June 5, 1967, through the October War and the extended peace process that started with President Sadat's visit to Jerusalem, and throughout the years that followed.

The Palestinians have suffered a great tragedy. The Arab and Islamic peoples and governments have stood with them in a strong show of support, yet all the Palestinian and Arab efforts have ended in failure. Many have used the Palestinians, and many have exploited the Palestinian cause, to achieve their own narrow ends. Egypt has worked consistently toward achieving their liberation, despite all the difficulties and divisions among Arabs and Palestinians, the criticisms and squabbles. Some in the Arab world, and indeed in Egypt, felt that we needed to press on with the October War until the Palestinian goal was realized, namely reclaiming every inch of their homeland intact. They ignored the inequitable balance of power between the Arabs (including Palestinians) and Israel, and assumed that the western world and the United States would just leave Israel at the mercy of what they viewed as Arab and Islamic aggressors. They pretended that the Arabs were capable of coming together and mobilizing their forces against the west and Israel during that period of western advancement and Arab backwardness.

Egypt's decisions from June 9, 1967, until today have been aimed at getting rid of the fallout from Israel's act of aggression and the Arabs' defeat, followed by building a suitable modality that allows the Palestinians to establish a Palestinian state on what remains of Mandatory Palestine, the principle being two states on Palestine's land, one Israeli and the other Palestinian. Egypt has achieved some successes, and encountered some setbacks. It still embraces and assists this just cause, in the face of occasional absurdities and blackmail.

The reader will note that the first chapter of the book covers what I call the silent and secret war between Egypt and Israel. In it, I present my personal experiences, which I feel are important to set down, not only in memory of a member of Egyptian Intelligence who worked tirelessly for years against Israel, but also to underscore the great efforts of this Egyptian national apparatus from its inception in 1957 to the present.

Mention of my personal experience in this field, while extremely limited and not to be compared with that of actual Egyptian Intelligence agents, may help the reader understand the dimensions of the conflict. It was not only a military effort, nor a diplomatic challenge. Egyptian Intelligence has made remarkable efforts to supply Egypt with the information it needs to succeed in its confrontation with Israel.

I now return to the defeat of 1967, to say this: it was a profound and shattering blow to every Egyptian of that generation, and it sorely intimidated anyone in a position of responsibility or on the way to assuming one. I speak of those Egyptians born in Egypt between 1914 and the start of the Second World War, who lived through the Second World War—the generation, in other words, who were between twenty-two and fifty-three years of age in 1967, the most influential and productive age group in any nation. This crushing blow intimidated that generation, but it did not break them. They stood firm, and struck back. For a long period, they prepared their counterstrike. I know, for I was one of them.

In June 1967, I was twenty-five years old. I was already an aficionado of war, military life, and strategy. I had been living in the Royal Egyptian Air Force Base (renamed the Egyptian Air Force Base after the 1952 revolution and the union of Egypt and Syria) since before 1952, closely following the work of my father, the pilot Ali Ahmed Aboul Gheit, throughout my formative years. I followed the battles of 1948–49 with a great deal of confusion and incomprehension. My father was away every day, and came home very late at night. My mother was always worried. Every night, when he came in to kiss me goodnight, I would ask, "Where do you go every day? What do you do?" He would reply, "I was bombing the enemy." When I went outside to play with the other pilots' children, it was only natural that we played war and "air raid." This was how I first learned about enemies and war.

I would listen with great attention to my father's chats with his fellow pilots. I recall many of their names even today. I also began to learn the types of aircraft then in use in the Egyptian air force—fighters, bombers, and U.S.-made Dakota and Commando transports, tweaked by Egyptian technicians for use in bombing enemy airfields and installations. We called them "the colonies" in those days. Later, over the decades, they came to be called "the settlements." I also learned the names of our military airfields—Almaza, Cairo West, Anshas, and Bilbeis—upon which the Egyptian air force depended.

The 1948–49 wars were a tragedy for the Egyptian army. They were sent into battle unprepared, without any conception of the abilities of the Zionist gangs supported not only by the west but also by the Soviet Union, along with the rest of the Eastern European countries that were completely subservient to the Soviets' will. No one in Egypt after 1949 realized that Israel was on the verge of seizing the cities of Rafah and Arish toward the end of the conflict. We should have known about Israel's burgeoning capacities.

I have read extensively about this war. I have also attempted to study the conflict in Sinai when the Turkish-Ottoman army conducted a raid on the Suez Canal and attempted to invade it in 1915, as well as Lord Allenby's campaign in which he invaded Palestine and Syria in 1917. The Egyptian army's movements in the 1948 campaign lacked a strategic vision and ignored the lessons of then-recent history, namely the First World War, or indeed of ancient history, namely the Egyptian army's battles in the Mamluk era and all the way back to Ancient Egypt. Egypt's military

leaders were blind to the pivotal importance of the city of Bi'r al-Sab',
currently Beersheba, which was in fact the key to the entire Egyptian
campaign. Egypt paid the price not only for a feeble strategy, but also for
many other reasons known to experts, about which much has been written and which are outside the scope of this book.

For all that, I would like to relate a brief anecdote that reflects just
how little we knew about the details of this war. In 1958, I heard my father
tell a story about the pilots at Almaza Airfield just a few days before the
Zionist state was declared on May 14, 1948. Some of them proposed an
air raid the moment Israel's statehood was announced, to bomb the Jewish
Agency in Tel Aviv and destroy the Israeli project in one fell swoop, not
to mention Ben Gurion and his men. Some of these pilots, enthusiastic
young Egyptians, took to searching for a detailed map of the city in hopes
of pinpointing the Agency headquarters to facilitate the attack—imma-
ture to say the least, not to mention unrealistic.

The next attempt to engage with Israel militarily came in 1956, when
I was fourteen. Both Egypt and Israel had by then expanded their military
capacity considerably. There were now MiG-15s and 17s in the Egyptian
arsenal, replacing the UK-made Second World War Hurricanes and
Spitfires and American P-51s. The British Vampires and Gloster Meteors,
though, had not been retired from active duty. The Ilyushin Il-28 and
English Electric Canberra bomber aircraft had replaced the 1940s-gener-
ation Lancaster and Halifax Sterling aircraft that my father flew. We also
had a very limited number of Flying Fortress B-17s. This was the entire
arsenal of the new Egyptian air force in 1956. On the Israeli side, there
was an array of Dassault aircraft: the French-made Ouragan, the Dassault
Mystère, and the Dassault Super Mystère. France had begun supplying
weapons to Israel to repay Egypt for Cairo's support of the revolution in
Algiers.

Israel was a close observer of the Soviet arms deal with Egypt in
1955–56, and Egypt's rapprochement with the Soviet bloc to obtain
weapons. What is certain is that Israel, and the western powers behind
it, decided to stand against Egypt and abort this burgeoning relationship
between Cairo and the capitals of the Eastern bloc, in addition to those of
the Warsaw Pact. When Egypt regained the Suez Canal via nationalization in 1956, Israel seized its chance. The battle of 1956 was an excellent
opportunity for the United States to inherit the spoils left by the aging
empires of Britain and France.

My father was at the time second in command of the Egyptian Eastern
Air Command in the Suez Canal. His living quarters were the Galaa
camp in Ismailiya, from where he traveled regularly to our home near the

Heliopolis Airport, and where we spent long months between furloughs. With the start of Israel's aggression against Egypt, fully coordinated with France and Britain, on October 28, 1956—I see no need to go into details which others have covered and the reader knows well—I saw my father telling his comrades in the air force, who had attended extensive training sessions at the Royal Air Force College in Andover (where I accompanied him in 1955–56), "It is extremely important to prepare for what Britain may do immediately after the implementation of the joint British–French warning to cease warfare between Egypt and Israel, and for both parties to move ten kilometers away from the canal to the east and west of the waterway. This will place the canal under the de facto control of the two colonial powers, England and France."

The Egyptian Air Force Command, as I understood later from my father, was working independently of the rest of the army in Sinai. We tried to avoid this lack of coordination when the Israelis next struck in 1967. In any case, Egypt's efforts at the time were concentrated on protecting the air force from the strikes it would inevitably sustain with the start of Britain's military action against Egypt. My father, just a few months back from a year of study in Britain, had an understanding of how the British would conduct aerial operations in such conflicts. The Royal Air Force would first focus on enemy airfields, air bases, and installations by conducting night raids and high-altitude bombardments aimed at crippling the opponent's abilities and closing their airfields, concentrating on the runways. At dawn, it would commence with attacks on aircraft on the ground, which would be unable to take off because of the lack of runways. Another option would be to lay bombs, or timed explosives, along the runways, threatening anyone who used them.

A great many Egyptian air force commanders studied in Great Britain in the years that followed the 1952 revolution; they therefore knew what was coming. They had no night-flying fighters to defend their forces and installations. Their efforts over the days that followed, therefore, concentrated on concealing our aircraft, to protect them from being bombed on the ground. Highways were used as runways. Unfortunately, Egypt's highways at the time were few and ill-equipped. These places were called "secret airfields" at the time, although there was nothing secret about them! Everyone knew about them, where they were located, and what they were for.

The Egyptian air force commanders' predictions came true. Our bases and installations were attacked. It was a terrible night. I recall the heavy bombardment on the night and evening of October 30: violent tremors rattled through our home, at the officers' housing near Heliopolis

Airport, and the Egyptian air force headquarters. We eventually had to leave, and spent a few days at my aunt's house. My mother's sister lived not far away, in Ismailiya Square in Heliopolis.

Sure enough, the French—or Israeli, I should say—Mystères and Super Mystères attacked our airfields at dawn, after the British bombers had incapacitated them the night before, in an attempt to destroy our fighters and other aircraft on the ground. Credit where credit is due: I saw Egyptian fighters chasing off the attackers on October 31, and pitched air battles raging over the Cairo suburb of Heliopolis.

Egypt's pilots, while outnumbered, proved their courage and tenacity in defending the skies of the capital city, and elsewhere. Effort and ability can only go so far, however, in fighting the resources of an empire.

My father came home to Cairo on November 2. The air force headquarters at the Suez Canal had been vacated, and all airfields there were out of action. He immediately set out to rehabilitate what fighters and bombers we had available, and rebuild what air bases remained deep within Egypt. The battle caused heavy losses for Egypt's army and air force. The city of Port Said was occupied. However, the intervention of the United States and the Soviet Union to stop operations against Egypt, coupled with the fact that Egypt was clearly prepared to keep resisting and fighting, aborted the plot. Egypt won strategically and politically, despite its heavy losses on the military front.

The military errors in battle did not go unnoticed, nor did the insufficiencies in Egypt's performance in all its military fields. However, the fighting spirit of the combat units, the pilots, and others may have led to the lessons of the battle being forgotten—in other words, there was no frank and objective discussion of the mistakes that were made. The times did not allow for it.

Ten years were permitted to pass, from 1957 to 1967. We spoke exclusively of the success of the battle at the Suez Canal, while all shortcomings were swept under the carpet. We paid heavily for this in June 1967.

At the time, I hungrily devoured every scrap I could read on the battles of 1956. Between 1957 and June 1965—the year I joined the diplomatic corps—I pored over books on warfare and strategy. I make no boast when I say that I read dozens of books in that period, by the greatest writers on strategy, warfare, and international relations. The year I spent at the Military Technical College in 1959 only whetted my appetite for reading on this subject. It is my conviction that this had a decisive effect on the formation of my character, worldview, and values.

My increasing reading, for longer and longer hours every day—even during the academic year—were making me increasingly doubtful of our military capacity, especially with Egypt's military venture at the time, in Yemen. This had a negative impact on the abilities of the Egyptian army, from October 1962 up to our defeat in June 1967. I often discussed these subjects with my father, who retired from active military duty in 1962, with the enthusiasm of youth coupled with information from my reading, especially on the Second World War on all its fronts. I was gradually moving toward a more profound and wide-ranging understanding of what lay behind these battles, their technical details, the types and capacities of their weaponry, their military tactics and commanders—their command styles, how qualified they were, and how they had earned their stripes. I thought out loud and discussed all this with my classmates, the young officers who graduated from military colleges between 1962 and 1965.

At this stage, I was preoccupied with, not to say apprehensive about, our military capacity, a matter I discussed with many of my friends who had an interest in our war with Israel. These were years of continual talk of combat, of challenges, of (on Israel's part) diverting the course of the River Jordan, of Arab unity and shared Arab army action. Our group included Mohamed Assem Ibrahim. The son of an army general, he joined Egyptian Intelligence after his graduation in 1966. He spent nine years there before passing the qualifying exams and moving on to the Foreign Ministry. His illustrious career in the ministry includes posts as Egyptian ambassador to Ethiopia, Kenya, Sudan, and Israel from 1995 to 2008. As a young man, I spoke with a great many junior officers, including Ali Abd al-Moneim Mursi, Sherif al-Hakim of the Artillery Corps, Hamdi Khattab from Air Defense, and many others, all my colleagues either at school or at military college. I also discussed the war with some other friends in the air force, such as Ahmed Sadek al-Gawahirgi, Kamel al-Mawawi, and many others.

My overriding preoccupation was that Israel might attempt to destroy the Egyptian air force with a surprise strike on a Friday morning, which is a general holiday for our bases and airfields. What reinforced this feeling was that I had often observed large numbers of pilots and military men on Fridays congregating at the sporting and social clubs in Cairo, leaving only skeleton crews at the bases. We discussed this discreetly, allowing our imagination full rein on how and when the Israelis would strike. We read often of Nazi Germany's Barbarossa strike against the Soviet Union, and how the Luftwaffe successfully destroyed the Soviet air force with a surprise preemptive strike at dawn on June 22, 1941. Thousands of Soviet aircraft were destroyed on landing strips and runways, with no resistance. I recall that some of our air force commanders resisted strongly when Egypt began to discuss and implement the new Soviet combat organization, and Soviet combat approach, starting in 1959–60. They kept saying that the Soviet Union was hardly a role model insofar as air forces went!

I spoke to my father about this. He was an expert on the use of aerial force: he had served in the air force directly on graduation from the Royal Egyptian Air School in April 1939 and remained there until 1962, and had been on many training courses in the United Kingdom. He discussed it with me, but told me to concentrate on my studies and career. "Don't think so much of war!" he told me. "It won't go that far."

It was the summer of 1964. The African summit was held in Cairo in July of that year. Israel attempted to embarrass Egypt by breaching Egyptian airspace in Sinai with several Mirage aircraft. They were confronted by Egyptian fighter aircraft, but the latter were slow and ineffectual. To a young man like me, already carrying a deep-rooted fear, this event sounded a definite and loud alarm.

On a Saturday morning in August 1964, I was at Nuzha Airport in Alexandria, getting ready to return to Cairo after two days in the famous resort city. Suddenly, I saw Lieutenant-General Mohamed Sidqi Mahmoud coming in, getting ready to board the same plane as me. I knew him very well, as my father was director of the Air Navigation School at Dekheila Coastal Airfield, west of Alexandria, when Sidqi Mahmoud was commander of the Airfield Station from 1950 to 1952. We were also neighbors in the officers' quarters at Air Force Command from 1952 to 1957. I sat next to him on the plane and spoke to him with quite extraordinary boldness about what preoccupied me, namely my fear of a sudden Israeli airstrike on Egypt.

To his credit, Sidqi Mahmoud listened attentively to my thoughts, though I was only twenty-two at the time. Finally, he said briefly, "It's impossible. Israel can't carry out a surprise attack of that kind." He went on to say that many of our bases and main airfields were out of Israeli air striking range.

For years, I buried myself in my diplomatic work. The Israelis struck on June 5, 1967. I buried myself again in books about war and strategy, and anything and everything related to armed confrontation between nations. It was still June 1967 when my father came to me and said, "We should have let you join the army, Ahmed." But I was not destined to serve in the army.

Much has been written—thousands of pages and millions of words—on the different aspects of that war, and the negative Arab and Egyptian aspects it revealed. But the truth of the matter is that many of the faults and errors were already known to a number of the junior to middling commanders in the Egyptian army and air force. Egypt's presence in Yemen from 1962 to 1968 had a severe negative impact, although it is not within the scope of this book to expand on this. Also, the management of the armed forces, and the system used for promoting officers and army commanders, was fundamentally flawed. One of these flaws was the routine dismissal of commanders and granting of civilian posts, justifying this as "improving the civilian structure of the state by nourishing it [sic] with military men," without the slightest understanding of the effects it would have on the efficiency of military leadership, to say nothing of the civilian branch. One day, in the spring of 1966, I spoke about this with a very close friend of my father's, Staff Major-General Abd al-Moneim Riyad, who is now a household name. I still recall his evident terror at what might befall me if I ever made these opinions public. "Never, ever say that kind of thing again!" he said firmly. "Not to me, and not to anyone else." I got the message.

Back to August 1964, and my meeting with Mohamed Sidqi Mahmoud on the flight from Alexandria. I suggested he prepare for surprise maneuvers one Friday morning, to test the efficiency of the air force at that time: a surprise full air drill. The man listened again, intently, then replied curtly, "Impracticable. Impossible. The political and security status of the nation won't allow it." His response reveals a great deal of what was wrong with the Egypt of the time, along with its armed forces. The attack of 1967 plunged it into the worst possible strategic circumstances any army could face.

Now to the second half of this book, which in truth could be a book unto itself. It covers Egypt's efforts to effect peace with a view to ending the Arab–Israeli conflict and finding a solution to the Palestinian problem, so as to allow the Palestinian people to reclaim rights to their land. This half covers all that occurred as I saw it or took part in it, starting with President Sadat's historic visit to Jerusalem in November 1977, up to my appointment to the post of foreign minister of Egypt in 2004. My part in the peace efforts throughout my years as the head of the Egyptian diplomatic corps from 2004 to 2011 is documented in my book on Egyptian foreign policy, *Shahdati: al-siyasa al-kharijiya al-misriya 2004–2011* (My Testimony: Egyptian Foreign Policy, 2004–2011), published in Arabic in January 2013. It may be useful to consider it a companion volume to this one.

As I was saying, the second part of the book starts with Chapter Fourteen, with the events of the Mena House Conference, held as a direct result of Sadat's visit to Jerusalem and the Ismailiya Summit that followed, after which Israel presented its plan in an integrated proposal for an Arab–Israeli settlement, covering Palestine and the occupied territories in Sinai. This half of the book covers the efforts of the Political Committee and the Military Committee, both Egyptian and Israeli, formed at the start of operations at the Ismailiya Summit. It goes on to describe the obstacles Israel placed in the path of the negotiations and Egyptian negotiators' rejection of the Israeli propositions. The situation became more involved; Egypt redoubled its efforts to win over the United States to its way of thinking and to pressure Israel to soften its position. This effort continued for months, from January 1978 until the Camp David Summit in September of that year.

At this point in the book, there is an evaluation of the way the United States succeeded in securing the agreement of the two sides, convincing them that each had achieved its main goals in going to Camp David, even though both sides had, of course, been obliged to make some (possibly vital or essential) compromises. The United States used every carrot and stick in its arsenal to make this deal a reality.

After this, I demonstrate Egypt's attempts, after the signing of the peace treaty in Washington, to link the Egyptian and Palestinian peace processes, accompanied by Israel's maneuvers to completely separate the two. The following chapters offer an overview of the preparations for the Madrid Summit, and the Oslo Summit after it. Finally, I show the role of the United Nations in convincing the countries of the world of the need for a Palestinian state side by side with the state of Israel, via the important Resolutions 1397 and 1515—the first-ever Security Council resolutions in the history of the Palestinian conflict to directly address the establishment of the state of Palestine.

Part 1
Witness to War

1 Silent War, Secret War: 1968–73

War begins not with the roar of gunfire but with months, indeed years, of painstaking preparation. The tasks are varied and endless, but the most important are performed in silence: covert operations aimed at divining the enemy's intentions and capacities, while preserving your own secrets. Such operations are an integral part of armed conflict before, during, and after the first shot is fired.

In the 1973 war, more commonly known in the west as the Yom Kippur War, and the politics that followed, both Egypt and Israel engaged—had to engage—in continual, unrelenting espionage against one another. Many of these tales have come to light on both sides, starting with the Lavon Affair in 1954, when Israel attempted to sabotage Egyptian–American relations and panic Egyptian Jews into emigrating to Israel. Others have become common knowledge and found their way into Egyptian pop culture and drama, such as the case of famous Egyptian spy Ra'fat al-Haggan or the bombing of the drill Israel imported from Canada to extract oil from our regional waters in the Red Sea. There is a long list of intelligence and counterintelligence operations between the two countries, which had varying degrees of success. One of Israel's successes was blocking Egypt's Nasser-era attempts to collaborate with German experts and scientists on developing and producing Egyptian missiles similar to those used by Germany in the Second World War. It is common knowledge that the Mossad was one of the most powerful intelligence agencies of that time. It is also no secret that the first generation of that agency's main operatives—polyglots from various countries, with the loyalty of Jewish communities there—originally manned the Allies' covert operations in the Second World War. These operatives were well-versed in covert operations before Israel was even declared a state.

The upshot of all this is that reconnaissance, observation, intelligence gathering, and counterintelligence operations were always difficult tasks for Egyptian Intelligence, especially as that agency admittedly, at least at the start, lacked the experience, expertise, and human resources of its Zionist—and later Israeli—counterpart. With the reader's permission, I will share an anecdote about an affair that took place nearly forty-three years ago—a covert operation against Israel. Naturally, no classified data will be disclosed, even though this was a long time ago; I mean merely to recount decisive Egyptian successes I witnessed in the silent war against Israel.

The story starts when my wife Leila and I landed, two months after our marriage, at Nicosia Airport, on September 3, 1968, on an Egypt Air flight in the late afternoon. The flight, on an Antonov An-24, took over two hours. The Egyptian national carrier used that model for short flights at that time. It was a relatively long flight; there were airspace restrictions in Egypt due to the state of war at the time, so all Europe-bound flights had to take a circuitous route, first southward to southern Cairo, then west to Fayoum, keeping a healthy distance from the defenses and air bases in the Nile Delta and well out of range of their ground-to-air missiles. No sooner had we stepped out of the aircraft when I was welcomed by a smartly dressed man, dark-skinned and wiry, who introduced himself as Magdy Omar, first secretary at the Egyptian embassy. I already knew that he was also the head of the Egyptian Intelligence station in Cyprus. This double duty was common practice at the time in most countries; it facilitated the operations of intelligence officers under the umbrella of their countries' embassies abroad. The Israelis followed the same protocol; in fact, it remains in use by many countries today.

Magdy welcomed us warmly as though he had known us for years. We had been introduced to his good wife a few days before in Cairo, where she was on vacation with their new baby Mohamed. Magdy's demeanor at the airport, and the way he was treated, indicated that airport officials recognized him as a personage of some importance. They showed him great respect and seemed eager to help him in any way possible—an indication of the good relations between Egypt and Archbishop Macarius' Cyprus. Egypt has always stood with that island nation against British occupation and assisted the efforts of Ethniki Organosis Kyprion Agoniston (EOKA) against British forces, which used their military bases on the island to bomb Egypt in 1956.

Gradually, over several months, I got to know Magdy Omar better. With the speed and profound understanding of an intelligence officer, he too familiarized himself with my personality and my career. We grew closer, and he took note of how interested I was in his work and how much I liked his style. My passion for military matters became clear; not only military history, but weaponry and armaments, fighter and bomber aircraft, and so on. We slowly became friends. From him, I learned the methods of covert intelligence, information gathering, intelligence analysis, and how to enlist agents and friends, and to fulfill Egyptian interests in handling opponents and enemies. Magdy Omar and his men were a hive of worker bees, humming along intelligently yet circumspectly, in a location teeming with intelligence apparatuses from all over the region, indeed the world, all working toward the interests of their own countries. It was only natural that all these competing intelligence teams on the island of Cyprus were the best of the best, the elite of their respective countries, with each state bent on achieving its interests via this vitally located island. As I grew closer to Magdy Omar, instead of watching him work at a distance I took part in some of his operations. But it was still at a distance; there must always be distance between the professional diplomat and the intelligence agent masquerading as a diplomat. However, what we shared was a loyalty to the interests of our country.

One day in October 1969, I walked into my office to find the secretary—a local, a Greek Cypriot—saying, "There's an elderly man here asking to speak to the person responsible for cultural activity at the embassy." That was me. I went to the meeting room off the main reception office to hear him out.

"I have a collection of 16-millimeter films of nature reserves I took when I lived in Rhodesia (currently Zimbabwe), full of plants and wildlife," he noted. He added that he was currently showing the films at schools in Cyprus for a nominal fee. He also said that he made regular trips to Israel to show them at various schools. I would like to remind the reader that television in 1969 was still in its infancy and lacked the variety of natural history and science channels we now take for granted. As soon as he said he made frequent trips to Israel, I leaned forward in my seat. Now decidedly interested, I went about finding out exactly what he sought from this interview. He said he would be happy to go to Egypt to show his films at schools in our country in exchange for a small living wage.

I told him I would have to check with my superiors in Cairo. He left, promising to come back in a week, during which time he would be showing his films in schools in Paphos, a district in the western part of the island, prior to a three-week trip to Israel. During the meeting, I learned a few things about his background and profession: he had been a railway engineer in India during the Second World War, then spent the remainder of his life traveling among India, South Africa, Northern and Southern Rhodesia (today, Zambia and Zimbabwe, respectively), and Great Britain, during which time he had learned to take photographs and make films. I hurried to Magdy Omar and told him about what had happened with the gentleman. We wondered whether he was bait. What was his real objective, and his hidden motive?

Magdy Omar sent to Cairo for any information about this man. He also asked some colleagues of his in the countries where the mysterious man had resided to find out more about his alleged stay there. The day after I met the man—not a young fellow by any means, for he was in his mid-seventies—he was back at the embassy, asking for another meeting! This time, he offered to leave a copy of one of his films with me for us to send to Cairo and watch at our leisure, to assess its usefulness and suitability for viewing in Egyptian schools. "Where are you staying in Nicosia?" I asked him. I also asked him to provide the names of the schools in Cyprus and Israel where he showed his films.

As we spoke, I noticed—and this was, let us note, a conversation between a twenty-six-year-old and a man in his mid-seventies—that he was wary of every question, answering as guardedly as possible. He seemed nervous, which made me even more apprehensive that he was some sort of mole sent to find out more about us (the embassy, I mean) and what we were really doing in Cyprus.

I kept the reel. Magdy Omar and I discussed the issue at length, and the man's odd insistence on visiting Egypt. We agreed to visit him at his hotel that same night, to check the veracity of the information he had given us.

At 1900 hours, I went to his hotel and asked for him. I was surprised at his apparent shock and his refusal to come downstairs to meet me in the lobby. He absolutely insisted that I come up to meet him in his room. I must add here that, to put it kindly, this was the most modest hotel in Nicosia.

Up in his room, I found a dismal standard of living indeed: the man was in dire need of assistance to keep body and soul together. I told him we really had no use for the film he had left with me, and that I would call him when the response arrived from Cairo.

Magdy thought long and hard about this person, contemplating the possibility—and usefulness—of enlisting him in our intelligence operations on Israeli soil. Having assessed the situation, we agreed that I would be the one to make the attempt to enlist him.

This process proved extraordinarily difficult due to his suspicious nature; he refused to take anything at face value. He was eventually persuaded to work for our side, and visited Israel many times, bringing us a variety of important information that eventually proved invaluable. This information cannot, as mentioned above, be described in detail, even after all these years. Unfortunately, after a long while, he was eventually detected and captured by Israeli intelligence. After his trial, he was released due to advanced age. Most probably, Israel never did find out just how much information we obtained thanks to this man, nor its true value.

I must admit to experiencing a great deal of personal conflict when he was caught. I felt his pain and suffering in Israeli prison. Still, I knew that Egypt's interests trumped any personal emotions. When he was finally sent home after his release, we paid him in full as per our agreement.

I resumed assisting Magdy Omar in Cyprus. We did anything and everything to uncover the enemy's secrets and networks. I know for a fact that our labors bore fruit in terms of assisting Egyptian Intelligence operations in Cyprus. Some great successes were the result. There was a constant battle to enlist agents and sources, fueled by enthusiasm and patriotism. Sometimes we sensed danger, feeling that our enthusiasm and zeal might provoke the enemy into actions that might endanger us or our families. Still, we were emboldened by knowing that our colleagues and friends were fighting on the front. The late Magdy Omar, who died in mid-2009, used to say, "The Israelis know that if they hurt us, there will be repercussions that'll hurt them as well." By this, he meant the mutual understanding in the intelligence community that neither side should engage in personal attacks against its counterpart.

Nevertheless, I was always checking everything: my apartment, my car, the routes I took, and so on. The minute I got home, I would search everywhere in the apartment, looking into things, afraid of explosives. I assiduously applied every rule of personal safety just as we had been trained at the Foreign Ministry back home.

I hope that this chapter's account of my experience in Cyprus—just one of many that I personally witnessed or took part in—has helped to illustrate the sterling performance of Egyptian Intelligence and its agents. This apparatus performed with great efficiency in locations around the world during that era, from Europe to Africa. They fought this secret war in silence and altruism, in preparation for the military confrontation they knew was coming.

Today, I reaffirm my conviction that with imagination, daring, and determination, nothing is impossible: they are the recipe for success in covert operations against an opponent as efficient as the Mossad. I end this chapter by saying that Magdy Omar and his men in Cyprus from 1968 to 1973 had these vital components of success in generous supply.

I must not forget to give a certain Egyptian citizen his due. A Coptic Christian, he is a man I remember well. He lived in Cyprus from the mid-1950s and was in the maritime shipping business. His initials are R.K. He was an active and loyal member of the intelligence services who took many risks and accomplished many missions for Egypt and our country's interests. He died in 1989. It is in his memory and the memory of my dear friend Magdy Omar, and all those who assisted them, that I write this chapter.

2 Twenty-Four Decisive Hours in My Life with Hafiz Ismail

On the morning of Saturday, October 6, 1973, a watershed day in the history of Egypt, I was out strolling with my lifelong friend, Ahmed Maher al-Sayed, in the garden of Abd al-Moneim Palace, a small villa in Heliopolis, in a mainly residential area close to what is now the presidential palace in al-Qubba. We noticed that a great many people were looking out of their windows intently, intrigued at the sudden appearance of a number of the Presidential Guard in the garden of the villa and all around it, plus a number of officials in civilian clothes. This activity was accompanied by the din of cleaning staff and maintenance workers repairing or replacing phone lines with newer ones offering better networks—networks able to ensure efficient communications with the palace to prepare it for its new occupant, the Egyptian national security advisor, and his staff. This personage was Mr. Mohamed Hafiz Ismail. At that time, he was mandated to assist President Sadat by managing the diplomatic and political side of the October 1973 strike.

We were discussing our preparations, what the military action we were planning might have in store, and simultaneous and concordant diplomatic and political maneuvers. That day, we were overcome by anticipation and not a little apprehension regarding what might or might not come to pass. For no matter how intently we examined the efforts made and the preparations in progress, the in-depth planning for everything—of which there was a great deal, and in which every element of the national security apparatus was taking part, including operatives working with Hafiz Ismail (a collection of the best young men from the Ministry of Defense, Egyptian Intelligence, the Ministry of the Interior, and the Foreign Ministry)—we were by no means certain that military action was indeed in the offing, and that our forces were indeed about to storm the Bar-Lev line. This would initiate a major military operation into which Egypt would pour all its efforts, an operation which might lead to great military and diplomatic success, or to ignominious defeat that would damage Egypt's standing in a manner unparalleled in the twentieth century.

It was a great gamble, requiring the most ingenious and insightful preparation. It had been skillfully concealed, with the highest level of strategic deception. I say gamble because the truth of the matter is that despite the hundreds of thousands of troops that Egypt mobilized in preparation for this large-scale military action, Israel had military superiority over Egypt and Syria in the form of U.S.-supplied weaponry and aerial forces. However, the joint Egypt–Syria strategy would force Israel to fight on two fronts, one to the far north and the other on the Suez Canal. This was intended to push Israel to divide its forces and resources, and prevent its army from mustering the entirety of its forces to face either one, thus annulling Israel's military superiority.

We saw Hafiz Ismail's late-1960s model black Mercedes approaching the outer gates. He alighted from it, a tall, wiry figure with a sharp, serious face, and hurried to the door of the palace, quickly climbing the steps and disappearing inside. "Don't you notice something, Ahmed?" Ahmed Maher asked me.

"What?" I said. "How grim he looked? Or do you mean the way he rushed in, ignoring two of his close assistants?" (I meant us, of course, walking in the garden—there was no way he did not notice we were there.)

"No," said Ahmed. "I mean that he was smoking a cigarette, although it's Ramadan and everyone is fasting! What could possibly be so serious as to make him break his fast in public like that?"

With that, we both went inside to start work in our brand-new offices. We had only moved into the palace the night before, on October 5, that is, and were still finding our way around the rooms, corridors, internal and external phone lines, and so on. Abdel Hadi Makhlouf, the office director for the national security advisor, was on his way to Hafiz Ismail's office on the upper floor of the villa. He stayed inside for half an hour, then popped outside. "The Advisor wants to see you." (We all called him the Advisor.) Bringing a small notebook, I hurried in with Ahmed Maher. Neither of us wanted to keep the great man waiting.

Even today, I still remember the sight of Hafiz Ismail in his shirtsleeves, his jacket discarded on a chair. He handed an envelope to Ahmed Maher.

"Please deliver this to Dr. Ashraf Ghorbal, assistant to the national security advisor." Ghorbal was in charge of media coverage and crisis management, with a special focus on the United States and other western powers, including Europe. "Dr. Ashraf is currently manning the media front at the Egyptian television headquarters in Maspero." Under no circumstances, he said, was Ghorbal to open the envelope before 1330 hours on this historic day. "He is to give orders for Egyptian radio and television to broadcast its contents at that time." He added that he would telephone Dr. Ghorbal to make sure that the sealed envelope had arrived safely. It was a little before 1030 hours. He went on, "In this envelope is a bulletin from the Egyptian armed forces to the effect that the Israeli air force launched an attack on Egyptian bases in the Red Sea and on the front, at 1330 hours today. Egyptian forces responded with military counterattacks all along the frontlines."

"Are our operations scheduled to start at 1330 hours?" Ahmed Maher asked. "While the envelope's being opened and broadcast?"

"Egypt will commence military operations," responded the national security advisor, "at 1405 hours."

"I don't quite get it, sir," said Ahmed Maher uneasily. "Wouldn't that be alerting the enemy in Sinai to our movements over half an hour before the fact?"

After a moment's thought, Hafiz Ismail nodded. "You have a point. Let's make it after 1400 hours, no sooner than that."

I exited Hafiz Ismail's office full of apprehension. I feared for my country, for my friends in the military, and for our future. I genuinely dreaded a repeat of that black day in our modern history, the defeat and subsequent humiliation of June 5, 1967. To calm my nerves, I took to telling myself that our armed forces were well-prepared, that a strike like the one we had suffered in June could not be repeated, and that this time it was we who would take the enemy by surprise. We had trained hard, we had learned from our defeat, we had prepared our army well.

On my way out of the office, I met Abd al-Fattah Abdullah, a minister of state at that time. He was quartered in the palace with us, as assistant to President Sadat, who was living in al-Tahra Palace, another more beautiful and luxurious palace. I had no knowledge of his duties or why he was stationed there, but I found out in the days that followed that President Sadat wanted him to attend all the working sessions, conferences, and other meetings at al-Tahra during the upcoming military operations, as well as attend to related diplomatic and political tasks. On the second floor, I should explain, there were bedrooms, one of which was Hafiz Ismail's, the other Abd al-Fattah Abdullah's. That worthy greeted me with the sternness common to military men when some important event is drawing near. I had seen it often in my life with my father, Air Force General Ali Ahmed Aboul Gheit. Abdullah went on his way, saying to Chief of the Cabinet Abdel Hadi Makhlouf, who was standing in the hallway that overlooked all the second-floor rooms, "I'm off to al-Tahra Palace to see the President, Makhlouf."

I was overcome with worry. We would not be able to defeat Israel's long reach, I felt, despite all our superior preparations, despite the War of Attrition that had trained, tested, and honed our forces, and despite the wall of anti-aircraft missile launchers we had formed over the past three years. I had a sneaking suspicion that our move to this palace reflected a fear that our main offices—in Abdin Palace, in the center of downtown Cairo—might be attacked. However, the real source of my unease was that President Sadat had taken up residence in al-Tahra Palace, in Heliopolis, closer to the military command centers and bases of operations in the deserts that then surrounded Heliopolis and Nasr City. I would have liked to see him take up residence in more modest quarters. However, in the days that followed, I was to discover that the president had selected this location in order to conduct many high-level political and diplomatic meetings with presidents and ambassadors of various countries, whom he might need to meet during this period of armed clashes.

In the days that followed, I read a great many minutes of the meetings between President Sadat and world leaders, prominent among them ambassadors from Britain, Iran, France, and Russia. These were recorded in their entirety by Abd al-Fattah Abdullah, and Dr. Makhlouf would often ask me to supervise the transcription of the recordings and convey their contents to various official bodies. These minutes reflected the president's confidence and belief in the military action that Egypt was taking, in that we possessed the element of surprise and thus would outstrip them before they had a chance to react.

"Has the Advisor told you what's happening in a few hours?" Makhlouf asked. We replied in the affirmative, whereupon he said, "We need to get ready." He called for a general meeting of the staff—Farouk Baraka, Ehab Wahba, Ahmed Maher, Ahmed Adel, myself, Maher Khalifa, Salah Sha'rawi, Gamal Barakat, and others in an elite group of national security experts—to assign duties and shifts for the coming twenty-four hours, and to organize communications, agree on how reports would be presented, give instructions on the use of the telephones, and familiarize us with the codenames for the top men in government (prepared by another assistant to the national security advisor, the distinguished ambassador Osman Nouri). We waited, biting our nails.

Worry twisted my insides. I remember writing that down in my diary: it was important, I remember feeling at the time, to document this decisive moment in our history. I set down several paragraphs on the evening of October 5 as soon as we had moved to the palace. One of them read:

> 2145 hours: Clearly the organizational side is not very strong. We have been given no duties so far. Not optimistic. Afraid the enemy will find out about our preparations, esp. as many now know of our intentions to strike.

I wrote also:

> We must start at once, or the enemy will abort us.
> Tried to sleep. Failed. I must be very tense.

These were my diary entries, as I mentioned above, for October 5. In any case, we waited. Hours and minutes passed like eons. As soon as the clock struck 1400 hours, the first communiqué was broadcast, the one Hafiz Ismail had sent to Ashraf Ghorbal to be read out.

During the heavy hours of waiting, things began gradually to improve. We were able to make telephone calls now, a luxury not available to ordinary citizens at that time—the communications apparatus of the state was in a deplorable state pretty much throughout. Military operations commenced with the first airstrike, coordinated with artillery fire across the Suez Canal. My diary entries at the time were like this:

> I can't believe how fast they're crossing, although they're so many.
> The reports coming to us from the army say that the forces are at
> around 2,000 yards. In my estimation, they need to go in deeper or
> else the enemy will pose a threat to the bridgehead. The enemy will
> not respond until tomorrow, Sunday, or even Monday, October 8.
> Everyone's starting to become hopeful, but I prefer to remain cautious.
> It's the best thing to do with armed conflict.

I had my own reasons, and justifications, for this extreme unease. The news had come in from Syria on October 4 that the Russians were pulling their experts out of Damascus, quite visibly and publicly. The Russian ambassador to Cairo had had a meeting with Hafiz Ismail on October 4 at noon, in which he had asked him directly, on instructions from Moscow, whether Egypt and Syria planned to break the ceasefire with Israel. The question took Hafiz Ismail by surprise. "He took his time thinking before he answered," said my colleague Farouk Baraka, whose job it was to record the meeting. After nearly half a minute of silence, he advised the Russian ambassador to take it up with President Sadat at their meeting the next day. In my estimation, Hafiz Ismail was trying to conceal the attack, and obfuscate the timing of the operation as much as possible for the Russians. This was why I feared our plans would be revealed, and fall prey to a preemptive strike from the Israelis.

However, the Russian ambassador, who was widely and deeply versed in Egyptian affairs and the measures Egypt was taking, made his report to Moscow and came back the next day, Friday, October 5, with a message from the Kremlin to President Sadat. The Arabic translation, I noticed, was surprisingly unidiomatic and badly written—odd, because we knew that a great many Russian diplomats spoke exceedingly fluent Arabic. In any event, the message consisted of a warning to Egypt of the consequences of any military operation against Israel. It spoke of how Egypt's military was unequal to Israel's, and predicted that Egypt might well be heading for a second crushing defeat if it went ahead and joined Syria in mounting an offensive against the Israel Defense Forces' fortification on the Bar-Lev line. Such a defeat, the message predicted, would deal a blow to Egypt's status that would be almost impossible to overcome.

For all these reasons, I was uneasy in the extreme. The writings of Israeli military experts that came out after the war will reveal, I have no doubt, that my fears were justified. Israeli intelligence reports dated October 5 and at dawn on October 6 state that Egypt and Syria were on the verge of a military strike, breaking the ceasefire; they recommended that Israel make a move at once to avoid sustaining heavy losses at Arab hands.

Israel finally made a decision to wait and see: if the forthcoming Arab strike did indeed take place, they would make the appropriate response at the time—the same fatal error, ironically, that President Nasser committed in June 1967, deciding to wait for Israel to strike first rather than initiate armed operations on the Egyptian side.

At the end of my shift, I returned to my home in Heliopolis, and went to bed at 2300 hours on Saturday, October 6, leaving another shift of colleagues working with Hafiz Ismail in the palace. Throughout the long hours from 1400 on October 6, Hafiz Ismail had been in constant contact with President Sadat to inform him of developments in the international political situation, especially the communications arriving from the United States, and the telephone conversations with Dr. Mohamed Hassan al-Zayyat, the foreign minister, then in New York. It was this worthy man who received the now-famous telephone call from Henry Kissinger at dawn on October 6. Having received intelligence that Egypt was mobilizing forces at the front, the U.S. president sought to reassure Egypt that Israel had no intention of conducting any strikes against our armed forces. Zayyat conveyed this message to Hafiz Ismail, possibly at the exact moment Egyptian military operations were starting across the Suez Canal. Ismail was calm, alert, and in control. His significant knowledge and experience were palpable. I must admit that, although I was relatively green, I had a great many conversations with him about the military experiences of various states and their statesmen in a number of wars, foremost among which was the Second World War, on which Ismail had written a good deal of riveting and enjoyable work in the 1950s, which I read before my tenure under him in the 1970s. He had a keen intelligence, a profound investment in his responsibilities, and a range of exceptionally astute context-based responses, influenced no doubt by his own reading on military history and the general strategies of states that had engaged in military conflict.

I woke extremely early on Sunday, October 7, and wasted no time getting to Ahmed Maher's house in the work car. We hurried to the palace, and I immediately delved into the reports from the previous night and the dawn, prepared by the night shift team for the national security advisor. My main concern was the Israeli air force's actions against our air bases and our forces on the front. I started with the previous night's reports and the ones dated October 7, and immediately my fears began to be allayed. The Israeli air force attempted to bomb our main bases; our fighter aircraft had been waiting and fought them off. The Israelis lost the advantage and their control of Egyptian skies. I wrote in my diary:

> Air force losses insignificant. Our air force extremely effective. Our MiG-21s defended our skies successfully.
>
> The bridgeheads are still very narrow. Heads of infantry divisions rose to fame as the most important corps in the Egyptian army. Forever inscribed in the annals of history are the Nineteenth Infantry Division, commanded by Brigadier General Fouad Afifi, and the Seventh Division, commanded by Brigadier General Ahmed Badawi, both divisions of the Third Army, as well as the Sixteenth Division, commanded by Brigadier General Abd Rabb al-Nabi Hafiz, the Second Division, commanded by Brigadier General Hassan Sa'da, and the Eighteenth Division, commanded by Brigadier General Fouad Aziz Ghali, infantry divisions of the Second Army. Each of these had an armored division in addition to their armor, that is, a total of around one hundred tanks for each frontline infantry division that crossed the Suez Canal on that glorious day.

The strip is 2.4 km deep. The Second Army is doing better than the Third Army. We have at least four hundred tanks east of the canal. The Third Army had to use the Second Army's bridges to cross, as the earth barrier (Bar-Lev line) was denser and more tightly packed in the south than in the north, and resisted the power of the water cannons to dissolve the dust and rocks of the Bar-Lev line.

A telegram arrived from Dr. Zayyat detailing Kissinger's call to him in New York demanding that Egyptian forces retreat to the west of the canal and saying that Egypt continuing military action may lead to negative consequences: the tide may turn against Egypt. In my estimation, what America cares about now is to provide Israel with an opportunity to launch a counterattack. My reading of military reports indicate this may come on Monday, October 8.

As soon as I had read the reports from the previous night and that morning, we started working industriously. The twenty-four hours since Hafiz Ismail had told us of the timing of the Egyptian attack felt like years.

3 Egypt and the October Victory

I n June 1999, I walked into the main banquet hall at the New York Hilton. I was there in my capacity as permanent Egyptian representative to the United Nations to attend a reception held by the Seeds of Peace organization. His Majesty Abdullah II and Queen Rania of Jordan were also in attendance, as well as our then-ambassador to Washington, my dear old friend Ahmed Maher. Seeds of Peace was founded by an American gentleman following the Oslo Accords of 1993: he wished to provide an opportunity for young people from Israel and Palestine to meet at annual camps for several weeks annually in order to get to know each other and build a healthy relationship for peace. Circumstances at the time permitted this type of thinking.

There were more than a thousand people at the party. I schmoozed with the attendees, meeting and complimenting, doing my diplomat's duty and searching for a VIP to meet or from whom to garner some valuable tidbit of information. Suddenly, who should I glimpse but former Secretary of State Henry Kissinger. I knew he had also been the national security advisor during President Nixon's first term.

I made my way over to him and introduced myself. He was standing with a group of American guests; still, he greeted me warmly and said in his trademark heavily German-accented English that he was always glad to meet the Egyptian ambassador. "I have great respect for Egypt." Our country, he said, was the real key to peace in the Middle East and the Arab region, and the most capable of providing great leaders. The US, he added, might not always agree with our leaders' vision, but Egypt's leaders always had America's respect because of their country's standing and weight in the region.

We started making small talk. I let him know that I had read his books, and truthfully told him that I had learned a great deal from them about international relations and military strategy, particularly regarding nuclear armaments. I mentioned specific books of his that I had read over the years, especially *The Necessity for Choice*. This seminal work established Kissinger as an American authority on nuclear strategy on the level of such greats as K.J. Holstetter, Herman Kahn, and Maxwell Taylor. I also spoke of *The White House Years*, his memoir about his tenure as national security advisor from 1968 to 1972, and *Years of Upheaval*, about his tenure as secretary of state from 1973 to 1976. Kissinger was impressed and pleased, especially when I mentioned his Harvard thesis, "A World Restored: Metternich, Castlereagh and the Problems of Peace 1815–1822." He wrote it at the end of the 1940s, after participating in the war against Germany. This started a conversation that lasted more than half an hour, with us gradually drifting away from the other attendees until it was just the two of us discussing political affairs. Suddenly, I launched my missile: "Did you know, Your Excellency, that your conversation with Dr. Zayyat in the summer of 1973, specifically when you said, 'I have no time to waste on the Middle East right now. You lack the ability to modify your relations and/or the balance of power in the region, and the capacity to achieve anything militarily. You also refuse to acknowledge the necessity of paying the price of your defeat'—did you know that those words contributed to, indeed pushed us to, war?"

His shock was palpable. His face darkened at hearing this testimony, as my words gave the impression that Kissinger encouraged the Egyptians to launch a military action against Israel. He began vehemently to deny that he had been urging us in any way to undertake any military action, even though we came to that conclusion after Kissinger's meetings with Dr. Zayyat and other Egyptian statesmen.

The fact is that from the start of 1973, Egypt had been continuously working to expand its military capabilities (via new fighter bombers, ground-to-ground missiles, and whatever other weapons President Sadat could, with great difficulty, convince the Soviets, to supply to Egypt that year) and, on a different front, to reach a political settlement with Israel without resorting to war. This was the job of Egyptian National Security Advisor Hafiz Ismail, who held meetings, consultations, and conversations with Kissinger himself. There was a meeting in New York in February 1973, and in the suburbs of Paris in May of the same year, all organized by the Central Intelligence Agency in collaboration with

Egyptian Intelligence, of which Hafiz Ismail was head in 1970. In August he had high-level meetings with Ceauşescu, then president of Romania, who had a good relationship with Golda Meir, and with Tito, president of Yugoslavia. Egypt also attempted to come to an understanding with Israel with a view to finding a political solution to the conflict, offering many options. Ceauşescu attempted to convince President Sadat of his—that is, Ceauşescu—potential as a mediator between Egypt and Israel, and that he was doing his best to facilitate Egyptian–Israeli proximity talks with a view to arriving at a final or transitional recommendation. Tito was making efforts along the same lines. This led Sadat to send his national security advisor to consult with these leaders regarding the possibility of moving toward a peaceful resolution, and thus obviating the necessity for war or armed action. These efforts came to nothing. Egypt proposed a settlement with Israel, going to the UN Security Council in July. Egypt won fourteen votes in support of its proposed draft resolution, although it was ultimately vetoed by the US. Egypt's peace efforts stalled, and it became clear that we were heading for military action.

At the reception, Kissinger flatly refused to acknowledge my explanations and vehemently denied that his words to Hafiz Ismail were the impetus behind our armed action. Indeed, he contended that he told us back then, "I'm busy with the Vietnam War negotiations in Paris. I have no time to waste on a cold case and Egypt's stubborn refusal to pay the price of the 1967 defeat."

I met Kissinger again socially in New York in 2000. He approached me and made a point of repeating his categorical denial that he bore any responsibility for Egypt's resorting to a military solution in 1973. My own assessment is that Kissinger wished to deny any responsibility for that war, for fear of being accused by certain circles in the US and Israel of indirectly egging the Arabs on to armed action against Israel.

Allow me for a moment to digress from 1973 and skip forward to January and February 1974, the year when Hafiz Ismail left office. Dr. Abdel Hadi Makhlouf, office manager for the national security advisor, called me into his office. In his trademark quiet manner, he said, "Ahmed, you know the room adjoining my office in Abdin Palace? A big room with one of the biggest armored safes in Egypt. It contains some of the most crucial—and classified—historical documents in Egypt." I nodded. "Now that our tenure with Hafiz Ismail at the Presidency is almost over, he has entrusted me with creating a complete archive of these documents. They cover internal Egyptian affairs. There are blueprints for Egyptian political and/or military actions concerning the October War and the time leading up to it." He gave me fifteen days to archive this mountain of papers, a treasure trove of information and historical documentation.

I entered the room and opened the safe. Opening the files, I dutifully set to archiving and filing. Instead of working a few hours every day, I got lost in reading. I devoured the papers. All the information that I never knew—indeed, that many people in the office of the national security advisor, Ambassador Makhlouf and Ahmed Maher al-Sayed excepted, never knew—was laid out before me. I had my hands on the minutes recorded by Ambassador Osman Nouri, assistant national security advisor, and Ambassador Makhlouf, of a vital meeting dated September 30, 1973. The meeting was headed by President Sadat, and every Egyptian political leader was present, including Mahmoud Fawzi, Mustafa Khalil, Mamdouh Salem, and Ahmed Ismail. "We are going to war," said the president, "and we must all prepare ourselves." Some objections were voiced. Some of those present opined that Egypt could make another attempt to negotiate a peaceful settlement, citing Egypt's difficult situation and the unequal balance of power with Israel.

The discussion went on for pages and pages. Dr. Mahmoud Fawzi, the former foreign minister, said that he appreciated the need for the armed conflict. He told a parable about when he was a young diplomat in his thirties stationed in Japan. At the time, he said, he was enrolled in samurai fighting classes on how to use a *katana* and *wakizashi*. One day, he went into class, dressed as a samurai, *katana* tucked into his belt. "Where's your short sword?" his trainer asked. "You have only your *katana*." Samurai generally carry two swords, the *katana*, a blade longer than sixty centimeters, and a *wakizashi*, or short sword for close combat or in case the *katana* is lost or broken. Fawzi concluded, "Egypt lost our *katana* in 1967; no matter whether we have exchanged it for a longer, sharper one, or whether we only have a short sword, we must use whichever blades we have in hand to achieve the objectives of the upcoming military action—the objective of moving the peace process forward, and creating a new military and political balance with Israel that can impose on both Israel and the US to cooperate with Egyptian demands for full withdrawal from Sinai."

This led to a heated discussion in the historic meeting. Hafiz Ismail said—in one of his interventions—that in light of some of his colleagues' fears about the results of the upcoming military action, we might move gradually toward Egyptian military actions resembling those of the War of Attrition that lasted from 1967 until the ceasefire in July 1970. The national security advisor proposed military–political initiatives to liven up, as it were, the Egyptian frontlines short of engaging in outright hostilities, thus avoiding the negative consequences of a full-scale military action. Field Marshall Ahmed Ismail Ali, then defense minister, disagreed. His evaluation stemmed from his conviction that "Israel will certainly not confine itself to a limited response to any limited Egyptian military action, or an Egyptian attempt at livening up the front. Israel knows it cannot support the burden of an extended military mobilization, nor a months-long extended attrition in the form of small, dispersed operations, especially since Israel knows that Egypt's military and air force have upped their efficiency over the three-year ceasefire period," meaning from July 1970 to September 1973. It followed, he went on to say, that Israel would immediately escalate, with maximum force.

Ahmed Ismail opined that the ideal method of military action would be to deal a major, extremely violent blow via massive Egyptian mobilization across the Suez Canal. Israel's counterstrike would have to be absorbed, and protect the Egyptian areas of Sinai that had not been taken, followed by the imposition on Israel of Egypt's vision for a political solution.

President Sadat ended the meeting, saying, "Let's do what must be done for the future of the country, to get this settled."

The military action commenced on October 6. This action clearly and honorably expressed the clarity of the Egyptian vision, reflecting what Carl von Clausewitz wrote in the eighteenth century. War is a continuation of politics by other means. War should use the highest degree of armed force to impose one's will on one's opponent. Finally, defense, after military action, is the strongest form of battle. All of these elements were put into practice with great maturity, efficiency, and discipline by Egypt's armed forces.

A final point remains: there is a political objective to every war, which armed action seeks to achieve. In the case of Egypt, it was abundantly clear that the objectives of armed action were to reclaim a broad strip of Sinai, strike out at counterattacks, and achieve a ceasefire. Having imposed its vision—documented in Sadat's presidential order to the Egyptian armed forces to initiate combat on that momentous day—Egypt commenced negotiations from a new balance of power with Israel, eventually achieving Israel's full withdrawal from Egyptian territory in Sinai. One cannot help admitting here that as a result of this armed action, Israel had only two options: to accept the results of the conflict and withdraw from Sinai, or to allow the Egyptian *katana* to remain hanging over their heads, in the form of a continuing threat of expanding Egypt's small strip eastward by degrees commensurate with the growth of our armed forces' capabilities.

Everyone working in defense and Egyptian national security was acutely aware of this. Everyone was worried about how we would strike against Israel and how the coming battle would be managed, politically and militarily. And, although still a young diplomat, I had ideas I was encouraged to present to the national security advisor. This important man always encouraged me and other members of his office staff to discuss strategic affairs related to the coming war and how we could manage its progress in a manner best suited to our interests. We sought to secure a lively diplomatic process within a time frame that took into account military requirements until an accord was reached.

I had my own discussions and memoranda with Hafiz Ismail. One day in June 1973, a few months before the war, I wrote that we must prepare a surprise strike aiming to achieve limited objectives on the other side of the Suez Canal in Sinai, after which we must transition to diplomatic efforts in the form of direct or indirect negotiations with Israel, until it agreed to withdraw from Egyptian territory. I presented my memorandum to Dr. Abdel Hadi Makhlouf, who presented it to the national security advisor, who unfortunately kept it. (I always enjoyed reading his astute comments and observations, written in his trademark flowing hand.) Dr. Makhlouf's response reached me a few days later, and treated me to an extensive response to my memorandum, handwritten by Hafiz Ismail.

> Aboul Gheit,
> Your memorandum raises a number of issues related to military action. I cannot say I agree with you.
>
> 1. As I understand it, you are assuming:
>   a. A surprise Egyptian strike.
>   b. A rapid blow to achieve specific objectives.
>   c. Israel accepting the results and agreeing to a ceasefire.
>
> Perhaps you remain preoccupied by the image of operations in 1967; you seem convinced that these can be repeated.
>
> 2. There are a number of considerations that lead me to differ with you.
>   a. It will be difficult to strike a strategic blow to take Israel by surprise; war might begin before we start it.
>   b. Egyptians do not like to plan or execute Blitzkrieg-style actions. The nature of the positions we are faced with, the defenses, the Israeli vanguard, and the use of aerial forces will lead to a slugging match, with the edge to strength rather than agility.
>   c. American intervention to bring about a ceasefire (which you assume we will accept) assumes Israel being defeated in western Sinai, and

our destruction of most of its armed forces. The reverse is true: the US will sit back and wait as long as Israel possesses the capability for counterattack. Still, operations may well be drawn out, and we must plan for that. This requires a very special type of planning.

d. This raises the question: When and how will operations cease? I believe that we should not start unless we estimate that it is within our capacity to achieve a certain objective: to stir up the situation so as to allow for political action afterward, or provide a path to Egypt's future security, securing maritime traffic in Suez and the Gulf, and draining both Egypt's and Israel's capacities, thus leading them to deescalate gradually, if not for good.

e. These are just thoughts, which may need further contemplation and analysis, to form a conception of how war may be started— and finished. Please return this document.

Dr. Abdel Hadi Makhlouf took the beautifully handwritten note back to Hafiz Ismail. I was not to see it again until many years later, when Dr. Makhlouf brought it into my office in the Foreign Ministry in 2009, saying, "I kept this for thirty-six years." What a surprise! But what was more shocking, in my estimation, was the realization that Hafiz Ismail's intention was to conceal from me, and from others in his office, Egypt's real intentions and objectives for armed military intervention, and the way this action would be managed militarily and diplomatically.

Now, after so many years, I can see that we—especially national security advisor Hafiz Ismail, with his instincts and diplomatic and military experience—had a specific view of how both aspects, military and diplomatic, of this battle could be undertaken. Despite his accurate estimation that it would be difficult to catch the enemy off guard, tactically and strategically, Egypt managed to take the enemy by complete surprise.

Back to the armed efforts of October 1973. President Sadat, as far as the diplomatic management of the dispute was concerned, kept all lines and channels open to all powers, foremost among which was the Soviet Union, which had covert or overt tensions with Egypt in the previous three years. The Egyptian president kept the lines open with them with a view to securing military and international political support. He also kept communications open with the U.S. president and his secretary of state, Henry Kissinger.

From October 7 to October 28, with the start of the ceasefire, messages between the two sides were constantly shuttling back and forth. By the end of this period, Sadat and Nixon had exchanged fifteen messages. Twenty messages were exchanged between Hafiz Ismail and Henry Kissinger. I must mention here that Ahmed Maher al-Sayed, Hafiz Ismail's diplomatic consultant at the time and foreign minister of Egypt from May 2001 to July 2004, was the one who conducted all of these communications, under the direct command and supervision of the national security advisor, who worked to convey President Sadat's vision, demands, and position to his U.S. counterpart.

President Sadat continued waging the diplomatic battle by means of constant communication with the British, by virtue of their close relationship with Washington; with the shah of Iran, whom Sadat saw as a potential ally who could be enlisted into working on the Americans; and, naturally, a number of other parties. A never-ending stream poured into Egypt of ambassadors, envoys, and messengers from other countries, with whom Sadat kept the lines of communication open with a view to putting an end to the fighting, circumstances permitting, in the service of the strategic objectives of the war.

Two pivotal points remain. The first concerns a message that had everyone talking: Hafiz Ismail's message to Kissinger nearly forty-eight hours after the start of the armed action, in response to a communication from the U.S. secretary of state. "Egypt," it said, "has no wish to broaden or deepen the confrontation." It has been said by some, including highly knowledgeable analysts and people of high standing, that Egypt's action rashly exposed its intentions and gave Israel and the US carte blanche in choosing their own responses, diplomatically and militarily. But I want to go on record to say that I disagree. The US and many Arab parties spoke of the possibility of Jordan launching its own front, further complicating things with Israel. Pressure was applied to Jordan to expand the conflict, and to join Egypt and Syria in their efforts. There were somewhat apprehensive messages from the US warning of this possible development.

Meanwhile, Israel ordered airstrikes on Egyptian forces in the Nile Delta, close to the front. During an Israeli air raid on Tanta Air Base, soon after the Egyptian MiG-21 aircraft proved their efficacy, an Israeli fighter aircraft—mistakenly, under threat from Egyptian aircraft, or deliberately—bombed a village close by. Newspapers from the time bear this out. In any event, President Sadat attempted to keep the lines of communication open with the US, and at the same time to limit the confrontation with Israel to the front lines in Egypt and Syria, keeping things contained for diplomatic and political reasons in the event of a ceasefire becoming necessary. Despite his rage at the attack on civilians, Sadat assigned Hafiz Ismail to give Kissinger, who was in intensive communications with Egyptian Intelligence and the Central Intelligence Station in Cairo, the message mentioned above: "Egypt has no wish to broaden or deepen the confrontation." This was a clear reference to his lack of encouragement to Jordan to open fire, although the Arab pressure from without and popular pressure from within did finally lead Jordan to send an armed brigade via Jordanian territory into southern Golan for a confrontation with Israel on Syrian soil.

Hafiz Ismail's communication was an extension of the message that Egypt had no desire to deepen the clashes by resorting to striking civilian targets. This was not impossible, for Egypt at the time had an arsenal of Scud-B missiles well capable of striking Israeli territory in Negev. This veiled threat appeared to achieve its end: there were no more strikes on any Egyptian cities or villages far inland. There were no more civilian casualties in Egypt.

It is my understanding—to the best of my ability as an analyst—that Hafiz Ismail strongly believed in maintaining a limited zone of military action, and that this was what he conveyed to Kissinger, in a message authored by his political advisor, Ahmed Maher. This is the reason, I believe, we were shocked when our leadership was accused of inadvertently betraying both the details of Egypt's military strategy and its limited nature to Israel and the US. In my opinion, the critics may have made the mistake of linking the two points above in their reading of Hafiz Ismail's response to Kissinger, and thus incorrectly concluded that this message led to a third Arab party joining the battle and the targeting of civilians in airstrikes.

My evaluation is borne out by the army's efforts to develop the attack on October 14, moving eastward toward the Sinai straits, where the attack ceased in the evening after the troops sustained heavy losses. This was also the source of the attempt to develop the attack south of the front, by sending in the First Mechanized Infantry Division toward Ras Sidr, also aborted under heavy Israeli attack.

The days of armed conflict were behind us. Fighting ceased. The front finally fell silent on October 28. Major-General Abdel Ghani al-Gamasy met with General Aharon Yariv to agree on the procedures required for a stable ceasefire. We were still staying at Abd al-Moneim Palace in Heliopolis—an extremely ascetic campsite for the national security advisor, who, I remember, insisted that we subsist on army rations. I developed an aversion to black-eyed peas and zucchini with tomato sauce and rice that lasted for years. I was forced to eat nothing else for a month!

My final point on Egypt's ability to achieve its military ends by armed means, and the end of the conflict, is my utter conviction that Egypt fully achieved its political objectives—albeit over the long term—via armed conflict. This conflict's success, and the fact that it ended with Egypt still in possession of active and capable armed forces, should not conceal the magnitude of the dangers with which it was fraught, nor the efforts expended to achieve its ends. There was suffering; there was hardship; there were great sacrifices, which can only be fully understood by those who took part in this Herculean task. The Second Army was under threat; the Third Army was under siege. Still, Egyptian insistence and the will to fight and foil the enemy's plans staved off all their attempts at defeating us. On the diplomatic front, this side of the confrontation showed exemplary creativity and initiative: our objectives were well-conceived and pursued without fear or hesitation.

On October 28, 1973, the war achieved its political ends, placing Egypt on the path to a final settlement that gave rise to Camp David and the Egypt–Israel peace treaty. What is certain, what has become abundantly clear in the fullness of time, is that once the battle was over, Egypt regained its strategic balance vis-à-vis Israel, both on the battlefield and in the region—a balance that had been lost for over six years, since the defeat of 1967. Egypt's armed forces compelled the US to finally take serious action to achieve a political settlement that, while slow to arrive, led to Egypt regaining and asserting full ownership of all of Sinai and returning to the international borders of 1906 between Egypt and Palestine/Israel. The presence of active and alert Egyptian armed forces capable of taking action against Israel, in addition to an air force with proven efficacy in battle, plus a concentration of efficient Egyptian naval units controlling the southern part of the Red Sea, convinced the US beyond any reasonable doubt that Egypt could, if it wished, repeat the exercise at any moment it saw fit. This led the US to conduct the first serious efforts—via Secretary Kissinger—to defuse the Egypt–Israel military conflict, which led to a threat to the world in the form of potential nuclear war between the two superpowers in the final week of October. This paved the way for efforts to reach a political solution which, albeit in stages, achieved all the objectives of the military action Egypt was forced to undertake when its diplomatic efforts failed.

The war reaffirmed Clausewitz's saying that war is a continuation of politics by other means. Sadat—and his advisor (*mustashar*) Hafiz Ismail—were well aware of this, strategizing with depth and maturity. Some in Egypt, and maybe also in Syria, imagined, conversely, that war ought to continue until the enemy is roundly defeated and absolute victory is achieved. Not only do I disagree with this way of thinking, but I also see it as myopic, ignoring the balance of power between Egypt and Israel at the time and the positions and policies of the two superpowers of that era.

4 American Assessments of the Situation

The previous chapter gave a brief overview of Egyptian diplomatic efforts to get things moving on the political front in the early months of 1973. Egypt sought to convince the United States to accept its view, namely that it would be dangerous to continue the deadlock in the Egyptian–Israeli situation, and of the consequent importance of the US putting pressure on Israel to relinquish its stubbornness and make sincere and real efforts—led by the US and with support from the Soviet Union—to achieve peace with Egypt and withdraw from Sinai to the 1906 Egypt–Palestine borders, conceding complete Egyptian sovereignty over that territory.

Egypt, as I mentioned, reached out to the US. The Egyptian national security advisor agreed to an initial meeting with his counterpart, Henry Kissinger, to look into possible ways and means of reaching an Egypt–US agreement that might open a serious path to—and perhaps the start of moving toward—a peaceful settlement. Long before the October crossing of the canal, on February 25–26, 1973, a meeting had been arranged for the two parties on Long Island, not far from New York City, for consultations. Although I was not party to these consultations, which were only attended on the Egyptian side by Hafiz Ismail, Abdel Hadi Makhlouf, Ahmed Maher al-Sayed, and First Secretary Ehab Wahba, all from Hafiz Ismail's office, I was able to read the transcript of those meetings upon their return. I was also briefed by Ahmed Maher on many of the details. US official sources published, years later, a number of details of this meeting.

Today, we may assess this initial Egyptian–American meeting as an attempt by each party to find out where the other stood. The Egyptian side reaffirmed Egypt's commitment, to date, to finding a peaceful solution to the dispute via faithful implementation—and clear interpretation—of Security Council Resolution 242, as well as Egypt's readiness to negotiate the required settlement as envisaged by the resolution. On the American side, Kissinger said at the Paris meeting on May 20, that the US was prepared to take responsibility for getting the situation moving. However, the US was very clear about Kissinger's take on how to deal with the situation: he proposed slow step-by-step activity over a long period, possibly two years or more, which might be built on a temporary settlement as a first stage, followed by a final and durable settlement after a certain period of time. The American side also made it clear that they found the possibility of success remote if a final settlement was sought via a single step. The reason for this is that the US was convinced that the matter was complex and convoluted, with many other considerations beyond the Egypt–Israel situation and affecting other Arab countries involved in the conflict.

The general impression on both the Egyptian and the American side after this first meeting was positive, despite a certain degree of natural suspicion of the other's motives, thought processes, and intentions. They showed readiness to move forward and hold more of these talks, to look into what kind of agreement might be reached regarding ideas to open the way for a legitimate move.

In the wake of this initial meeting, there was a great deal of talk about the importance of Egyptian military action, and the necessity of not relying completely on American statements of goodwill. Israel would not comply with anything that ran counter to its hopes of imposing its will on the Arab states, by dint of its military superiority and the impact of the invasion. The Egyptians, as everyone recalls, threatened international actors that they would not wait too long; after all, it had already been nearly six years since their land was invaded. It was not too farfetched, they intimated, to imagine Egypt breaking the ceasefire or conducting a military operation. In fact, an American document declassified in 2000 (in accordance with American law) states that the US, like the other superpower at the time, was closely following Egypt's preparations. This document, dated April 1973, indicates that the US was aware of Egypt's war efforts, having made "an observation of hostile intent." The author outlines these observations as follows:

- In the first quarter of 1973, Sam-6 anti-aircraft batteries were moved from Aswan and surrounding areas to within thirty kilometers west of the Suez Canal. The Americans also noted much development in the batteries of Sam-2 anti-aircraft missiles, with a clear uptick in their operating efficiency.
- About thirty French Mirage 5s were brought in from Libya, which had signed a contract to buy them in 1969 with the intent of allowing Egypt to use them in any confrontation with Israel. Egyptian pilots were also being trained on this aircraft. The aircraft, the report said, had already arrived in Egypt.
- Sixteen Hawker Hunter older-model fighter aircraft were brought in from Iraq, with Iraqi pilots, and Egyptian pilots were being trained to use them. Egyptian air bases started using these in April 1973.
- Egyptian heavy bombers were moved from Aswan to areas surrounding Cairo, especially the Cairo West Air Base, which had always been a base for these bombers. The U.S. report adds that there were no indications of these bombers being moved or equipped with air-to-ground missiles. The latter were used in the October War to great effect, destroying Israeli radar stations and command communications and controlling Mount Umm Margam in Sinai.
- In April 1973, the alert status of the Egyptian air force was raised, and Egyptian air squadrons were redistributed and their combat efficiency increased in preparation for being commissioned for new combat missions in light of the arrival of the fighter bombers from Libya.
- A great many army units, including Special Forces units, were moved from all over Egypt to areas close to the Suez Canal. The US received information about major plans for an Egyptian crossing of the canal, choosing a time when the moon would be full. The American report even mentions May 19 and June 16, 1973, as possible dates for a large-scale Egyptian military operation.
- Jordanian sources—with British support, the U.S. report says—expressed their concerns as to the repercussions of the situation, due to Egypt's insistence on conducting a large-scale military operation regardless of the outcome. Moreover, the U.S. assessment says that available information indicated that King Hussein of Jordan had told Israel he feared that the situation would deteriorate militarily if things remained as they were, with Israel refusing any move to initiate a real peace process.
- There were indications of Egyptian attempts to arrange an Arab oil embargo against western nations that stood with Israel in case of military action.

- The U.S. document illustrates this by saying, "Such action on the part of Egypt will be consolidated and increased in the coming period, in order to achieve one or both of the following objectives: either an actual Egyptian military operation across the Suez Canal, or convincing international actors to intervene between the two parties to the dispute, achieving a political breakthrough in the situation." The American document goes on to say, "Egypt may attempt to invade areas east of the Suez Canal for a few days only, so as to force an international intervention; Egyptian troops are established in strength in areas east of Cairo all the way to the Suez Canal."

- The U.S. assessment report states that while it was difficult to be sure of Egypt's intentions, it was imagined that President Sadat had not yet made a final decision with regard to the form, scale, or timing of any military action. The Egyptian economic situation, it adds, was in decline; however, the assessment was that these conditions would not impose their weight on President Sadat or drive him to large-scale military action, since the Egyptian president was well aware that a failed military operation might have the effect of removing him from power.

- The U.S. assessment document, declassified in 2000, concludes that, after close monitoring by American sources, "it is most probable that President Sadat will await the proceedings of UN debates in May before making a decision on this matter." This was the effort undertaken by Egypt at that time to convince the Security Council, ending with the U.S. veto in 1973.

- The report goes on to mention more U.S. surveillance of movements surrounding the preparations for an armed battle between the Arabs and Israel, however concluding that in order to promote the building up of Arab diplomatic pressure on international powers, a number of Moroccan military armored units have been observed moving to Syria. Soviet transport ships were used to transfer the Moroccan equipment from Algerian ports. Twenty Algerian MiG-21s were moved to air bases in Libya, with the objective of raising the efficiency of Libyan air defenses, while remaining close to Egypt's borders should they be needed for any battle with Israel. There was also news that Algerian MiG-17 and MiG-15 fighter aircraft were being moved to Syria.

- The report also mentions Jordan: "The greatest weakness on the Arab front is Jordan's refusal to place its forces under the command of the joint Egyptian–Syrian leadership. However, it can be noted that there is currently [April 1973] tension on the Lebanese–Israeli borders.

The Palestinian resistance may take advance action, leading to the eruption of the situation on all fronts, especially the Egyptian–Israeli front. This may drag Jordan into any major warlike confrontation."

- As far as Soviet movements go, the U.S. document reveals close monitoring of Soviet positions. This indicated that the Soviets desired a degree of continued pressure on both the US and Israel. Still, they—the Soviets, that is—definitely did not desire any military action using advanced Soviet weaponry that might result in a new Arab defeat, thus negatively impacting on the policies of the Soviet leadership, in particular Brezhnev, who was eager to maintain the U.S.–Soviet pacification that had been in effect since mid-1972.

- The U.S. document mentions confirmed intelligence that the Soviets requested that Syria not enter into any armed confrontation with Israel, and to inform the Egyptians of that intention. To reconfirm this, Soviet Minister of Defense Marshal Grechko brought it up during his meeting with the French chief of staff. He asked his French counterpart to try and influence Egypt to move away from armed conflict.

- The American assessment came to an additional conclusion, namely that the US ruled out any flare-up of hostilities prior to the end of the UN session scheduled for May 1973. Egypt, the report concludes, would not undertake any large-scale military action in the coming few weeks—around six weeks.

This U.S. assessment—conveyed no doubt to Israel, which country's information and intelligence services were certainly instrumental in the compilation of the report—reveals that both the US and Israel were closely and carefully monitoring the framework in which Egypt was operating. The fact is that reading this document shows the seriousness and dedication of Arab efforts conducted via their armies. Morocco sent troops to Syria and Egypt (although U.S. intelligence did not specifically mention that development); Algeria sent aerial forces to both Libya and Syria; and, last but not least, Morocco sent ground units, whose equipment was transported by Soviet supply ships to protect it while being transported across the Mediterranean, and used Algerian ports for that purpose. Doubtless, Algeria's permission for this equipment to pass through its ports and across its soil, accompanied by Moroccans, represented a significant step that reflected Algeria's commitment to supporting Syria and the Arab East in their confrontation with Israel. When I say the 'Arab East'—Egypt and Syria—this of course meant that the Arab nation was united, and that its western side supported its eastern side in carrying out a consolidated military action.

Some Arabs who read about these events may be provoked by the U.S. document's statement that the Jordanian leadership informed Israel of the possibility of an upcoming military action by Egypt and Syria. My own assessment today—and at the time—is that Jordan, like Egypt and Syria, was using the possibility of military action against Israel to induce flexibility in that state's position or to motivate western powers to pressure Israel to reach a settlement with the Arabs. As for the US, note that Jordan refused to place its army under joint Egyptian–Syrian command. This may well be explained by the bitter defeat experienced by Jordan in 1967, which seemed to dictate caution and a reluctance to embark on a new venture. This is especially valid in light of what was being bandied about at the time by both Israel and the west, that Jordan could serve as an 'Arab Palestinian state'—a catastrophic suggestion, especially given the demographic imbalance between the two countries, namely that Palestinians far outnumbered Jordanians.

The American document also offers an assessment of the Egyptian economic situation, saying that President Sadat was capable of withstanding economic pressures and managing their threat to internal stability in Egypt. In truth—again—a reader of the minutes today, or indeed back then, of Sadat's meeting with the Egyptian National Security Council on September 30, that is, six days before the battle with Israel, would be convinced that these economic pressures had a decisive role in driving the Egyptian president to the necessity of taking action and attempting to find solutions to the Egyptian predicament. Without this, Egypt would have eventually fallen prey to economic and military failure.

The official U.S. assessment of the Egyptian and Arab situation at the time made it clear that the Americans—naturally—ascribed great importance to U.S.–Soviet relations. They appreciated that the Soviets would not accept Egypt embarking on a war, thus revealing the inadequacy of Soviet weaponry in a repeat of 1967's humiliation. The Americans shared this view, which shaped a great deal of Kissinger's actions vis-à-vis the 1973 battle and his insistence on not allowing U.S. weapons to be defeated by its Soviet counterpart.

It can be gleaned from the report that there were additional factors driving the U.S. assessment of the situation: not only the international détente achieved by the Moscow meeting between Brezhnev and Nixon in late 1972, but also the agreement between the leaders of the two superpowers on the importance of relaxing the military tensions in the relationship, and in every international issue of mutual interest, foremost among which, of course, was the tense situation in the Middle East.

Egypt had in fact been preparing for a large-scale military operation across the Suez Canal in March–April 1973. The Egyptian timeline originally set April as the month for that cross-channel leap. Israeli documents and writings post-October 1973 show that Israel was monitoring these preparations and getting ready for them. A review of Israeli military and media activity at that time shows that Israel was conducting small operations against Syria with the aim of convincing everyone of its ability to crush the Arabs. The media preparations conducted by Israeli military personnel and politicians were of course known to the Arab side; the Arabs were busily making preparations to stand up to these, while Egyptian diplomatic efforts continued unabated in hopes of achieving their ends. Egypt ultimately decided to give diplomatic efforts one final chance to achieve the desired goal, which is why President Sadat chose to defer military action instead of launching it in April as planned.

The postponement worked in favor of Egypt's strategic deception plan when the time came for Egypt to strike across the Suez Canal. Israel had observed Egyptian preparations in April, as had the US (as evidenced by the declassified document); Israel already had been making preparations and mobilizing. The joint Egyptian–Syrian strike never came. When the military action came on October 6, it took Israel by surprise, as it decided not to mobilize anew in response to the Egyptian preparations it observed. The mobilization had cost Israel a great deal in April 1973, after all. The Israelis saw the October mobilization as a toothless repetition of what had gone on earlier in the year. Israel thus ignored the writing on the wall, paying a hefty price for its clash with the Arabs.

In February 2013, I read a number of U.S. analyses of the possibility of Egyptian military action against Israel—documents written either in the days leading up to the fighting or during the clashes of October 1973. These were published by an American intelligence research center in January 2013, and dealt with the CIA's success or failure in its surveillance of the war operation. The documents revealed recognition on the part of the US that the Egyptian strategic and tactical deception, on the military and political fronts, had fully achieved its objectives as far as the US and Israel were concerned. In fact, the CIA went so far as to present a report on possible developments in the situation to Henry Kissinger on the evening of October 5, in which it ruled out any direct Egyptian military action against Israel. When the fighting broke out, the documents took to saying that the war would be short-lived and end with a crushing defeat for the Arabs. The US, they said, would have to pressure Israel to accept a ceasefire within a few days. However, Egyptian military obduracy managed to give the lie to all these assessments and expectations.

It may be relevant here to go back to the communications between the US and Egypt in early 1973 in preparation for another meeting between the national security advisors of the two countries, in a suburb of Paris, for further talks on how to start the ball rolling on serious peace efforts. This was in accordance with Egypt's decision to allow more time for American–Egyptian efforts to produce a peaceful settlement and explore the possibility of the Security Council and the UN intervening, in the hope that the latter could have some influence on Israel.

The meeting was held on May 20, 1973. Hafiz Ismail, accompanied by the Egyptian working group, met with Kissinger, who had also come to France as part of a schedule of meetings and efforts to settle the Vietnamese crisis, whose negotiations were moving forward at that time.

The Americans had raised two points with Egypt at their previous meeting in the US in February. The first was that the US was offering a move toward a settlement in gradual increments or steps. It is noteworthy here that Kissinger stuck faithfully to this during all of his negotiations with Egypt, even after the October War. It led to an extended peace process, which started on November 7, 1973, with Kissinger's arrival in Egypt, and ended with the second disengagement between Egypt and Israel in May 1975, as well as the implementation of a series of additional Israeli withdrawals deep into Sinai, allowing for the reopening of the Suez Canal to international shipping and the repopulation and rehabilitation of the Suez Canal cities.

The second point Kissinger discussed with Hafiz Ismail was his request that Egypt come up with a new vision or put forth an initiative that would leave the way open for the US to put pressure on Israel to take steps to reach a settlement and final peace. However, the US made clear that it could not guarantee Israeli compliance, nor its own ability to apply pressure on the Israelis successfully, due to the internal situation in America.

The Paris meeting, held at a villa owned by a CIA official, began with Kissinger reaffirming that he had no intention of making promises he could not keep; that the US wanted to tell Egypt that its role in the Middle East was independent of Israel; and that the US, as a result of Israel's internal situation and the hard line taken by Israel's leaders in preparation for the upcoming elections, could not guarantee that its views and voice would be heard in that country.

Hafiz Ismail responded by saying that recalcitrance was one of the inherent qualities of the Israeli stance, election or no election. The US, he added, could not claim with any truth that it was powerless to pressure Israel—the shipments of U.S. armaments were still flowing, after all, and there were contracts in place to supply more U.S. fighter jets to Israel over 1974–75, a fact that raised profound concerns in Egypt. What made matters worse, Ismail noted, was that the US was pushing the Soviet Union to agree to more Soviet Jews emigrating to Israel, to say nothing of the financial incentives the US offered the Soviets to agree to this.

Hafiz Ismail moved on to the substance of the meeting. He made it clear that Egypt was quite prepared to sign a peace treaty with Israel. This was the Egyptian response to the U.S. request to offer a new initiative. The Egyptian national security advisor then discussed the American idea of a gradual Egyptian–Israeli settlement, saying that Egypt feared, with good reason, the US' talk of an interim or temporary settlement. The reason, naturally, was that an interim settlement has a way of taking on permanence, accompanied by a cessation of efforts to achieve peace or the US losing interest. It was therefore essential, according to Ismail, to look into how the proposed interim settlement could be linked to the final settlement, within a strict time frame. What was required if Israel agreed to the American plan, he said, was that both sides, American and Israeli, announce that this interim step in withdrawing from Sinai—in exchange for security guarantees for Israel—would be a part of a comprehensive peace process with an acceptable time frame.

It was now Kissinger's turn to speak. He asked Hafiz Ismail about the Egyptian areas for negotiation, with a view to creating an agenda for them. He said that it was difficult for the US to accept any Egyptian attempt to agree (with the US) on a precise interpretation of the disputed articles of UN General Assembly Resolution 242 of November 22, 1967, generally considered the basis for any settlement, while compiling the general areas. Ismail retorted that the general areas constituted the agenda for negotiations and that it was necessary to elaborate them in some detail so that Israel would not equivocate. The Egyptian national security advisor went on to criticize the U.S. position in assisting Israel's nuclear program. Kissinger cut him off, insisting that the US would never assist any party in acquiring nuclear weapons or the knowledge to develop them; indeed, he said, the US was constantly badgering Israel to join the Nuclear Non-Proliferation Treaty. He asked the Egyptians to give him details of any specific occurrences where the US had assisted Israel in building military nuclear capacity.

Hafiz Ismail went on to explain the course of Egyptian diplomatic efforts, affirming that Egypt had resorted to the United Nations and reopened the Middle East issue before the Security Council to obtain adequate interpretations not provided by the Security Council resolution of 1967. He then alluded to the fact that Egypt had no desire to push forward with military operations, and that this was only on the table because of Israeli intransigence. Egypt, Ismail said, was following the Vietnamese people's fight; he emphasized that his country was keeping a careful eye on how this extended conflict was unfolding. Kissinger heard the innuendo and responded with some disgruntlement that it was dangerous to compare the situation in Vietnam, which was a fight that had been going on for years because of completely different geographical and topographical circumstances than the deserts of the Middle East. In Egypt, he said, we must recognize that desert battles and military clashes are always time-limited and conclusive in their results. They are different from jungle fighting. Kissinger stated quite clearly that, in his view, any military undertaking by Egypt would have negative consequences for Egypt, and damage its standing in the region.

It was now Hafiz Ismail's turn to speak. He said that the initiative President Sadat had charged him to convey to the Americans aimed at transitioning from a state of war to a state of peace. Egypt, he said, was asking the US to offer a clear American interpretation of UN Resolution 242, directly from the White House. He said that Egypt expected the US to officially announce its acceptance of Egypt's borders with Palestine/Israel—a view that it expected would include complete Egyptian sovereignty over Sinai.

Kissinger responded with what may be called a great deal of evasiveness. There might not be an issue with accepting Egyptian sovereignty; however, there were security arrangements for Israel that must be guaranteed. Kissinger hinted that he could see the US accepting nominal Egyptian sovereignty, although he was aware that Israel would be inflexible about its security concerns.

The second Egyptian–American meeting was drawing to a close. What with consultations and lunch, it had lasted about four hours. The Egyptians promised to let the Americans know President Sadat's decision, and his view on the American proposal of a gradual, step-by-step settlement. Kissinger asked in return that the Egyptians postpone raising the issue at the Security Council until after the Soviet–American summit in Washington on June 18, 1973. Something might come out of it that would be relevant to the Middle East. Hafiz Ismail said that Egypt might look into postponing the United Nations, but added that the US needed to commit to affording that effort a real chance with the Security Council.

Both sides agreed on the possibility of arranging a third meeting, to look further into the chances of achieving a peaceful settlement. The reader must take note of the extra attention given by the Egyptian national security advisor to these meetings, which revealed a great deal—for the first time—about America's ideas for reaching a settlement. Hafiz Ismail, it must be noted, tried to convince President Sadat, during the Egyptian National Security Meeting on September 30, to postpone this major step and leave room for a third meeting with Kissinger, which might bear the fruit that Egypt sought via armed action. President Sadat's mind, however, was made up. His position was only reinforced by the U.S. stance at the Security Council in June–July 1973, which can only be described as absolutely negative.

Finally, I would like to convey some of the conclusions reached in this meeting via an official U.S. document prepared by Alfred Leroy ("Roy") Atherton, then deputy assistant secretary of state and later ambassador to Egypt, and presented to Kissinger to be sent on to the White House. It was released in 2001 as part of the thirty-year declassification program. This document included a statement that Hafiz Ismail made it clear to Kissinger during a private conversation between them, just before that day's working lunch, that Egypt was completely prepared to sign any peace treaty in accordance with the American concept offered to Syria and Jordan in Paris. Hearing this, Kissinger asked about Egypt's vision of the nature of the peace with Israel, how any Egypt–Israel accord would affect the Palestinian question, and the situation between Syria/Jordan and Israel. The Egyptians did not explain their vision in detail, but they did insist on the US' announcement of Egypt's full sovereignty over Sinai.

Both sides left the CIA representative's villa in the suburbs of Paris with an understanding that there might be yet another meeting, and that Hafiz Ismail would respond to the Americans with regard to the relevant questions and ideas. Each went home. They would only meet again after the end of the armed conflict, in October 1973. What is certain today is that anyone who reads the results of these meetings and the elements that made them up cannot miss the fact that many American ideas were advanced and implemented in the years to follow.

5 The Battle Approaches

In this chapter, I reexamine what I have called the time leading up to battle, and the crises of the first week of war. Two main points must be stressed, and anyone following the conflict closely, who lived through those days, will recognize the importance of mentioning them before launching into an overview of that historic conflict.

First, I am writing today of events that occurred forty years ago. During those days, I recorded a great deal about the events in diaries, documenting my observations. I commented on what I observed moment by moment. Today, so many long years later, I have gone back to reevaluate what I wrote in the heat of the moment, reaching conclusions about my observations at the time and their continuing effect on Egypt, its view of war, and its exigencies today. Of these diaries, I need to emphasize that I was writing about my personal experiences, not relying on the writings of others who might have taken part in some way or another in the events. I am not writing in order to respond to anyone's evaluation or to any issues. Finally, it is not my intent to review or evaluate the writings of Arab or foreign military analysts or historians who have attempted their own analyses of this conflict as a whole or even its minute details—quite the contrary. It may appear sometimes that I disagree with them, but what is certain is that what I write now has its source in meticulous records made at the time the events were actually taking place, as I lived, read, or experienced them.

These diaries were made from October 5, 1973, at 2130 hours, to 1700 hours on November 25, 1973. That is when the diaries stop. I attempted, when writing them, to set down with great brevity what was happening for the duration of those fifty days—a great deal. I regret this somewhat today; history was being made before my eyes, and perhaps I should have recorded a great deal more than I in fact wrote down. However, my method was influenced by the great number of diaries I had read by important military and political figures of the past, especially from the Second World War—figures like Franz Halder, chief of the Oberkommando des Heeres staff, and Field Marshall Alanbrooke, chief of the Imperial General Staff during that war, among other famous and influential individuals. Their diaries are short in length, precise in nature, and avidly read by great strategic commentators. For a great many students of military strategy, they still light the way toward understanding the philosophy of the clash of powers in war as a means to achieve countries' and societies' objectives, and the combination of diplomacy and war when great powers and peoples engage in conflict.

Some may imagine that I seek to compare myself to these great figures of history, that numerous company of outstanding military and diplomatic leaders who have left us their enlightening observations. But the truth is that my goal in 1973, as it is today, consisted in showing my countrymen what I saw at the time, aside from any duties I may have undertaken or positions I may have held—up to foreign minister of Egypt, the greatest Arab country and one of the most influential powers in the affairs and development of the Arab region.

The second point I would like to emphasize also has to do with the mission I undertook at the end of my journey in the service of Egyptian society, namely the responsibilities of foreign minister of Egypt. In that role, my task was to plan Egyptian diplomatic affairs and implement a successful and influential foreign policy to protect and secure Egypt's national and strategic interests, in a region plagued by tensions morning and evening as a result of this event or that.

The obligations of my past public service bind me even today: I shall always scrupulously avoid speaking of subjects that might negatively affect our relations with other parties. On the other hand, I am no less scrupulous in reporting my observations and thoughts utterly honestly; I recorded these with the reverence due the written word, and great care for accuracy and clarity. All of us who worked with Hafiz Ismail could sense that something great and momentous was underway. This feeling intensified in light of a great many indications, of which I took precise, written note.

The most important of these indications of approaching war was what I noticed on a day in August 1973: the name of then Brigadier General Taha al-Magdoub, chief of the planning branch of the Armed Forces Operation

Department, on the national security advisor's meeting agenda. That day, I saw that scowling, swarthy military man, with typical Egyptian features, walking down the long corridor in Abdin Palace to Hafiz Ismail's office. Along that corridor were situated the national security advisor's office and that of the presidential secretary for information, a post then occupied by Dr. Ashraf Marwan. I noticed at the time—or think I noticed—that he was wearing dark khaki battle dress and a green beret.

This visit was repeated—to my surprise—two more times. None of us at Hafiz Ismail's office, except for Ambassador Abdel Hadi Makhlouf, office director to the national security advisor, knew the reason behind these visits between Taha al-Magdoub and Hafiz Ismail. However, I must admit that when I was given the chance to open the iron safe I mentioned before and examine the documents and records pertaining to the war, I found out that Taha al-Magdoub had been sent by Ahmed Ismail Ali, commander in chief of the armed forces and minister of war at the time, to keep Hafiz Ismail abreast of the general framework of war plans, its strategic and mobilization goals, and its desired time frame. In my estimation, the cooperation between these two men—these two military giants, if I may say—was always optimal: they exchanged a great many ideas and proposals, sharing their information and views openly while displaying no sensitivities or competitiveness. Their main concern was the army: how best to build its capacities and abilities, and supply it with all the available resources to strengthen it for an upcoming battle that would restore Egypt's dignity and recover Sinai, a main objective on the path to a possible settlement to the Palestinian issue.

Both Hafiz Ismail and Ahmed Ismail Ali were old-school Egyptian military men. As young men, they witnessed the Second World War being waged in the Egyptian desert. Doubtless this left its mark on them, both in terms of understanding military strategy and the use of armed forces within a general strategic framework, and the tactical details of how to use forces and weapons in all-out war, especially in the desert. This was the necessary introduction, and basic training, that polished their abilities for a confrontation with Israel in the Naqab (Negev) desert and in Sinai. Both were deserts where it was necessary to learn from the lessons of those who had trodden this path before.

These two men had also studied all modern military operations in North Africa, whether of the British Eighth Army under Montgomery and his predecessors, or the Germans' North Africa Corps under "the Desert Fox," Erwin Rommel. Hence, they both understood the effects of each specific weapon on the outcome of a battle. They equally grasped the role of the tank as the master of desert warfare, but also the effectiveness of antitank RPGs in open desert country. They understood, to expand upon this, the effect of infantry soldiers stubbornly standing their ground. They were well aware of the dreadful power of aircraft to cause ground troops heavy losses during open movement, and hence the importance of concealment and camouflage, and similar arts. These two great men had been awarded the highest academic degrees in the 1950s, from the Royal Military Academy Sandhurst in Camberley, Surrey, and the Frunze Military Academy in the Soviet Union. They shared a great mutual respect, and a keen understanding of both the capabilities and the limitations of a given military force.

After the war—I have mentioned the circumstances of how this came about—I was granted access to the general framework of their plans, Granite 1 and Granite 2, which Taha al-Magdoub had, at Ahmed Ismail Ali's request, entrusted to Hafiz Ismail for discussion with the commander in chief. I find myself pausing for a moment here to say that I thought it very odd for Hafiz Ismail to have mentioned the subject of that conversation at the Egyptian National Security Council Assembly on September 30, headed by President Sadat, and his differences with the commander in chief, especially as the documents in his office revealed the general framework of the war and the strategy for its military management. From some people close to Field Marshall Ahmed Ismail, I learned that he, too, was rather surprised by the position and vision that Hafiz Ismail presented to him on that day. However, what is certain is that this event did not affect their relationship, which remained strong to the end.

It remains to say that Brigadier General Taha al-Magdoub's visits were not the only indication of war. Also telling was the sudden frequency of foreign diplomats contacting Egyptian ambassadors in different capital cities, all warning against the dire consequences of any military action. These included Russian statesmen who remained unconvinced of Egypt's military ability and capacity, in a wide-scale battle with Israel, spanning the entire Suez Canal front, the Mediterranean, and the Red Sea. Naturally, as an Egyptian, I am inclined to believe in my country's capabilities and its military capacities. Regardless, I believe that the root of our profound difference of opinion with the Soviets was their failure to understand the magnitude and profundity of the national humiliation we had suffered in 1967, and our desire to reclaim the honor of our military and our country.

In this the Soviets appeared not to have recalled their own lessons of the Second World War, when the Red Army emerged victorious. When defense of the nation and its honor motivates soldiers to commit their lives, armies—from the lowliest private to the commander of the main formation, or the entire army—can rise to the most severe challenges and pressures. With such motivation, responsible use of their capacities, proper insight, and adequate training and armaments, they rush aggressively to accomplish their mission, however impossible it may appear to others who fail to understand the power of the soldier's will.

Indications continued during the summer months of 1973 that war was fast approaching. Israeli air reconnaissance attempts were intensifying, both on the front and deep within Egypt. Many intelligence reports sent to the president's information secretary, with standing orders that the national security advisor always receive a copy, reflected an Israeli desire to find out intensively and minute by minute the movements of Egyptian forces, especially the air force, and to gauge their reactions to the Israeli sorties.

During this period, various world leaders sought to convince Egypt to seek peaceful, diplomatic solutions. Among them were Romania's Ceaușescu and Yugoslavia's Tito, who were widely seen as influential within Egypt and whose support for such diplomatic initiatives thus was presumed needed.

Amid these maneuvers, communications, and movements, Egypt was engaged in preparing the groundwork to reduce Israel's, and thence the US', capacity for diplomatic evasion at the Security Council, in an attempt to strip them of a great deal of their international support—support that would be urgently needed by Egypt if it did enter into armed conflict. Hence, Egypt presented the issue once again to the Security Council. However, to safeguard the secrecy of the Egyptian movements and objectives, and the reason behind Egypt's call for a Security Council session, Hafiz Ismail sent me on a one-night mission in July to meet with our foreign minister, Dr. Zayyat, who was then in Paris. I was to bring him written instructions on the framework of our goals, in light of sensitive information that reached Egypt after Zayyat had already left Cairo for Paris and London for consultations with his French and British counterparts, hoping to isolate the Israelis and Americans.

August 1973 arrived in a buzz of planning and organization. Diplomatic preparations were at their height. In the second half of August, I accompanied Hafiz Ismail and the office director for the national security advisor Dr. Abdel Hadi Makhlouf to Romania and Yugoslavia. We met President Ceaușescu at a resort in Mangalia, on the Black Sea. Hafiz Ismail explained Sadat's vision to Ceaușescu, mentioning his readiness to start indirect negotiations or proximity talks via Romania. He asked for Ceaușescu's assessment of whether Golda Meir, prime minister of Israel at the time, had enough power and negotiating clout to accept a withdrawal from Egyptian lands and move toward an equitable settlement for Palestine, or if she still clung to her insistence that there was no such thing as a Palestinian people—to the extent that she once referred to herself as "We, the Palestinians," denying the existence of that suffering people. We went on to convey the same messages to President Tito, in an even lovelier resort, the breathtaking Croatian city of Dubrovnik. Both leaders promised to convey Egypt's views to Israel, whose eventual responses were chilly and arrogantly phrased.

Egypt set out on the course of war through the sweltering heat of August. The Egyptian public spent a preoccupied summer, full of speculation. I could see that hard times were ahead, and that I needed several days to recharge my mind and body. I needed to spend some time with my wife and son. Having obtained permission from Dr. Makhlouf for a short vacation, I took a trip to Alexandria.

In Alexandria, as was my habit every summer, I visited a close relative of mine, Vice Admiral Fouad Zikri, at his home in the beach suburb of Agami. As a thirty-year-old diplomat, I had an especially privileged relationship with a man who had twice been admiral of the Egyptian navy, once from 1967 to 1969 and again from 1972 to 1974. Zikri appreciated my interest in—my passion for—studying military history, war strategy, and the lives of historical figures, especially military leaders. He was something of a naval historian himself: his time spent studying in Britain and fluency in English had greatly broadened his knowledge. He was widely and deeply read in naval battle strategies, especially during the First and Second World Wars.

Our discussions were rich and varied. He was a serious and precise interlocutor. I told him of the indications I had noted, and that I felt it signified something momentous approaching, especially since the start of September 1973 tensions between Syria and Israel were escalating. Fouad Zikri's comments were extremely guarded: "We will cut off their communications and block their naval routes. We will strike a forceful blow. We will confound their plans and teach them a lesson." Since I knew him well, I assumed he was merely expressing his patriotism and his love for his country. I only understood what he meant after the war started, when Egyptian naval units revealed their presence at the entrance of Bab al-Mandeb and at the shores of Yemen—a message to Israel that controlling the Sharm al-Sheikh Straits, or Tiran and Sanafir, would do them no good, as we could close the Red Sea to Israeli maritime traffic, cutting off access to the port of Eilat.

I profoundly admired this man, who excelled at his command of the Egyptian navy in extremely difficult circumstances. He conducted its battles adroitly, showing great acumen and caution, achieving remarkable results that affected the outcome of the battle, especially toward the end.

Over the years, I visited him many times, sharing a viewpoint or some detail that I had read in an article or book on naval battles. He was always a fount of expertise, not only as a navy man but also in his capacity as an expert historian with profound knowledge of virtually every aspect of naval history.

As we were talking at his home on the coast, the radio blared. It was an announcement of an aerial battle that day between Syria and Israel. Israel announced that it had brought down thirteen Syrian MiG aircraft. Zikri froze in shock and worry. We had only just been talking about a number of meetings between Egypt and Syria that had taken place in Alexandria, at the highest level, bringing together the commander in chief and the Egyptian commanders of the armed forces with their Syrian counterparts—meetings I knew of and knew that Fouad Zikri had taken part in. Zikri leapt up and launched into a flurry of telephone calls to the naval operations room, then to the armed forces operations room. He returned grim-faced: the Israeli announcement was in all probability accurate.

Only later did I find out that it was not only Fouad Zikri who was deeply troubled; all the leaders of the armed forces shared his emotion. They were, after all, preparing for the October military action and count-ing on Syria's participation to disperse the enemy's efforts and fragment Israel's abilities with strikes from the north and south. I recall a conver-sation with then-President Hosni Mubarak about his experiences in the battles of 1973, during which I mentioned my experiences with Fouad Zikri—whom the former president admired a great deal—and that con-versation in September 1973, after the news that a number of Syrian fighter planes had been downed. Mubarak told me that he, too, had been stunned by these losses and consumed with worry over the abilities, or lack thereof, of our ally, which would be fighting alongside us within a few short weeks.

The reader may recall that the first of the previous two chapters dealt with the start of the war and offered a record of the approach of battle and the first twenty-four to thirty-six hours. The second chapter dealt with the cessation of hostilities and the achievement of the objectives of war as set out by President Sadat and carried out by a sagacious and fully knowl-edgeable command of the armed forces, by an army well-trained, for over six years, to perform its tasks and what these tasks required. This chapter aims to cover the remaining days of that first week of war, including the crisis, or crises, that occurred, and always do occur during battles and armed conflicts, which served to reveal their leaders' depth and determi-nation, or lack thereof, with the accompanying results of victory or defeat.

One such example was immediately forthcoming, on Monday, October 8, according to my diary. On that day, Egyptian troops were still flowing into Sinai, the bridgeheads reaching as deep in as fifteen kilometers behind enemy lines. These five divisions succeeded in consolidating their positions into two bridgeheads: the Third Army in the south and the Second Army in the north. On that day, military intelligence reported that the efforts of the enemy's air force were dispersed on our front, and that its ability to jam electronic signals was limited. It became clear that Egypt had destroyed the Bar-Lev line, in which the enemy had placed a great deal of faith. The army waited for the Israeli counterstrike, which never came. Our forces repulsed the Israelis' several disperses counterstrikes, dealing them heavy losses.

Meanwhile, there were indications that Syria was also achieving great successes in the Golan; their armored units had almost reached Upper Galilee. However, the Israeli air force was concentrating on repulsing the direct Syrian threat to Israel, and Syria ultimately sustained extremely heavy losses. Soviet sources began to speak of a Syrian desire for a cessation of hostilities, content with its successes so far. In my diary dated Monday, October 8, at 2330 hours: "Syria is leaning toward a ceasefire. The Soviets are repeating this in several capital cities." I felt intense worry—fear, even—about the repercussions of this situation if it should prove true. Israel might accept the ceasefire, leaving their army free to concentrate on the Egyptian front. My diaries for October 8 end at 2400 hours, with:

> The Soviet military command is notifying us, based on their close observation of the progress of fighting, that it is concerned that our bridgeheads lack sufficient depth of penetration. President Sadat is reassuring them that we will persist in deepening these bridges, and bring them together into two main ones.

Tuesday, October 9, came. At 0200 hours, my diary reads:

> Enemy attacks are still isolated and unable to breach our bridges. Enemy air force activity has failed to achieve its intent, namely blocking the consolidation and preservation of supplies and equipment and ammunition to the two armies in Sinai.

Syria reappears in the diaries:

> Our information from the Soviets, and our other official sources, reflects that Israel has forced the Syrian army to withdraw once again

from the Golan, with debilitating losses. The Syrian forces fought with incomparable courage, especially the armored units, which sustained great losses.

In addition, Israeli armored and aerial forces have launched intense activity focusing on the Egyptian front, in attempts to breach the bridgeheads, especially in the central sector of the Second Army, or to breach the missile battery defenses on the west bank of the Suez Canal.

The 0200 entry on October 9 reflects the difficulty of the situation and the approaching crisis. Minister Abd al-Fattah Abdullah, minister of state for cabinet affairs was with President Sadat at Tahra Palace and had attended and taken part in every meeting held by the president with ambassadors and other statesmen. He returned to Abd al-Moneim Palace, also known as Hurriya Palace, to transcribe the recordings of the meetings that had taken place that day. Dr. Abdel Hadi Makhlouf tasked me once again with supervising—and assisting—the typist on duty. All the contents of these documents were extremely classified, not to mention the additional effort required to decipher the arcane and baffling handwriting of Abd al-Fattah Abdullah!

The contents of the minutes shocked and disturbed me. Leonid Brezhnev, the general secretary of the Central Committee of the Communist Party of the Soviet Union, and the main Soviet decision-maker via the Politburo of the Communist Party, said that Syria wanted an immediate ceasefire. Brezhnev not only encouraged this, but also urged President Sadat to accept it, for fear that the military march might continue into Damascus. Not only would this, needless to say, pose a catastrophic threat to the region, it would also seriously damage Soviet interests in the region and its relationship to the other superpower. I must admit that I was terrified at the danger posed by this Soviet message. However, Sadat's response was decisive: Egypt would persist with armed confrontation until Egypt's political objectives were achieved in their entirety.

"This is a historic occasion with Syria," I wrote in the same paragraphs penned in the small hours of October 9. I went on to say:

> The president is sending an envoy to the Syrian president to impress upon him the importance of pushing on with the battle, switching now to defensive mode, with the objective of attrition; more military must be requested of the Soviet Union as part of the military supply, and the slow-moving Iraqi army must be brought into the war effort.

Now, in my overview of Tuesday, October 9—the daylight hours of that day—comes the time to record the events of 1830 hours.

> The situation is good. Extremely heavy enemy losses. All counterattacks repulsed. Enemy is exhausting its forces in parts, not as a comprehensive whole. Their losses are a direct result of their hasty efforts to make a dent in our forces. The 190th Israeli Armored Division is a good example. Ahmed Ismail telephoned Hafiz Ismail at 1600 hours to tell him that the Israeli armored divisions facing our forces are no longer able to fight. Hafiz Ismail says the army will advance when the stage of reorganizing and rearranging for the famous and much-talked-about regrouping effort is completed.

—an effort which I shall discuss in more detail later.

I must not forget to mention another event which took place that day—a day when all the news from the Egyptian front was positive. I had a chance to converse with Hafiz Ismail on the balcony of the palace that evening. Now he felt he could meet with any Israeli official on the spot—Yigal Allon, to be specific. The man with the different ideas for reaching a settlement with the Arabs. He was prepared to meet him anywhere, now that the army had struck and revealed the limitations of their capacities.

I was astonished at the boldness of his thinking, and this initiative. The truth was, however, that his attitude reflected how deeply he appreciated the results of military action, and his intention of using these successes to achieve the required political advantage and aims. My diary at 2000 hours on Wednesday, October 10, says:

> The Soviets are pressuring the president to agree to a ceasefire. The president categorically refuses. He raised his voice with the Soviet ambassador and threatened to expose the Soviet position. He also demanded that the Soviets keep up the flow of equipment, bridges, and aerials needed for the missile batteries, as well as an urgent air bridge—or else he would tell the entire Arab nation the truth. Clearly the Soviets are under pressure from the US, which is doubtless what President Sadat fears as well.

The decisive paragraph that day—indeed of the first week of war— deals with Sadat's telephone call to President Hafez al-Assad. The Syrian president indicated his conviction that Syria's military position was very good, and that they had fought back the Israeli incursions and put a stop to them. The Egyptian president informed his Syrian counterpart of Egypt's position vis-à-vis the Soviets.

After this talk with the Syrians came the report of the Egyptian president's envoy to the Syrians: he assured the president that they were going ahead with military actions. I must admit that the diaries reveal, for the first time, my concerns about the Soviets' position, and doubts about the Soviets held by many Egyptian statesmen. There were also some concerns and misgivings about the Syrians' vision of, and objectives for, the war. The two Arab parties had been coordinated militarily but their diverging political positions urgently needed coordination.

The Soviets' attempt to convince Sadat to accept a ceasefire, in my estimation, was due to their fear that the US might throw its full military might into supporting Israel, leading to the latter's military victory—a blow to Soviet interests. When Sadat rejected their position outright, they felt a need to salvage their relationship with Egypt, despite any doubts, distrust, or suspicion. Soviet leaders thus decided to re-supply both the Syrian and the Egyptian armies, making up for their losses. However, what is certain is that Soviet actions reflected the fact that the Soviets preferred the Syrians over the Egyptians—or, at least, reflected their perception that the Syrian army was in need of immediate and urgent support and assistance, while the requests of the Egyptian army evidently constituted a secondary priority.

According to my diary, the Soviets, having made the decision to provide military supplies, moved a number of Soviet armored vehicles to the port at Odessa, loaded with tanks to be delivered to Soviet ships for immediate departure. Confirmed intelligence available to us at the time indicated that the Soviets sent four hundred Soviet-made tanks between October 8 and 11. These arrived in Latakia on October 11 and were immediately offloaded for use by the Syrian army, which had lost a large number of tanks. The Israeli air force also stayed away from the Latakia port at that time, due to strongly worded Soviet messages that any attack on Soviet ships en route to Latakia or in the port would have serious consequences.

Meanwhile, Egyptian armed forces were awaiting the arrival of a large number of missile batteries, which Israel was destroying heavily to render the Egyptian air defense vulnerable and make it fly blind. We were also expecting a shipment of Volga longer-range missiles for the defense of our forces deep in Sinai. Doubtless those who planned the Egyptian attacks had timed them so as to ensure Egyptian ground troops would never find themselves outside the defenses afforded by their umbrella of anti-aircraft missiles. The plan also ensured that Egyptian capacities would not be exhausted in possibly destructive clashes with Israel. Herein lay the importance of air defense to the philosophy of battle; President Sadat's contacts and meetings—revealed by his meetings with the Soviet ambassador—focused on the need for this type of supplies in particular.

The moment to develop the attack was approaching. It was the moment we had all been waiting for, ever since our troops leapt onto the Bar-Lev line and destroyed it, rebuffing the dispersed counterattacks. Some felt we were leaving it rather too late; others understood the need to completely secure the troops against Israeli airstrikes, as mentioned above. In the early days, the Israelis concentrated on Syria, which received the opening strike of the battle. In the estimation of some at the time—myself among them—the Israeli focus on Syria defied all logic, since experience with this kind of conflict imposes on rear-echelon strategists to concentrate on the stronger power, the one with the greater capacity to defeat them, and only then to turn their attention to the weaker and less dangerous attacker. What was certain, however, is that Syrian armored vehicles drawing near to Upper Galilee imposed another strategy on the Israeli military leadership, namely to put Syria first. This was the source of the predicament in which the Syrian army found itself, which led to extreme sensitivity on the part of the Soviets—mentioned above—and the Syrian leadership. It also imposed on Egypt a move toward developing the battle, with an attempt either to reach the Sinai passes or to try and relieve the pressure on Syria with large-scale ground operations on the Egyptian front.

This brings us to the second crisis of the war. In parallel with the intensification of battle, Sadat's communications with foreign leaders intensified, as did his proactive diplomatic activity, even as the armies clashed. It may be useful here to glance at my diaries for Friday, October 12, and Saturday, October 13. They largely reflect the delicacy of the situation, which we had already intuited. At 0150 hours on Friday, I wrote:

> Syria's military situation not good at all. Israeli armored vehicles advanced toward Damascus, in a five-kilometer penetration. The Syrians are attacking violently to repulse the intrusion. What will happen if Syria withdraws from the battle? We will of course keep going. Have we lost the initiative? Perhaps. We're still waiting for the Volgas. The Soviets tell us they should arrive today or tomorrow. Clearly the battle will last longer than I originally imagined. Perhaps another fifteen days. The Israelis will soon focus the thrust of their efforts against us. The president is pressuring America via the oil-producing countries of the Gulf, especially Saudi Arabia. Also through

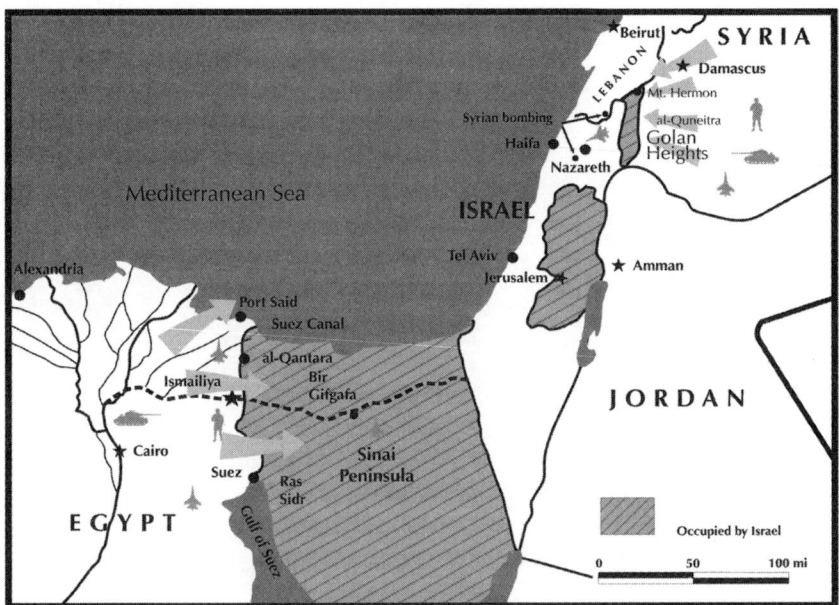

The crossing of the Egyptian canal by Egyptian forces and Syria's attack on the Golan Heights. Based on a map published in *TIME* magazine, October 1973.

continuing talks with Kissinger via Hafiz Ismail. We have warned the Americans that if the Israelis keep bombing civilian targets in Egypt, we will retaliate in kind. This is our second warning.

The Soviet air bridge to Egypt has been going on since yesterday. Will we have time to use the new missiles? Will we receive enough of them to make a meaningful difference? I hope so.

Additional bridge equipment has arrived. I imagine that the enemy will attack us fiercely soon. We will fight them off and defeat them, then move forward under missile cover; in fact, we might move forward much sooner, perhaps even before the enemy's major attack.

The situation is delicate; I don't think it is yet critical. Perhaps in two days' time. We are faced with three Israeli fighting groups. Advisor Hafiz Ismail is exasperated by the Syrian situation and has become extremely short-tempered.

My entry in the early hours of Saturday, October 13, focused on Syria:

The Syrian counterattack has managed to fend off the Israeli penetration. Everyone is optimistic. Syria will repulse it.

6

The October War: Military and Diplomatic Efforts, Coordinated

Years ago, I read Sir Winston Churchill's quote about Admiral John Jellicoe, whom Churchill famously dubbed "the only man on either side who could lose the war in an afternoon." Churchill was the head of the Royal Navy during the First World War until he left his post in 1916, after Britain's failure to take Gallipoli, and the attempt to penetrate the Dardanelles. Jellicoe had been the admiral of the Royal Navy in the Battle of Jutland—the British navy's first and last clash with the full force of the Imperial German Navy's High Seas Fleet, in 1916. The British navy was unable to achieve a decisive defeat and destroy what was, after all, a navy comparatively lacking in experience and weaker in ability, under the leadership of Admiral Scheer. The battle was over in a day. One of history's greatest naval battles ended in British losses, in terms of main ships, greater than those Germany sustained.

The battle was the subject of much discussion, spoken and written, after the fact, and the discussion did not wane even after the end of the First World War in 1918. Much of it focused on the odd reserve of Admiral Jellicoe, and asked why he had not invested his far greater superiority in a more aggressive approach. This was the subject of Churchill's famous quote, giving Jellicoe his due. The defeat of the Royal Navy on that day would have doubtless led to a complete defeat of Great Britain in the fierce and furious battle with Germany on the European continent.

I have my reasons for introducing this chapter with a reference to the Battle of Jutland. Egypt, I always felt, burdened Ahmed Ismail Ali, commander in chief of the Egyptian armed forces, with heavy responsibilities.

The man shouldered these with aplomb, accurately estimating the precise abilities of our armed forces and what they were capable of doing. He also grasped the required objectives and the ways and means of achieving them, and finally, the methods that could be used to motivate the armed forces and their main branches to achieve the military objectives—and thence the political objectives—of war. With his depth of experience and wisdom, Ahmed Ismail Ali was keenly aware that Egyptian military operations across the Suez Canal were not only about destroying the Bar-Lev line. Breaching this heavily guarded line, starting with its broad water barrier, with all its stations and fortifications, was not an easy task—certainly as daunting a challenge as anything faced by First World War soldiers. Ali knew that beyond this, his mission also included taking the strip that extended all along the east bank of the Suez Canal, striking back against Israeli counterattacks; securing an end to armed confrontation; and ensuring the presence of capable, effective, and dominant Egyptian forces on the ground in Sinai itself, even if only on a strip as narrow as ten to fifteen kilometers. This would be the proof that Egypt had destroyed the theory of Israel's security, as immune from any outside intrusion on the Bar-Lev line, and had the means to impose on Israel and the US the necessity of moving toward a political settlement.

Hence Ahmed Ismail took control of all his forces with an iron grip. He absolutely forbade any of his main Second and Third Army forces from hastily succumbing to the temptation to leave the bridgeheads of the five infantry divisions. Indeed, he fought hard against any notion of making an immediate move to exploit the preliminary opening success of the battle, namely the destruction of the Bar-Lev line. Instead, he sustained his infantry divisions' strategic focus on defeating all the armored counterattacks, and maintaining a presence on the lines that had been established from the start to accomplish Egypt's preliminary military objectives and the longer-term strategic and political goals of its military action.

Egypt's early success came at a price far lower than that estimated by the military and political leadership. This placed Ahmed Ismail Ali under pressure: he was urged to consolidate his successes by allowing, indeed directing, his forces to Mitla and Gidi, the two main passes deep inside Sinai. Some also mentioned in their postwar analyses that Golda Meir was shocked by the capitulation of Moshe Dayan, then minister of defense, and General Shmuel Gonen, chief of the Southern Command. In a stormy meeting on October 9 at the Southern Command Base in central Sinai, they asked Meir to look into withdrawing the Israeli forces standing against the Egyptians deep into Sinai, behind the Sinai passes. Meir, however, absolutely forbade it. She decided to appeal to U.S.

officials, asking them to move immediately to supply Israel with all the weapons and ammunition it needed.

Subsequent years have revealed that, at the time, there was some disagreement in Washington between the Department of Defense and the State Department about the Arab reaction, specifically the Arab supply of oil to the western world. The matter was resolved in favor of the State Department, led by Kissinger, who said that Soviet weaponry could not be seen to vanquish U.S.-made armaments. America's decision was made: Israel would receive everything it needed and more, and every U.S. naval and air resource would be pressed into service to achieve this end.

I remember here—in response to those who say that the attack should have been developed starting October 10, after Israel's armored counterattacks had been repulsed—that Ahmed Ismail Ali was well aware that the Soviets had no desire for the Arabs to breach the ceasefire, and had been against it from the start. Egypt and Syria had succeeded in putting massive strategic and political pressure on the Soviet Union to supply them with weapons, enabling the Egyptian army and air force to build their capacity, especially between October 1972 and October 1973. Indeed, it would not be going too far to say that Egypt succeeded not only in giving Israel and the west the impression that it was militarily unprepared, but also in fooling the Soviets, who imagined that its cadres and leadership were unqualified to put these weapons to use in the hands of Egyptian soldiers. It follows that they imagined Egypt's commander in chief had no wish to find himself—amid the exigencies of the battle he was being urged to wage—at the mercy of the Soviets for essential munitions and supplies. This was the source of his conservation of forces, resources, and efforts. This was the controlling ethos of the Egyptian position from preparation for battle until it finally drew to a close.

Reports from our embassies and diplomats on their discussions with their western counterparts indicated—from my reading of them—that everyone expected the Soviet weaponry in our possession to become obsolete within two years, and that it was hard to imagine the Soviets agreeing, or being persuaded, to make up the Arab shortfall by supplying us with new state-of-the-art aircraft, tanks, and heavy artillery. I am convinced that Ahmed Ismail Ali realized that losing his army a second time, or repeating the defeat of 1967, would be the fatal blow to Egypt. Israel would of course count this as a success, tightening its hold on Sinai for decades, perhaps generations. This explains his clear circumspection and iron control over the army, and his refusal of the temptation of development and its possible merits. He could see only too well the downsides.

National Security Advisor Mohamed Hafiz Ismail, in his analysis of this viewpoint, writes in his book on Egyptian national security and the October War:

> With the completion of the armed forces' direct objective on 10 October, I must indicate that I—in talks with Lieutenant-General Ahmed Ismail Ali before the war—am aware that he had no intention of moving in as far as the mountain passes. The instructions of the ops center of General Command were that the objective was to take the passes; however, these were meant to motivate the junior leadership to keep going, during the bridgehead-building stage, until they reached the direct objective intended by the army.

I must reaffirm my conviction that when a state and/or society takes the path of armed conflict, it is the duty of diplomacy to safeguard the successes of military action and not allow them to be held back, and also continually to work toward finding opportunities to achieve the ideal strategic and political situation when a ceasefire should occur. This, in my estimation, was the chief preoccupation of Hafiz Ismail and his team.

The Egyptian army mobilized and continued with its preparations and fortifications on the east bank of the canal, until the first crisis of battle. We continued calm diplomatic efforts, while holding our breath in anticipation. We were waiting for the moment when, in our estimation, Egypt would achieve its military objectives, at which point we could work toward reaping the political profits. From the outset, the deterioration on the Syrian front imposed on Egypt the need to relieve the pressure on the Syrian army by drawing some of the main Israeli forces to the Sinai front. However, the Israelis—starting on October 12—were already pushing a great many of their main units toward Sinai, as shown by an Egyptian reconnaissance report by elements spread out deep within Sinai behind enemy lines. On that same day, large numbers of mobile bridging equipment were observed, indicating Israel's intent to cross the Suez Canal.

I was extremely puzzled when reading this report, presented to Hafiz Ismail. How could the Israelis imagine that they would succeed in displacing the concentrated Egyptian forces in their path? How would they deal with the armored and mechanized Egyptian divisions stationed west of the Suez Canal, close to the waterway, the Fourth and Twenty-First Armored Divisions, and the Sixth and Twenty-Third Mechanized Infantry Divisions? In any case, this information clearly did not faze President Sadat, who insisted on developing the attack, nor did it affect the plans of the General Command under his direction. On October 13, several of us learned in the office of Hafiz Ismail that a heated argument had taken place between commander of the Second Army, Major-General Saad Ma'moun, and General Command in Cairo. Ma'moun, for long hours, opposed the concept of developing the attack, in order to preserve his forces and the balance of the army on both sides of the Suez Canal. While arguing with General Command, he had a mild heart attack, which forced him to step aside. Major-General Saad Khalil replaced him as the head of the Second Army.

My diary entry for Saturday, October 13, 1700 hours:

> Our forces are currently faced with three main fighting groups. In my view, Damascus cannot fall. The Israelis will not attempt to enter into an Arab city of such a size and population. Syria will fight off the penetration.

I added in the diary that the British ambassador had awakened President Sadat at 0400 hours on October 13 to give him a message from the British prime minister. The message was that Secretary Kissinger had asked Sir Alec Douglas-Home to make a proposal to the Egyptians, the gist of which was that Israel would not refuse a ceasefire along the current battle lines if Egypt was amenable to the idea. Sadat refused this overture, in the absence of a consolidated political horizon for dealing with the conflict and its political aftermath.

The Soviet ambassador had also contacted the president directly a few hours earlier, in the early hours of October 13, calling upon him to consider a cessation of hostilities. In the diary for the same day, I wrote:

> The Soviets are worried about their relationship with America. Also, they must be concerned about the situation with the regime in Syria. According to the record of the call made by Mr. Abd al-Fattah Abdullah, minister of state for cabinet affairs, the president asked that any ceasefire be accompanied by an agreement on a plan for the Israeli withdrawal from Sinai, including a time frame for the withdrawal, and that a peace conference be held, attended by the two superpowers.

I also wrote this:

> The president has an admirable clarity of vision. He sees
> - That Israel is attacking Syria for political, not military ends—for future negotiations. Israeli military officials are seeking some

appearance of victory to conceal the strategic shock they have undergone.

- The main front is the Suez Canal. It is this that will decide the outcome of the conflict. The battle now is Egypt's, not Syria's. The turning-point will be the Egyptian army's success at striking the Israeli army in Sinai, and foiling the latter's plan of attack against the Egyptian army.

The points that Sadat addressed with the ambassadors of both the Soviet Union and Britain were the same ones Hafiz Ismail covered in his first written communication to Secretary Kissinger on the evening of October 7: "Egypt's unchanged goal is achieving peace in the Middle East, not a partial settlement. It follows that Israel must withdraw from all the occupied territories, at which time Egypt will be prepared to take part in an international peace conference under appropriate supervision."

Messages began to flow thick and fast between Hafiz Ismail and Kissinger. On October 9, Ismail sent a message saying that Israel must withdraw to the June 5 borders before a peace conference could be held to set out the details of an agreement for a permanent peace. Egypt, the message said, had no objection to an independent international presence in Sharm al-Sheikh to ensure the freedom of international navigation in the Straits of Tiran and Sanafir. With that, Ismail and Kissinger began to set out their positions in more detail. It became clear, however, that the American side was still somewhat evasive and frequently prevaricated to waste time in anticipation of some Israeli military success on the ground. For example, Kissinger's messages began to ask what Egypt meant by withdrawal from "all" the occupied territories, whether such a withdrawal would precede or follow the peace conference, and so on.

A new message from Hafiz Ismail reiterated his vision, the one conveyed to Secretary Kissinger at the start of the clashes. There were many considerations for the position in which President Sadat found himself, and Hafiz Ismail was clearly committed to carrying out the president's instructions. It was certain, however, that Egypt's distrust of both Israel and the US weighed heavily on the ultimate decision-maker, causing him to refuse an end to armed conflict, especially given his concerns that the US and Israel were only seeking a temporary or tactical ceasefire, after which Israel would resume its military operations against us. What was also certain was that Egyptian political leaders discussed the option, especially given the escalating Soviet pressure for a ceasefire. Hafiz Ismail's message, referenced above, which he later published in his memoir, *Amn Misr al-qawmi fi 'asr al-tahaddiyat* (Egypt's National Security in the Age

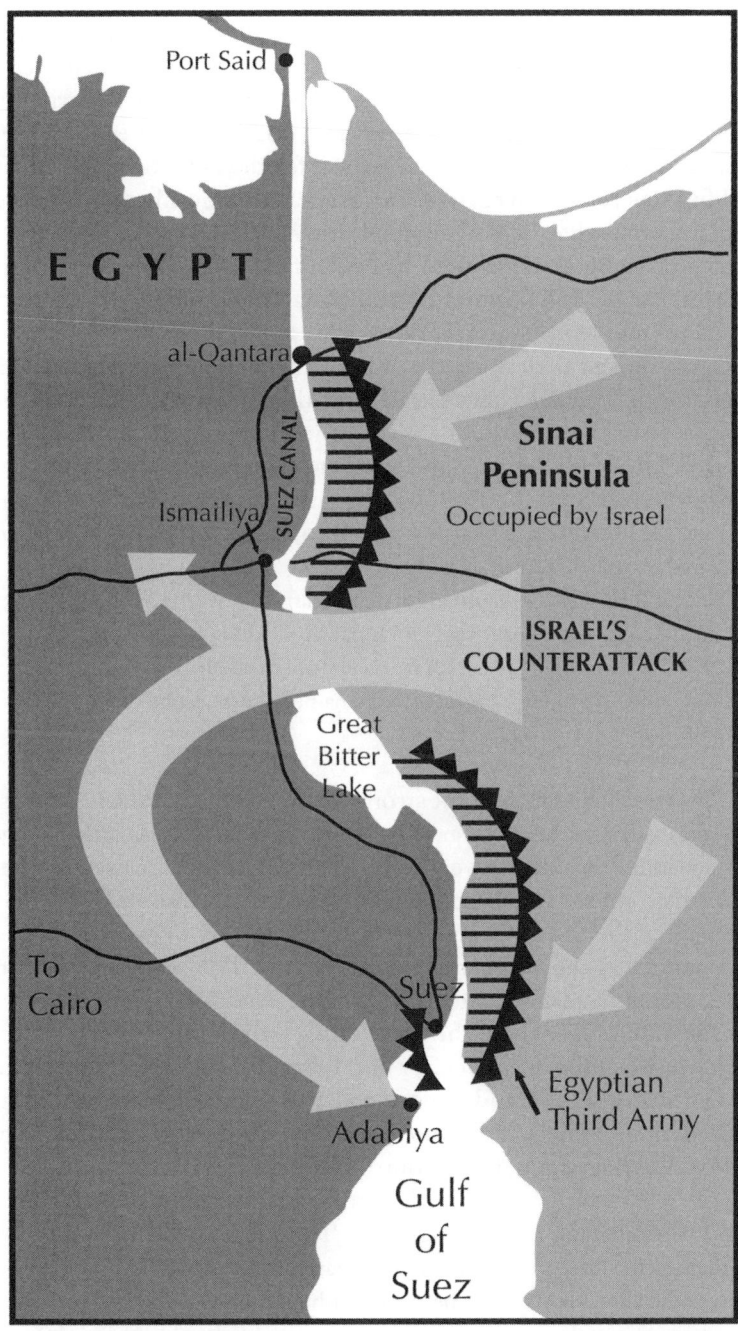

Port Said

E G Y P T

al-Qantara

SUEZ CANAL

Ismailiya

Sinai
Peninsula
Occupied by Israel

ISRAEL'S
COUNTERATTACK

Great
Bitter
Lake

To
Cairo

Suez

Egyptian
Third Army

Adabiya

Gulf
of
Suez

Israel's counterattack. Based on a map published in *TIME* magazine,
October 1973.

of Challenges), mentions that Dr. Mahmoud Fawzi, the foreign minister, feared a negative reaction from the ranks of our armed forces if they were ordered to stand down at a time when Israeli forces were suffering heavy losses, yet still advancing toward the east bank of the Suez Canal. Fawzi proposed that Israel announce its respect for the neighboring Arab countries' full sovereignty over their own lands, and officially demand a ceasefire. The fact is that Hafiz Ismail's writings were very much in line with my own thoughts at the time. I had been following all the developments via the messages and minutes of Abd al-Fattah Abdullah, as well as other documents and telephone recordings.

Egypt moved to develop the attack. The pause for mobilization from October 6 to 13 would have lasted until the end of armed hostilities had it not been for the situation in Syria, which imposed the need for a move eastward. I learned that the development of the attack, intended to relieve the pressure on Syria, at President Sadat's insistence would start late on October 13. However, it was postponed to dawn on October 14. My diary on Saturday at 1700 hours states:

> An American SR-71 reconnaissance aircraft flew over the Nile Delta
> and Cairo, to the Suez Canal and Sinai, and left via Arish on the way
> back to where it had taken off from, an American air base in Europe.
> It was at an altitude so high that it remained out of range of Egyptian
> fighters and anti-aircraft missiles.

This reconnaissance flight strongly affected battle developments: the aerial photographs America gave to Israel revealed that the main Egyptian units stationed in reserve west of the Suez Canal had crossed to the east bank, which meant intent to develop. The images also revealed that the west bank of the Suez Canal was now largely empty of main heavy forces. The enemy was thus prepared for our strikes. The battle moved into an unprecedented, delicate, and critical phase.

Our forces launched the developing attack on October 14. The attack paused in the evening after our forces had sustained heavy losses— between two hundred and twenty and two hundred and fifty tanks and armored units. These were no doubt serious losses. In my diary on Monday, October 15, at 0700 hours, I wrote:

> It is clear that our attacks have ceased. This will have serious conse-
> quences for the battle. It is also important not to abandon our initiative
> over the enemy, or we will be struck without mercy. We must keep the
> pressure on with active attacks.

Years later, I noticed that Hafiz Ismail had come to the same conclusion, which he laid out in *Amn Misr al-qawmi fi ʿasr al-tahaddiyat* (Egypt's National Security in the Age of Challenges):

> The attack launched by our forces in the daylight hours of October 14 achieved its objectives even before the forces left their bases at the bridgeheads. Since October 13, Israeli attacks on the Golan front had ceased, and the threat to Damascus had been averted. However, with the end of the development battle on the evening of October 14, the Egyptian military command had exhausted our forces' energies, proving the advantage of the initiative we had achieved since October 6. The fact is, however, that this initiative had been slowly eroding ever since we stopped advancing in favor of pausing for mobilization, thus handing the initiative, ultimately, back to the Israeli military command.

I am completely convinced that Ahmed Ismail Ali and the military command that faced this extremely difficult and delicate situation on the evening of October 14 made the prudent decision. By pausing the attack, they spared more heavy losses of their forces needed for the future of the battle, and to deal with the Israeli counteroperations revealed by reconnaissance and observation seventy-two hours earlier, that is, on October 11 and 12.

Hafiz Ismail continued his analysis of the events of October 14:

> The matter merited a struggle to re-arm and rearrange our units that had been in battle, reassembling and redistributing them within the coming twenty-four to forty-eight hours, in preparation for the next stage of enemy operations, which was of course inevitable. We needed to take into account that the failure of the Egyptian attack on October 14 was the real starting point of the Israeli counterattack.

Hafiz Ismail's points and anaylsis were not unfamiliar to the Egyptian commander in chief's. The president worked to obtain the maximum military support necessary for this upcoming critical stage of armed conflict. My diary for 0700 hours of Monday, October 15, noted that, "Egypt has obtained two hundred tanks from Yugoslavia. They are slated to be sent to the port of Alexandria in a few days. There is also talk of tanks from Morocco, Algeria, and Libya."

I opened this chapter with Churchill's reference to Admiral John Jellicoe in the First World War as "the only man on either side who could lose the war in an afternoon." Ahmed Ismail Ali, the commander in chief of the Egyptian armed forces, likewise could have lost the war in the afternoon of October 14, 1973, if he had insisted on pushing his attacks forward to the mountain passes, which had been the goal of the original plan.

7 Accepting the Ceasefire

The few days that followed Israel's success in repelling Egypt's efforts to develop its attack on October 14 were accompanied by important developments that had a great effect on the form our military action took, and on diplomatic efforts. On October 16, President Sadat presented an integrated vision for Egypt's proposed settlement to the Egyptian People's Assembly. He presented a consolidated account of what he had discussed with the ambassadors of the main countries involved during the previous few days, including the content of Hafiz Ismail's messages to Kissinger in the first week of the war. Sadat affirmed that Egypt's ultimate goal was to reclaim our territory in Sinai, liberating it from Israeli occupation. He reiterated that Egypt was prepared to accept a ceasefire on condition that Israel withdrew from all our occupied territory, under international supervision. Egypt, he said, was prepared, as soon as the withdrawal was complete, to attend an international peace conference at the United Nations to set out protections and safeguards for peace in the region, on the basis of the legitimate rights of all of its peoples.

The president stated that Egypt was prepared to start clearing the Suez Canal immediately and opening it to international navigation. This proposal, naturally, reiterated the legitimate rights of all the peoples of the region, as well as protections and safeguards for peace in the region— all of which Egypt took steps to achieve from that moment on, through to the Camp David peace talks and the signing of the Egypt–Israel peace treaty, including at the Geneva Conference in December 1973.

At the same time that President Sadat was making his speech at the People's Assembly, Golda Meir, then prime minister of Israel, was making a short statement on Israeli radio, the gist of which was that Israeli military units and special forces had crossed the Suez Canal and begun armed operations between the cities of Ismailiya and Suez. Hafiz Ismail, as part of his communications with Kissinger, conveyed to him an Egyptian vision close to what the president presented in his speech, although it went a bit further than the introductory vision that Sadat gave to the people. On October 10, Ismail demanded that Israel withdraw within a specific time frame to the lines of June 5, 1967, under the supervision of the United Nations, noting that war would be over as soon as the withdrawal was complete. He also demanded that after this withdrawal the Gaza Strip be placed under UN supervision until such time as the Palestinians had the right to self-determination.

Kissinger's response to Sadat's speech at the People's Assembly came quickly. So did Hafiz Ismail's message of October 9 mentioned above. It became clear that the US "wishes to end the current clashes and fighting, in circumstances that will facilitate moving forward toward a final settlement." This was a telling paragraph in Kissinger's message, as it revealed what the U.S. side was working toward during the second week of fighting: namely, assisting Israel with every possible military support so as to restore its military and strategic balance with Egypt, allowing Kissinger to play the role of mediator and move toward a resolution to the conflict.

Kissinger reiterated to Hafiz Ismail that the Egyptian vision put forth in Sadat's speech, and the messages from the Egyptian national security advisor, could only be achieved through a protracted war. Egypt, he said, should look into limiting its goals; this insistence on achieving the full extent of its desired goals would mean a continuation of armed conflict, which threatened to erode all the Egyptian successes to date. Kissinger focused on his demand for a ceasefire along the current lines of battle, securing an agreement from the warring parties that they would start negotiations under the supervision of the United Nations, and the establishment of a full and equitable peace based on Resolution 242, taking into account the importance of the balance between sovereignty and security. Kissinger wrote to Hafiz Ismail on October 14 that America would work to supply Israel with equipment and consumables, seeming to be speaking of ammunition, which is of course consumable by its very nature. However, the truth of the matter was that the Americans went ahead and supplied the Israeli side with a great deal of heavy equipment, firepower, tanks, antitank missiles, and other weaponry of that kind. My diary from 0700 hours on October 15 reads:

This last message makes it clear that the American decision to start the supplies flowing is using that the Soviets are supplying Egypt and Syria with what they need as an excuse to keep fighting. Kissinger said in his message that the US would cease this flow of supplies as soon as the fighting stops; he added that he would like to continue "this useful consultation," and that he had asked Israel not to attack civilians. He said he had also obtained Israel's agreement to cease firing on the current positions, but it was Egypt that refused.

Naturally, anyone reading these messages today, and linking them to the developments on the ground starting on the evening of October 15, would conclude that the US had decided, in the wake of Egypt's rejection of a ceasefire, to create a fundamental shift on the ground. It aimed to restore the balance (as the Americans saw it) and help Israel to countervail the Egyptian gains of destroying the Bar-Lev line and reestablishing military control of a ten- to fifteen-kilometer strip extending the length of the east bank of the Suez Canal.

This exchange of messages and positions between Egypt and the US, and President Sadat's frank presentation of his vision to Egypt and the international community, coincided with an important visit to Cairo by Alexei Kosygin, premier of the Soviet Union, on the evening of October 16. It was clear that President Sadat had chosen the timing of his speech to the People's Assembly to coincide with Kosygin's arrival. He aimed to present the consolidated Egyptian position in a way that would not allow Kosygin to affect our decision to keep working toward the goals of the conflict, and to reject Soviet calls for a ceasefire along the current lines of battle in the absence of a clear political view of the required settlement. My diary for 0100 hours on Tuesday, October 16, reads:

> Kosygin arrives in Egypt today. He will try to pressure us into a ceasefire. The president will make his speech to preempt Kosygin and take the initiative on the five points. This will force the Soviets into a confrontation with the US, who have already taken the decision to provide military support to Israel; this may lead to a political crisis.

My diary also mentions President Sadat's efforts to make use of his strong ties to the shah of Iran to soften the American stance. He kept up the highest degree of communication with the shah all the time, from the start of military operations, via the energetic and efficient Iranian ambassador stationed in Cairo at the time. The shah, for his part, was responsive to Sadat's efforts, replying to his messages and doing his best to influence the Americans in favor of Egypt. I doubt that this was very far from the president's thoughts, as evidenced by his reaction to what the shah went through later and his granting the shah political asylum in Egypt.

At this point in my narrative, it is important to return to what Hafiz Ismail mentioned to me in the early days of the conflict. The gist of what he said was that he had no objection to a meeting with Yigal Allon, the Israeli deputy prime minister, who had proposed a draft Arab–Israeli settlement a few years before—especially now that Egypt had moved beyond the humiliation of 1967. My diary for 0100 hours on October 16 speaks of this, as I had discussed it again with the national security advisor, indicating the importance of what he said on October 9, of being flexible in our thinking, and of not refusing direct meetings with the Israelis, especially now that we had trounced them. Hafiz Ismail responded that it was Syria he worried about, as they had lost actual land. He wondered how that country could be satisfactorily compensated. The other Arab countries that had rushed to take part in the war with small units would also constitute a problem.

My narrative now takes me to Kosygin's visit and his extended one-on-one sessions with President Sadat, in which the aim was agreement not only on the form of Egyptian–Soviet coordination in communications with the Americans and with the UN Security Council, but also on the type and amount of equipment and armaments the Soviets would supply to us. I remember reading the minutes of one of the president's meetings with the Soviet ambassador to Cairo the day before Kosygin's arrival, in which Sadat said, "Please tell my friend Alexei Kosygin to prepare himself and prepare deep pockets. I will put my hand in them and scoop out as much equipment and weaponry as I can, as well as anything else our fighting forces need."

There was a clear understanding between the Egyptians and the Soviets at the end of Sadat's meeting with Kosygin, who left Cairo on October 19, just as the Egyptian military position came under threat. The Soviets would try to get the US to agree to a U.S.–Soviet attempt to secure a ceasefire, with Israel's withdrawal to start immediately after the ceasefire, in compliance with Resolution 242, as well as joint U.S.–Soviet guarantees of the implementation of each aspect of the agreement. It was at this exact moment, as a result of conversations between some members of Egyptian Intelligence, that I learned that Egyptian military intelligence had concluded that Israeli forces were extremely numerous, as a result of surveillance of Israeli forces' communications and observations of the number of logistics units and accompanying medical units west of the Suez Canal. This did not bode well.

As soon as Kosygin arrived in Moscow, he asked the Americans to send Kissinger to the Soviet capital immediately for consultations on what they could do together to contain the fighting and possibly end it, and to move toward a satisfying settlement and an international conference.

Although I am speaking primarily of diplomatic efforts, I find it necessary to mention the military situation, which indicated that we were surrounded by threats to the successes we had achieved thus far in the conflict. My diary for Tuesday, October 16, at 1720 hours, reads:

> The enemy has penetrated the gap between the Second and Third Armies, and is sending in amphibious forces via the Great Bitter Lakes opposite the Deversoir region. The enemy is attacking the west bank of the Suez Canal in an attempt to destroy our forces' bridges and our anti-aircraft missile batteries, which are impeding their fighter bombers' ability to fight our forces.
>
> Our armored forces, especially the Twenty-First Armored Division, fought back valiantly until 1400 hours today.
>
> We will lose the initiative with our current inaction. If we do not move fast, we will lose heavily.
>
> What is the enemy's objective with these attacks? Is it to develop the attack toward the west? Perhaps.
>
> I feel extremely resentful at this flurry of enemy activity, activity that our own inaction served to bring about.

The entry for Wednesday, October 17, at 1500 hours, reads:

> Suspicious silence. Extremely violent fighting in the axis of the Sixteenth Infantry Division of the Second Army. No communiqué, no news, no reports.
>
> Do the enemy operations seek to break through the gap [between the Second and Third Armies] on the eastern and western banks of the Suez Canal?
>
> Its forces in the west must be neutralized, at once, so that such an attempt is not repeated.
>
> It is clear that the enemy has started to fight its Egyptian battle, although its Syrian battle is not—and cannot be, as yet—concluded. The enemy cannot seriously envisage being able to successfully conclude a battle for Egypt.

Long years after I wrote this evaluation of the situation, I was granted access to a British official document that dealt with this period of the conflict. According to the report, prepared for the eyes of the British prime minister at 1130 hours on Tuesday, October 16, 1973, "The Israeli forces in Syria will most probably attempt to establish positions that threaten Damascus, but that also require fewer forces to secure them, allowing the Israelis to move their forces to the Sinai front." Naturally at the time I had no way of knowing that Israel would, in the coming days, transfer their forces to the Suez Canal front to attack the Egyptian forces stationed there.

The fighting continued over the next few critical days. My diary for 0800 hours on the morning of Thursday, October 18, reads:

> Yesterday's battle was critical in the extreme. The enemy seeks to establish a bridgehead on the western side of the Great Bitter Lakes from which to strike at our army.
>
> Our armored forces are striking at them from both sides.

The diary resumes at 0100 hours on Friday, October 19:

> We have lost the initiative, and shall pay the price.
>
> It is clear that the enemy has massive forces capable of dealing with us on the western side of the Suez Canal. However, the national security advisor is confident that we will succeed in this military clash.
>
> We must strike at the Israeli bridgehead, then strike at the penetration in the east.
>
> We must seize the initiative by means of effective action, or the situation will deteriorate, compelling us to withdraw the army from Sinai to confront the penetration in the west, or else lose it.

At 1700 hours on Friday, October 19, I wrote:

> Israel is attempting either to secure a bridgehead and await a cease-fire—meaning that Israel has not been defeated—or else to encircle the Second Army. The latter is an extremely difficult operation, requiring a great deal of effort; I doubt that Israel possesses the forces to achieve such an objective.
>
> The national security advisor says in his conversations with us that the US and Israel are working to get everyone out of this on even footing, making it easier to reach a subsequent settlement.
>
> Hafiz Ismail remains optimistic, thinking of how we will conduct the ceasefire as agreed with Kosygin, and how to work toward a disengagement of forces and the means of implementation, and how we will

deal with the Israeli bridgehead on the west bank of the canal when the ceasefire comes.

The moment of crisis came on Saturday, October 20:

> Our forces are trying to close the breach in both east and west and sustaining insupportable losses; but they are fighting with desperate ferocity.

In the next two short days, we approached a ceasefire. At 0815 on Sunday, October 21, I noted in my diary that Presidential Secretary for Information Ashraf Marwan had arrived at 0200 hours to meet Hafiz Ismail, who took him to see President Sadat. They returned after a short time, when the national security advisor asked the deputy chief of Intelligence, Rif'at Hassanein, to summon the representative of the Central Intelligence Agency in Cairo and have him send a message to Secretary Kissinger, in Moscow at the time, informing him that Egypt agreed to a ceasefire on the present lines, and to holding an immediate peace conference, on condition that the US and the Soviet Union guarantee the cessation of hostilities and Israel's withdrawal.

It is clear that the decision was imposed on us by the harsh military situation. Hafiz Ismail notified us that after President Sadat visited the command center and was reassured about the confrontation plans vis-à-vis the Israeli penetration, the commander in chief took the president aside and told him that he needed to build reserves—which required time to prepare—to resume armed conflict with the Israelis on the east and west banks of the Suez Canal. Ismail Ali had no objections to a ceasefire at this point, to allow time to rebuild our logistical side.

I added in my diary at the time that the ceasefire might be achieved in about three days, and that it was imagined that Israel would also agree to a ceasefire. The Americans would no doubt leap at a ceasefire on the present lines, that is, with Egypt in Sinai and Israel west of the Suez Canal, achieving the balance Kissinger was seeking to simplify diplomatic efforts to reach a settlement. The summary of all this—the truth that was visible to me in 1973, and of which I became more convinced while rereading my writings at the time and the writings of others, foremost among which were those of Hafiz Ismail—is that our abortive attack on the entrances to the mountain passes in Sinai on October 14 and our heavy losses that day gave Israel the opportunity to counterattack and breach our defenses in the east. The Israelis leapt into the space left unguarded by Egypt and thereby affected the balance of power and the military equilibrium between the two parties. There can be no doubt that the Americans throwing their full weight into the conflict, providing Israel with virtually unlimited supplies, was the primary factor, not only in allowing them to penetrate the lines but also essentially to stand against the development of the Egyptian attack. It is not going too far to state that fighting on the Syrian front from October 13 to the ceasefire announcement on October 22 had its own effect, allowing the Israelis to advance their forces southward, to Sinai. This was revealed by the developments in the battle, and affirmed by international reports.

The fact is that the lack of effective precautions on the Egyptian side allowed the Israelis to move westward and broaden the threat they posed to the Egyptian forces. What is incontrovertible, however, is that the strength of the Egyptians' military performance, their solidity, and their insistence on continuing to apply pressure on the Israelis on the west and east banks of the Suez Canal—as well as Egyptian ambushes in that region, which cost the Israelis dearly and caused heavy losses on their side—played a role in bringing the Israeli leadership to the conclusion that the most they could achieve was a measure of equilibrium with Egypt, which could pave the way for active negotiations.

Kissinger and the US maneuvered to achieve this result, liberating each side from the consequences of feeling vanquished by the other. It did, in fact, have the effect of opening up the diplomatic and political path after the fighting stopped. But it is also quite futile to deny that Egypt's strategic success was the basis for moving the situation forward and reestablishing the strategic balance in the Middle East, which largely limited the effects of the 1967 defeat on the relationship between the two parties.

8 The War's Final Week

We were sitting together, Ahmed Maher al-Sayed and I, at 0200 hours on October 21, during the night shift on the first floor of Abd al-Moneim Palace, then in use as Advisor Hafiz Ismail's headquarters. We conversed in low tones in deference to our proximity to the sleeping quarters that housed both Hafiz Ismail and Mr. Abd al-Fattah Abdullah, minister of state for cabinet affairs, who was tasked with attending and recording all of President Sadat's meetings and telephone calls during the day shift, and for long hours during the night.

Some may imagine, when I speak of Abd al-Moneim Palace, that it was a huge palace with dozens of rooms and ballrooms. It was a misnomer, though, as the place was only a relatively small villa. The level where we two Ahmeds sat—Ahmed Maher and Ahmed Aboul Gheit—consisted only of a dining room, or 'a hall' as they called it, that opened onto three small rooms used as the offices of the national security advisor, and two bedrooms as noted above. At the very end of the dining room was a small desk bearing a number of telephones and other communications equipment connected to Abdin Palace, the main headquarters of the Presidency. A pretty folding screen concealed whoever sat at the desk from the eyes of those in the rest of the dining room.

We were speaking, Maher and I, of the developments and dangers in store, which had started to weigh heavily on this bloody conflict, and the conflagration of war east and west of the Suez Canal. I personally had started to realize, at least forty-eight hours before, the unwelcome

83

direction in which the war was heading. My diary, in which I wrote whenever I had the chance, said, at 0100 hours on Friday, October 19:

> We have lost the initiative, and will pay the price. However, Hafiz Ismail seems calm and confident.

This lasted until 0500 hours on October 18.

> It is clear that the enemy is in possession of massive forces capable of dealing with us on the western side of the Great Bitter Lakes. It is also clear that we are not being decisive enough in dealing with them.
>
> We must strike at the Israeli bridgehead that threatens to unbalance our forces on the eastern and western sides of the front, then move to strike at the penetration between the Second and Third Armies.
>
> We must seize the initiative by means of effective action, or the situation will deteriorate, compelling us to withdraw the army from Sinai, or leave the men in danger there.

I should note here that, while writing this, I was closely following what was happening, scrutinizing everything I read and saw, mostly military and political reports. However, my conclusions were clouded by the mystery of war, where nothing is certain. Even though these reports and briefings, meant for the eyes of the national security advisor, were as up-to-the-minute as possible, oftentimes they were preempted by events, making them reports on what had already happened—sometimes as long as several hours before—rather than advance information.

The second point I beg the reader to excuse is the way I fluctuated, sometimes wildly, from deep pessimism to cautious optimism in my diary, which was my state as I followed the events unfolding before my eyes, even though we were mostly kept abreast of all developments and their implications for the war.

The third and final point I urge the reader not to ignore is that, however hard the battle, however dark the days, Egypt successfully achieved its goal with this war: it forced the Israeli army into a protracted conflict in which Israel lost a great deal of its military capacity and was stripped of its status as the actor in charge, which it had enjoyed since 1967. The end of the conflict also saw Egypt in possession of massive military capacities on both the east and west banks of the Suez Canal. The Egyptian air force was active and effective during and after the war. Finally, Egyptian naval forces closed Bab al-Mandeb and prevented Israel from using the port of

Eilat, freezing and neutralizing the Israeli presence in Sharm al-Sheikh. Morale was high in the Egyptian armed forces after the war with Israel, emboldening them to repeat military action if Israel refused to respond to the logic of withdrawal and settlement.

Suddenly, as Maher and I sat there, Dr. Ashraf Marwan looked in. He glowered at us and said, "Please wake Hafiz Ismail at once." He then entered the advisor's room, spoke with him briefly, and left immediately after.

Hafiz Ismail came out of his sleeping quarters, and so did Minister Abd al-Fattah Abdullah, who had also been woken up. The national security advisor strode frantically down the long hallway, then disappeared down the stairs, still tucking in his shirt. He was due to meet President Sadat at 0200 hours on Sunday, October 21.

The events of the previous two days had culminated in this moment of truth. On Friday, October 17, at 1700 hours, I wrote:

> The enemy bridgehead has an armored division of around a hundred tanks.

The events of the following days, and the studies written after the fighting was long over, show that the Israeli army had three to four armored divisions stationed in the west. There are also questions in the diaries as to the enemy's true intentions—on which more later.

> The objective of all this Israeli activity is either to obtain a bridgehead, however small, and await a ceasefire . . . so that Israel will not have been "vanquished" in the clash with Egypt . . . or to attempt to encircle the Second Army north of the Lakes in the area around Ismailiya City, . . . a difficult and labor-intensive undertaking. I doubt that the Israelis possess the forces to achieve this objective.

On the diplomatic front, the diary says:

> Consultations with the Soviets—Kosygin and his visit to Cairo—covered the possibilities of a ceasefire in force at the positions where the parties were stationed, provided certain guarantees were received from the two superpowers to guarantee Israel's speedy withdrawal of Israel from Sinai in accordance with Resolution 242. What Hafiz Ismail is currently thinking of is how to achieve a ceasefire and a disengagement of forces, how to deal politically with the situation with the Israeli bridgehead in our territory west of the canal, the peace conference we

have been calling for as soon as the ceasefire comes into effect, and forming a force manned by the two superpowers tasked with effecting a disengagement between the forces.

The diary for the same day, Friday, October 19, at 1700 hours, reads:

The attempts to close the breach east of the Suez Canal in Sinai have had no success. The Twenty-Fifth Armored Division withdrew from the south to join the bridgehead of the Third Army, and elements from the Twenty-First Armored Division from the north to the bridgehead of the Second Army, which sustained heavy losses.

It becomes clear in the following paragraphs, which I started recording at 0150 hours on Saturday, October 20, that I was overcome by pessimism. I wrote:

The Israeli bridgehead is still active. I have begun to doubt our ability to beat it back. If we do not succeed in striking them within the next few days and hours, and destroying this clear and present threat to our forces, we will not achieve the objective of the war: complete Israeli withdrawal by means of political negotiations.

These words, which I have conveyed with all honesty from my diary, are indicative of the concern and unease that ruled us all. I shall seize the opportunity to repeat a conversation I had with Hafiz Ismail at around noon on Friday, October 19. Much of the staff had left the palace to pray at a nearby mosque, while I remained on shift. I sat in a great hall on the ground floor equipped with a long table that we used for meetings and writing, when the national security advisor walked in, in his shirt-sleeves, and started to talk. He spoke of the situation, going up to the giant map on the wall that faced the conference table. Intelligence officers Maher Khalifa and Nabil Hassan, both experts in information and assessments regarding Israel, who had been brought in to join our office staff, always used this map to point out developments in the course of the war. The two men's military experience and extensive training enabled them to understand and analyze the situation in order to remain in constant communication with Center#10, the General Command headquarters, and with Egyptian Intelligence headquarters to confirm and check their information.

Hafiz Ismail stood at the map and began to explain the importance of General Command immediately realizing the need to establish a new command, independent of the commanders of the Second and Third Armies, whose job was to deal directly with the Israeli penetration west of the Suez Canal and the Great Bitter Lakes. It became clear in the course of his comments that such a command would be in control of our available forces. These forces, he explained, needed efficiency, and it was unacceptable to have the two armies fighting over their command among themselves. The command he was proposing, he said, would ensure maximum efficiency and avoid any issues with task distribution that might be caused by a confusion of command and commanders.

I believe General Command did eventually adopt a similar view, once the ceasefire proved durable, and that it was now preparing to liquidate the Israeli pocket west of the canal, in November–December 1973. At that time, Major-General Saad Ma'moun was entrusted with the task of commanding all the forces, plus the Egyptian reserves, for the purposes of Operation Shamel. The objective of this operation was to eliminate the Israeli pocket if matters failed to move in the direction of a settlement or an Israeli withdrawal to the east of the Suez Canal.

Ismail's words and explanations to me reflected not only his wisdom and understanding of the situation the army was facing, but also the tension from which he suffered at the time, as did we all, and his worry about the situation's potential outcomes. However, I was sensitive to his implicit criticism of what matters had come to. At one point he said, "There needs to be at least one effective commander who can shoulder responsibility, who can move on the ground amid threats! A battle can't be managed remotely, after all!" This might well have been an allusion to General Command being situated in the desert of Heliopolis and not near the front lines, close to sensitive areas in Ismailiya and Suez and the nodes of communication and transportation in that region. While Lieutenant-General Saad Shazli was sent to the Second Army on October 18, this was not the guiding principle behind the action.

Years after this conversation, I can safely say that Hafiz Ismail's outburst was a product of both his frustration and his reluctance to appear to be critical of how General Command was running the battle, which is why he said it when alone with me, even though he later revealed a lot of what he had been thinking and feeling during those dark days in *Amn Misr al-qawmi fi 'asr ayn; al-tahaddiyat* (Egypt's National Security in the Age of Challenges), which came out in 1978.

One final point remains concerning what I thereafter dubbed the 'conference room conversation.' At around noon on that day, Friday, October 19, Hafiz Ismail expressed his discomfort regarding Commander in Chief Ahmed Ismail's relationship with Chief of Staff Lieutenant-General

Shazli, and its effect on how the war effort was being managed. Many in the know recognized that the relationship between these two men was strained, not just from the start of hostilities or preparations for war, or even with the major disagreements around developing the attack, but from the first time they clashed in the Congo in 1960. Back then, Ahmed Ismail was the military advisor (*mustashar*) to Ambassador Mourad Ghali, while Shazli was commander of the Egyptian parachute battalion that formed part of the UN peacekeeping force. There was no reason for a clash, as there was no organizational overlap between them—at least, that is how it should have been.

Back to 1973. Hafiz Ismail and Abd al-Fattah Abdullah came back after a short meeting with President Sadat at Tahra Palace. He had entrusted the deputy head of Intelligence with contacting Kissinger via the Central Intelligence Agency and informing him that Egypt accepted a ceasefire on the present lines for both parties to the conflict. Kissinger had just arrived in Moscow at the invitation of General Secretary Brezhnev, in the wake of Kosygin's return from Cairo and the understanding he reached with Sadat on the elements of the settlement.

Today, nearly fifty years after the war, I relive the stressful moments when Ahmed Maher took down the message Hafiz Ismail dictated to him, headed for Kissinger in Moscow, after which Ismail immediately went back to bed. It was around 0400 hours. Calmly, Ahmed Maher and I went downstairs to the ground floor of the palace, leaving a member of the secretarial pool to monitor the telephone station in case any calls came through in the early hours of that day, now October 21. We tried to relax, but it was hard. Instead, we took to discussing and analyzing our predicament, especially the fact that we were now in a race against time. We needed a ceasefire to rebuild the required reserves to continue the military confrontation and put an end to the Israeli presence west of the Suez Canal. We got no sleep that night. Years later, I learned from Hafiz Ismail's book that he could get no sleep either.

Those were trying times, hours of tension that I recorded at 0815 on the morning of October 21, knowing that Kissinger was in consultations with the Soviet leadership, seeking a vision acceptable to both superpowers. My diary for that day reads:

> The president met the Soviet premier on Saturday, October 20. He told him that the Egyptian armed forces were still trying to beat back the Israeli bridgehead, and demanded tanks for Egypt immediately, as hundreds of American tanks were pouring into Israel. We also need 9M14 Malyutka missiles, which proved their effectiveness in the battles

of recent weeks to destructive effect on the Israeli armored forces. In the meeting, Sadat also said that we need aerials for our missile batteries, most of which are currently nonoperational. He—the president, that is—wants to get all the air defense batteries operational at once, which would be a surprise to the enemy.

I must admit that in those trying times, I felt a good deal of rage at our method of dealing with the Israeli bridgehead, or what came to be called the 'breach pocket,' especially as Israeli operations revealed an appetite for risk due less to military know-how and more to complete and full information on the Egyptian theater of operations, helpfully provided through American reconnaissance.

With the arrival of the vanguard of the air bridge of American supplies to Israel, the theater of operations was laid wide open for an Israeli counterattack. I can say now that I was—and still am—convinced that establishing an Israeli pocket west of the Suez Canal always had the potential to turn into an unprecedented catastrophe for Israel, if Egypt had managed to strike it after rebuilding its reserves, given the fast pace at which this was happening. Any reasonably well-informed person with sound judgment would conclude from the battle developments that the breach in the west should have been dealt with from the first moment, and should never have been underestimated. Nothing would have been easier than destroying all of Israel's forces west of the Suez Canal between October 15 and 19. Hafiz Ismail's words echo in my head, speaking of the differences between Ahmed Ismail and Shazli, and their dispute over how to deal with the breach on the east bank of the Suez Canal and the presence of the Israeli pocket west of the canal—an issue that was extensively analyzed and discussed. Some proposed moving armored units from the east bank to the west of the canal to take care of the pocket, and some proposed holding the positions of the Second and Third Armies in the east, with all their main units, with no change, and managing the battle with whatever reserves remained available to General Command and the two armies west of the Suez Canal.

The truth of the matter, I am now convinced, and have been for many years, since the end of the conflict, is that Sadat took the more courageous path in dealing with the situation. It was clear to him that the Israeli forces in the pocket were far too massive for the Egyptian forces facing them, and could not be dealt with at that time and in those circumstances. Withdrawing some forces from the east and moving them west of the canal was fraught with its own dangers. It would have weakened the ability of the forces to maintain the bridgeheads in Sinai under

Israeli pressure, especially given the massive flow of supplies from the US to Israel via Arish and the paucity of Egyptian reserves west of the canal—Egypt having sustained losses at the hands of the more massive Israeli forces in the pocket. Any attempt to tackle the pocket would probably have necessitated a complete withdrawal westward, reversing all the gains achieved by the crossing and doing away with any possibility of a satisfactory settlement for our side.

Therefore, President Sadat sagaciously agreed to the ceasefire proposed by the Soviets. However, as I wrote on Saturday, October 21, at 1340 hours:

> The upcoming settlement, partly in light of the battles still raging, and partly in light of what international sources—including the US—are saying, is likely to take the form of Israeli withdrawal from Sinai in stages, over a year, and disarmament in the entire Sinai Peninsula, while allowing Israel [maritime] access to the Straits of Tiran and Sanafir and the right of passage through the Suez Canal once the war is over, recognition of the state of Israel, and the signing of a peace treaty.

All day on October 21, we were unsettled and concerned, watching the Moscow consultations between Kissinger and the Soviets, who had already been notified of Sadat's message to Kissinger that he agreed to a ceasefire starting the moment Hafiz Ismail delivered this message. A paragraph from Hafiz Ismail's *Amn Misr al-qawmi fi 'asr al-tahaddiyat* (Egypt's National Security in the Age of Challenges) reflects the strain of that day:

> From the window of my room overlooking the palace garden, I saw some of my assistants conversing. I went downstairs and joined them; I was not entirely sure what had caused us to move so fast toward a ceasefire that was not conditional on Israeli withdrawal from Sinai. I had a vague sense of impending doom.

I was astonished to read these words from the national security advisor, and his ignorance of the reasons for the ceasefire in particular. It was clear that our armed forces had suffered west of the Suez Canal and urgently needed several weeks to regroup and rebuild their reserves, after which they could resume fighting if needed. I believe Ahmed Ismail had apprised Sadat of that situation on the harsh night of October 20.

I say today that the days that followed the conversation between Ahmed Maher al-Sayed and me, and possibly Abdel Hadi Makhlouf, on the morning of October 21 decisively clarified Sadat's snap decision to agree to the two superpowers' urgings for a ceasefire: it was to salvage the goals for which Egypt had entered into that historic military conflict with America and Israel.

In the afternoon on October 21, we received word that the Americans and the Soviets had approved a draft resolution to be presented to the rest of the Security Council members in New York, calling on the warring parties to implement a ceasefire and start proceedings for an international peace conference on implementing Resolution 242, under appropriate supervision. The Americans and the Soviets sent messages to Egypt making reference to guarantees of the immediate and complete implementation of Resolution 242. The Soviets also conveyed additional reassurances to Egypt that the ceasefire would indeed be implemented. An urgent Security Council meeting was held on October 21, during which the famous Resolution 338 was passed, to the effect that:

- All parties should cease all firing and terminate all military activities within twelve hours in their present locations;
- The parties should implement Security Council Resolution 242 (1967) in all of its parts; and
- Concurrently with the ceasefire, they should start negotiations with the aim to establish a just and durable peace in the Middle East.

At 1900 hours that Sunday, I held my breath, waiting for the ceasefire. I was following the developments and operations on the ground. A slightly calmer atmosphere was starting to prevail after two extremely stressful days, especially as I noted some improvement in the military situation—or so I fancied. My diary for 0150 hours on Monday, October 22, reads:

The military situation has improved relatively. Our armored vehicles west of the Suez Canal are pushing the enemy to a fixed bridgehead that can eventually be liquidated. At least that is our assessment based on reports from military intelligence and reconnaissance that arrive every few hours. Two hundred T-62 tanks should be arriving tomorrow or the day after; the Soviets have activated the air bridge with supplies. The Second Army's missile batteries have regained their capacities. There are Soviet promises to urgently supply us with 85 MiG-21 fighters.

Military intelligence reports at the time also mentioned that the Sixteenth Division and the Twenty-First Armored Division, on the right flank of the Second Army, had borne the brunt of the Israeli penetration. A deep dent had been made in their positions and they had been driven several kilometers north of the bridgehead, but they had achieved, along with the Fourteenth Armored Brigade (of the Twenty-First Division), some success and had somewhat rectified the situation. These reports, along with our completely foggy knowledge of the situation, led some of the staff of the national security advisor's office to convince him that any decision to cease firing should not be respected, and that he should not encourage that it be accepted. To make matters worse, some of us imagined that our political and military commanders had failed to observe, in the fog of battle, that our situation was not so bad.

I was convinced that agreeing to a ceasefire was the ideal path to take, given the lack of reserves that would enable us to strike back at the enemy in the west. I was also convinced that continuing to maintain an active, effective, and influential presence east of the Suez Canal was essential to achieving a timely political settlement, especially as I was confident that the Israeli pocket west of the canal could be dealt with at a later stage, provided the needed supplies arrived and if things failed to move politically toward a peaceable settlement. This was especially true as the Soviet ambassador had assured President Sadat at 2230 hours on October 21, when he delivered Brezhnev's message on the Soviet–American position on the ceasefire, that the international conference would be held at the UN, and that both sides—Soviet and American—guaranteed the required withdrawal.

In another conversation I had with the national security advisor at 1300 hours on October 22, Hafiz Ismail said he was aware that, despite the ceasefire coming into effect in a few hours' time, the fighting would most probably go on for another couple of days, requiring another UN resolution to cease all firing. This opinion of his was doubtless based on a wealth of experience dealing with Israel: that state was well known for noncompliance with any commitments when at war with Arabs. This was especially true since the prevailing assessment was that the Israeli presence west of the Suez Canal was fraught with weaknesses and insufficiencies that the Egyptians could not fail to notice—at least this was the Israeli thinking. Consequently, it was Hafiz Ismail's estimation that the Israelis would try to expand the boundaries of the pocket, and perhaps even expand military operations to besiege or encircle one or both of our armies.

"But isn't it dangerous to implement a ceasefire while Israel has a presence in the west?" I asked, suggesting that it would be beneficial to drag our feet until such a time as the pocket was liquidated or otherwise addressed. I and others like me, far from the battlefield but close to news of the battle, obviously had no knowledge of the dangers of which President Sadat was aware, or which he was briefed on by Field Marshall Ahmed Ismail Ali, then minister of war. A great many commentators on the war have failed to take these dangers into account when evaluating the military and political angles at the time.

9 The Post-Resolution 338 Crisis

On the morning of October 23, Ahmed Maher and I were walking in the palace gardens discussing the situation, and what developments we could expect. I must offer some background on why we, the two Ahmeds—Maher and Aboul Gheit—could always be found together at every turning-point of the war. The office staff had divided themselves, on Ambassador Makhlouf's instructions, into permanent working groups. Maher and I were in the same working group, which, as luck would have it, witnessed perhaps every one of the important moments in that war. As I was saying, we were walking in the gardens when the national security advisor himself came down to us directly from his sleeping quarters and launched into a long and detailed monologue. The two of us remained silent, allowing him to think aloud and come to his considered conclusions about what was facing us.

In the national security advisor's assessment of Egypt's management of the confrontation, President Sadat was working in the absence of what Hafiz Ismail saw as sufficient support from his senior advisors and had been left alone to shoulder all the consequences of the political and/or military decisions, except for a few conversations with some statesmen close to him from time to time. My own thoughts, after all these years, are that perhaps Hafiz Ismail imagined that some individuals might have had a negative impact, while others were conspicuous by their absence from any constructive input to an overview of the situation.

After around thirty minutes of talking as we walked from one end to the other of the small palace gardens, Hafiz Ismail left us to get properly dressed and leave for his meetings with some of our most senior government officials, main political figures, and members of the National Security Council. It was said that they had five or more meetings with major statesmen, including Vice President Hussein al-Shaf'i, former Prime Minister Dr. Mahmoud Fawzi, Acting Prime Minister and Minister of Information Dr. Abd al-Qader Hatem, former Minister of Transportation and later Prime Minister Dr. Mustafa Khalil, Minister of Industry and later Prime Minister Dr. Aziz Sedki, and Minister of the Interior Mamdouh Salem. He spoke to them about the need to stand with the president and not abandon him. It was only later that we found out that Hafiz Ismail's discussions with at least four of the five (or more) officials had reached the ears of President Sadat in a way that misrepresented Ismail's intention as a wish to restrain the president's autonomy. This, as it turned out, was a step toward the national security advisor being relieved of his duties and being given new, different ones.

In my estimation, this matter, assuming the story is not apocryphal, was not the only reason for Hafiz Ismail's eventual dismissal from office. I shall go into that on another occasion. What is important, as I recall, is a discussion I had with Ahmed Maher a few weeks after Hafiz Ismail left, as Maher and I awaited transfer to diplomatic posts where we could continue to serve our country. During that period, we spent most of our time after hours in the Heliopolis Sporting Club in the Heliopolis suburb of Cairo. As it happened, we were discussing the war and national security (there was no shortage of these discussions in the period from February to March 1974) when Ahmed Maher said, "Do you know, Ahmed? I almost told him not to go to any of those meetings. I almost told him to talk to the president directly, if he was convinced of what he was saying, so as not to give the wrong impression. Oh, well."

I recently mentioned this story to Dr. Abdel Hadi Makhlouf, office director of the national security advisor, in a meeting at my new offices in the Foreign Ministry. In any case, the full story of what Hafiz Ismail felt and his assessment of that challenging time can be found in his brilliant memoir, *Amn Misr al-qawmi fi 'asr al-tahaddiyat* (Egypt's National Security in the Age of Challenges).

At many stages of the military conflict, which lasted over three weeks, U.S. Secretary of State Henry Kissinger, held a great many of the strings. In the period that followed the cessation of military operations, and until he left his post on January 20, 1978, with the arrival of the Carter administration to the White House, Kissinger held the reins of all the efforts to reach a political settlement, and dictated its pace, working toward peace and stability in the Middle East and the US having the upper hand in the region and its future.

Readers of Kissinger's writings on this conflict, with which the Nixon Presidency had to deal at one of its most trying times, Watergate, will note his influence on U.S. foreign relations. This was a time when President Richard Nixon was largely preoccupied with efforts to save his administration. President Sadat remained in constant contact with the Americans, and entrusted Hafiz Ismail with the task of continuing to exchange messages with the highest frequency. President Sadat wrote his own messages and had discussions with Nixon, which gave both parties the opportunity to assess the situation. I say here that Hafiz Ismail told President Sadat that Kissinger had mentioned visiting Israel on the way back from Moscow, after Resolution 338, with the express purpose of impressing upon the Israeli leadership the importance of complying with the ceasefire, discussing the peace talks, and the role of the two superpowers in the talks. Sadat then asked Ismail to arrange an invitation for a similar visit by Kissinger to Egypt, to reaffirm the balance of the relationship. Kissinger made his excuses, however. I believe, then as now, that he was aware how difficult the coming days would be and that his appearance on the Egyptian and/or Arab stage was a step for which the time was not yet ripe. By this, I mean because of the armed conflict, the end of which was not yet secured.

October 23 and 24 brought a shock that unsettled everything: Israeli armored forces succeeded in reaching the port of Adabiya, south of Suez, on the western bank of the Gulf of Suez, in the shadow of the Ataqa mountains. They attempted to enter Suez and lay siege to the city, as well as to two divisions of the Third Army east of the canal. I made an entry in my diary at 1400 hours on Wednesday, October 24, before we received news of the outcome of what later came to be known as the immortal Battle of Suez. This battle revealed a great deal about the war, especially in these dark days, and showed that there could be shining moments, too, decisive for the war and its future developments. I would like to add here that I and a great many of Hafiz Ismail's office staff went to Suez on a one-day visit immediately after Israel's withdrawal from the pocket in Deversoir, and witnessed a great number of Israeli tanks and armored vehicles, completely destroyed, at the entrances to Suez, in what would turn out to be the decisive battle in this war. We saw Egyptian military capacities, which were in the possession of the army in the area under siege. That diary entry reads:

> The enemy is encircling the Third Army. President Sadat is talking
> with Brezhnev, general secretary of the Central Committee of the
> Communist Party of the Soviet Union, and the leader of the USSR,

demanding immediate intervention in accordance with Soviet promises and guarantees given to us and which encouraged us to agree to the ceasefire. Military operations on Israel's part must cease immediately. The USSR and USA must oblige them to comply. The president has sent a similar communication to Nixon in the light of the same promises made to us by Kissinger.

Suez highway blocked at Kilometer 102. Third Army bridges cut off—or at least dismantled to avoid destruction by Israeli air and missile forces, which can now see them.

Many breaches in anti-aircraft missile battery defenses. Egyptian air force making valiant, desperate, and matchless efforts, sustaining some losses, to achieve army's objectives and defend ground troops.

Will the Third Army east of the Suez Canal be forced to surrender? Or will these experienced divisions—the Nineteenth and the Seventh—fight?

The diary continues amid the fog of war. I must emphasize here that the war—any war—often looked dark, and there were moments when things could go either way. What is incontrovertible, though, is that the troops' dedication and sacrifice, and the wisdom, maturity, and realism of the command decisions, in a situation where you and your enemy are ultimately in the same boat, always achieve the better outcome if only you can go the distance.

Our efforts to secure the divisions on the east bank of the Suez Canal and in the city of Suez continued on October 25. The pace of Egyptian communications stepped up, both with the Americans and the Soviets. We took it to the Security Council. A new resolution was passed, Resolution 339, just as Hafiz Ismail predicted. The Soviets had the sense that any new Israeli success, and any new Egyptian failure, would have severe repercussions on the image of the Soviet Union. Brezhnev intervened sharply with Nixon. The Soviets decided to give the US the impression that they intended to intervene to disengage the forces themselves.

The Americans responded to the challenge, at least in appearance, and placed American forces worldwide on alert. Still, the Americans knew that allowing Israel to go beyond its previously arranged parameters might waste a monumental, historic opportunity for the US to take the reins in the Middle East and turn the situation completely to its advantage. This is the background to Nixon's message of October 25 affirming that Washington would make Israel comply with the ceasefire. The information available to us about our military supplies was that our armed forces had started to receive a good number of tanks: a hundred T55's from

Yugoslavia, as well as an expected two hundred T62's within a few hours, by the end of October 25. We absolutely needed those armored vehicles and supplies to rearm and regroup our units, which had sustained heavy losses over three weeks of fighting. We also received tanks from Libya, and some from Algeria.

What preoccupied me, and indeed everyone working in the office of the national security advisor, was how to guarantee the safety of the Third Army divisions on the east bank of the Suez Canal, and how to get supplies to the city of Suez, which had soundly defeated an aggressive attempt by Israeli armored forces to take the city, thanks to a concerted effort on the part of its citizens, most of whom remained in their homes.

We kept up pressure on the Soviets and the Americans all of October 26 and 27. At the height of the crisis on October 24, President Sadat called for joint Soviet–American forces to proceed to the area and ensure the disengagement of the forces. However, as they could not come to an agreement, to say nothing of being aware of the dangers of armed conflict (which I dismissed as being for form's sake at the time), what eventually came of this pressure was the creation of a new emergency force for the Middle East, dubbed the second United Nations Emergency Forces (UNEF-II).

Under Soviet, American, and international pressure, a message arrived from Kissinger on Saturday, October 27, conveying the views of Meir's government on the ceasefire and the situation of the Third Army, which clearly had successfully aborted any attempts to push it back or force it to surrender. Via Kissinger's message, Golda Meir proposed that Egypt send a high-ranking officer to meet with the Israeli chief of staff, or even the Israeli defense minister, at a time and place of our choosing, to look into finding an honorable exit for the Third Army.

Hafiz Ismail convened a high-level meeting from 0400 to 0600 hours on October 27, which was attended by Commander in Chief Ahmed Ismail Ali, Abd al-Fattah Abdullah, and Ismail Fahmy, the acting foreign minister in the absence of Dr. Mohamed Hassan al-Zayyat, who was in New York for the three weeks of the war (an overly long absence in my estimation, which should have been cut short with the start of operations on October 6). The Egyptian response to Kissinger's message, mentioned in my diary of 0800 hours on October 27, was that Egypt would send a major-general to Kilometer 100 on the Suez road to meet with an Israeli counterpart and consider the details of implementing Resolutions 338 and 339. Egypt proposed a complete cessation of hostilities at 1300 hours on October 27. The Egyptian missive added that the meeting would take place at 1500 hours that afternoon. The Egyptian delegation would be accompanied by a logistical fleet of sixty-ton supply vehicles for the Third Army and the city of Suez. I noted in my diary, "I believe Israel will agree."

Hafiz Ismail had notified us that the army and its commanders were insistent that if Israel did not allow the supply fleets into Suez and to the eastern divisions of the Third Army, we would strike hard to clear the passage by force, especially as the military equipment promised by our friends and allies had begun to arrive to our units. The Egyptian logic was that UNEF-II and UN observers had started to arrive and take up their positions, and that it would be possible, in the presence of these units, to clear the path by force.

The following hours revealed continued tensions between the two superpowers. Egypt went on calling upon the Americans and the Soviets to ensure that Israelis returned to the lines of the ceasefire declared on October 22. Those days proved that whatever successes Israel won, it still had a long way to go to achieve any real objectives or break the will of the Egyptian army. This was especially true since Egypt held a lot of cards with which to apply pressure. First, it had the newly supplied divisions at the head of the Third Army. Second, it had the success of Suez's citizens, army personnel, and police force in fighting off the invaders and causing heavy losses for Israel. Also, the Egyptian armed forces continued applying pressure from the west, in the direction of the Suez road. Egypt was quickly building up and regrouping the Fourth and Twenty-First Armored Divisions and the Twenty-Third and Twenty-Sixth Infantry Mechanized Divisions. It also enjoyed high capacities in the region of Ismailiya and to the east of the Suez Canal among the divisions of the Second Army.

It is important at this stage to note that Meir's messenger via Kissinger had not come out of nowhere. It was preceded by a British proposal to the Soviets, conveyed to us by the Soviet ambassador in his meeting with President Sadat in the early hours of October 26, that Egypt return Israeli prisoners of war and withdraw all Egyptian destroyers and units at the entrance to Bab al-Mandeb, which were blocking Israel's trade and maritime traffic and forcing it to use the port of Eilat. In return, the British message said, Israel was prepared to withdraw to a reasonable distance, allowing the Third Army direct communication with the rest of the Egyptian army.

I felt a certain satisfaction at reading the transcript of this meeting. I was reminded of my conversation with Vice Admiral Fouad Zikri in the second week of September, particularly his words: "We will cut off their communications and block their naval routes. We will strike a forceful blow. We will confound their plans and teach them a lesson." The man was as good as his word. He can rest in peace knowing he kept his promise to his country. At his mother-in-law's funeral in 2010, I was stunned to see the seemingly endless line of Egyptian naval officers in full dress uniform offering their condolences at Cairo's famous Omar Makram Mosque, more than a quarter of a century after Fouad Zikri's passing. Egypt never forgets her duty and loyalty to those of her sons who give their all.

My record of the events of those few days was handwritten in pencil at 0800 hours on Saturday, October 27. The time was so stressful, and morale so low, that I could no longer record events moment by moment as I did at the start of the war. "The president agrees in principle, especially as the Soviet ambassador insisted that Britain tell them that Israel will accept if the offer is made." This was diplomat-speak for Britain looking into the matter in advance with Israel. I mulled it over and asked in my diary whether the initiative was an independent attempt by the British to test the waters. I quickly answered that I thought not; therefore, it was an attempt by Israel to test the waters, to try to make some gains, before being obliged to allow supplies to pass to Suez and the Third Army in the east.

I also wondered whether the Israeli personage due to meet with us at 1500 hours on October 27 would ask the same question, especially as the British assured us, when presenting the idea, that it represented a separate and independent agreement between Egypt and Israel, completely apart from the comprehensive settlement, with the sole purpose of resolving the closing of Bab al-Mandeb and thus the Straits of Tiran and of finding a land link between the forces in Suez and the rest of the Egyptian forces.

A message arrived from Kissinger proposing that he visit Cairo on November 6 for a day to look into all the elements of a settlement and the implementation of Resolutions 242 and 238. Egypt welcomed the visit. From Hafiz Ismail's documents and his meetings with President Sadat, I gathered that Sadat planned to make specific proposals to the Americans, before Kissinger arrived, covering:

- Israel's withdrawal to the lines of October 22, which had been transgressed, not to say ridiculed, by its breach of the ceasefire in Resolution 338, in exchange for Egypt returning the Israeli prisoners of war and reopening Bab al-Mandeb.
- Israel's withdrawal, a short time later, east of the Sinai passes, in exchange for Egypt starting to clear the Suez Canal.
- Upon Israel's withdrawal from the west bank of the Suez Canal, the commencement of a peace conference. Egypt might send, starting immediately, the vanguard of a delegation to Geneva or New York to look into the preliminary procedural elements of the conference.

My diary for 0100 hours on Sunday, October 28, says that the meeting between Egyptian and Israeli military officials had been set for 2400 hours on the previous day, October 27. There had been some confusion, as the Israelis had proceeded to Point 110 in the direction of Suez, while the Egyptians had gone to Kilometer 101. The situation was salvaged, and Major-General al-Gamasy, head of the Operations Department, met General Yariv, and the Americans promised that a thirty-vehicle logistical supply convoy would be allowed in that very night. Hafiz Ismail mentioned the possibility of a military operation to clear the path by force, under the oversight of the UN, whose forces had started to take up positions between the two sides. Later, at 1715 hours on October 28, my diary notes that General Yariv said he "had no instructions to look into returning to the lines of October 22, or withdrawing." Instead, he brought up navigation in the Red Sea and in Bab al-Mandeb, and the exchange of prisoners of war. The meeting was characterized by mutual respect.

Today I say what I said then: Kissinger's desire to come to Egypt made it clear that he would not allow the Egyptians and the Israelis to agree among themselves, that is, as the UK had proposed. We should not have expected, therefore, any results from the talks between our military officials, other than a mutual understanding regarding not breaching the ceasefire, supplying the besieged city, and other organizational issues and lines of communication between two armies should be entirely open during the ceasefire.

I learned that Ismail Fahmy, the acting foreign minister, was due to leave for Washington on October 28 for meetings with Kissinger and possibly Nixon. Dr. Zayyat was finally about to return to Cairo from New York. I noted in my diary:

> I think Zayyat is on his way out, very soon. Ismail Fahmy has proved himself to the president during this month of conflict, and during this crisis. In my estimation, the president will make good use of him as foreign minister in the upcoming negotiations, especially as his tensions with Mourad Ghalib, the foreign minister during 1972, were well known, when Ismail Fahmy directed harsh criticisms at the Soviets, which made Mourad Ghalib suspend him. Fahmy's removal from the post of ambassador to Germany in 1973 and appointment as minister of tourism, and his constant writing to President Sadat offering his view on the situation and its developments and suggestions on how to move on the level of the United Nations, and his evaluation of the chances of implementing Resolution 242, were all indicators that he was being groomed to serve as foreign minister instead of Zayyat, who

was undoubtedly absent from the internal scene at a decisively significant juncture.

I sensed a great deal of frustration and anxiety in how Hafiz Ismail
was handling a number of things—so much so that Ahmed Maher was
prompted to say to me, "I'm sure there's quite a struggle at the top," that
is, in the highest echelons of power, adding that there was a strong conflict of opinion. Hafiz Ismail, he predicted, would not remain in his position very long in the presence of Ismail Fahmy, in whom Sadat had placed
his trust during that month of conflict. On occasion, I myself felt quite
critical of the national security advisor. He was not assertive enough, I
felt, in defending his ideas and viewpoints to the president, nor did he
insist on meeting him on a daily basis during that time, which would
have consolidated his influence. However, Hafiz Ismail clearly saw what I
could not at the time: the power struggles, the people involved, and their
inclinations. This was told to me by Ahmed Maher, who was far closer to
Hafiz Ismail than I was.

Ismail Fahmy's mission was to influence Kissinger and the US to
present a proposal bearing some resemblance to what President Sadat had
outlined above. Personally, I had little hope of the mission succeeding, as
Kissinger was meanwhile pursuing his own ends in person during his visit
to Cairo. At the same time, the president was talking to the Soviets about
what Hafiz Ismail had revealed to us, namely his intentions for a powerful
strike to clear the path to Suez if we sensed no real commitment from the
Americans and the Soviets.

In the years that followed the war, a great many claims and assertions
have been made attributing nonexistent or wholly imaginary powers to
the Israeli army. Israeli Prime Minister Golda Meir, Minister of Defense
Moshe Dayan, and Chief of Staff Eli Azer, in addition to the senior and
main division commanders of the Israeli army west of the Suez Canal,
Avraham "Bren" Adan, Kalman Magen, and Ariel Sharon, were stopped by
the UN, which forced them to cease fighting before they had completed
their mission. The truth is that these claims, in my estimation and that of
a great many military commentators, are unrealistic in the extreme, not to
say in conflict with what actually took place on the ground.

Although a great many of the Egyptian reserves sustained heavy
losses in the west because of misuse, poor mobilization, or unclear missions carried out under pressure, Israel's defeat by the city of Suez shows
that the Israeli forces, on the outskirts of that courageous Egyptian town,
were exhausted and suffering from heavy losses unprecedented in Israel's
history, namely the loss of between five and six hundred tanks, which

stripped them of the ability to push forward and launch new attacks. They had gone as far as they could go, under circumstances that were already set to change in favor of Egypt if it continued rebuilding its forces at the same pace. This was evident in the preparations for Operation Shamel, which aimed to liquidate the Israeli pocket, in addition to digging in defenses and antitank trenches in the region of the pocket. This indicates Israel's awareness that it would certainly be targeted by an Egyptian military operation west of the Suez Canal.

As for Sharon's boast that he arrived within a short distance of Ismailiya and was on the verge of entering, these are empty words. The Egyptian defenses standing firm to the west and south of the Ismailiya road, the fierceness of the units and unyielding special operations forces, and the paratroopers who fought on the platforms all caused the defeat of Israel's military efforts at capturing Ismailiya. Israel's withdrawal to a safe distance from the city revealed that while the Israelis had done their best, their best was not enough, especially in light of the Second Army presence. There was nothing for Israel to do but wait for the next Egyptian strike aimed at liquidating the pocket.

When the ceasefire became more stable, an article appeared in Egypt's most prominent national newspaper *al-Ahram*, written by the well-known journalist Mohamed Hassanein Heikal, then editor-in-chief of the publication. It was on how Egypt had managed the battle. Hafiz Ismail, I could tell, was extremely upset by what it said. The national security advisor's assessment was that the article damaged the commander in chief's standing under already extremely difficult circumstances, at a juncture that would not allow for it. Hafiz Ismail said,

> Whatever you say about Ahmed Ismail, you have to give him this: the man fought, and succeeded in demolishing the Bar-Lev line. All these magnificent forces and iron-willed commanders were under his leadership. He bore the brunt of the confrontation with Israel that followed, then achieved the objective of the war, and ended the conflict at the right time, preserving the effectiveness and capacities of the armed forces, inflicting heavy losses on Israel. Finally, his assessment of the situation was so accurate that the Supreme Commander was warned of the importance of achieving a ceasefire in a time frame not exceeding seventy-two hours.

What is certain, in my estimation, is that this opinion, expressed by Hafiz Ismail and many others, has been written by a number of commentators and discussed in analyses of what could or could not have been done—a discussion that will probably go on for years. What is also certain is that the names of Ahmed Ismail Ali, Mohamed Abdel Ghani al-Gamasy, Mohamed Ali Fahmy, Hosni Mubarak, Saad Ma'moun, Abd al-Moneim Khalil, Abd al-Moneim Wasel, Fouad Zikri, Yusuf Afifi, Ahmed Badawi, Abd Rabb al-Nabi Hafiz, Hassan Abu Sa'da, Fouad Ghali, al-Urabi, Qabeel, al-Zumur, all the joint chiefs of staff and their staff, and many, many others—all these, I say—will remain in Egypt's memory for centuries to come.

Those were dark and difficult days. But they were wonderful by any standard for they restored the honor of the Egyptian military.

10 Attempts to Extricate the Third Army

N ow that the military confrontation was over, Egypt had its main forces on the east bank of the Suez Canal. Israel, meanwhile, had succeeded, with massive U.S. support, in establishing an Israeli army pocket stretching from the south of the Cairo–Ismailiya road to the Mount Ataqa region and the port of Adabiya overlooking the Gulf of Suez in the region west of the Suez Canal. It has also besieged the city of Suez and a large portion of Egypt's Third Army east of the canal.

Despite the Israeli presence west of the canal, the Egyptian military command was aware that we had achieved, to a great extent, the strategic objectives of the war. It had imposed on the US, and hence Israel, the inevitability of taking into account Egypt's demand for full control of the Sinai Peninsula in any negotiation process, even a years-long one. The military command also recognized that the Israeli side had placed itself in a position of massive risk if Egypt should decide to resume fighting and force a passage into Suez, backed by the Third Army or the Badr forces, in position east of the canal. The days following the ceasefire were characterized by valiant efforts by the Egyptian army to rebuild its reserves and to cluster around the Israeli presence in the west with a concentration of Egyptian troops so unprecedented that it forced Israel to maintain defensive positions. Israel's main forces were threatened by this siege just as they themselves were laying siege to the Egyptian Third Army. The exit for Israel's forces through the Suez Canal, and to Egyptian soil outside of Sinai, was extremely narrow, offering only a few kilometers overlooking the canal in the pocket. Any experienced military tactician knows that such a position is extremely vulnerable, and poses a severe threat to the balance of forces.

Egypt was well aware of this. Egyptian political leaders, though, thought it important to try and arrive at a peaceful political settlement that would allow them to reap the fruits of the war in a timely manner. They focused on the strategic goals, putting aside small-scale maneuvers and eschewing unnecessary risks—an approach characteristic of President Sadat in his every major action.

Anyone who has followed Egyptian efforts at the time can tell that Egypt, immediately following the ceasefire, also engaged in negotiations along three interrelated axes: a political settlement embodied by the first Israel–Egypt Disengagement Agreement in January 1974, followed by the Sinai Interim Agreement of 1975, and the visit to Jerusalem in 1977 that led to the Camp David negotiations and the Egypt–Israel peace treaty.

In contrast to the earlier chapters, which spoke of my experiences with war, without any reference to peace, this chapter will call attention to the peace efforts. My reasons for this spring from the fact that, in addition to closely monitoring all the negotiations after the ceasefire, I took part in every delegation and kept tabs on every Egyptian effort that followed Sadat's visit to Jerusalem. I was with Ahmed Maher al-Sayed in the Egyptian negotiating delegation that visited Jerusalem in 1978, at the establishment of the Political Committee preceded by the Mena House Conference in December 1977. During that conference, I was private secretary to Dr. Esmat Abdel Meguid, head of the Egyptian delegation during that opening meeting of Egyptian and Israeli diplomats. He occupied the post of permanent Egyptian representative to the United Nations, and had been called in from New York to assist with the negotiations on the strength of his experience and profound insight into the Arab–Israeli conflict.

I took part in the negotiations attended by Egyptian foreign ministers, starting with Mohamed Ibrahim Kamel at Leeds Castle, followed by the Camp David Summit in September 1978, and the Madrid Summit in 1991, when the Egyptian delegation was headed by Amre Moussa.

These were long years of superhuman effort by Egyptian diplomats, and for Egyptian diplomacy. The real start was the defeat of 1967, and they came to full fruition when every inch of Egyptian soil was regained from Israel with the Taba ruling of 1988.

I would be remiss if I did not mention a great many respected Egyptian diplomats who took part in this process, and who were wise and experienced beyond their years despite their youth at the time. They were committed to the future of their country, no less than the brave soldiers of the armed forces and the members of other Egyptian security apparatuses. Foremost among them was of course the brilliant ambassador Osama al-Baz, and the team that worked the hardest at the start of the negotiations: Ambassador Abdel Raouf El Reedy, Dr. Nabil al-Arabi, Ahmed Maher al-Sayed, and Amre Moussa.

I mentioned the three axes of Egyptian negotiations immediately following the ceasefire. Ismail Fahmy, President Sadat's special envoy, went to Washington on October 29 for consultations with the Americans. This move occurred in parallel with the talks at Kilometer 101 in Suez between Major-General Abdel Ghani al-Gamasy and General Aharon Yariv, the personal representative of Prime Minister Golda Meir. The Egyptians were preparing to execute a central element of Resolution 338, which called for negotiations between the concerned parties. In my estimation, then as now, the siege of the Third Army forced President Sadat to take steps he would not have taken if the front had remained as it was on October 20, for example. The president signed off on the start of talks at Kilometer 101 to spare the Third Army unnecessary risk. He also attempted to push Israel, using U.S. pressure, to return to the lines of October 22. These were attempts I was certain would fail, as their implementation would place the Israeli army in great danger. Meanwhile, although Ismail Fahmy's visit took place in this context, its goals were far beyond returning to the October 22 lines. The visit reflected all that Sadat had worked toward over the previous three years, from when he launched his initiative in May 1971 through to the subsequent moves toward the US.

This stage of the process, with its three axes, lasted from October 28, 1973, to the Disengagement Agreement of January 21, 1974, achieving the withdrawal of Israeli forces from the west bank of the Suez Canal to the entrances to the Sinai passes. This stage also witnessed two developments that proved pivotal to the Middle East conflict. The first was the gradual sidelining of Egyptian–Soviet relations and the start of a decline in Soviet efforts in the Middle East, which culminated in Egypt's work against the Soviet invasion of Afghanistan in December 1979. The second development, more important in my estimation, was the dawn of Egyptian–U.S. relations that led to a strategic volte-face in Egyptian foreign policy. Egypt sought the US' friendship and began depending on the Americans to facilitate negotiations to retrieve Egyptian land from the clutches of Israeli occupation.

These two developments were accompanied by an additional element, namely a deep rift between Egypt and Syria concerning the rationale for the war and its strategic objectives. The rift surfaced periodically in the years after 1973, and may continue even today. "War is a continuation of politics by other means." Sadat was aware of the wisdom of Clausewitz's famous dictum, and applied it with great dedication, attempting to reach a political settlement via armed conflict.

The reader is no doubt impatient for details on these axes I keep mentioning. I will be quick and say that the objective of Ismail Fahmy's visit to Washington and the start of negotiations between al-Gamasy and Yariv at Kilometer 101, as I mentioned, was to end the extended siege on the Third Army and the city of Suez, as well as to signal to the US the importance of making the most of the Egyptian overture, embodied in the frequent messages between the Egyptian national security advisor and his U.S. counterpart, and between Presidents Sadat and Nixon. These messages were numerous, going back and forth both during and after the war.

In fact, the US was fully cognizant of the importance of making the most of this opportunity, afforded by the diligence of the Egyptian diplomatic corps, to deepen Egyptian–American cooperation. The Americans' commitment to the settlement process was clear starting from October 28, as indicated by their insistence on logistical support fleets reaching the besieged city and army, and not allowing Israel to engage in its usual prevarication or to threaten the safety of the Third Army in any way whatsoever.

Kissinger's writings, as well as those of Israeli diplomats and Egyptian statesmen—Mohamed Hafiz Ismail, Ismail Fahmy, and al-Gamasy—reveal the efforts made by both the Egyptians and the Americans to secure the arrival of supplies and rebuild the trust lost between Cairo and Washington.

The American efforts, born of the Egyptian–U.S. understanding, bore fruit in the form of a thirty-vehicle logistical support fleet entering Suez and heading to the Third Army as soon as the ceasefire came into effect. My diary for 1715 hours on October 28 reads:

> In addition to this first logistical fleet, the initial al-Gamasy–Yariv meeting was held at 2400 hours last night. Clearly, the Israeli side has no instructions nor desire to discuss retreating to October 22 lines, where Israel and Egypt were supposed to stay when the October 22 ceasefire was announced in accordance with Resolution 338. However, Israel crossed these lines and, in the period from October 22 to October 27, expanded its presence in the Israeli pocket, besieging the Third Army. The Egyptian objective during Presidential Envoy Ismail Fahmy's visit to Washington and Major-General al-Gamasy's visit to

the discussion tent at Kilometer 101 was to contract the Israeli presence back to the October 22 lines.

I added later in the diary that the Israeli side was raising the issue of navigation in the Red Sea, the need for the Egyptian navy to end the siege on Bab al-Mandeb, and the exchange of prisoners of war.

The first meeting between Egyptian military officers and their Israeli counterparts since the 1949 Armistice, according to Major-General al-Gamasy's report to the commander in chief, President Sadat, and Hafiz Ismail, his national security advisor, was conducted in an atmosphere of mutual respect. I wrote at 1330 hours on Tuesday, October 30:

> The three meetings held so far between the Egyptian and Israeli sides, attended by the United Nations representative, are deeply respectful; some feel that this respect might turn to amity, since al-Gamasy and Yariv appear to have broken the ice usually characteristic of such opening communications, especially ones held after violent military clashes that have only ended a few days ago.

The meetings also made it clear that the Israelis wanted their dead, who had fallen behind our lines, and to exchange wounded and imprisoned soldiers. Al-Gamasy responded that the issue of prisoners of war was linked to the Israelis returning to their points of retreat, which could be agreed upon between the two parties as the lines of October 22—or an approximation of them. This appears to have been the first sign of Egypt's flexibility, other than its insistence on raising the siege on the Third Army. "Go back to the Deversoir and the surrounding areas," was the gist of al-Gamasy's words, "and then we can speak of POWs and those killed. The Egyptian armed forces find it unacceptable that the Third Army remains under siege."

The record of the third meeting between Yariv and al-Gamasy, on October 30, shows that the Israelis called for political representation in the talks, so that both sides could begin to discuss the nuts and bolts of the ceasefire. Hence, Egypt promoted Major-General al-Gamasy to assistant deputy minister of war, which conferred new capacities on him and authorized him to speak to political issues as well as military ones. The meeting records show that al-Gamasy was entrusted with the task of laying out the Egyptian concept for military disengagement to the Israelis. This plan consisted of the Israelis withdrawing from the area west of the Suez Canal to a new line east of the main passes deep in Sinai, in return for permission to exchange prisoners of war and wounded soldiers and to conduct searches for the dead. It also included raising the Egyptian siege on Bab al-Mandeb, starting to clear the Suez Canal, and planning the peace conference. My diary for that day reads:

> During the next few meetings, I believe that both sides will come to an agreement on POW issues, and on permanent supplies for the Third Army and the city of Suez. Today, October 30, we will start to give them a list of the names of Israeli POWs in our custody; we have also agreed on an immediate exchange of POWs and wounded. It is an urgent Israeli demand, to which we agreed in exchange for allowing supplies to the Third Army.

The prevailing impression among us back in Egypt was that Golda Meir's choice of General Yariv reflected her wish to send her own man, as it were, to bear the responsibility of negotiating with the Egyptians, and precluded Moshe Dayan, then minister of defense, from sending one of his own, far more inflexible men. Major-General al-Gamasy confirmed this impression. Yariv, he said in a report to the political top brass, was Meir's man, and in addition to clearly being balanced and fair was also in direct communication with Israeli political leaders, which made him effective in case of any complications.

This brings us to the visit of Ismail Fahmy, President Sadat's envoy, to Washington, DC. The announcement that Fahmy had been appointed foreign minister came when he was in the U.S. capital. At 1345 hours on October 30, I wrote:

> Ismail Fahmy will lay out Egypt's vision for the next steps, which are to call for:
> - An Israeli withdrawal to October lines 22.
> - The Egyptian vision for disengagement of forces (retreating from the west to the east of the passes, the Bab al-Mandeb issues, the POWs).
> - Setting a date for announcing the resumption of Egyptian–American diplomatic relations.
> - Setting a date for starting to clear the Suez Canal.
> - The timing of the peace conference, with all the relevant details, and the stage during which it will be held, plus how all this relates to Israel's withdrawal from the west of the Suez Canal. In my estimation, Israel will categorically refuse this proposal.
> - Final withdrawal and the importance of carrying it out in a single stage, not in staggered stages.

- Ending the state of war with the completion of withdrawal, and allowing passage of Israeli ships in the Suez Canal.
- The status of Sharm al-Sheikh: international forces, or not?
- Looking into the suggestion that two politicians from the US and the USSR oversee the ceasefire.

I added in this entry that Ismail Fahmy would have a hard time negotiating this deal. According to my diary, during our daily dinner with Hafiz Ismail, in the presence of Ahmed Maher al-Sayed, I said as part of a conversation assessing the war:

- Egypt has achieved the objectives of the war. The Egyptian armed forces not only were not destroyed during the bloody conflict, but also remain capable of actively working to impose the inevitability of making a political move, as we are now witnessing.
- Our armed forces managed to put a dent in Israel's security by closing Bab al-Mandeb, thus rendering worthless Israel's control of the Straits of Tiran.
- Indications are that we need to succeed, therefore, in forcing an Israeli withdrawal within the space of a few months, in exchange for concessions to Israel in the matters of passage in the Suez Canal, ending the state of war, and guarantees of the borders of Egypt and Israel in accordance with international law.

Now we come to the results of Foreign Minister Ismail Fahmy's visit to Washington. I recorded the preliminary information that was in his telegrams to President Sadat, copies of which were given to Hafiz Ismail in his capacity as national security advisor. My diary for 2315 hours on October 30 reads:

Kissinger made it clear in his meeting with the Egyptian foreign minister that he was aware of the issue of the Third Army, and that he planned to take it up in his meeting that very evening with President Nixon, to look into taking a firm American stand on this issue. Kissinger then spoke about the Arab oil embargo, saying it weakened the internal capacities of the U.S. administration, and thence the administration's ability to apply pressure on Israel. He added that he was convinced that a Third Army surrender was not in anyone's interests.

I added here:

> As if they genuinely thought they could eliminate these Egyptian units, tried by the fire of an unprecedented battle, and as if the Egyptian reserves already in place around the army would allow the enemy to threaten the Third Army without retaliating by inflicting similar punishment on the Israeli pocket.

I wrote, as well, that Ismail Fahmy appeared optimistic that he would get Nixon's view of the matter on the evening of October 30. I added a significant fact: the Information Department said that the Third Army only had enough provisions to last thirty-six hours at most. This may explain why Ahmed Ismail Ali, Hafiz Ismail, and President Sadat all said the same thing virtually simultaneously to the Americans, the Soviets, and Egyptian statesmen: that the Egyptian army would work to create a path for the Third Army, by means of a large battle if necessary.

My record resumes at 2050 hours on Wednesday, October 31.

> We are closer to success in settling the matter of the Third Army. This will be achieved either through a permanent settlement by which they are provided with food and water daily, but no weapons or ammunition—of which, incidentally, they already have plenty—or by guaranteeing Israel's withdrawal to a new line allowing the Third Army ground forces contact with Egyptian army forces west of the Suez Canal and south of the Israeli pocket. President Sadat's instructions to the foreign minister in Washington also insisted he present the Egyptian proposal for a disengagement of forces in full. The president, however, was insistent that no POWs be exchanged without a withdrawal to October 22 lines—the same principles Major-General al-Gamasy discussed with Yariv at Kilometer 101.

The telegrams from the foreign minister flew thick and fast. I took brief notes on everything I read. My diary at 0800 hours on Friday, November 2, states my conviction that the foreign minister's telegrams reflected the importance of cautious optimism. Ismail Fahmy's telegram to the president said that Nixon would make Israel carry out Egypt's proposal for disengagement. Nixon had said to the minister that the Egyptian proposal was constructive, while Kissinger considered it reasonable.

Now, I will point out something extremely important that Minister Ismail Fahmy said. I made careful note of it. Our foreign minister asked the Americans for written assurance that the forces in the Israeli pocket would not launch military operations west of the Suez Canal. I was extremely put out by this request. I imagined that if the Americans were to offer us such assurance, they would ask for Egypt's assurance in return, which we could not give while our territories remained occupied. Our refusal to comply with such a request would give away our intentions, which could not be revealed at this juncture. A great many officers in the army were already preparing for a fresh strike to clear the path for supplies to the Third Army and to cut off the path of retreat for the Israeli pocket via the Israeli bridges on the Suez Canal.

Looking back on these events with the benefit of hindsight, I think it most likely that Minister Fahmy had decided on the importance of achieving stability on the front and ensuring that neither of the two parties would try to rock the boat during this delicate phase of negotiations. It may have been his view that it was important to test the veracity and credibility of U.S. intentions toward us.

In any case, Minister Fahmy got his written assurance and brought it back to Cairo. I wrote after reading it:

> The phrasing of the assurance is unpleasant, characterized by vague language. Kissinger merely initialed it.

Ismail Fahmy recounted what he covered in his meetings with Kissinger and Nixon. They had both made no secret of their admiration for Egypt's military and political actions. The US, they said, would send a highly respected American personage to be their point person in Cairo. They assured him that the US was capable of helping Egypt achieve its goal of an Arab–Israeli peace. They of course mentioned the oil embargo, and spoke of the need to lift it. Both Kissinger and Nixon hinted that it was far better for the Egyptians and Americans to meet directly, without any 'third parties' being involved, which was a tacit request to get the Soviet Union out of the picture. My diary says of this:

> It is quite dangerous to remove the Soviets; the US will have us all to themselves.

Ismail Fahmy's meetings with Kissinger continued. I went on summarizing the transcripts I read. At 2315 hours on November 2, I wrote,

> Kissinger is up to tricks, prevaricating and possibly reneging on his agreement. He has told the foreign minister that he needs more time to convince the Israelis to accept Egypt's proposals for a disengagement of forces.

Kissinger said on November 3 that he needed to convince Golda Meir, in Washington at the time, to accept the Egyptian proposal. That Saturday at 2230 hours, I wrote,

> Kissinger may be trying to stall any agreement that might be possible in Washington with Ismail Fahmy, and to wait until the secretary of state's visit to Egypt on November 7, so as to bring all his efforts into one big achievement.

I added at 0800 hours on Monday, November 5:

> Kissinger is still prevaricating and equivocating with our foreign minister. He [Kissinger] says he needs more time to go back to the October 22 lines, and "might," he says, tell us the results of his efforts in his upcoming visit to Cairo. He says he is also looking into a way to get over the issue of the October 22 lines.
>
> In his final meeting with Ismail Fahmy before the latter left DC to await the U.S. secretary of state's visit to Cairo, Kissinger floated the question of whether we could move directly to the peace conference without looking into the matter of the lines of October 22. He added that he planned to discuss the Egyptian proposal for disengagement of forces during his visit to Cairo. Finally, Kissinger said that he needed at least two months to manage to convince Congress and American public opinion of the new U.S. policies and systems for dealing with the Middle East crisis. He said he intended to put forth a U.S. proposal for peace after this.

I must mention here that, during his discussions and consultations with Nixon and Kissinger in Washington, Ismail Fahmy was insistent that it was dangerous for the US to keep supplying Israel with weapons. Egypt and the Arabs, he said, had been shocked, indeed outraged, by the US supplying Israel with weapons in the thick of battle, which threatened all of Egypt's military successes at the time. Four Arab foreign ministers, of Algeria, Morocco, Kuwait, and Tunisia, must be singled out for thanks, as they went to Washington on October 17, met with both Nixon and Kissinger, and strongly raised the same issue. Kissinger's response was that he had waited a number of long days, watching the Soviets send military supplies to Egypt and Syria at the start of the war, and waiting for it to stop. He said he had noticed that the Soviets gave the Arabs all the military supplies they needed. He had counted three hundred Soviet military aircraft, and saw no signs of this stopping, which, he said, had imposed on the US the necessity of waiting no longer, now that the Soviet Union had made clear its intention to support the Arabs. As for Nixon, his response to Fahmy was that the US had decided that it was essential to work toward restoring the military balance between the two parties—a view echoed by Kissinger. The U.S. shipments were simply counterbalancing what the Soviet Union was sending to the Arabs, they said, and included no attack weapons—as if M16 tanks do not constitute attack weapons!

Ismail Fahmy's response was that this military supply had not only reversed a great deal of the Egyptian military success, but also assisted Israel to the extent that it would be difficult to make Israel respond to political and diplomatic efforts after the ceasefire. I read recently, for the second time, Minister Ismail Fahmy's memoir, entitled *Negotiating for Peace in the Middle East*. I advise anyone with an interest in this era to read the book, which reveals more details on what I am discussing. For more information, the reader may also wish to read the U.S. State Department's declassified documents on Minister Fahmy's visit to Washington, from October 29 to November 2, 1973. They were declassified between 1999 and the end of 2000.

Now allow me to return to the third axis of Egypt's maneuvers: the preparations for negotiations with Israel. President Sadat asked the Soviets to send one of their elder statesmen to discuss the negotiations with us, whereupon they sent First Deputy Minister of Foreign Affairs Vasili Kuznetsov. At the time I believed, in line with what Hafiz Ismail wrote in *Amn Misr al-qawmi fi 'asr al-tahaddiyat* (Egypt's National Security in the Age of Challenges), that it would have been more appropriate for the Soviets to send the experienced and powerful Foreign Minister Andrei Gromyko, who enjoyed decision-making authority and a stature equal to Kissinger, who had by then announced his upcoming visit to Cairo.

Anyone with knowledge of second-tier Soviet statesmen will conclude that however admirable their professionalism and profound their understanding, they were hampered in—not to say prohibited from—decision-making by the rigid Soviet hierarchy. In any case, Kuznetsov held talks with Sadat and Hafiz Ismail on a number of points related to preparing for the peace conference, which it was agreed should take place in Geneva.

The consultation between Egypt and the Soviet Union made President Sadat more determined not to hold a peace conference as long as the matter of the October 22 lines remained unresolved. However, Sadat decided during his talks with Kuznetsov to accept—or rather, to prepare to accept—the peace conference, while continuing his efforts to convince the Israelis to withdraw to the October 22 lines, on the understanding that the conference would commence as soon as they complied. The Egyptian national security advisor's comments on his meeting with Kuznetsov indicated that Egypt was not that insistent on its presence in Bab al-Mandeb. Finally, both Sadat and Hafiz Ismail made use of Kuznetsov's visit to emphasize the importance of continued military support for Egypt.

President Sadat then received the Soviet ambassador on November 5, and asked him to urgently supply Egypt with MiG-21 fighter aircraft. He requested large quantities of Malyutka antitank missiles, T-62 tanks, and shoulder-portable Strela surface-to-air missile systems. In the same meeting, the Soviet ambassador presented Sadat with a message from Brezhnev, which complemented the heroism of the Egyptian army and said that it had worked miracles using state-of-the-art weaponry. Having read the message, I commented in my diary:

> It's as though the Soviets can't believe it themselves, although they are on record as being against military action before! Brezhnev's message went on to warn the Egyptians against Kissinger and what the Soviets called "his tricks," describing him as a servant of imperialism, and stressing that Egypt ought not be fooled by what he said.

My diary for November 5 at 2330 hours reads,

> The president is telling many of his Arab guests that the Israeli army west of the canal is in a huge trap. We can strike them, but we are attempting to balance the benefits of striking at the Israeli army with the benefit of complying with the ceasefire in order to achieve our political goals, without any bloodshed on our side.

As I will soon discuss Kissinger's visit to Cairo, whose important effects we were all awaiting, I find it essential to quote from Hafiz Ismail's book his comments on the Soviets and the Americans, their relations with Egypt, and Egypt's position vis-à-vis the two superpowers. The national security advisor notes,

> President Sadat kept the pressure on the Soviets to fully arm our forces, which he had broached in his meeting with the Soviet ambassador, so we could be in a position to clear a path to our forces east of Suez by force, in case diplomatic efforts failed. Therefore, the president made no secret of his impatience with the Soviets' position when their response to his requests fell short of our goals.

Hafiz Ismail comes to a final conclusion regarding the Soviets' actions toward us:

> The Soviets contributed once again to their own loss of initiative. The initiative, having slipped through their fingers, went to the Americans, who stood prepared to respond to Egypt's direct needs, namely the opening of supply lines to the east of Suez, even if they did consider the possibility of Israeli forces returning to the October 22 lines remote. This reinforced the American role: the US became solely responsible for any movement forward by applying pressure on Israel. Until the end of the road, the US did not allow the initiative to slip away again.

11 Kissinger and Reaping the Rewards

Everyone was eagerly anticipating Kissinger's arrival. It was the secretary of state's first visit to Cairo. It turned out to be the first of many, which led to great developments in Egypt–U.S. relations, many advancements on the issue of the settlement both on the Egyptian–Israeli and Syrian–Israeli fronts, and finally to a sea change in the approach to the Palestinian question, which—despite sheaves of agreements and accords, and Arab and Israeli actions—was, and remains, the core of the conflict in the Middle East.

As I was saying, we were all filled with anticipation. Hafiz Ismail's office, under the immediate and wise supervision of Ambassador Makhlouf, worked diligently to get all the documents in order and present the requisite memoranda, evaluations, and analyses. Kissinger's usual way of thinking and working was analyzed, extrapolating from his actions in the Vietnam War, back when he assumed his post as the national security advisor in January 1969 in the Nixon administration's first term, and when he assumed the mantle of secretary of state during the transitional period in Nixon's second term, which the president never completed due to Watergate.

Hafiz Ismail greedily devoured every scrap of information we gave him on Kissinger's negotiation style. In summary, Kissinger divided issues under negotiation into numerous small parts. He started with the easiest to agree on, hoping to reach an easy yes, build trust, and reinforce his role as a man capable of achieving what others could not. Gradual success, in steps, was his way, affirming the importance of the US.

121

On the evening of November 6, the U.S. secretary of state arrived in Cairo. President Sadat met with him on the morning of Wednesday, November 7. My diary on November 8, 1240 hours, reads:

> The president and Kissinger have quickly reached an accord aimed at securing stability on the front, and have sent it to Israel with Kissinger's assistant in the State Department:
>
> Egypt and Israel must strictly comply with the ceasefire called for in the UN Security Council Resolutions, starting with 338.
>
> Talks must start immediately between the two countries, with the aim of settling the issue of a return to the lines of October 22, as part of a plan to agree on a disengagement of forces and cessation of hostilities under UN supervision.
>
> The city of Suez must receive daily rations of food, water, and medicine, and the wounded will be transported out of the city.
>
> There will be no restrictions on non-military supplies being transferred to the eastern bank of the canal.
>
> UN-affiliated checkpoints shall replace Israeli checkpoints on the Cairo–Suez road. Israeli officers may be allowed to take part in searches and check the nature of non-military supplies alongside the UN representatives at the Suez end of the road.
>
> As soon as UN checkpoints are established along the Cairo–Suez road, the exchange of POWs, including the injured, will commence.

On the same day, my diary reads:

> Kissinger spoke with President Sadat, proposing that the Third Army withdraw to the western bank of the Suez Canal, that is, to its original position before commencing the crossing, in exchange for a complete Israeli withdrawal from the pocket in the west, and their return to the east of the canal in the position currently held by the Third Army— the same rash proposition made by General Yariv to Major-General al-Gamasy in the talks at Kilometer 101 on the Egypt–Suez desert road, and also by Kissinger during Minister Ismail Fahmy's visit to Washington. Indeed, it is the same proposition made by Kissinger to Hafiz Ismail on the second day of the launch of the Egyptian military operation, October 7. President Sadat categorically rejected this proposal, just as all the statesmen above had rejected it before.
>
> Kissinger then proposed to the president that the retreat to the lines of October 22 be linked to the agreement to a disengagement of

forces, that is, disengagement of the Egyptian and Israeli armies, and the gradual withdrawal of Israel to the eastern bank of the Suez Canal.

Kissinger also proposed that the parties look into holding the peace conference referred to in Resolution 338 in early December, attended by both the US and the Soviet Union, which would also take part in all the committees. He responded positively to an Egyptian proposal for a similar ceasefire between Israel and Syria, on the model we had started upon with the Americans with regard to the Egyptian front.

Kissinger finally mentioned a number of points he believes to be of importance, mainly ending the oil embargo to the US, and ending the Arab petroleum-producing states' productivity reduction, as per their October 20 decision. For my part, I still think that that Arab step was influential and important—but I'm also convinced it came too late. It should have been carried out, and prepared for, as soon as the US adopted pro-Israel positions and provided military support; in other words, a week earlier. Perhaps our Arab brethren's unpreparedness to enact such a step as soon as the war began, and the fact that they were not informed of the precise timing of the military strike, slowed their response to the situation. In any case, President Sadat was adamant about linking a return to pre-embargo levels of production and export to an Israeli withdrawal, although he did not go into specifics.

Kissinger also spoke to President Sadat about Egypt's closure of Bab al-Mandeb to Israeli shipping and maritime trade. He hoped, he said, that we would quietly raise this siege. I must add here that Egypt deliberately ignored the passage through Bab al-Mandeb of an oil tanker flying the Liberian flag, on November 1, on its way to the port of Eilat, as an indication of Egypt's flexibility if the US retained its positive position, and if Israel responded to Egypt's requirements. This ship was the subject of a heated discussion between the Egyptian national security advisor and the commander in chief of the Egyptian armed forces, Ahmed Ismail Ali. The latter wanted to sink it, especially as it was in the sights, and within the range, of one of our submarines in the area. But Hafiz Ismail preferred to leave it alone, in order to safeguard the mission of Foreign Minister Ismail Fahmy, who was at the time in Washington, DC, while still letting the Americans know that our position had not changed and that we reserved the right to enforce our rights in the future.

The day of that event, I had written,

This step means that we are ceding part of our control over the Red Sea.

There is no doubt that it is being done in return for allowing supplies to reach Suez and the Third Army.

In the middle of all this, President Sadat, back from a whirlwind visit of Kuwait and Saudi Arabia on November 2, issued strict instructions to block any and all ships headed for Eilat. Finally, it was agreed that diplomatic relations between Egypt and the US, which had been cut in 1967, would be restored.

Today, I find myself meticulously rereading the diaries where I mention all these meetings. I was unhappy with some of what I was recording, within the limits of my vision and experience at the time, and the information and interpretations available to me. I wrote, for example,

> All Hafiz Ismail's office staff are worried, even unhappy, about the results of the meeting. The Americans have cleared a passage to the Third Army in return for an exchange of POWs and the clearing of Bab al-Mandeb, while Israel remains in position and refuses to withdraw to the October 22 lines.
>
> This leads me to conclude that the siege of the Third Army will go on indefinitely. The six points that were agreed upon have been linked to a disengagement of forces, and it will take months to look into that and reach an agreement. Israel will do all it can to achieve gains that we cannot grant. Israel will try and link the disengagement to future steps, and thence to a final settlement; that, too, will take time, perhaps six months. During that time, the Third Army will have grown lax under siege.

While writing this book, I asked myself: Did we possess the military capacity at the time to force a passage through to the Third Army? Or did we need more time? These are questions to which only a select few of Egypt's military commanders know the answer: those who know the background to the situation, the capacities of the armed forces, and the shape and form of our military support, forces, and equipment that were starting to pour in from every direction.

It is important to mention Sadat's meeting with Lieutenant-General Pyotr Nikolayevich Lashchenko, the senior Soviet expert in the Nasser era, at 1130 hours on November 6, the day before his meeting with Kissinger. The president insisted on demanding MiG-14 fighter aircraft. Lashchenko hinted indirectly that the Soviets did not have enough of that type of plane! The president also asked for modified SAM-6 missiles to combat AGM-45 Shrikes, which Israeli fighters were using heavily against our anti-aircraft missile battery radar. Lashchenko again responded that the Soviets had nothing new in their possession, nor modified beyond what we were already using. President Sadat asked for thirty M500 (MiG-25) aircraft immediately. Lashchenko said that thirty aircraft would have little effect—meaning the reverse, namely that we might as well do without.

The Soviet general then added, despite all that had just been said, that his experts would study Egypt's demands and requirements and do their best to respond to them. He went on to say that the Israeli forces west of the Suez Canal were in an extremely precarious position and could be wiped out by a military strike, and that he—Lashchenko—could not tell who was the besieged and who was the besieger.

President Sadat agreed. He added that Ahmed Ismail had prepared for a massive military strike, to be carried out if needed.

"But why not just carry it out?" asked Lashchenko. "In accordance with Resolution 242, to say nothing of the return to the October 22 lines?"

President Sadat, it is worth mentioning, was trying hard to keep up positive relations with the Soviets. Despite his openness to, and orientation toward, the promising American path, he was aware that arming the Egyptian forces was the way to secure American and Israeli flexibility. Only this way could a satisfactory settlement be reached. He therefore kept trying to get whatever he could from the Soviet Union. This explains why he granted another audience to the Soviet ambassador on November 11, repeating his request for the MiG-21 fighters, especially as he judged the Egyptian air force, after its losses and sacrifices, to be in a precarious situation. To justify his demand for more fighters, Sadat made it clear to the Soviet ambassador that Egypt had more tanks in the west, and that the enemy was uneasy as a consequence, which drove them to attempt airstrikes against us. This was why we needed to be prepared for a confrontation.

The president emphasized our capacity to liquidate the Israeli pocket in the west. He concluded by expressing some frustration and resentment regarding the Soviets' attitude, and requesting that he be kept apprised of Soviet actions and interpretations of the situation. He affirmed that their continued failure to send the fighter planes was a clear message to us. The ambassador promised to convey the situation to Premier Brezhnev in full, and asked if we would accept other types of fighter aircraft. I remember writing in my diary, upon reading the minutes of this talk, "I hope the Soviets don't mean to send us MiG-17s!" Finally, Sadat said that he found any Soviet suspicions of Egypt and Egyptian actions unacceptable.

This brings me back to the six points, my reading of them during Kissinger's visit to Cairo, and the effects of the visit. I request the reader's patience as I quote from Hafiz Ismail's book:

The president summarized the results of Kissinger's visit during his meeting with his assistants, saying that most of their time was spent on how to achieve a disengagement of forces between Egypt and the US, not Israel as we had been thinking! "We have entered a new chapter in our relations with the US," he said. He viewed the US as the only party capable of moving the situation forward without any collaboration with the USSR.

These words clearly reflected Egypt's future orientation. The Soviet reaction, represented by Lashchenko's positions, made it clear that the Soviet Union had no intention of further strengthening Egypt or building its capacities without promises and pledges that Sadat had no intention of giving, or even considering, in his current situation. Once again the decision was made. Egypt moved toward a gradual, step-by-step path of rebuilding trust with the US.

On November 11, as soon as the six points were set out and signed off, President Sadat issued instructions to Major-General al-Gamasy to start working on a disengagement of forces with General Yariv. They resumed their meetings directly the next day. It may be relevant, when discussing the six points, to mention that the Egyptians were not happy with Israeli leaks and statements to the effect that the list included a clause raising the siege on Bab al-Mandeb. The Egyptian foreign minister requested a suspension of any announcement of an agreement pending clarification.

The Egyptians began to notice that the Israelis had started creating a problem—a series of problems, in fact—in order to hold up the arrival of supplies to Suez and the Third Army. This became so bad that Brigadier General Ahmed Badawi, commander of the Seventh Infantry Division and of the Badr forces in the east, began to send his food and water rations back. He poured away a number of jerry-cans of water into the sand, as the Israelis and the UN observers watched. This was met with great respect among Egyptian military leaders; it revealed the man's mettle. Many predicted a brilliant military career for this commander, which came true when he was appointed minister of defense. Badawi was just one of the Egyptian military commanders who was treated unjustly after the defeat of 1967, like Lieutenant-General al-Orabi, commander of the Twenty-First Armored Division and the future chief of staff. Both had suffered defeats, yet, bloody but unbowed, they remained ever loyal to their country.

Upon the signing of the Six-Point Agreement on Sunday, November 11, the same day and the same month as the signing of the Armistice during the First World War, I wrote:

There will be endless controversy around this agreement. There will be conflicting interpretations. But what is certain is that we are on the path to a settlement. We need to mobilize the maximum political and military pressure to speed it along. A settlement could be built, initially, on Israel's withdrawal to the east of the Sinai passes, thinning out the military presence on the east bank of the Suez Canal, and bringing in international peacekeeping forces.

I expressed my hopes and expectations that this might be completed within two months, or maybe six weeks, when the peace conference would be held.

The week after Kissinger's visit to Cairo, Egypt began to implement the six points and establish a secure and unbroken supply line for the Third Army and Suez, as well as prepare for the peace conference in Geneva. In parallel, it worked to advance Egyptian–American relations, while not giving up on a last attempt to preserve its relations with the Soviet Union. Finally, it worked to bolster its hand through active cooperation and coordination with Arab countries, especially oil-producing ones, and patient and constructive collaboration with Syria to preserve the unity of our partnership in war—especially as the Syrians, in the view of many Egyptian statesmen, were being obdurate and rejected any attempt to follow up on military gains with careful political action.

Today, I believe we ought to have done more to convince the Syrians that the active, fast-paced Egyptian maneuver was the right way to exploit the flurry that followed war and the twin military pressures on Israel's armed forces hundreds of miles apart. We should also have tried to safeguard Syria's trust in Egypt's intentions. I thought then, and still do, that both sides fought magnificently, in accordance with a clear strategy of dividing Israel's capabilities by making it fight on two fronts. However, Syria and Egypt did not manage to work together seamlessly during the operation management stage. This would have required a great deal more preparation, coordination, and consultation before, during, and after the commencement of military operations. This is where I think the lapse occurred. What is certain is that the two parties were not in agreement on the final goals of the armed conflict. I am also certain that they lacked a clear vision of what would happen when the fighting was over, and the required study of possible scenarios and planning for various alternatives.

The relations between Egypt and Syria were sometimes strained, to be sure. Many have written, including Mahmoud Riyad, then secretary-general of the League of Arab States, that the leaders of both states were suspicious of each other's intentions. Syria was convinced that Egypt had jumped the gun and acted on its own, while the consensus in Egypt was that the Syrians had not understood the need for political action as soon as the dust had settled. Furthermore, the Syrians believed that Egypt had no reason to agree to a ceasefire. All this strained relations almost to the breaking point, and I recall that while preparations were under way for the Geneva Conference, there were conflicts between Egypt and Syria so severe that the transcripts of some telephone conversations between the countries' foreign ministers showed them to be openly belligerent and confrontational. I must admit I was shocked. Again, I do appreciate that the lack of mutual understanding of the objectives of military action and the lack of agreement between the partners on a shared political framework made things difficult. It led to a gradual, then final, parting of ways, which culminated in President Sadat's peace initiative in November 1977, despite sincere attempts to consider Syria's interests and defend Syria in its confrontation with Israel and the US.

Over the past couple of years, I have read a number of books on the Second World War and the meetings between the Allied leaders, Britain and the US, on the political and military fronts. These books reveal how far the two parties were willing to go in their coordination with each other, getting over arguments and disagreements and arriving at under-standings and compromises. This was not merely a war against Germany, but also against the disagreements that divided them as allies. They worked together to defeat Germany and the Axis powers. My estimation today is that the Egyptian and Syrian military and political leaders should have intensified their coordination and meetings, and sought to arrive at a mutual understanding, so as to not allow things to decline as far as they did in November 1973.

I recall the last axis of Egyptian action, namely the large-scale disen-gagement of forces. This mission occupied Major-General al-Gamasy and General Yariv for a few weeks after the Six-Point Agreement of November 11. In parallel, the Egyptian political side was working on it, represented by President Sadat and the Egyptian Foreign Ministry. These efforts, if they reveal anything at all, show how systematically the Egyptian side worked to achieve its aims as soon as the fighting stopped, advancing an approach whose ultimate destination was the liberation of Egyptian soil, while working toward a Palestinian settlement. I must admit that the pas-sage of time shows that Israel's strategy of stalling and prevaricating with both Egypt and the US was successful. It allowed the settlement process to flag after 1975, losing its pace after the Sinai Interim Agreement, also known as the Second Disengagement Agreement, and resulting in almost total stasis afterward. The situation was so bad that Sadat was driven to come up with another adventure: not a military one this time, but a political act that many considered shocking, especially Arabs. I will discuss this below when I cover the Middle East peace efforts.

Before I return to the Kilometer 101 negotiations, and the preparations for the peace conference, I believe it is important to mention the relationship between Hafiz Ismail and Ismail Fahmy, the new foreign minister. Fahmy believed that Egypt's foreign minister was the one who should communicate with the U.S. secretary of state, not the national security advisor. The political developments that led up to the preparations for the Geneva Conference meant that the Foreign Ministry, not the National Security Department, should handle these preparations—which it did. This was when Hafiz Ismail began to be pushed aside, especially as he seemed alienated by the speed with which President Sadat was moving toward the US.

There were conflicting currents, as it turned out, in the upper echelons of Egyptian leadership: some tacit, some explicit. The foreign minister's role expanded, while the national security advisor's role diminished. All of us, Hafiz Ismail's staff, recall Ismail Fahmy ordering Makhlouf to give him a full copy of every communication that passed between Hafiz Ismail and Kissinger during the weeks of the war, on the president's instructions. "Why did you not provide the Foreign Ministry with a copy of these messages?" Minister Ismail Fahmy asked, whereupon Makhlouf responded that they were highly classified by order of the president himself. When instructed otherwise, he immediately provided the requisite copies. I would be remiss not to mention that Hafiz Ismail's messages to Kissinger were not to him as U.S. secretary of state but as U.S. national security advisor, until he was succeeded by Brent Scowcroft.

In any case, the tensions gradually dissipated when Hafiz Ismail was relieved of his responsibilities in February 1974. We returned to the Foreign Ministry and other Egyptian apparatuses from which we had been on loan to the Egyptian National Security Department, headed by the Presidency, with the start of Minister Ismail Fahmy's preparations for the Geneva Conference. The few paragraphs I recorded in my diary at the time show that preparations were well under way. There was talk of preparations for Egypt, Jordan, Syria, and Israel to participate in the conference, as well as some talk of a Palestinian and a Lebanese delegation taking part in the next stage of the conference.

The next stage never came. Syria was absent from the first. The conference lasted a day, then broke up without making any progress.

The focus returned to the Kilometer 101 talks and Kissinger's communications with the Egyptian Foreign Ministry, with the aim to agree on the disengagement of forces that President Sadat had negotiated with Kissinger on November 7. My diary for that period, specifically on Tuesday, November 13, at 1800 hours, reads:

> Ahmed Maher is basing what he says on his conversations with Hafiz Ismail on an Egyptian-American understanding, which I have previously noted in these diaries, on a disengagement of forces taking Israel to the east bank of the canal and paving the way for a comprehensive settlement of the conflict, in closely connected stages.

Kissinger also spoke with Sadat of the importance of reaching a Palestinian settlement—according to what I set down at 2300 hours on Thursday, November 15—namely that a Palestinian state be formed in the West Bank and Gaza with borders defined by the Arabs. This was proposed in a conversation between President Sadat and the Jordanian foreign minister, sent by King Hussein that day.

The talks between al-Gamasy and Yariv continued, and the argument continued on both sides, on the interpretation of the Six-Point Agreement or on the definition of the disengagement of forces. On November 15, at the eleventh meeting between the two sides, General Yariv proposed an understanding that underscored the importance of the talks not ending with a clear 'victor' or 'vanquished.' He said that Egypt's efforts to return the inhabitants of the Suez Canal area to civilian life were important to achieving the disengagement. Another important element was Israel's retreat to strong defense lines that would deter aggression and remove the need for building new interim lines, with a future stationing of international peacekeeping forces between the two sides as the withdrawals developed. Yariv also emphasized that direct communications between Egypt and Israel were not important but essential—a point to which Israel assigned central importance. Major-General al-Gamasy asked if this meant that Israel was offering to withdraw far east of the Suez Canal, without the Egyptian forces having to withdraw to the west. Yariv said yes. He added, however, that this would have to be "accompanied by a thinning of the Egyptian presence the length of the eastern bank of the Suez Canal, to assure Israel of Egypt's good intentions, so that we can move forward together toward more settlements and withdrawals at a future stage."

In my diary for 2400 hours on Friday, November 16, my own question was:

> Should we accept? Should we agree to a curtain of forces? I doubt it. . . .
> We might agree to a presence of one and a half divisions in the east. The future will reveal both parties' stance and their intentions.

But the main point I need to make clear is that the Egyptian armed forces were heavily massed, in hitherto unprecedented concentration, around the Israeli pocket. They were always provoking and baiting the Israelis. The Israelis were therefore so apprehensive about a surprise attack that they raised a number of fortifications, including a deep and wide antitank trench. Israel's withdrawal after the Second Disengagement Agreement in Aswan on January 21, 1974, revealed that there had been a massive concentration of Israeli forces inside the pocket. This indicates that if the Egyptians had attacked, a huge battle would have ensued, possibly surpassing all the battles of the October War, especially as the battlefield would have been packed with massive numbers of troops in a small area.

When the Israeli forces eventually returned east via the bridges, watched by and within striking range of our troops, the Egyptians counted over six hundred Israeli tanks, in addition to thousands of other vehicles. Despite what Yariv had said, the talks that followed revealed that the Israelis were reneging on their agreement. There were words between the two sides. Egypt was starting to lose patience. I could sense it in the conversations of our office staff. There were conflicting opinions: some said we should make a military move, while others said we should take the Israelis to the Geneva Conference while they still had a presence in the pocket, arguing that the military pressure of such a presence, coupled with the length and breadth of the area over which its communications and transport networks were spread thin, and therefore weakened, would force Israel to be flexible politically. Foreign Minister Ismail Fahmy's opinion, I wrote in my diary, was that Kissinger should be urged to end the Israeli presence west of the canal before the Geneva Conference began, so that the negotiations could take a positive strategic orientation.

The messages between Fahmy and Kissinger became more frequent. We were still receiving copies of all the assessments and information submitted to the president from all state quarters, especially the Ministry of Defense, the Foreign Ministry, the Ministry of the Interior, and Egyptian Intelligence.

Kissinger kept up the pressure on the subject of allowing the passage of trading vessels via Bab al-Mandeb. The Americans notified us that a number of ships headed for Eilat would pass through the straits within a few days, around November 20 or later. The Egyptians responded: "You need to notify us of the name of every ship in advance." The objective, of course, was to claim some semblance of control over the straits, although the Egyptian decision at the time was to quietly lift the siege.

The twelfth meeting between al-Gamasy and Yariv was held on Tuesday, November 20. I wrote,

No agreement. The Israelis offered to withdraw to the east bank in exchange for thinning out the Third Army, while the Second Army remains unchanged. We refused. Both sides maneuvered for a long while, without settling on a final strategic position. It became clear that the Israelis were playing for time.

A message arrived for Hafiz Ismail from Kissinger on Wednesday, November 21, in which he responded to the message he had received from the Egyptian foreign minister on the disengagement of forces before the Geneva Conference. Kissinger's message read that the Geneva Conference would be delayed until December 17. It was ultimately held a few days after that, on December 21.

Kissinger requested to visit Egypt on his way back from Syria on December 14. He disapproved of Egypt's insistence on, or discussion of, the disengagement of forces before the Geneva Conference. Kissinger's message revealed his attempts to bend the positions of both parties to serve American interests.

Al-Gamasy and Yariv worked to try and speed up the steps of the disengagement. They held two meetings on November 22 and 23. At 1700 hours on Friday, November 23, I wrote,

> I believe that the two sides are on the verge of reaching an agreement. Israel is now offering a withdrawal to the east bank, at a distance of 12 kilometers from the front lines of our forces in Sinai, while keeping a symbolic curtain of our forces in the east. Al-Gamasy responded with an Egyptian proposal that Israel withdraw to a distance of sixty kilometers from our vanguard, which Israel rejected.

I was certain, I wrote then, that we would arrive at an agreement guaranteeing Israel's withdrawal to the Sinai passes. Our forces would remain in their current positions, albeit considerably thinned out, with international peacekeeping forces deployed between them, plus the peace conference. The Egyptian and Israeli sides negotiated points for some time. I imagined, from all that I read at the time, that we were genuinely close to coming to an agreement. But suddenly the Israelis became inflexible, and we were forced to go to Geneva without results.

Kissinger came back to the region in May 1974. Documents declassified in later years revealed that Kissinger had intervened with the Israelis and imposed a slowdown, so that it would be he and not the parties concerned who phrased the agreement, which was to become the First Disengagement Agreement, signed on January 21. (The reader may note that I have made no mention of the details of the disengagement, or of the Geneva Conference: I prefer to leave the telling to those who took part in it and wrote about it.) I recall that we—Hafiz Ismail's office staff—visited the front in Suez and the Third Army on January 25. I saw the flower of the armed forces, the true fighting spirit of our military. The equipment was in tip-top shape; the people were unforgettable. I saw the true mettle of Egyptians faced with a challenge.

Hafiz Ismail was in Aswan, on the sidelines during Sadat's meetings with Kissinger. He then returned to Cairo, and found another way to serve his country. In *Amn Misr al-qawmi fi 'asr al-tahaddiyat* (Egypt's National Security in the Age of Challenges), he writes:

> Just as the signing of the Disengagement Agreement represented an end to the complex military situation on the Egyptian front, and a stable starting point for Egypt's foreign relations, it was the start of a new stage. I felt it was time to step away from the inner circle of the president's men, after twenty-nine months as national security advisor, in compliance with what was agreed upon in a meeting with President Sadat.

Our work with Hafiz Ismail at the National Security Advisory was at an end.

12 Back to the Decision to Go to War

On the evening of September 30, 1973, six days before the Egyptian army crossed the Suez Canal, Dr. Abdel Hadi Makhlouf hosted a Ramadan iftar at the offices of National Security Advisor Hafiz Ismail for the small group of Foreign Ministry diplomats who worked under him. The company was small: Counselor Ahmed Maher al-Sayed, First Secretary Ehab Wahba, First Secretary Ahmed Adel, Second Secretary Farouk Baraka, Third Secretary Mohamed al-Gawwali, Third Secretary Ahmed Aboul Gheit, and Third Secretary Hussein Shalash. There were also some members of other Egyptian national security apparatuses, including Egyptian Intelligence and the Presidential Guard, and a few economic experts. It was a small but highly disciplined group, comprising a profound knowledge of every field of the Egyptian state: economics, supplies, security, foreign relations, and developments on the military front. We received regular, possibly daily, reports on the enemy's activities and movements on the front, in addition to their reconnaissance along the ceasefire lines, and even enemy attempts to breach deep inside to glean information about our forces, armaments, and so on.

Speaking of this, I recall an extremely precise report that Hafiz Ismail wrote of an Israeli aerial reconnaissance in May 1973, explaining in detail the air routes and the probable objectives of the flight in the report being prepared by Military Intelligence and Reconnaissance. Two Israeli Mirage aircraft had flown a reconnaissance mission in the area between the southern banks of the Great Bitter Lakes and the city of Suez, flown southward to the middle of the Egyptian coastline on the

Red Sea, then flew northward, and returned, via a point close to Sharm al-Sheikh, to their own air base in Sinai. Hafiz Ismail wrote in his report: "The enemy's reconnaissance over Alexandria and the Nile Delta will intensify in the coming period." I remembered this prediction, and took note of its importance. Hafiz Ismail's prediction regarding an increase in reconnaissance attempts meant that the enemy was trying to obtain information because certain issues were preoccupying them, perhaps to do with Egypt's intentions or changes in Egypt's situation. I discussed this with Ahmed Maher, saying it was strange. Why would Hafiz Ismail be expecting this to happen? I came to the conclusion that the mention of Alexandria—the port, that is—meant that we were due to receive new equipment, which the enemy sought to find out about.

"That's true," Ahmed Maher said, "it's an accurate reading of the situation." There was a shipment of Sukhoi Su-17 bomber fighters and medium-range Scud-B missiles on the way as a result of a new Egyptian–Soviet understanding, itself a result of the contracts signed between Egypt and the Soviet Union in late 1972. Hafiz Ismail had told Maher about these developments in one of their discussions.

After the meal, we sat quietly chatting. The host received a telephone call; he talked a little and then returned to make his excuses, as he had to go to meet Hafiz Ismail, who had been on the phone. We all left. A few days later, the October War began. In January 1974, as I wrote earlier, Makhlouf asked me to inventory, record, and archive the most important documents, and I made a meal of it, devouring as much information as I could. The process took many weeks. I read the minutes and transcripts of President Sadat's meetings, encounters, and negotiations with Soviet leaders from late 1970 until mid-1973. I noted the tug-of-war between us and the Soviets concerning our military position, our needs in terms of weaponry and equipment, and our desire to increase our deterrent capacity so as to impose our will on the Israelis—at least with regard to control of our land and airspace.

That was when I noticed that many of the discussions were related to our need to arm and reinforce our air capacities sufficiently to repel any Israeli threats deep inside Egypt—always our greatest fear. We also focused on increasing our air defense capacities and multiplying their batteries, protecting Egypt's ground forces and all the vital areas in Egypt with an effective air defense umbrella—one of the strongest air defense systems in the world at the time.

During this archiving process, I had the golden opportunity to read an important document related to President Sadat's meeting on September 30, the same night of the iftar we attended at Makhlouf's invitation. It turned out that our host had left the dinner to attend the president's meeting and transcribe all of Sadat's discussions with the leaders of what came to be called the Egyptian National Security Council. I mentioned the contents of the minutes of this meeting in an article published in *al-Ahram* on October 6, 2009. A few weeks later, in July 2010, I received a surprise phone call from Abdel Hadi Makhlouf. He asked me to send over a car for him to give the driver an envelope whose contents he wanted me to see.

I opened the envelope and was astonished. Dr. Makhlouf had kept a copy of the minutes of the meeting—that historic meeting where they had prepared for the October War! The document I had read in Abdin Palace in January or February 1974 was the complete transcript. And here I was, thirty-seven years later, holding the original document in my hands, in the handwriting of Abdel Hadi Makhlouf. I began to try and decipher the mysteries of its author's handwriting. Again I read the transcript, tears in my eyes. What wonderful days! What mighty challenges! The president's will to fight was strong and clear. His insistence and clear-sightedness revealed a deep faith in God and country.

Many of my compatriots under fifty years of age today will not fully comprehend what that generation of Egyptians lived through during the October War, nor the profound shock and dismay of June 5, 1967. The Israeli strike was painful, but it did not finish us. What it did was infuse us with an urgent need to restore our pride and preserve Egypt's role and influence as the country that had long defended the region, its culture, and its civilization, for over a thousand years. The need to recover our status weighed heavy on this generation. Determination, hard work, planning, training, confrontation, and defiance, and everything positive, came together in the Egyptian psyche: the granite of Aswan, or perhaps the harshness and invincibility of the Darb al-Arba'in desert.

I would be remiss if in this chapter I did not speak of the contents of this transcript—the historic transcript of the decision to go to war, and the different inclinations within the meeting, manifested in the discussions between the senior officials of the state.

The meeting commenced at 2130 hours at the home of President Sadat, on the Nile, in Giza. First, a welcome was extended to the attendees, who included Foreign Minister Mahmoud Fawzi, Minister of Industry Dr. Aziz Sedki, Minister of War Ahmed Ismail Ali, Minister of Information Abd al-Qader Hatem, Minister of Supplies Ahmed Thabet, People's Assembly Chair Hafiz Badawi, Parliamentary Legal Advisor Dr. Abd al-Aziz Kamel, Minister of the Interior Mamdouh Salem, Speaker of Parliament and Legal Advisor to Sadat Dr. Hafiz Ghanim, Political Advisor and Minister of State in the Presidency Dr. Hassan al-Tohami,

National Security Advisor Hafiz Ismail, Minister of State for Cabinet Affairs Abd al-Fattah Abdullah, and Assistant to the National Security Advisor Ashraf Gorbal. Minutes were taken by both Dr. Abdel Hadi Makhlouf and Osman Nouri, assistant to the national security advisor.

The president said he was holding the meeting to put everyone in the picture, with the goal of going over the general situation in Egypt and moving to confront the challenges of our situation. The president went on to explain: "None of Egypt's leaders over the past five thousand years had to face the situation we are currently in. No Egyptian official, in seven thousand years of recorded history, has had to confront the challenges facing the president today. These circumstances impose on the author of Egypt's decision, and this small group of Egyptian decision-makers, the duty of making a momentous resolution. Egypt must choose for itself, not leave the decision to be made by others."

President Sadat went on to analyze the domestic and international situation and how it related to our conflict with Israel. What was certain, according to the president, was that the US was continuing to offer full support to Israel, despite the latter's military superiority to all the Arab states combined. It was therefore obvious that the US was actively working to impose Israel's conditions on Egypt, as well as Israel's view of how it should relate to Egypt and the Arab–Israeli conflict. Washington, in an attempt to achieve its ends, was floating some ideas with the aim of getting the situation moving, including the reopening of the Suez Canal, followed by the start of negotiations between Egypt and Israel. The situation, and the suggestion, represented a grave danger: the focus would be on opening the canal and affording Israel passage, absent any comprehensive settlement of the conflict. This would represent a partial, flawed, and indeed dangerous solution, greatly threatening Egypt's interests.

The president explained the elements of how Egypt was moving to confront the "stalling" of Israel and the US, to quote Sadat. "Instead of accepting the U.S.-Israeli proposal, we took the issue to the Security Council, where we achieved quite a victory in July 1973. We managed to isolate Israel and the US, and got fourteen votes in support of the draft resolution for a settlement against the U.S. veto. This shows the strong international influence of the Egyptian and Arab view."

The president also brought up the Egyptian efforts on the Arab front, in preparation for the diplomatic war with Israel. He explained his attempts to secure a groundwork of deep-seated Arab cooperation, despite the usual disparities and differences among Arab countries, which prevented the mobilization of resources in support of Egypt in its diplomatic and military efforts.

He went on to say that the Israeli threat was not confined to Egypt and Egyptian soil, nor even to Palestine and the rest of the Arab occupied territories. The threat, he said, extended to all of us, which could be easily spotted by a careful observer. The distance between Ras Mohamed in Sinai (near Sharm al-Sheikh and Ismailiya), for example, was the same as the distance between Ras Mohamed and Medina (in Saudi Arabia), or Ras Mohamed and the southern Egyptian town of Sohag—a point that would surely not escape the enemy. Kuwait and Saudi Arabia, the president said, were currently purchasing weapons for Egyptian use.

The president then spoke of the domestic situation. The Egyptian economy, he said, was drained. This was a drain he believed to be more dangerous than the military threat. Prices had become dangerously high, and economic growth was at a standstill. Sadat spoke of the danger of confining efforts to reach a settlement with Israel to the two superpowers, while Israel went on building settlements on our land in Sinai. Domestically, this would lead to a despair-based eruption. Such an eruption would achieve every objective Israel had desired from 1967 without a single shot being fired.

As for the Soviet Union, Sadat said that while it was true that the Soviets stood with Egypt and had pledged support, they still did things the old-fashioned way, giving weapons in a manner that allowed them to retain the key to the situation. Finally, he said, "Egypt's armed forces have been preparing from October 1972 until today—September 30, 1973—to build up massive capacities and capabilities for military action. The next step is for us to take the decision to initiate armed conflict." He asked for everyone's views on this decision, saying that this generation of Egyptians had a duty to hand to the next generation a stable situation and a homeland free of occupation.

This powerful introduction reflects Sadat's resolve to go to war. He did not, however, discuss the timing of the battle, its objectives, and its philosophy. The reactions of those present reveal a great deal about how difficult the situation was domestically, while also bringing to light some differences of opinion about what form the battle should take. Some spoke of the difficult situation on the Arab front, what with the differences between Arab countries, and the negative impact this would have on Egypt's ability to mobilize a comprehensive and integrated Arab position. What was needed at this moment, the attendees argued, was more time for Egypt to re-mobilize Arab energies. It was essential that Egypt not go to war alone, or bear the burden in isolation; therefore, they concluded, six more months were needed, for more political preparations, and to allow for absolute Arab participation and Arab financial support for Egypt to be secured.

The supply minister spoke up. He said he must inform the president and those present of the supply situation in the country. The most important thing for Egyptian citizens at this moment when Egypt is on the verge of a war, he said, is securing supplies and basic commodities and organizing supply chains, ration cards, and so forth. What was crucial was for commodities to remain available all through the period of armed conflict. Minister Ahmed Thabet went on to explain, in great detail, the difficulties facing the supply of foodstuffs in the country, including a shortage of rice and the hurdles faced by the Supply Ministry, the Ministry of the Interior, and the Ministry of Agriculture in planting rice. Farmers, he said, were stockpiling it against a hoped-for price increase. He went on to speak of the difficulties facing the government in supplying oils and fats, which had to be imported, and the need for hard currency to purchase wheat from foreign markets. He reiterated the importance of having three- to four-month reserves of basic commodities such as rice and wheat, and other basic needs, before the start of war, especially as Egyptian ports and maritime routes might come under fire, which would necessitate alternative ports of supply and other measures. The minister said, "Farmers must be made to hand in their stocks of all crops." He concluded by saying that the current picture, as he saw it, was that the Egyptian supply apparatus was as yet unprepared to supply the required amounts of all basic commodities for at least ninety days. He therefore requested a little extra time to make this available, by purchasing from abroad, given the requisite financial resources.

Others spoke of the necessity of knowing the time frame for armed action in order to respond to the supply requirements. They mentioned that the government had the powers necessary to ensure that people stuck to ration cards and farmers complied with delivering crops to government supply centers. After much discussion, it transpired that although the majority favored going to war, they felt it was important to agree not only upon the objectives of armed action but also on the war's time frame and methods. Mention was made of the possibility of a war of attrition more prolonged and on a broader scale than the one between Israel and Egypt from 1968 to 1970.

The minister of war cut in, explaining with great clarity and credibility, "Our current circumstances, military and otherwise, will not allow Egypt to liberate its land in a single blitz. The state of the armed forces is reassuring, but time, developments, U.S. support of Israel, and the fact that the Soviets will be close-fisted about offering Egypt an unlimited supply of weapons mean that military developments will go against Egypt if we drag our heels." He added that he could not see Egypt liberating all of Sinai with the available resources and noted that "the disparity between the Israeli and Egyptian armies is widening, with Israel on top. Our weapons are crumbling in our hands. Our ammunition is running out. The Egyptian troops have remained more than six years in the trenches, with what that means for morale. Morale is half the battle."

The minister objected to what some of those present said about starting with attrition, which could then be converted to all-out warfare. While there needed to be a battle, he said, it must be prolonged, with an extended time frame, not, say, a forty-eight-hour clash. Ismail explained his plan for battle, referencing his intent to strike a central, powerful blow at the enemy and absorb the enemy's counterstrike. This, he said, must be done urgently. Circumstances did not allow for a delay of months, as some had suggested.

The talk then turned to the objectives of armed conflict. There was discussion of implementing Security Council Resolution 242 and the importance of preparing a comprehensive Egyptian position with a unified view of exactly what Resolution 242 meant to Egypt, as well as of agreeing on what to do about acknowledging the state of Israel. Dr. Ashraf Ghorbal said that we must understand that contemporary wars were shorter in duration; the era of protracted wars that lasted for months and years on end was over. It would only take days, he said, or weeks at most—not months. He affirmed that we would be forced to respond to the international situation. The world no longer accommodated prolonged wars, he said; it was not in our hands alone. Since the international community and the relationship between the two superpowers would not allow for such a protracted war, he concluded, it followed that we must work to achieve the greatest military success in the narrowest-possible time frame, then move immediately to settle Egypt's issues with Israel through political channels. The Arab–Israeli conflict as a whole, he appended, would take generations to resolve; we needed to hand the next generation the best possible incarnation of the Palestinian issue, insofar as it concerned our own interests.

The discussion turned to the important issue of oil, and how to use it as a weapon in armed conflict. Dr. Aziz Sedki said that the oil supply must be used as a weapon, because cutting off the supply of oil would force everyone to move. Dr. Ashraf Ghorbal said we must not work to cut off the supply of oil to the outside world, as this would lead to a war against the Arabs. Decreasing production and limiting exports, he said, could achieve the required effect.

Hafiz Ismail spoke. "It is important," he noted, "to define our vision of what was meant by peace." He went on to say that Egypt needed to specify where it stood on the Palestinian issue and how to settle it, affirming the importance of an Egyptian–Syrian conception of how to settle the conflict, shared by Jordan. He added that attempts had been made in early 1973 to reach an Egyptian–American understanding leading to a change in the situation and in America's handling of its relations with Egypt. As for Israel's occupation of our territories, the two attempts made in February and May of 1973 had not led to any breakthroughs. This led him to believe in the importance of making a final overture to the US before engaging in military action against Israel. He believed that this new round with the Americans—Kissinger, to be precise—should be conducted in November–December 1973, after the Israeli elections, and also to give President Nixon the opportunity to get through the issues facing his administration at that time. He said the goal was to reach an understanding with the US on the basics of a political settlement that could then be the umbrella for direct and indirect negotiations, under UN supervision, for a permanent settlement.

In preparation for this step, the national security advisor added, we needed to keep our troops on high alert, to confront Israeli provocations. We should not allow an operation like the last Syrian–Israeli air battle, in which Syria lost a great many fighter aircraft, to go by without an assertive response. If the Israelis decided to go to war, we needed to be prepared to meet them. We were faced, then, with two possible forms of battle. The first was the vision of Commander in Chief Ahmed Ismail; the other was what certain of us had spoken of, namely a war of attrition. "In truth, my view," said Hafiz Ismail, "is that both are possible in succession. One of them can follow the other. What is certain is that, after three years of this ceasefire, we need to plumb the capabilities of our forces, and how deep the enemy's defenses are. We must, therefore, plan for an extremely complex battle for the crossing."

"We must look into another option," Ismail continued, "that will allow us to break the stalemate and arrive at an accurate reading of the enemy's capacities before launching into the main battle. With the start of this great battle of attrition, we can escalate in the entire region on the oil supply front. If there are indications that our side is winning, we can then launch a large-scale military operation. This is where we must identify the political goal of the large-scale operation, especially as a military operation will leave our resources drained to the last drop—rehabilitating our forces will take ten to fifteen years—and there will be a deadlock for years, Egypt in the west of Sinai, Israel in the east. Every element of this situation requires careful study. We also need to study the domestic front with the same care, and guarantee the minimum of people's supplies and basic needs. It will also be necessary to pay attention to the media battle, domestically, in the Arab world, and internationally."

Dr. Mahmoud Fawzi cut in: "There are many considerations that make me optimistic. There may be clouds on the horizon, but the future is still bright. There have been many changes: the first is within us. We can now see clearly and interpret what is happening. We have our ducks in a row as far as the use of oil and energy goes. Everyone knows that now. Our Arab brethren are on board with us in the matter of using oil supplies as an effective weapon. We must study the matter comprehensively, and create an operations room to study all the elements, over the next three months. We need to prepare for a military action based on firm political and economic groundwork. In any case, it's best to abandon this defensive stance of ours, and go on the attack. *Katana* or short sword, we need to use whatever sword is available to us. This is not to advocate taking risks, but circumstances force this step—the fact is, we are already at war. The battles are continuous. It will be a disaster if the domestic situation collapses without a war. This is why we insist—why it is our duty—to go to war. We have no choice. In addition to continued military escalation, we must prepare—when necessary—to move. Our move needs to increase the pressure on Israel and the US gradually, avoiding all haste, especially in the matter of oil. Finally, Egypt cannot shrink back and remain under occupation. Therefore, there is nothing for it but all-out war. There must also be an effective battle on the media front, offering a fresh view of the confrontation."

Minister of War Ahmed Ismail spoke up in response to Hafiz Ismail and Mahmoud Fawzi. "Israel today," he said, "may well initiate military action against us as soon as it senses or observes any preparations for armed action by the Egyptian armed forces. It will achieve military successes at our expense, at least in the early stages of battle. It follows, in my view, that we must start operations from our side, with the element of surprise."

He went on to respond to additional points raised by the national security advisor. "It would be more prudent, naturally, to acquaint oneself with all the enemy's abilities and capacities in detail. However, circumstances may not allow for this. Therefore, the operations must be based on the resources and capacities available to Egypt. We must admit that we won't liberate Sinai in a single strike. It is impossible to launch a new war of attrition. We shall work within the limits of our resources—realistically. The enemy has the edge in state-of-the-art weaponry and aircraft. However, this does not mean that the enemy will necessarily win a battle against us. We now possess the means to conduct reconnaissance and find out the situation in Israel, which information will have a positive impact when the fighting starts."

Then, President Sadat took the floor. "Everyone around the world thinks we're dead. That's why no one's doing anything. When they offer us suggestions, they are ideas that serve Israel's interest—and then they wonder why we refuse the Americans' offers! In everyone's judgment, our position is defensive: they think we are incapable of attacking. If this goes on, it's certain death for Egypt.

"We cannot accept this despair. We can only do one thing: stand up to Israel. If we are incapable of doing it, we must tell the people the truth. If we break the ceasefire, that means that we are alive and that we *can*. The other considerations—supplies, needing more time, and whatnot—I have no intention of letting those stand in our way. I say, the armed forces must accept the challenge. I'm not telling them to get Sinai back in one big blitz. I'm telling them to tell the world, *we're alive*.

"Egypt can't wait forever. We've got to move. Everything around us is pressuring Egypt to cave in. We won't allow it."

In response to Hafiz Ismail's suggestion of a third round of talks with the US, with a view to reaching an Egyptian–American understanding, the president said, "Kissinger sent us a message last month requesting just such a meeting, which I think is completely useless. He will offer us half of Sinai back, the reopening of the Suez Canal, and some compromise between Egyptian sovereignty and Israel's security. Remember what [U.S. Secretary of State William P.] Rogers told [Soviet Foreign Minister] Gromyko: 'Israel must reap the fruits of its victory.' Hence, I disagree with any opinion advocating a third round of talks with the US. They will lead nowhere."

Dr. Fawzi requested the floor once more, saying, "There can't be any harm in trying to reach an understanding with the Americans, or giving them another chance to hear our side."

"We've already explored their position twice earlier this year. That's quite enough," retorted the president.

"It might be advisable to try a third time," replied Dr. Fawzi.

Mamdouh Salem interjected, "We can try. After all, we don't want permanent enmities. We need to take our domestic situation into account."

"I don't take the domestic situation into account," Sadat retorted. "A smart man can take a hint. We're in too deep. The situation is clear: I can't wait another six months or a year. We must recognize that the losses of war are always less costly than the costs of preparation. If we lose facilities worth $100 or $200 million to the war, that will definitely cost less than the armed forces cost in a year. We're currently paying $700 million a year—far more than we can afford. We've got to say no to the US and Israel. We're going to fight."

The meeting was nearing its end. The possibility of using an oil embargo was raised again. The president reiterated his conviction that the Arabs would move to assist us, only with care and circumspection, so as not to turn things against us.

The decision to go to war now taken, the national security advisor took the floor a final time. "There are important sectors of the government that need to be warned of the outbreak of war. They'll need four or five days to get fully prepared. We'll also need an operations committee to manage the running of the country and fulfill the requirements of this conflict."

The president agreed at once. Abd al-Fattah Abdullah was nominated chief of staff for President Sadat, to oversee the running of operations and position coordination, in full cooperation with the national security advisor.

Just before the session was concluded, Dr. Ashraf Ghorbal said, "Immediately the battle starts, we should launch a peace initiative with constructive suggestions, to emphasize Egypt's positive attitude—with the understanding that these suggestions can be implemented as soon as the fighting stops."

Again, President Sadat approved this proposal, saying that this would be the preparation and conflict management stage. We needed, he said, to be prepared with many alternatives and suggestions.

The meeting concluded at 0200 hours on October 1. The decision for war had been made.

Upon reading this overview of that strategic and historic meeting, the reader may arrive at a number of conclusions. First, President Sadat was the real force behind the decision to go to war, the main agent and initiator. Egypt would not have engaged in this military operation without his vision and analysis of the extremely difficult situation in which the country found itself.

Second, the discussions reveal a complete accord between Sadat and Commander in Chief Ahmed Ismail on how to manage the armed conflict, the objectives of the military strike, and the limits of its abilities.

Third, the Egyptian armed forces were well aware that the Israelis' capacities surpassed theirs at that point in time; however, they were confident in their abilities to achieve a successful crossing of the Suez Canal, do some damage to the enemy, and impose their view of the pace of the battle.

Fourth, some Egyptian senior officials envisaged, indeed suggested, the possibility of postponing armed conflict for several months, in order to better prepare for it, especially domestically. Others thought that domestic unrest in Egypt could be brought under control by preemptive security procedures. However, President Sadat categorically rejected all these suggestions.

Fifth, a number of senior officials who attended the meeting had hidden worries and doubts about other Arab countries supporting Egypt during the armed conflict. Some even called for Egypt to continue asking the Arabs for more financial support, if it was to conduct a successful and effective military action.

Sixth, President Sadat and Hafiz Ismail were well aware of the requirements and needs of preparing a state for battle. This is why there was a clear division of roles and tasks, assigned specifically to each of the officials taking part. Egypt moved with comprehensive coordination on the domestic, foreign, and military fronts, with a circumspection that afforded it the opportunity to bring all tools to bear on the objectives of the military action, and the Egyptian and Arab efforts that followed in terms of political pressure on the US and the west in general to gradually soften Israel's positions.

Seventh, President Sadat's management of the two prongs of battle—military and political—inevitably attracted some criticisms from various quarters, in particular Sadat's refusal to accept the Soviet–UK proposal for a ceasefire early in the morning of October 13, and his insistence on developing the Egyptian attack at dawn on October 14. Some said that Sadat took these decisions all by himself, which deeply damaged the Egyptian position—and there may well be some truth in what they say. The president might have done well to consult and take advice from more of his counselors and assistants. Still, this is the nature of war, with all its twists and turns—especially given this man's commanding presence and overpowering influence. The manner in which other historical figures managed similar battles, with Nazi Germany, for instance, may be enlightening. These well-known personages—Churchill, Stalin, and Roosevelt, as well—had their own way of seeing things and their own convictions as to the right way of doing things, which, too, might have led to their own brand of losses. Still, what counts is the outcome. In the end, the outcomes were positive, in the war with Germany, and also in ours with Israel.

Historic times, fateful decisions. Ultimately, the final assessment of the war, its operations and outcomes, our possible errors and successes, will be the province of history.

13 The War's Objectives and Outcomes

Over the years, many, including influential figures, have alleged that the October War was a fabrication—that it was not a real war but just for form's sake, undertaken only for Egypt to have the opportunity to achieve a settlement that unjustly favored Egyptians at the expense of the rest of the Arabs. This talk was at its peak after President Sadat's peace initiative, which naturally gave rise to a great deal of controversy. I categorically reject such claims, which indicate that the blood of the soldiers martyred in this unprecedented conflict with Israel was mere fodder for an expensive charade. Some have even gone so far as to say that Egypt deliberately notified the Americans of the limits and boundaries of our military objectives for attacking across the canal, to guarantee that they would understand and thus respond to the effort and its requirements. As if wars can be planned like some elaborate piece of theater! As if such a thing could be kept secret! As if countries great and small are incapable of accurately assessing their opponents' intentions and capabilities or judging what warring parties in a conflict like that in the Middle East can and cannot do!

I can say with the greatest confidence that any follower of the strategic and tactical situation and the abilities of the Egyptian armed forces would reliably come to the same conclusion: that if these forces thought to storm the Suez Canal and take the Bar-Lev line, they would have had the choice of either holding their position in a bridgehead of limited width for an unspecified time or working toward the vitally important Sinai passes, especially the ones on the southern axis of the Suez Canal front.

147

The method and structure of the Israeli mobile air defense on the southern Egyptian front may indicate how the Israelis envisaged this. In Israel's estimation, if the Suez Canal fortifications should be destroyed and the Egyptians succeeded in establishing a bridgehead the length of the frontlines east of the canal, the Israeli armored and mechanized forces would rely on a base of operations on the higher ground east of the canal for defense or attack, working against the Egyptian presence east of the canal either by eliminating it or by creating a breach to the water, which would allow Israel to cross to the western bank to encircle or invade.

It follows that any serious student of Egyptian intentions—as demonstrated by the positions adopted by President Sadat, Field Marshall Ahmed Ismail Ali, and other high-ranking Egyptian officials at their meeting on September 30, 1973, which was covered in the previous chapter—will see that everyone knew the Egyptian armed forces were inferior in capacity and ability to their Israeli counterparts. Therefore, the High Command, including the supreme commander, decided to task the Egyptian forces with a large-scale military operation suited to their capacities, by no means aimed at liberating Sinai in a single strike. As Ahmed Ismail Ali said, "We will work realistically within our limits. The enemy has superior weaponry and a better-equipped air force; that does not mean that they will win the battle."

It may also be deduced from this that Egypt sought to enter into a calculated conflict, so that the armed confrontation would end with it achieving clear and effective military successes. This, in turn, would not only lead to a fundamental shift in the positions of the opposing forces on the ground, but also break new political and strategic ground for Egypt. One Egyptian action in particular was extremely prudent, flexible, and effective, namely, opening the door for relations with the US and responding to the American request for dialogue, despite the heat of battle and the certain knowledge that the US would stand by Israel and provide every possible resource to defeat the Egyptian military effort. The events of the conflict also highlighted the effectiveness of Egypt's highest decision maker in presenting his ideas and initiatives, both via dialogue with the Americans in the form of Hafiz Ismail's messages to Kissinger and Sadat's to Nixon, and in public stances by the president, such as his speech to the Egyptian People's Assembly on October 16.

Any observer of Egypt's positions may note that these initiatives were clearly not spur-of-the-moment, or a sudden action born of the first ten days' success in battle. They were planned well in advance, as evidenced by Dr. Ashraf Ghorbal's speech on September 30 on the importance of proactively proposing Egyptian initiatives and perspectives that reflected

Egypt's desire for a political settlement despite the war. These proposals, and their many elements, were of course well known to all of us in the national security advisor's taskforce long before the war.

The results of the 1967 confrontation had come as a shock to every Egyptian. What is certain is that all Egyptians, whatever their political leanings, felt that Egypt would not be rehabilitated without a counterstrike that matched what Egypt suffered at Israel's hands on June 5, 1967. Egyptians were profoundly cognizant of the reasons behind the defeat. This is why they did their utmost to remedy those ills in 1973, as much as circumstances permitted. They knew that the Egyptian armed forces should not again be placed in the political, strategic, and military predicament that led to their earlier defeat. Therefore, Egypt's participation in the war in Yemen was terminated and the not insignificant number of troops brought home. They were rearmed and equipped with highly qualified military commanders, then rigorously regrouped. They recovered their military discipline, and were kept apart from any political conflict between the higher echelons of the state administration, which readied them for the military operations in October 1973.

Again I must speak of this generation of Egyptian youth, in their mid-twenties, or perhaps a little older, in 1967. This generation—my generation—served as battalion and company commanders, the leaders of the small units that fought in the war of attrition, the battles in the trenches, the cannon blitzes, and the air sorties, while I was a young diplomat at the Egyptian embassy in Cyprus. To tell the truth, I was ashamed of myself when I saw my friends heading to the front in their dozens, waging war and facing fighter planes, separated from their families and children, while my family and I were living in Cyprus, engaged in diplomatic efforts that can bear no comparison to the crushing wheel of war. I decided I would bear it no longer; I began to take part in intelligence operations, and took my place as a determined volunteer engaging in covert ops against the enemy.

Our generation, I suggest, had this certainty: that we would have to rehabilitate our country's status. It followed that as soon as I joined the national security advisor's taskforce in early August 1972, I threw myself into every possible activity that might serve Egypt's strategic goals politically. I even dared, with the encouragement of Dr. Abdel Hadi Makhlouf, our office director, and Counselor Ahmed Maher al-Sayed, to write on some of the military matters about which I always avidly read.

Hafiz Ismail was kind enough to read the writings—ideas and initiatives—I showed him every week. All of us at the National Security Advisory were aware of the importance of creative thinking and being proactive with initiatives and suggestions aimed at enhancing the effectiveness of

Egypt's efforts. Those were tense but inspired times. There was an overpowering sense that we must all rise to the challenge. I remember reading
some of the diaries I wrote back then: they were chock-full of the ideas
that preoccupied me at the time. For example, one of my diary entries,
dated June 1973, and presented to the national security advisor, dealt with
strategic deception in preparation for war:

> On Preparing for Military Conflict with the Enemy and a Plan for
> Strategic Deception
> 1. There is a general consensus on the necessity for a plan for military
>   and strategic deception, to be implemented upon the initiation of
>   military conflict with the enemy. The objectives are concealing the
>   timing of commencing military operations and the directions and
>   axes of the attack.
> 2. Naturally, such a deception plan must be commensurate with the
>   size of the planned operations and the required objectives.
> 3. Assuming Egypt should resort to military conflict with the enemy,
>   the following points should be looked into as potential elements for
>   an Egyptian strategic plan:
>   a. Possibly using the person of the president of the republic as an
>   element of this plan, to mislead the enemy about Egypt's intent
>   to go to war and its timing, by means of:
>   • A presidential visit to an Arab country, say, Algeria, on D-day -1.
>   The Egyptian media should cover this visit and mention con-
>   spicuously that the purpose of the meeting is to study the tense
>   political and military situation in the Middle East, and guaran-
>   tee Algeria's participation in the impending conflict, mentioning
>   that the visit will last for, say, two days.
>   • The president returns in secret to Cairo the same night he
>   leaves.
>   • These movements on the part of the strategic/military
>   deception team may give the enemy a false sense of security,
>   assuming they do not wish to make the first strike. The enemy
>   may well think that Egypt cannot initiate large-scale military
>   operations until the president returns from abroad. Note that
>   the job of the military deception team will be to conceal the
>   preparations for operations, their timing, or the axes selected
>   for military action.
>   b. Possibly using the following in the service of strategic deception:
>   • The minister of war, or a lookalike, visits another Arab country
>   on the same date, at the peak of military and political tensions,

on the pretext of garnering more support and for the same purposes mentioned in the previous point.

- Making use of the political and military tension leading up to
the start of military operations in a presidential call for an Arab
summit—not actually to be held—ostensibly to study specific
responsibilities of the Arab nation in this conflict with Israel,
announcing a proposed start date after the commencement
of military operations, say, D-Day +3. The enemy might well
succumb to the impression that any Arab action will only come
after the (illusory) conference is over.
- The Foreign Ministry could send a telegram or two to all
our diplomatic missions abroad, saying, for instance, that the
enemy has hostile intent and requesting that our embassies
intensify their efforts to infer Israel's intent on this front. The
embassies could be informed in code of the characteristics and
evidence of Israel's general mobilization for war. These telegrams, if intercepted and decoded, could convince the enemy
that Egypt, as usual, is awaiting the Israeli strike and does not
intend to strike first.

4. There are most probably dozens of points that could be added to
the strategic defense plan on the domestic and international fronts.
Forming a committee made up of members of the Foreign Ministry,
the Ministry of War, the Information Ministry, and Egyptian
Intelligence should be looked into, with the purpose of making an
integrated plan to be carried out at specific times in the development of the situation, as armed conflict draws near. Such a committee should have a grasp of the entire Egyptian plan for how this
conflict is to be approached.

I am convinced that anyone reading this memorandum, and seeing
this way of thinking, more than forty years later, will come to the conclusion that the matter of war, confrontation, armed conflict, and rehabilitating our pride was a common theme in every department of Egyptian
national security. The preparations for Egyptian military action were in
full swing.

I prepared another memorandum, on which Hafiz Ismail commented
at length. Looking through my old papers, I found yet another note to
Hafiz Ismail, dated December 5, 1972. In this one, I suggested a well-
thought-out aerial clash with the enemy's fighter planes to inflict losses
at the same time as Egypt brought its case before the General Assembly,
convincing the international community of the urgency of the situation

and the possibility of deterioration, which might then convince the major powers to intervene and try to help reach a settlement. It read as follows:

> On the Situation in the Middle East
> 1. The Middle East crisis is currently moving within the following parameters:
>   a. Political Egyptian action at the General Assembly.
>   b. Reactivating Syrian military activity on the Golan Heights front.
> 2. It is imagined that the atmosphere within which this crisis operates will allow Egypt to conduct an isolated and limited military operation in the form of a pre-planned and pre-prepared aerial engagement.
> 3. Such an engagement would provide Egypt—providing it inflicts heavy losses on Israel in terms of fighter planes, or at least achieving a balanced battle outcome—the following benefits:
>   a. Pressure at General Assembly debates.
>   b. Reaffirming the danger of things blowing up in the region, especially as such incidents are followed by great media attention worldwide.
>   c. Demonstrating to other Arab countries Egypt's participation in the escalating military activity in the region.
>   d. Attempts to affect the enemy's view of the Egyptian armed forces' capacities.
>   e. On the domestic front: raising the armed forces' morale.
>   f. After analyzing and measuring the Israeli reaction, it can safely be concluded that Israel has no desire to move the situation militarily on the Egyptian front. This was made clear as soon as the most recent operations started on the Syrian front. It follows that a strong Israeli military reaction may not be expected to this isolated and limited Egyptian action, viewable as a typical skirmish similar to those that occur routinely from time to time.

The national security advisor read, with close attention, the memoranda, that I and other members of the office staff presented to him. If the ideas piqued his interest, he would have long conversations with the team member in question or—surprisingly—send back a reply, long or short, beautifully handwritten on the document itself. He would often initial the document, and command some action, or indicate that he was apprised of its contents, as occurred with the one quoted above.

In this tradition, I showed him another paper I wrote in mid-July 1973, in which I suggested that we make use of the current deadlock in the military situation, and the Security Council's failure to adopt Egypt's draft resolution on a general framework for a settlement due to the American veto, to send our armed forces for a limited surprise attack, which I called Operation Powerful Raid. The plan consisted of sending in a special ops division, landing from the air in Sharm al-Sheikh, to destroy the enemy's equipment and apparatuses in that area in half a day, withdrawing in the evening or at dawn. I spoke of the importance of establishing air control in the area, and defended the concept in my document, saying it sent a serious message to the enemy that Egypt had teeth, and that it would force the Israeli command to keep its forces in a broad strip of confrontation at high levels of alert and emergency status. This would, of course, affect the enemy forces' morale.

Hafiz Ismail read my document and initialed it; I did not dare to ask him what he thought of my suggestions.

Weeks passed. I went abroad with the national security advisor on a short mission to meet the Romanian president, Ceaușescu, and the Yugoslavian president, Tito, to discuss their views on the ability of the Israeli prime minister, Golda Meir, to reach a peaceful settlement with Egypt. This mission occurred in response to an invitation by the two leaders to President Sadat to send an Egyptian official to speak with them about some offers being made by Israel. These attempts revealed that the Israeli offers were no more than an agreement to a partial Israeli withdrawal from the Sinai passes and the reopening of the Suez Canal and repopulation of the towns along the canal.

In Romania, on a beach in the Mangalia resort on the Black Sea, Hafiz Ismail took to recalling what he had read, and his passion for Second World War subjects. He looked shrewdly—piercingly—at me. "I can't agree with what you said. I can't go along with us exposing our forces in an air transport to the risk of heavy losses. That's what your suggestion could lead to, Ahmed."

He went on: "You're assuming we'll achieve airspace control over Sharm al-Sheikh. That's an extremely tall order. Our aerial forces in the area are insufficient. Our fighters don't have the sufficient range. You're thinking of an air blitz like the 1942 Dieppe Raid, aren't you? That was an unmitigated disaster for the Allies. The Canadians lost a great many men; the Allies lost close to five thousand, killed, wounded, and captured. Their morale was severely shaken. I can't agree to an operation of that kind."

That was when I realized that he—Hafiz Ismail—had not only read my document but also thought it over deeply, taking it in completely thanks to his study of the Second World War. I must admit that I had the same thought after reading about the Dieppe Raid that he mentioned in response to my idea.

The focus of everything I did with the national security advisor was always how to secure a political atmosphere that provided all the means for an Egyptian military strike capable of changing the balance of the situation. The strike finally did take place, and achieved its military and political objectives. We succeeded in getting the stagnant situation moving, and in the direction of a political settlement, thanks to the effectiveness of our capable and efficient armed forces, in no small part due to the stern Arab oil embargo, and also thanks to the U.S. push to take responsibility for peace.

Much has been said, and much asked, about why Egypt did not press on with fighting during the difficult time our forces had in the breakthrough area and the Israeli counter-crossing. Those commentators never realized that Egypt received all of its armaments from the Soviet Union, which prioritized Syria as the recipient of massive weapons aid. Attempts by President Sadat, and Egyptian commanders and senior officials, to convince the Soviets to supply us with large amounts of equipment and fighters, which would allow us to strike at the breach, were met with complications. The Soviets had observed our shift toward America: the closer we got to Kissinger, or to Washington, the further the Soviets retreated. This was the complex kernel of the situation. We could see that the US, after the military strike, was the key to achieving a settlement, yet we hoped to keep our high military capacity thanks to the Soviets, who distrusted Egypt's intentions. Still, the Soviets had not entirely lost hope for keeping up good relations with Egypt.

The battle of 1973, like the tragedy of 1967, revealed that those who do not manufacture their own weapons, or possess a speedy, unbroken, and reliable source of weapons from abroad, will always be vulnerable to pressure, and must avoid entering into large-scale armed confrontation. Losing one's weapons without an appropriate and assured replacement means that one loses heavily.

Many discussions have covered the Egyptian armed forces' delay in developing the attack by destroying the Bar-Lev line fortifications. Many say that our armed forces should have moved quickly to consolidate the victory, arrive at the passes, take them, and block the enemy from returning to the west of Sinai. During these first days of Egyptian success, I wrote notes to myself constantly on the need to keep going and the importance of consolidating our victory. At 0200 hours on Wednesday, October 10, three and a half days after the start of operations, I wrote:

There is apprehension about the American stance.

I then asked myself if we could convince the Americans that we had no intention of pushing on with military conflict past the Sinai passes. This was the first time I mentioned the passes as an Egyptian military objective. I went back to this issue at 1900 hours that day:

When do we push on to the passes?

The battle went on; the attack was developed on October 14. The situation became precarious after that, culminating in the ceasefire on October 28. Many at the time realized that it was essential to develop the attack and reach the passes as soon as the enemy's ineffective counterattacks between October 8 and 10 had been repulsed. However, once the window of opportunity was closed, it would have been a mistake for the Egyptian army to develop the attack. It needed to stick to stalwart defense, the same defense that had vanquished all the counterattacks, and kept their armored forces as a strategic reserve, on the east or west banks of the canal.

I say today that if we had held our ground while developing the attack, we would not have been in the position we ended up in after October 16. The Egyptian–Israeli settlement would have come about much faster, instead of taking from November 1973 to April 1982. That said, I believe the same settlement would eventually have been reached, with the same parameters and agreements, after the president's shock visit to Jerusalem.

President Sadat's visit to Jerusalem was a development of the attack, and a leap forward in the service of a national goal, a strategy in which military and political action alternated in playing the leading role. Great errors were made in combating the breach and the counter-crossing. But when our forces regained their equilibrium, it became clear that Israel had placed its forces within Egypt's reach. Consequently, the Egyptian and Israeli sides both settled, with enthusiastic help from the Americans, on the importance of not renewing clashes and returning to political action via U.S. assistance and mediation.

A final point: the true reasons for the delay in deciding to develop the attack. Was the real motivation for the delay to take the pressure off Syria? Although this interpretation is accurate to a certain extent, the truth of the matter as I see it is as follows: After the success of the canal crossing, destroying the Bar-Lev line, our forces' demonstrating their effectiveness in beating back the immediate Israeli counterattacks, and Egypt's air force proving itself—an outcome that was by no means certain—President Sadat decided to develop the attack on the basis of these successes, without taking into account the risks and consequences of failure. This is why I say that Sadat caused negative consequences by throwing caution to the winds. But this is the nature of war, sometimes obscuring the bigger picture in fog.

There are a number of conclusions I would like to draw at the close of this segment on the October War. First, the change in the Egyptian military command, that is, the appointment of Major-General al-Gamasy as chief of staff to replace Lieutenant-General Shazli, was no reflection on the abilities of the latter. One of the things we have learned from the First and Second World War is that when commanders disagree and conflict rears its head, political leaders—in this case, President Sadat—intervene. Sadat had no choice but to remove Shazli and choose Ahmed Ismail, who was in tune with his line of thought and followed the president's military commands with the ultimate objective of advancing the situation politically and putting an end to the conflict while Egyptian forces still had a presence east of the canal and still possessed the ability to fight.

I remember meeting Staff Major-General Hosni Mubarak, commander of the Egyptian air force, for the first time at Abd al-Moneim Palace, when he came for two days in succession late in the evening to meet with Sadat while we were in the thick of battle. This was in the decisive days of the war, when the challenge was at its height, in the period starting on October 18. I saw a military man with exemplary calm, speaking of complex issues with profound analytical perceptivity, without losing his cool or appearing in any way tense. I remember speaking with Ahmed Maher al-Sayed, who, like me, was astonished at the calm on the face of the commander of the air force—a man with a great deal on his shoulders in this delicate situation. He accepted the national security advisor's invitation to dinner before going to meet President Sadat at Tahra Palace.

Second, the outcomes of the war began to appear very early. The US committed to implementing a political settlement, which ultimately returned all the occupied territories of Sinai to the motherland. It may well be said that we could have pursued another course; however, what is certain is that President Sadat had come to the end of the road with the Soviets at the end of 1973. It was a parting of ways. Egypt was quick to reestablish strategic relations with the US. Egypt faithfully implemented Lord Palmerston's dictum: "Nations have no permanent friends or allies, they only have permanent interests." Egypt primarily pursued its interests. It also remained committed to helping Syria, and standing behind the Palestinians' rights.

Kissinger's maneuvers were effective and garnered both Israeli and Egyptian approval. The fact is that Kissinger's intervention provided them with a good justification for not repeating the conflict after the ceasefire, following October 28. This guaranteed that each party would be heard on their pressing interests, simultaneously facilitating the US' successes in the region that would keep it influential there for decades.

Third, the years that followed the 1973 armed conflict, in which the political settlement began in stages, concurrent with the end of the Vietnam War, were a time of great political and strategic expansion for the Soviet Union. The Soviets' influence became felt through their Cuban partners and the international and African left in areas such as Angola, Mozambique, Ethiopia, and others. This was followed by the Soviet Union's invasion of Afghanistan, whereupon the west began to combat the Soviet expansion. This was especially true once the US realized that defeat in Vietnam was inevitable, having been forced into strategic defense.

The west began to apply pressure on the Soviets. The arms race began anew, reaching hitherto unheard-of heights. The Soviet Union's economy began to crack under the strain. It took less than two decades after 1973 for the Soviet Union to collapse completely. Some began to ask what would have happened to a country like Egypt, completely dependent on the competition between the two superpowers to build and equip its armed forces, using Soviet military support to stand against the Israeli expansion, if the Soviet Union had crumbled some twenty years earlier. The question is legitimate—especially as the 1973 conflict revealed the impressive attack, defense, and destructive capacity of Soviet weapons, which led, for example, to Israel losing over eight hundred tanks on the Egyptian front alone. Making up losses on this scale was not something either Egypt or Israel could have done at the time—not even today, in fact—without the assistance of a superpower, of which, since the end of the Cold War, only one remains. It was a good thing that Egypt got rid of the Israeli invasion prior to the Soviet decline, or else, in my estimation, we would never have managed to liberate Sinai.

Fourth, assuming that Egypt could have somehow replaced Soviet sources of weaponry with some other international source, the developments in international armaments would have strained Egypt's resources to the utmost. In plain language, the emergence of modern tools of war, and new types of tanks and fighters, indeed the changing shape of modern warfare that began to emerge in the 1980s, would have taken their toll on an Egypt unable to finance its requirements for modern and expensive armaments. An MiG-17 in 1956 cost around £25,000; an MiG-21 in the early 1960s cost around £150,000; and a single F-14 in 1974 cost around $15 to 20 million. As of writing, in 2013, a brand-new U.S.-made state-of-the-art F-35 costs $110–150 million, depending on how it is equipped. A French Rafale fighter aircraft, comparable to its U.S.-made counterpart, will run the purchaser $100–120 million apiece. And so it goes for all the fifth-generation fighter aircraft. These are facts that need to be taken into account when speaking of war and peace.

I wrote a memorandum about this specific point on July 25, 1973, which I presented to the national security advisor on the same day. I include it here because it explains, to a great extent, the point of the analysis above.

On the Future of Armament in the Middle East

First: General

1. News agencies published a quote from the U.S. magazine *Aviation Week* that Israel expressed an interest to the US in obtaining the new F-14 fighter in the last quarter of the current decade, to gradually replace the Phantom, which will start to become obsolete in the 1980s.

2. News agencies also reported that the shah of Iran, during his current visit to Washington, plans to discuss the possible supply to his country of this new fighter.

3. It is already known that the U.S. plans to produce about four hundred units of this new fighter, which will enter into service in the U.S. navy in 1974.

4. This fighter costs $15–20 million.

Second: The Future of Armament in the Region

5. It may be said that the Arab–Israeli conflict over the past twenty years proves that the countries in the region have a relatively unchanging goal of obtaining the most modern weaponry possible. This has led to the outbreak of an arms race between the different parties concerned.

6. However, on the other hand, specific developments in different weapons are reflected in enormous production costs, which has limited the production quantity—and export sales—of each new type of equipment.

7. It may well be said that these developments and conditions, assuming they are correct, force Egypt to study their future ramifications when assessing the situation regarding the possibility of military conflict with Israel extending into the 1980s, as follows:

a. In the event that Egypt and Israel cannot reach a political settlement in the 1970s, will they continue their current arms race in the coming years?

b. Also, will Egypt's own capacities, unaided, be capable of keeping up with these developments in the 1980s? Will our technical and scientific knowledge, and Egyptian command and leadership, be suited to these new developments?

c. Will the numbers and stocks of each party's main weapons remain as is? Or will the rise in cost, as well as operating and running costs, force them to keep relatively far smaller quantities in stock? What advantages or disadvantages will this cause each party?

d. The final question remains, will it be in Egypt's interest, indeed within its capacity, in light of these developments to prolong the military confrontation with Israel into the 1980s, or could circumstances force an end to such a military confrontation in one form or another before things turn against Egypt completely?

8. In light of the above, it is possible that the reasons keeping Egypt from military action at the present time will continue, indeed escalate, to Egypt's detriment in the future. This seems to urge a reassessment of the situation. We need to find a solution in light of the current circumstances.

Fifth, the 1973 war revealed the Arab success in closing the technology and quality gap with Israel. The warring parties would need, if any such armed conflict continued in the future, to stockpile vast stocks of equipment and weaponry to be sure of quickly making up sudden and heavy losses. Not stockpiling would force each party to the conflict to rely on support from a superpower, which would impact the ability to maneuver and/or impose one's will on enemy and ally alike.

Sixth, Israel learned the lesson that if it closed all feasible avenues available to its opponents, the latter might find it in their interests to resort to war or military action, even if less well equipped than Israel. Israel thought that President Sadat, and Egypt, would not resort to armed conflict, seeing Egypt as a crippled nation unable to achieve victory or even stave off defeat. However, what Israel failed to take into account was that President Sadat found it useful to resort to war when there was a reasonable chance of achieving the military objectives of Egypt's armed action, followed by glittering political rewards.

Seventh, armed conflict brought to light that Israel should not have preserved the status quo—that is, the occupation of Sinai—after 1973. The myth of control over Sharm al-Sheikh as a central element of Israeli security was exposed: geography, on the one hand, and missile technology, on the other, were decisive in dispelling these concepts of security that Israel had clung to until the afternoon of October 6.

Eighth, Egypt's military and political prowess placed it in the most favorable position to regain control and full sovereignty over Sinai. The conflict revealed to Egypt, and primarily to the Israelis, that we had always underestimated our true military capacities: the results of the armed conflict, and the strength of our fighters, revealed an Egyptian mettle that should not be underestimated, in peacetime, at war, and in any confrontation.

Military action proved once again that the Egyptian side was definitely at a disadvantage as far as armaments were concerned. Any balanced and objective comparison of the armaments of Egypt and Israel will conclude that the M-16 tanks on the Israeli side were far superior to the Soviet T-55s and T-62s used by the Egyptians, and that the U.S. TOW antitank missiles were orders of magnitude more powerful than their Soviet-made counterparts, the 9M14 Malyutka missiles used by the Egyptian infantry. It is also safe to say that the battles of 1973 largely revealed Israel's advanced destructive antitank capacity, which limited the effectiveness of the tank as a main tool in battle. This forced modifications to the tactics and use of tanks in battle, as well as the need to protect tanks in different circumstances. The U.S. self-propelled artillery was definitely more powerful than the towed artillery provided by the Soviet Union.

Despite all this, the Egyptian ground forces accomplished their mission with notable success that commands respect. The air battles revealed that Egyptian pilots, trained on a punishing schedule over the years that followed the defeat, from 1967 to 1973, who lost a great many of their number in these training exercises, were able to rise above the limitations of their fighter planes and bombers, confronting more technologically advanced aircraft with a longer range and staying power in the skies. The main weakness of Egyptian pilots pre-1967, and in 1967 itself, was lack of training. As a result of lack of resources, some pilots trained as little as six or seven hours per month, whereas the standard for the North Atlantic Treaty Organization (NATO) or Warsaw was up to four times that. The Egyptian air force succeeded in securing the requirements of air control and direction during air battles, and protecting fighters and airfields during restocking and refueling on the ground. They were not only efficient, but also destructive to Israeli air and ground forces. The latter crumbled not only by dint of Egyptian resistance, but mainly because the strong Egyptian air defense and its varied technique afforded Egyptian ground troops the ability to cross the Suez Canal and confront the Bar-Lev fortification.

No doubt the crossing, with all its complexities, was far more difficult, at least in my estimation, than the crossings of the Soviets on the eastern front or the Allies in the west during the Second World War. The entire face of the Suez Canal was covered by heavy concentrations of Israeli fire, while the river defenses on the eastern and western fronts in the Second World War were riddled with gaps, which allowed the troops a less complex and risky crossing. The battle that Egypt planned was also completely subject to the geography and topography of the area, and therefore direct action on the enemy's defenses, based on the water barrier, with all the difficulties that this entails.

The battles of 1973 also made it clear that General Command had full control of its forces despite being far from the front in the desert of Heliopolis and often feeling the need to move to closer proximity to the fighting at the front. This was especially true in the challenging times of the Israeli breach, starting on October 15. As for the Egyptian navy, it largely achieved its objectives in the war. True, the Israelis were more aggressive in their attempts to attack our shores and ports, but the true reasons were clear to anyone who knew the background. Each Israeli naval sortie took place under the umbrella of complete local air control, when dinghies were sent to attack the Egyptian coastline. Every one of Israel's attempts, it is important to note, was aborted by the Egyptian navy, which prevented the raids from succeeding or achieving any of their goals.

Finally, there is the siege of Bab al-Mandeb, with all its results and effects on the general strategic framework of the confrontation, revealed to us by the British, who requested that the siege of Bab al-Mandeb—and consequently of the port of Eilat—be lifted, after consulting with Israel, toward the end of the conflict, in exchange for allowing ground communications between the Third Army's forces east of the canal and the main body of the Egyptian army in the west.

The new situation in the Middle East, for long years after this conflict, became obvious with the landing of a huge U.S. C5A Galaxy at Cairo Airport in April 1974, bearing the American equipment and vehicles needed to secure the visit of President Nixon—the first visit by a U.S. president since Roosevelt's visit during the Second World War. That day, I was at home, looking out of my window that overlooked the runway of Cairo International Airport. I thought to myself, "This might well have been one of the planes that transported the tanks to Arish Airfield, to the Israeli army in Sinai, to fight the Egyptians and block our progress. Oh well, this is the nature of international politics and national interests, changing one's position to achieve national interests at the highest level. Egypt, like any other international actor, seeks its own interests and those of the Arab nation."

Part 2
Witness to Peace

14 Sadat's Visit to Jerusalem

resident Nixon's visit to Cairo in April 1974 was the start of a new phase in the Arab–Israeli conflict, indeed in the Middle East conflict. I shall recount it as I experienced it: the events that I directly witnessed or took part in from the moment President Sadat launched his peace initiative in November 1977 to the Madrid Conference in 1991, and then later, from 1996 to 2004, when I occupied the post of assistant to the foreign minister and of permanent representative of Egypt to the UN.

The reader will notice that I am making no attempt at a complete chronology or exhaustive historical record of events. This has been done at length in volumes and studies since 1977, and perhaps to the present day. I will recount my view and assessment of that period in time from the standpoint of what I saw and did, and what I saw and did only. This has long been my principle.

On the evening of November 19, 1977, I sat in the living room of my home in Heliopolis watching in silence, and not a little trepidation, the landing of President Sadat's plane at Israel's Lod Airport on television. The plane taxied, approaching the greeting area, which was crowded with dozens of Israeli senior officials, journalists, and television cameras, all waiting for the door of the president's Boeing 707 to open. Every political leader in Israel was there, the same ones Sadat had fought against in October 1973. Among them were Golda Meir, whose party had lost in Israel's elections as a result of the war, and Abba Eban, who needs no introduction. Eban spoke fluent Arabic and was married to an Egyptian Jewess, whom he met while serving in Alexandria with Her Majesty's

Armed Forces in the Second World War. There were quite a few Israeli officials who were married to Egyptian Jewish ladies, such as General Chaim Herzog, who was a spokesman for the Israeli army during their wars with us, and then rose through the ranks to become Israel's representative to the UN in the 1970s and president of Israel in the 1980s. Moshe Dayan was there, too, then foreign minister of Israel. He had split from the Israeli Labor Party to assume his duties as minister. All the country's generals and politicians were there, in anticipation and possibly pride: there they were, on Israel's soil, during a historic moment whose like Israel had not experienced since its statehood was declared on May 14, 1948.

The door to the plane opened. History was being made. The Israeli chief of protocol mounted the staircase and entered the aircraft to invite President Sadat to accompany him outside. The famous official welcome followed; I shed a few quiet tears.

My son Kamal, not quite seven years old then, was with me in the room. The child looked at the television, then at me, and said, "What is it, Daddy? Are you crying? Did they beat us?"

I couldn't answer. I was truly at a loss for words to describe the situation, or even to grasp it. I was as yet uncomprehending of the consequences of the Egyptian initiative and how it would affect us, the Arab region, and the Palestinian question, not to mention the Arab–Israeli conflict with which I had lived my entire life, first in my father's house—my father the fighter pilot who had flown sorties against Israel and bombed its bases and armies—and later after I joined the Foreign Ministry in 1965, to fight its battles as a diplomatic soldier.

It is difficult to underestimate the effect of this shock. It required a lot of effort, thinking, and analysis to eventually understand the outcomes of such a step. We at the Foreign Ministry had lived our lives in direct conflict with Israel on the international diplomatic stage. I had just returned from New York a few weeks earlier, where I had been working with the Egyptian delegation to the UN from 1974 to October 1977. After this, things would no doubt be different. And I had no idea—no one had any idea—how to deal with it. Foreign Minister Ismail Fahmy had resigned. Minister of State for Foreign Affairs Mohamed Riyad had been relieved of his post for expressing doubts about the entire affair when asked to take on Fahmy's responsibilities temporarily. At the time, I was working with Amre Moussa, the director of the Department of International Organizations at the Foreign Ministry, who had strong ties to Minister Ismail Fahmy and Minister Mohamed Riyad. I had no confidence that he or anyone else would be spared. What would we do?

Those were hard times for us, especially as Dr. Boutros Boutros-Ghali was now the acting minister of state for foreign affairs and responsible for Egyptian diplomatic affairs. He was an outsider to the diplomatic service; he knew nothing about how we worked, how things were set up, or the people there. What was certain was that he was an expert in all things to do with Egypt's international relations, being a professor at Cairo University, as well as founder and editor-in-chief of a magazine dedicated to Egyptian foreign policy, published by the state-owned *al-Ahram* Press.

In any case, the days after Sadat's speech at the Knesset were enthusiastically covered by the international press. The hero's welcome Sadat received upon his return from Israel came and went. I recall that Cairo witnessed an unprecedented rally, when people from all walks of life took to the streets in support of Sadat's step toward peace.

At the Foreign Ministry, we began to acclimate to this step, and its ramifications. Still, some of us had a hard time making this volte-face, or understanding the consequences and changes that would follow. Abba Eban said on the day of Sadat's visit to Jerusalem, "The Middle East will never be the same." I believe that all of us at the Foreign Ministry, to varying degrees, had also come to this conclusion.

Egypt proposed holding a preparatory conference to study the peace process and the possibility of working toward resurrecting the Geneva Conference that had been held for one day only in December 1973. In mid-December, Egypt called for the new conference to be held in Cairo. It was clear that President Sadat, having shaken up the political and international situation, as well as our relations with Israel, had decided to quickly take the reins of political negotiation. He wanted to strike while the iron was hot, allowing Israel no space to wriggle out of the process with the pressure still on. Much of the international community, after all, had expressed its support for the step Egypt had taken, and for its motivations. Dr. Esmat Abdel Meguid, Egypt's permanent representative to the UN, whose office in New York I had left short weeks earlier, received Sadat's instructions via Dr. Boutros-Ghali, to come to Cairo immediately to head the Egyptian delegation, and also the Preparatory Peace Conference in Cairo. This eventually came to be known as the Mena House Conference, for the hotel where it was held on December 15, 1977.

Dr. Esmat Abdel Meguid was one of the first Egyptian ambassadors to express strong support for the peace initiative a few days after getting to understand it. To know Dr. Esmat is to quickly conclude that he is a man of principle: he thinks out his steps in advance, calculating them thoroughly, and then carries them out with skill and determination. At the time, he made the right choice, thanks to his wealth of legal and political knowledge and experience, as well as his familiarity with the Palestinian question and the development of the Arab–Israeli conflict since his work with the famous former Egyptian Foreign Minister Mahmoud Fawzi. He also had a wealth of experience with the UN, where he had by then been working for about five and a half years.

At that time, there was a working group composed of a small number of Egyptian diplomats known for their efficiency and secrecy at the Foreign Ministry, working quietly under the leadership of Dr. Osama al-Baz, office manager of the foreign minister, whose main task was assisting the minister in managing the Geneva Conference file, comprising all the efforts to resume the peace conference and get it moving. This group included, in addition to Dr. Osama al-Baz, the following ambassadors: Ambassador and Director of Political Planning Abdel Raouf El Reedy, Legal Department Head Nabil al-Arabi, officer in the Information Department Ahmed al-Zunt, Counselor Amre Moussa, the director of the Department of International Organizations, First Secretary Hussein Hassouna from the Office of the Foreign Minister, and First Secretary Mohamed ElBaradei, private secretary to Ismail Fahmy, and his close confidant. Although Ismail Fahmy had resigned, the working group managed by Dr. Osama al-Baz remained. Dr. al-Baz also occupied the post of director of the Political Office of the Vice President at the time.

Dr. Esmat Abdel Meguid arrived from New York in early December to head the working group and prepare for the Mena House Conference in anticipation of the start of negotiations with Israel. He attempted to call me in my office at the Department of International Organizations as soon as he arrived. I had left a little early, so he called me at my home and left a message with my wife Leila that I was to come and see him at the Shepheard's Hotel that evening. As soon as I received the message, I called him at the hotel, whereupon he asked my wife and me to come and visit him. The ladies, Leila and Iglal, his wife, could spend some time together while we talked about work. Dr. Esmat added that he had also invited First Secretary Salah al-Hindawi, who worked with him in New York. Coincidentally, Salah al-Hindawi and I had left New York on the same day, October 1, 1977.

As soon as Salah al-Hindawi and I joined Dr. Esmat, he said, "The upcoming task is the most critical one I have been assigned in my long career in the diplomatic service." This, despite the vast experience he had accumulated working with Dr. Mahmoud Fawzi, deputy prime minister and foreign minister of Egypt from 1953 to 1964, during the negotiations for the British evacuation of Egypt, the nationalization of the Suez Canal, the

Israeli withdrawal from Sinai in 1957, and other monumental challenges. He added, "This challenge means I must rely on my former aides"—he meant us— "most familiar with the way I think and run things, like the Egyptian delegation to New York."

Salah al-Hindawi agreed immediately, in advance, to whatever the head of the Egyptian delegation would dictate in the negotiations with Israel. As for myself, quite clearly and directly (I was always clear and direct with Dr. Esmat, whose greatest strength was appreciating honesty and understanding the other point of view) I said, "I don't have a full understanding of all the elements of the Egyptian initiative yet, although I know it's been two weeks since President Sadat visited Jerusalem." I added, "I might not be fully convinced of the initiative's effectiveness. I'm not quite sure it's led to good things on the Arab front, although I do appreciate that it's unleashed huge international support." I then pledged myself "a soldier in the Egyptian Diplomatic Service," and said that I could do nothing else but "fight for my country when my commander calls," in this case, Dr. Esmat Abdel Meguid. "I will carry out any tasks I'm assigned," I promised.

We then suggested he ask Minister of State for Foreign Affairs Boutros-Ghali to make us part of the Egyptian taskforce and of the delegation participating in the negotiations in the days to come. On the spot, he made a telephone call to Dr. Boutros-Ghali, who gave his immediate consent and called the Department of Diplomatic and Consular Affairs to take the appropriate action.

The two of us, Salah al-Hindawi and myself, started work the next day. We met Dr. Esmat Abdel Meguid in the office that had been Dr. Mahmoud Fawzi's when he was deputy minister for foreign affairs, during Mahmoud Riyad's tenure as foreign minister. He started to set up shop with our assistance, holding his first meeting with the above-mentioned working group on the crisis. What is certain is that Dr. Esmat Abdel Meguid's deep knowledge of these men, and of their leanings and abilities, greatly facilitated the running of the group. As head of the delegation, he started out by looking over the main documents and records he had not seen when away from home in New York. He then began to hold daily meetings with this group of capable Egyptian diplomats.

That they were exceptional diplomatic minds was to be proved by their accomplishments with the passage of time. Still, I must admit that there was some internal rivalry in the group and a few conflicts in the way they saw things on occasion, which could not fail to complicate matters between them, whether at the time or in later years. I might do well to mention one or two incidents that reflect a little of what I am saying. I suggested adding Ambassador Ahmed Maher al-Sayed, a rising Egyptian diplomatic star, to our working group. I broached it first with Dr. Esmat, who welcomed the idea. Still, experience told him to request that I speak with some members of the group to feel them out regarding adding such a weighty new member. I duly broached the subject with a number of team members and immediately felt resistance. I realized that the move would not be welcomed. I spoke about it with Dr. Nabil al-Arabi, who told me he had done the same thing before me, to no avail. One of these gentlemen—an influential personage—believed that Maher's presence would lead to tensions in the group, and that it was therefore best not to include him. Thus, the group lost (actually, as things turned out, only delayed by a few weeks, as I shall explain shortly) the opportunity to benefit from Ahmed Maher's hard work and expertise.

The second anecdote concerns the Department of Diplomatic Corps Affairs, which interpreted Minister Boutros-Ghali's instructions as being to add Ahmed Aboul Gheit and Salah al-Hindawi to the working group as 'secretaries to the head of the delegation' but not as members of the working group—quite a difference! Still, we sat with them and took full part in all the debates of the group, in Dr. Esmat's presence and in his absence. This was of course a power play on the part of *someone* or other, which we found out about immediately, but preferred not to bring up or get into any confrontations that might destroy the integrity of this important working group. The main task, after all, was to achieve the objectives of Egyptian diplomacy at an extremely sensitive and crucial juncture.

Such matters aside, I took to working diligently and industriously to acquaint myself fully with the situation and its ramifications, our negotiating style, and the limits of our actions at the upcoming conference, especially as Dr. Esmat had met with Vice President Hosni Mubarak in Heliopolis and then with President Sadat himself at al-Qanatir for instructions on running the conference and the negotiations.

We moved into the Mena House Hotel some days later, in preparation for our meetings with the Israelis. The head of the Israeli delegation was a Romanian-Israeli called Eliyahu Ben-Elissar, later appointed the first Israeli ambassador to Cairo after the signing of the peace treaty between Egypt and Israel.

Salah al-Hindawi and I worked directly under Dr. Esmat Abdel Meguid. We worked together to prepare his opening statement for the preparatory meeting, the intention of which was to prepare for a return to the peace conference that was held for only a single day in December 1973. This was the starting point for the statement. It was a strong statement, its main elements comprising everything Sadat had covered in his speech before the Knesset in Jerusalem.

To prepare himself for the negotiations, Dr. Esmat had asked Dr. Osama al-Baz, office director to the vice president at the time, to provide him with any documents that could assist him in preparing the Egyptian perspective at the meeting. He also headed a string of taskforce meetings, during which a preferred method for dealing with the Israelis was developed, and various scenarios that might arise from Israeli proposals or suggestions tested.

The Israelis arrived at Cairo Airport, whence they were whisked by Egyptian helicopter to an empty lot close to Mena House Hotel. The official delegation comprised Eliyahu Ben-Elissar, Meir Rosenne, and General Avraham Tamir, commander of the Planning and Policy Directorate of the Israeli army. I got to know General Tamir during my tenure as the private secretary of Deputy Prime Minister and Foreign Minister Kamal Hassan Ali, from 1982 to 1984. They each had a great admiration for the other. Kamal Hassan Ali saw Tamir as an Israeli statesman with a great desire for peace with Egypt and for building stable Egyptian–Israeli relations. In this period, I had the opportunity to converse with General Tamir several times, whenever he visited Egypt to meet Kamal Hassan Ali. Many times, I discussed the battles of 1973 with him, especially as he had served as the chief of staff of combat groups, led by General Sharon to the west bank of the canal after the Israeli army crossing.

15 The Mena House Conference

I will now turn to the proceedings of the Mena House Conference. The list of invitees was as follows: the UN; the US; Israel; Jordan; the Palestine Liberation Organization; Syria; Lebanon; and the Soviet Union. The flags of all these parties were flown; however, only the first three attended. All the Arabs, and the Soviets, were conspicuous in their absence. We all had the feeling that the Palestine Liberation Organization had missed a golden opportunity to embarrass Israel by sitting down opposite the Israelis; however, they turned it down, and their seat at the conference hall remained empty. We did notice that on the flagpole outside the conference hall, instead of the PLO flag, someone had apparently got confused and hoisted the flag for Yemen—a rather unamusing error we subsequently corrected.

Eliyahu Ben-Elissar, head of the Israeli delegation, asked to meet the head of the Egyptian delegation immediately upon his arrival. Dr. Esmat Abdel Meguid agreed, and the meeting was held in the suite of the head of the Egyptian delegation. The Israeli representative sat stiff and tense; he spoke fluent French and English. After they had exchanged the customary pleasantries and words of welcome, he opened his briefcase and took out a thick file, saying it was a draft peace proposal that it was his pleasure to present, from Israel to Egypt.

Dr. Esmat looked at him very coldly. "Put it back in the briefcase, and close it up," he said. "I have no authority to receive documents from any Israeli representative," particularly, Dr. Esmat went on to say, as this Mena House Conference was merely being held to prepare for the

173

logistical and organizational side of a return to the peace conference that was an extension of the Geneva Conference, not to discuss the elements of any Egyptian–Israeli peace.

Dr. Esmat had benefited greatly from the documents he had spent days poring over and reading closely, including the draft Israeli proposal the Americans gave to Minister Ismail Fahmy in September 1977, saying it was a proposal drafted by the Israelis that the Egyptians ought to look into and respond to with a counter-proposal, which they duly did. This draft Israeli proposal was a source of outrage to many members of the Egyptian taskforce. They had never seen it prior to its revelation by Ben-Elissar. Some of them spoke of their displeasure to Dr. Osama al-Baz, who explained why he had not shown it to them: Minister Ismail Fahmy had not wanted to reveal it, nor the Egyptian counter-proposal.

The Israeli peace proposal that Dr. Esmat Abdel Meguid refused to accept, knowing we already had a copy, was full of negative proposals, with which the Israelis always started negotiations with Arabs as a matter of course. The most important points were the goal of signing a peace treaty between Egypt and Israel leading to the normalization of relations, establishing diplomatic ties, and eliminating the threat of war. Each state was to recognize the rights of the other, as well as the rights of all the countries in the region, to sovereignty and independence within safe and recognized borders. Article 1 of the treaty, therefore, covered a declaration on both sides ending the state of war, while Article 4 stipulated that the borders between Egypt and Israel would be established by mutual agreement based on a protocol and a map appended to the treaty, and that both parties would unconditionally respect the integrity of the other's lands within its new borders. This paragraph revealed that Israel, even after President Sadat's initiative and the October strike, imagined it could still change the borders of Egypt or obtain territory from Egypt under pressure of invasion. Naturally, Israel's rehashing of an inequitable and flawed proposal in spite of the Egyptian president's initiative was an extremely disheartening indicator of what was in the pipeline for the negotiations.

The first and last session of the conference took place on Thursday, December 15. Dr. Esmat Abdel Meguid read the statement that Salah al-Hindawi and I prepared for him, based of course on his instructions. It included Egypt's call for complete withdrawal from the occupied territories, pursuant to Resolution 242, guaranteeing the Palestinian people's right to self-determination, and the right of all the states in the region to live in safety and security. The Israeli side responded with all the elements of the peace proposal mentioned above.

The meeting concluded without results, work on the conference ceased, and the Egyptian delegation stayed on at Mena House Hotel, reassessing the situation, looking into possible scenarios, and following up on developments. I noted with great astonishment that the head of the Israeli delegation wrote to Dr. Esmat Abdel Meguid on December 16, delivering a message from Israeli Prime Minister Menachem Begin—a positively honeyed message. He had no conception of what he was in for: to wit, a legal battle between the Israeli prime minister and Egypt's permanent representative to the UN. This would occur in just nine days at the Ismailiya Summit between President Sadat and Prime Minister Menachem Begin on December 25.

Menachem Begin wrote to Esmat Abdel Meguid:

Today, en route to the United States, in an effort to achieve peace,
I send to you on behalf of the Israeli people, all good wishes for the
Cairo conference. Everyone, everywhere, is praying and sincerely
hoping that the conference can be a basis for peace between Israel and
its great Arab neighbors.

There was no mention in the message of the Palestinian people, or their rights.

Menachem Begin returned from his visit to the US, whereupon President Sadat invited him to Egypt for more discussions on how peace could be achieved between our two countries.

I was sitting in my room at the Mena House at around noon on December 24, preparing some documents for the head of the negotiations delegation, who was getting ready to leave at dawn to take part in the Ismailiya Summit, in that city between Israel and Egypt. Suddenly, BBC Radio announced the news from Cairo that Ambassador Mohamed Ibrahim Kamel, Egypt's ambassador to Germany, had been appointed Egypt's new minister of foreign affairs.

I grabbed the radio and rushed to Dr. Esmat Abdel Meguid's room, knocking frantically. He stuck his head out of the door. "They've appointed Mohamed Ibrahim Kamel foreign minister!" I fairly shouted at him.

I fully sensed the dignity of that great man in that moment. All of us—or at least Salah al-Hindawi and I—had been expecting Esmat Abdel Meguid to be awarded Sadat's confidence, and the position, to lead the diplomatic efforts at this turning-point in Egypt's political and diplomatic affairs. "Mohamed is a friend," Esmat Abdel Meguid said with his customary calm. "I'll be able to work with him quite effectively to serve the country and get things done."

He was stoic, always ready to serve his country in whatever position he was allocated. Seven years passed until he was entrusted with the
task—by President Hosni Mubarak—of leading the country's diplomatic
affairs, in July 1984, after Kamal Hassan Ali left to assume the duties of
prime minister. At the time, though, I found myself torn between two
great men: Kamal Hassan Ali, whom I accompanied from the Foreign
Ministry to the Cabinet, having worked for him as a diplomatic consultant and private secretary, whereupon he decided he wanted me with him
in his new job, and Esmat Abdel Meguid, who wanted me with him for
the same post. I was obliged, with great discomfiture, to make my excuses
to Dr. Abdel Meguid. However, Dr. Esmat kept pushing me into high
positions at the Foreign Ministry over the following years, and brought
me back to work with him in my old post with his predecessor Kamal
Hassan Ali between 1989 and 1991.

I return now to those decisive days in 1977. Now that Mohamed
Ibrahim Kamel was foreign minister, I knew he would do his best to
exploit the abilities, knowledge, and culture of Ahmed Maher al-Sayed. I
called Ahmed Maher on the telephone at his home in Zamalek; he confirmed the news, saying that he had received a telephone call already from
the new foreign minister, asking him to come to his house immediately,
whereupon he had appointed him office manager and manager of ministerial affairs. "Get ready to work together again," he told me, referring
to our time together under National Security Advisor Mohamed Hafiz
Ismail from 1972 to 1974. "I have to prepare myself to suffer, listening to
the flow of your bright ideas and initiatives!"

For the rest of our team members, it was a new era as we acclimated
to working under a new foreign minister. Personally, I had no difficulty
working with either Ahmed Maher or the minister. I knew the latter
quite well, having served under him at the Press Office of the Foreign
Ministry in 1966, before he was transferred to Kinshasa, the capital of
Zaire—now the Democratic Republic of Congo—to be Egypt's ambassador there. Mohamed Ibrahim Kamel was Egyptian through and through,
extremely loyal to his country. He had sat with President Sadat in the
same prison cell, both political prisoners prior to the 1952 revolution. He
was decent, a heavy smoker, a friend to everyone—although not above
making pithy and accurate observations about them—inveigled into
the Foreign Ministry despite himself. It is my firm belief, after working
with him for a long time, that he had not been grooming himself for this
weighty responsibility at such a hard and challenging juncture.

I notified Esmat Abdel Meguid that Mohamed Ibrahim Kamel had
chosen Ahmed Maher al-Sayed as his office manager. "Excellent choice!"

approved Dr. Esmat, "I would have done the same if I had been appointed." I said then, as I say now, that this is high praise even for such an experienced thinker, not to say philosopher, as Ahmed Maher al-Sayed, whom we sadly lost in September 2010.

And now to the Ismailiya Summit. I did not take part, but Dr. Esmat Abdel Meguid and Dr. Osama al-Baz returned to Cairo the evening of December 25, directly after the summit concluded, and briefed us in the taskforce on all that had occurred. They also showed us all the arrangements and what had been agreed upon, and shared our tasks for the upcoming period.

When the pair of them met with the diplomatic taskforce and started to talk, we could feel the disappointment coming off them in waves. Clearly, this first summit with the Israelis had dashed many hopes. The Israelis, directly after the first session had commenced at noon on December 25, had proposed a new draft peace treaty between Egypt and Israel, dated December 24, the day before the Ismailiya Summit. To a great extent, it resembled the draft treaty the Americans had shown Minister Ismail Fahmy on September 19, and which Ben-Elissar had attempted to present to Esmat Abdel Meguid on December 14 at the Mena House Hotel. However, the Israelis had made a major modification to their plan to tempt the Egyptians, hoping to garner their approval for the new, equally flawed, plan. The proposal said, "Egypt will withdraw their forces to the international borders between Egypt and Mandatory Palestine"—the first indication of any Israeli admission of the existence of these borders since 1967. "This withdrawal will take place over two stages: the first to Arish/Ras Mohamed (east of Arish and west of Ras Mohamed), and the second to the international borders mentioned above, on condition that this final withdrawal be completed three to five years after signing the treaty."

The draft treaty went on to reveal the true intention of the Israelis, always part of any Israeli negotiations with the Arabs: namely, staying on Arab land and dismissing any withdrawal as unnecessary. The draft proposal states that, "Israeli air bases on Egyptian soil in Sinai should remain, between the Arish/Ras Mohamed line and the Egyptian international boundaries with Mandatory Palestine [Israel]." These were the air bases that had been heavily bombed by Egypt in 1973: Etzion, Eitam, and Ofira. They also wished to keep their electronic observation stations at Jebel Hilal and Jebel Harim, with mobile land and sea forces within Egyptian borders and in Egypt's territorial waters.

The Israeli proposal then moved on to what I can only describe as bare-faced impudence, stipulating that after withdrawal to international lines was complete, the Israeli settlements in this region, civilian of course, would remain in place on Egyptian soil with a UN presence in the demilitarized zone in the area mentioned above. These "civilian" settlements would also possess "defensive forces" on Egyptian soil to defend themselves. This presence would be subject to the jurisdiction of Israeli law and Israeli courts!

The Israeli proposal continued in this vein, disparaging the Egyptians by speaking of the "rights of Israeli and Arab civilians" living in Sinai to freedom of movement in the UN-controlled area, which could not be removed from Sinai without the agreement of the Egyptians and Israelis, plus a unanimous vote from the Security Council.

This draft proposal revealed once more the crass negotiation style that Israel was adopting in its negotiations with the Arabs, seeking to encircle and restrict future developments with numerous legal texts and loopholes aimed at ensnaring any Arab parties naive enough to agree to them. In truth, Begin's proposal was impossible for the Egyptians to accept. He seemed to have neglected to take into account that this was a proposal more suitable for a victor to propose to a vanquished party, and that this no longer applied to the balance of power after 1973. Egypt, as I explained above in the conclusion of "Witness to War," had armed forces capable of working effectively against Israel; it enjoyed a privileged position among Arab and African countries and internationally; and it had alliances in every quarter. Sadat's peace initiative had changed things, engendering proceedings and developments unprecedented in American and western thought in general, and in international Jewish and Israeli thought in particular. Here I must admit that only then did I begin to start to become completely convinced of the peace initiative, its reasons and goals, and what we could achieve for ourselves through it, if it was managed with profound professionalism in a balanced manner.

The two Egyptian ambassadors started explaining the proceedings of the summit. Dr. Esmat Abdel Meguid argued with the Israeli prime minister when he brought up the "right" to keep Egyptian and Palestinian lands under Israeli sovereignty. Egypt and the Arabs, Begin said, had conducted an aggressive attack against Israel in 1967, which conferred upon what he called the injured party the "right" to keep control of all lands that had become disputed territory. Esmat was scathing in his reply to the claim to Egyptian and Arab lands and the definition of "aggression," and with regard to UN Security Council Resolution 242 of November 1967. The heated argument convinced Israel in later years that "the Egyptian Foreign Ministry is so belligerent that it stands in the way of a settlement."

The ideas, proposals, and nomenclature of the Israeli prime minister show the degree of confusion and contradiction he was offering. Today, looking back on these proposals as the Palestinians are engaged in a similar battle of negotiation, we all need to go over what happened then and what is happening now. I would like to refer the reader to two books: Dr. Esmat Abdel Meguid's *Zaman al-intisar wa-l-inkisar* (Times of Victory and Defeat) and Minister Mohamed Ibrahim Kamel's *al-Salam al-da'i' fi Camp David* (The Lost Peace of the Camp David Accords). Menachem Begin spoke of the relations between Jews and Palestinians in the state of Israel as follows: "We have Arab Palestinians living in Israel. We have Jewish Palestinians living in Israel. Today Israel proposes in its negotiations with the Palestinians, nearly thirty years after the start of negotiations between the Arabs and Israel, the concept of the Jewish state and the acceptance thereof." I refer the reader to the speech of the then-prime minister of Israel, and even draw his or her attention to Golda Meir's words on the Palestinian–Israeli situation: "Who are the Palestinians you are talking about? WE are the Palestinians."

Back at the Ismailiya Summit, the Israelis proposed self-rule for the Palestinians directly for the first time, calling the Palestinians in Palestine's lands in Gaza and the West Bank "the Arab Palestinians living in Judea, Samaria, and the Gaza Strip." The suggestion again included the concept the Israelis had been clinging to since December 25, 1977, up to a few years ago, when it was forced, under Arab and international pressure, and the pressure of regional and demographic developments, to develop its stance with regard to self-rule and accept the concept of a Palestinian state, while continuing to work toward circumscribing it and stripping it of any efficacy, squeezing it into the narrowest of frameworks and imposing restrictions that would cripple its functioning. However, I am confident that it will be a long and uphill battle for them to ever achieve this. I trust that the Palestinians, with support from Egypt and the Arab nation, are capable of achieving the goal of establishing a viable state on the soil of the Palestinian lands within the 1967 borders. Egypt has always had powerful armed forces capable of imposing its vision and defending its interests; today, the Palestinians lack this capacity, which is what Israel knows in any negotiations with them. Still, the Palestinians' ability to reject Israel's attempt to impose a fait accompli will eventually force the Israelis, as Egypt did, to reach an equitable settlement. The alternative is the continuation of conflict for decades, if not centuries.

The Israeli proposal of December 1977 included:

- Doing away with the administration of Israeli military rule in Judea, Samaria, and Gaza (the West Bank and Gaza).

- Establishing a self-rule administration for the inhabitants of these areas by means of an election process for a ruling council.
- The right of all inhabitants over eighteen to vote in the elections for this administration and its council, which would then establish different departments for each branch of self-rule: education, health, industry, and so on.
- Israel to keep control of this region for its security and defense.

This proposal was the clearest-possible revelation of Israel's intention to remain in the occupied Palestinian lands in the West Bank and Gaza, while giving full rights to the Israeli civilians in these territories. The Israelis also revealed their plan to retain control of these areas by making the same proposals we hear today when they speak of the Arab threats coming from Jordan or beyond the Jordanian borders in Iraq. Today, they speak of threats from beyond Jordan in their resistance to establishing an effective Palestinian state, referencing Iranian threats and radical Islam that might grip Egypt or Jordan—all posited with the sole goal of keeping control and maintaining the occupation.

During a break between summit meetings, Dr. Esmat Abdel Meguid and Moshe Dayan had a long conversation. Dr. Esmat asked Dayan if the Israelis wanted the West Bank for historical or security reasons. "Both," Dayan responded. "We are Palestinian Jews. We have a right to the land; we also need to protect ourselves from Arab aggression, attacks, and threats."

Dr. Esmat responded that the Arabs would not see it that way, and thus conflict would continue. It did, in point of fact, and it escalated, attracting Islamist elements that had not been part of the equation. As long as the Israelis eschewed equitable moderation in a settlement with the Palestinians, this confrontation and this pressure on everyone would continue.

I recall another long conversation between the two Egyptian ministers who took part in the Jerusalem meetings for the negotiations of the Political Committee (which I will come to in due time), Mohamed Ibrahim Kamel and Boutros Boutros-Ghali, and the Israeli foreign minister at Lod Airport, as they awaited the return of the Egyptian aircraft to take the Egyptian delegation back to Cairo on the evening of January 18, 1978. The Egyptian ministers went over the same points that Dr. Esmat Abdel Meguid had covered with Moshe Dayan in Ismailiya. The Israeli minister reiterated his conviction concerning the rights of the "Palestinian Jews," as he called them, to live in all the lands of the West Bank, and the importance of the presence of the Israeli army to protect them from the aggression of external Arab parties and others beyond their borders. This same logic is being put forth today to defend the Israeli armed forces' presence in the Jordan Valley, even within the framework of a peace agreement allowing for establishing a demilitarized Palestinian state. I am confident now, as I was then, that the Palestinians cannot really accept any of the current Israeli proposals. I hope they will succeed, as Egypt did before, in achieving their goals of liberating all their lands from military Israeli presence, settlement, and occupation.

This brings me to the activity of the Egyptian taskforce managed and supervised by Dr. Esmat Abdel Meguid, with the active participation of Dr. Osama al-Baz. We drew up an Egyptian peace proposal to be presented to the Israelis at the Ismailiya Summit. It was important that the initiatives not come from the Israelis alone. Our proposal was that a statement be made about a settlement, as a declaration of its guiding principles, comprising the following important points:

- Israeli withdrawal from Sinai, the Golan, the West Bank, and Gaza, in compliance with Security Council Resolution 242 and the principle of the inadmissibility of the acquisition of territory by war.
- A guarantee of each state's full sovereignty over its own lands, via measures agreed upon between the two parties.
- An equitable settlement for all sides of the Palestinian question via the right to self-determination through negotiations with Israel held by Egypt, Jordan, and a representative of the Palestinian people.

The meeting issued a statement reflecting President Sadat and Prime Minister Dayan's agreement on the commencement of ministerial meetings between the two countries and forming two committees, one military and one political, to negotiate the ideas set forth by the parties during their meeting. This was agreed upon during a bilateral summit meeting attended only by the two of them. We therefore had to prepare for a new fight: how to establish the basis and principles that were to govern these negotiations.

March 1974. Ceremony honoring National Security Advisor Mohamed Hafiz Ismail, with ambassadors Talaat al-Shaf'i and Osman Nouri to his right and left, respectively.

March 1974. Group photograph of Hafiz Ismail's office staff at the National Security Advisory. Hafiz Ismail is in the front row, third from right, with Ahmed Maher al-Sayed standing directly behind him. Author appears top left.

January 1978. Coordinating meeting of Minister of War Mohamed al-Gamasy and Minister of Foreign Affairs Mohamed Ibrahim Kamel in Egypt in preparation for the start of operations of the Military Committee in Cairo and the Diplomatic Committee in Jerusalem. Author appears in center background.

January 1978. The only meeting of the Political Committees of Egypt, Israel, and the USA. Seated at the table (background, from left to right) are: Osama al-Baz, Boutros Boutros-Ghali, Mohamed Ibrahim Kamel, and Esmat Abdel Meguid. Behind them (also seated left to right) are: Nabil al-Arabi, the author, Ahmed Maher al-Sayed, Hussein Hassouna, and Amre Moussa. Moshe Dayan is in the foreground, second from left. Mohamed ElBaradei, slightly obscured, is behind Ahmed Maher al-Sayed.

September 1978 during the Camp David negotiations in Gettysburg, Pennsylvania.
Front row (left to right): Prime Minister Begin, President Carter, President Sadat, and
Moshe Dayan. Behind them, Ezer Weizman is standing to Dayan's left, with Ahmed
Maher al-Sayed immediately behind Weizman. Boutros Boutros-Ghali is between
Dayan and Sadat, and Mohamed Ibrahim Kamel is between Sadat and Carter. Hassan
al-Tohami, with spectacles, stands behind Begin, with the author behind al-Tohami.
U.S. Ambassador to Egypt Hermann Eilts is to the author's immediate right.

1984. Esmat Abdel Meguid (left) with the author at the seat of the Egyptian Cabinet.

1984. Prime Minister Kamal Hassan Ali with the author at the seat of the Egyptian Cabinet.

1999. President Yasser Arafat with Secretary-General of the Arab League Esmat Abdel Meguid, the author, Egypt's representative at the United Nations, and Hussein Hassouna, representative of the Arab League in New York.

16 The Ismailiya Summit

D r. Esmat Abdel Meguid concluded his instructions the evening of December 25 by telling us, "We have a new foreign minister today who will need all our support. I don't yet know whether I'm staying with you in Cairo or if I will be called back to resume my duties in New York. The main thing is for the working groups to keep up their efforts and discussions." He went on to tell us that it was up to us to prepare for the positions Egypt would take at the negotiations in Jerusalem, where the Political Committee talks would be held, attended by both countries' foreign ministers, and in Cairo, where negotiations were to be held between the defense ministers of Egypt and Israel on military matters and security requirements related to the goal of complete withdrawal from Egyptian soil.

President Sadat's instructions to Minister Mohamed Ibrahim Kamel were to keep Dr. Esmat Abdel Meguid in Cairo for a while, and to attend the Jerusalem negotiations himself in due time, so that the minister could benefit fully from Dr. Esmat's knowledge and experience with the Palestinian question in the upcoming negotiations related to this issue. This was when I began to realize that it was Egypt's sincere goal to work toward a comprehensive agreement between all the Arabs and Israel, putting an end to the Arab–Israeli conflict and establishing a comprehensive peace and stability for all concerned. I was convinced of the positive nature of this initiative and its ability to achieve gains and successes, which had hitherto been absent from joint Arab efforts.

In the days following the Ismailiya Summit, the Egyptian media was noticeably scathing in its criticism of the Israeli negotiating style. Sternly

worded articles were written by authors close to the Egyptian seat of
power: Moussa Sabry, Ali Hamdi al-Gammal, and the eminent writer
Salah Montasser, who wrote a vitriolic anti-Israel article published on the
front page of the premier national newspaper *al-Ahram*. Much was made
of "the Shylockian negotiating style." Naturally, this put Israel's back up:
the Americans stepped in to tone down the Egyptian criticisms.

We all met Minister Mohamed Ibrahim Kamel—a man, as I have
said before, with a modest and unassuming manner, and a deep faith in
his country's abilities. He enjoyed the security of firm convictions in this
period, convictions he never compromised, up to his resignation at the
Camp David Summit. Ahmed Maher al-Sayed, his office director (and
future foreign minister, as fate would have it), told me that I would be
working with the minister on the settlement file. This would bring me in
close contact with the minister. Minister Kamel told me that he knew me
well, and appreciated me. "I've a heavy workload for you!" he said. That
was the start of our working relationship, which remained close from
December 26, 1977—the day after the Ismailiya Summit ended—until
his resignation on September 22, 1978.

When I started working with the new minister, I intuited that despite
his budding conviction about the advantages of the Egyptian peace initiative—if effectively run—he still had a great many questions about what
had motivated President Sadat to take such a step, shocking everyone
with his visit to Jerusalem and getting the stagnant peace process moving
with a step unprecedented in its boldness. In the days that followed, I
wrote to him what I thought was a logical explanation for the president's
initiative. Here is the memorandum I presented to him, with the approval
of Ambassador Ahmed Maher al-Sayed:

> Four years after the shock of the war, and our strike at the Israeli army
> in Sinai, Egypt realized that the situation has clearly stagnated.
>
> The attempts to bring the Arabs and Israel together in a peace
> conference in Geneva have revealed Israel's continued stalling on pro-
> cedural issues; meanwhile, the Arab parties seem content to take part
> in the negotiations, while the Israelis persist in evasiveness, ignoring
> the core of the matter, and the possibility of serious negotiations that
> could open the door for a just and equitable settlement achieving
> everyone's goals.
>
> These points are doubtless known to President Sadat, despite then
> Foreign Minister Ismail Fahmy's conviction that he was getting close
> to achieving the goal of holding the conference, jump-starting serious
> negotiations with a strong and cohesive framework of Arab support.

I then spoke to Minister Kamel about a conversation I had with Second Secretary Mohamed Ahmed Ismail, my friend and a former classmate at Heliopolis Secondary School, and the son of Field Marshall Ahmed Ismail Ali, the same gentleman who informed me in October 1977 that Minister Ismail Fahmy, during his participation in the General Assembly in September of the same year, had entrusted him with a political report for the eyes of President Sadat. Ismail Fahmy had decided to send it with a courier and not entrust it to a diplomatic bag or a telegram, lest it be intercepted and decoded. That report, Mohamed Ahmed Ismail told me, was about Minister Ismail Fahmy's efforts to get the Geneva Conference started again, and his communications with the Americans and other parties to get this done. Mohamed Ahmed Ismail told me that he had presented the report to the Presidency in the first week of October 1977; however, President Sadat, upon hearing that the bearer of the report was none other than the son of Ahmed Ismail Ali, had asked Second Secretary Mohamed Ahmed Ismail to meet him in person at his summer house at al-Qanatir.

President Sadat met the young Mohamed Ahmed Ismail in his sleeping quarters at the summer house. He broke the seal on the envelope and read the report attentively. He looked up at the young man standing before him. "Have you any idea what's in this report?" The young diplomat said no. The president gave him a very brief outline, then asked, "What do you think of it?"

The young Mohamed Ahmed Ismail launched into a lengthy defense of the views of Minister Ismail Fahmy. Finally, Sadat held up a hand. "This isn't getting us anywhere. Things aren't moving. We need to shake things up. What we need is a shock, a big one." He thanked the young diplomat and dismissed him.

This was what Mohamed Ahmed Ismail told me, just before boarding his flight back to the Egyptian embassy in New York. We confabulated and shared our thoughts on what the president could possibly be planning.

The weeks passed slowly after that, until the president's visit to Jerusalem. I gathered, as Ismail did, that this was the "shock" Sadat mentioned at al-Qanatir in October 1977. The reader must remember that direct Egyptian–Israeli meetings had started in Morocco toward the end of September 1977, between Hassan al-Tohami and Moshe Dayan, attended by Kamal Hassan Ali, chief of Egyptian Intelligence, also in Morocco at the time.

I recounted all this to Minister Mohamed Ibrahim Kamel, reaffirming my conviction that President Sadat had not been at all certain that the Geneva Conference would be held at all, nor that it would have yielded

anything in terms of a real settlement even if it had gone ahead. My memorandum listed all the reasons and interpretations that, in my view, justified the initiative:

> What is being said is that President Sadat feels that the Arabs offered
> Egypt insufficient support in the aftermath of the October War—
> indeed, some went so far as to rudely refuse Egypt's requests for
> assistance during the period of economic and political policy transfor-
> mation launched by President Sadat. It is also said that the president is
> offended at how some of his emissaries were treated in Arab countries
> when they conveyed his requests for support of Egypt's economy, and
> for his ambitious projects.

I moved on to two elements that affected the president's decision to
launch an initiative. The first of them was things blowing up domestically,
in the form of the demonstrations on January 18 and 19. There was a
universal call to action, to hurry up with economic reforms to protect the
domestic front, especially as the enemy was still stationed in the greater
part of Sinai. The second, I said, was the Likud Party's rise to power in
Israel, in May 1977. President Sadat knew that the Likud was an extension of the extreme right-wing Herut, led by Menachem Begin, Ze'ev
Jabotinsky's prize pupil. Jabotinsky was the Zionist figure with the greatest hatred of the Arabs of Palestine. That party's ascendance to power in
Israel was an indicator of a hard-line right-wing period in Israel, the first
in its history since its establishment in 1948. It was a negative indicator
that imposed on the president the necessity to think deeply of how to
encircle the Israeli side and put Israel in a defensive position.

At this point, the US came on the scene, attempting to convey Israeli
attempts to open the door to Egypt via new views and stances—or, at
least, this was how the Americans made it seem. The president appreciated the possibility of checking the veracity of these views, agreeing to the
meetings between Hassan al-Tohami and Moshe Dayan in Morocco, and
followed up with the shock visit to Jerusalem.

The final reason, in my estimation at the time, was that with Egypt
having weakened its relations with the Soviet Union, the Soviet Union
had progressively restricted its military aid and weapons supply to Egypt.
President Sadat felt that the power relations between Egypt and Israel, as
well as the military balance, had started to skew in favor of Israel. He had
to make a move, and fast.

Minister Mohamed Ibrahim Kamel carefully read my candid brief.
We began preparations for the Jerusalem meeting on January 17. The

minister began to espouse the objectives of President Sadat's historic visit, and to openly express his conviction that the president had done the right thing. He spoke of what this visit could achieve for Egypt and the Arabs, especially if they succeeded in keeping up the pressure on the Israelis, and managed to get international public opinion on our side and to support our proposals.

The Egyptian taskforce's view was that communication and cooperation with the Americans needed to be one of Egypt's goals. Therefore, Minister Mohamed Ibrahim Kamel remained in close contact with the U.S. ambassador to Egypt, the experienced Hermann Eilts.

The US called for the Military and Political Committees to start their work. All of us on the Egyptian side, both diplomats and military officers, began to coordinate and prepare what we would propose at the negotiations, militarily, politically, and diplomatically, to achieve a settlement. A high-level meeting was held between the Egyptian minister of defense and the foreign minister on January 10, in preparation for the start of operations of the Military Committee in Cairo and the Political Committee in Jerusalem. This coordination revealed the importance to the Egyptian diplomatic service of avoiding a possible Israeli trap of being asked to draw up lines of withdrawal, (residential) settlements, and so on. These had been delegated to the Military Committee, and designated as details of the withdrawal, which was already agreed upon and outside the scope of negotiation, and therefore of diplomatic meetings.

As for the meetings in Jerusalem, it was agreed that these should cover a comprehensive political settlement between Israel and the Arabs as a whole, not only Egypt. The declared aim was to arrive at a mutually agreed-upon declaration of principles, on which upcoming negotiations and future elements of a settlement could be built. These, it was agreed, should not take too long. Both sides, Egyptian and Israeli, exchanged documents reflecting each party's view of a satisfactory declaration of principles governing the process. This was done via the US, which must be given all due credit for maintaining impartiality.

This was also a period of unrest in Iran, with the rise of Ayatollah Khomeini and the start of the shah's domestic issues. The US was focused on developments in the Iranian arena. President Jimmy Carter stopped over in Egypt for an official visit on his way back from India. Minister Mohamed Ibrahim Kamel met Secretary of State Cyrus Vance for the first time in Luxor. Their short meeting—no more than half an hour—built firm trust between the two men. I must say here that to meet Cyrus Vance was immediately to recognize him as a man of integrity. I had always seen him as one of the great American statesmen to emerge from the

First World War; one of those Anglo-Saxon gentlemen in the mold of W. Averell Harriman, Lafayette, Henry Wallace McLeod, George Marshall, and Harry Hopkins, who helped their country win the war and push the western world toward the Cold War, NATO, and other developments.

The Egyptians, as I have said, sought to secure the highest degree of understanding between Egypt and the US. Carter announced in Aswan, for the first time, an American stance more attentive to the Palestinian situation. The U.S. statement spoke of the need for a solution to the problem of Palestine from all sides—a solution, Carter said, that took into account the legitimate rights of the Palestinian people "to participate in the determination of their own future." This groundbreaking statement should have been singled out for building upon in the days and months that followed.

I had no way of knowing back then that I, still a young first secretary, would keep on dealing with this issue with successive colleagues at the Foreign Ministry, not only throughout 1978 and the Camp David Accords, but all the way to the Madrid Conference in October 1991, thirteen years later, and beyond, as a principal assistant to Foreign Minister Amre Moussa, from 1991 to 1999, and finally, as foreign minister myself, until 2011. The difficulty of reaching a settlement on this issue weighs on us even today.

I still remember the effort it took just to prepare for, and agree upon, a negotiation schedule. The Israelis were quick to offer, in early January 1978, a draft agenda. The document, dated December 31, offered details of the elements of the Israeli proposal. Ambassador Hermann Eilts wrote to our foreign minister about what his counterpart in Israel, Samuel Lewis, had said. Moshe Dayan had suggested a three-point working agenda:

1. Studying the issue of the status of the Israeli civilian settlements in Sinai in the area to the east of Arish/Ras Mohamed.
2. Principles of a peace treaty on both Judea and Samaria (by which he meant the West Bank) and the Israeli proposal for self-rule for Arab Palestinians living in Judea, Samaria, and the Gaza Strip.
3. The points that might be covered by the peace treaty.

The message asked Egypt to offer its own views and a counter-proposal, if it so wished. The U.S. message also communicated Moshe Dayan's urgings to Egypt to prepare a response quickly, so that things could move forward. Dayan had added that he was aware that disarmament in Sinai was the province of the Military Committee in Cairo, scheduled to start working a few days before the Political Committee in Jerusalem.

Finally, Dayan's message added that if the military meetings managed to disarm the Sinai Peninsula, the Political Committee could concentrate on political matters, such as the matter of the Israeli settlements in Sinai. If there was no settlement on disarmament, then that, too, might be discussed in Jerusalem and Cairo at the meetings of both committees, although the Israeli prime minister added that he was aware that this was a military more than a political issue.

The U.S. ambassador in Cairo affirmed at the end of his communication that he was merely a messenger, and that these statements did not constitute a reflection of the American stance.

In Cairo, we in the political taskforce and Minister Ahmed Maher al-Sayed read the message with a great deal of disgruntlement. It was clear that Israel was still stuck in the old way of thinking: they were making unfounded assumptions, foremost among which was Menachem Begin's demand, in his flawed proposal, to keep the Israeli settlements in Sinai, in addition to the issue of disarmament. Also, the Israelis were speaking of a settlement of the Palestinian issue in terms of mere self-rule for the Palestinians.

It also became clear that Israel was speaking of the plight of the "Arab Palestinians," a transparent ploy meant to convey that there were "Jewish Palestinians," that is, Israelis. This was in accordance with the attitude adopted by Menachem Begin in Ismailiya, and statements by Moshe Dayan, Golda Meir, and others that "Israelis are the Jewish Palestinians," and that there are "Arab Palestinians" living in disputed territory. We discussed the matter among ourselves. A draft proposal was prepared for Foreign Minister Mohamed Ibrahim Kamel, who agreed to present it to the Israelis via the US. It comprised the Egyptian view of the agenda for the Political Committee meetings, including,

1. An item specifically devoted to ending Israeli occupation of Arab territories occupied since 1967.
2. Guaranteeing the integrity of territory, and political independence, of all states in the region, by means of procedures to be agreed upon between all parties, on the basis of reciprocity.
3. Guaranteeing the right of all states in the region to sovereignty, integrity of territory, and independence.
4. Arriving at an equitable settlement for the Palestinian problem in all its elements, via negotiations attended by Egypt, Jordan, Israel, and representatives of the Palestinian people.
5. Ending all calls to war and establishing peaceful relations between the states in the region, in accordance with the UN Charter.

Naturally, the reader will notice that the Egyptian proposal has remained unchanged in essence over these forty years. Our focus, then as now, has been on ending the occupation, promoting everyone's right to live in peace, establishing a normal relationship under the umbrella of comprehensive peace, and finding a settlement of the Palestinian problem.

The Israelis were silent for ten days after the Egyptian draft schedule of negotiations at the start of January 1978. Then, a message arrived from Moshe Dayan to Mohamed Ibrahim Kamel expressing Israel's agreement to three of the points proposed by Egypt—with modifications that, in effect, gutted them. They also rejected Point One, withdrawal from occupied territories, and Point Four, finding a fair solution to the Palestinian question.

Dayan's message stated that Israel "naturally" agreed completely, without reservation, to the right of every state in the region to live in peace within its borders. He affirmed that Israel would be happy to accept any phrasing mentioned in Resolution 242. However, he said, Israel could not accept anything else: he went on to reject the proposals Egypt had offered in Ismailiya on December 25, mentioned above.

The Israeli foreign minister repeated Israel's position on "Arab Palestinians," as it related to Judea and Samaria. He then suggested that the Jerusalem negotiations focus on peace treaties, after which all the political and civilian issues could be discussed in due time, such as the matter of civilian settlements in Sinai. The Israeli message ended by reaffirming the Israeli vision, summarized in five points for a proposed agenda:

- Guaranteeing the sanctity of territory and the political independence for every state in the region via procedures that included the establishment of demilitarized zones.
- Guaranteeing the right to sovereignty, integrity of territory, and political independence for all countries in the region.
- Ending all calls to war and establishing peaceful relations between all states via the signing of peace treaties.
- The inclusion of political and civilian issues, such as the civilian settlements in Sinai, in any peace treaty.
- Agreeing on a statement on the Arab Palestinians living in Judea, Samaria, and Gaza.

Again, Israel was concentrating on the points it found useful for its own ends, at the forefront of which was ending the state of war and signing peace treaties. Meanwhile, it insisted on mentioning the Sinai settlements as a means of perpetuating these settlements' status. Finally, it sought to weaken the Palestinian angle, making light of Palestinians' rights in treating them as citizens, not a people with full rights, and completely ignoring the issue of withdrawal from occupied territories.

We on the Egyptian political taskforce went back to weighing the situation. The foreign minister agreed on January 12, 1978, to a new proposal to be submitted to the Israelis via the US, emphasizing that our conception of the agenda reflected, in essence, the letter and the spirit of Resolution 242, which emphasized the inadmissibility of the acquisition of territory by war, the result of which was our call for Israel to withdraw from the territories occupied in 1967. Egypt also categorically rejected Israel's omission of Egypt's demands for Israeli withdrawal from its territories from the proposed agenda for negotiations, and reemphasized its rejection of the position Israel had made public in Ismailiya, and that state's proposals on this issue. Egypt's offerings of alternative suggestions at the time were an affirmation that Israel must withdraw from Sinai, the Golan, the West Bank, and Gaza.

Minister Mohamed Ibrahim Kamel's message to Moshe Dayan said that Israel was assuming an absurd position, and explained its position in detail. The Egyptian message was curt, just this side of brusque, and hinted that our patience was wearing thin. The minister repeated the Egyptian position presented in the earlier draft agenda.

It appeared that the two sides, Egyptian and Israeli, would not be able to agree, without an intermediary, on an agenda that might open doors to the start of negotiations for the Political Committee in Jerusalem. The Americans realized it was important, indeed essential, to intervene to help them overcome their differences.

A message arrived from the U.S. ambassador for the Egyptian foreign minister, dated January 12. It suggested that the focus be on a declaration of principles for the negotiations and the settlement, since this was the preliminary goal of the Political Committee, while emphasizing the importance of achieving a settlement for the Palestinian problem and moving forward on this issue via an interim solution lasting roughly five years.

The American proposal, in sum, called for us to give U.S. Secretary of State Vance the opportunity to hold discussions in Jerusalem with Egypt and Israel on two main issues: guidelines for negotiations for arrangements for the West Bank and Gaza over a five-year period, and the principles for a settlement between the Arabs and Israel. The US then specifically suggested an agenda with three main points:

- A Declaration of Principles that would govern the negotiations and peace treaties in the Middle East, with a focus on issues related to peace, withdrawal from occupied territories, agreeing on safe and recognized borders, and an equitable solution for the Palestinian question.
- Guidelines for the negotiations for settling the Palestinian question in all its elements.
- The elements in the peace treaties between Israel and its neighbors in accordance with Security Council Resolution 242 dated November 22, 1967.

Once more, we and Israel were plunged into discussions of the U.S. proposal. Each party attempted to make gains that served its own views. On January 15, the US proposed a final draft agenda, which it viewed as fair. The final U.S. proposal had, again, three elements:

- A Declaration of Principles that would govern the negotiations aiming to achieve a comprehensive peace in the Middle East.
- Guidelines for the negotiations related to the West Bank and Gaza.
- Peace treaties between Israel and all of its neighbors along the lines of Security Council Resolution 242 dated November 22, 1967.

The Egyptian and Israeli sides agreed to start negotiations as part of the Political Committee in Jerusalem on this basis.

The Military Committee had already started work, holding its first four meetings on January 11 and 12, before the Egyptian diplomatic delegation arrived in Jerusalem on January 16. The Egyptian delegation was headed by Lieutenant-General al-Gamasy and the Israeli delegation by Ezer Weizman, both ministers of defense in their respective countries. The two sides' positions in these early rounds revealed a great disparity. The Israelis affirmed and reaffirmed their need for security, and how delicate their position was in this regard. Therefore, they were insistent on their air force using their air bases in Sinai, and the importance of their settlements remaining in place in the peninsula. They repeated a great many absurdities, including that allowing the settlements to remain would make them feel secure; that their presence at the Jura/Ras al-Naqab/Ras Nusrani Airfields was essential for the security of Sharm al-Sheikh, from which they were to withdraw; and that the airfield would make a good base from which to defend Eilat from Saudi Arabia and Jordan, not to mention that it was out of range of the Syrian air force.

The Israelis went on to say that they were mistrustful of the Arab situation, especially with regard to countries that had ties with the Soviet Union. They harped on their distrust of the major powers' assurances, including of the US. They then insisted that the settlements in Rafah and Yamit were a buffer against the Palestinian conurbation in Gaza. The Israeli presentation ended with a demand for guarantees in the form of control of these airfields and settlements; this was, they said, because of their distrust of future generations of Egyptians.

The Egyptian military side summarily dismissed all these demands and pretexts. They affirmed that they had no intention whatever, under any circumstances, of agreeing to study the possibility of security by means of giving up land or allowing for any presence on Egyptian soil in any way, shape, or form. On these grounds, the Egyptians refused the Israeli proposals, for their flagrant violation of Egyptian sovereignty and restriction of Egypt's ability to defend Sinai and the Suez Canal against future Israeli aggression. They concluded by saying, "The Israeli proposals reflect the expansionist designs of Israel, which we utterly reject. We cannot accept this under any circumstances."

For my part, having read the transcripts of these negotiations between military men, I can safely say that today is only a reflection of yesterday. Israel's attempts to subdue the Palestinians on various pretexts mentioned above are only attempts, in truth, to acquire land, which have been proven utterly illogical and unreasonable, not to mention untrue, by history and by reality.

The negotiations on the Military Committee level also revealed that, despite the agreement on an Israeli withdrawal to the international borders between Egypt and Mandatory Palestine, and the return of Egypt's sovereignty over Sinai, Israel still clung to airfields and settlements on Egyptian soil—in other words, it clung to the situation Menachem Begin mentioned in his peace proposal to President Sadat in Ismailiya on December 25, 1977.

On another front, the two parties agreed during these four meetings on January 11 and 12 on elements for mutual security, foremost among which was agreeing to demilitarized and partially militarized zones, and that the main forces for both parties in Sinai and the Naqab desert would pose no threat to either party.

17 The Political Committee and the Visit to Jerusalem

I n the Political Committee, we began to prepare for the visit to Jerusalem. Ahmed Maher entrusted me with the task of supervising all the important papers, both administrative and organizational, and pertaining to the content of the meetings. I stepped up my work and contacts with the Egyptian security teams who would precede us into Israel in order to secure the delegation's precinct, the rooms of its members, the meeting room we were to use, and the secure communications and telephone centers we would use in contacting Cairo, as well as the delegation's code room, the province of Egyptian Intelligence.

My main observation at that stage was that many in the Foreign Ministry and associated bodies were eager to be in the delegation. It became clear to me that many people were enthusiastic to find out more about Israel, its lifestyle and society, see for themselves what the situation was really like there, and find out how people lived: in short, everything about its affairs. I also noted that many experts on Israeli affairs at the Foreign Ministry were insistent on their right to take part and visit that country: this visit, they felt, and this role, represented a unique opportunity for them to find out more about Israel.

We started the process of supplying the American embassy in Cairo with all the names and details, tasks, passport numbers, and so on of the members of the delegation, to be conveyed to Israel to complete the tasks related to their admission to, and temporary residency in, Israel. One thing that had caught our attention in Cairo when the Israeli delegation arrived on December 13, preceded by a security detail to prepare the main group's rooms at the Mena House Hotel at the Pyramids, was that their actions at the hotel bespoke a certain entitlement. Nothing, they seemed to believe, should stand in the way of Israeli security and their efforts to ensure that there were no bugs in the rooms, telephones, walls, or furniture. We were shocked when the Israelis left the Mena House: the hotel management found that all the wires, telephones, walls, and pretty much all the furniture had been ripped apart and all but destroyed. The entire wing of luxury suites where the Israelis stayed needed extensive repairs, in the name of "security" and making sure the rooms, suites, and reception halls were free of Egyptian bugs.

When the Egyptian security delegation arrived in Jerusalem, they were the first to take over the rooms we had been given in Israel, on the topmost floors of the Jerusalem Hilton. We treated the room's appointments exactly as Israeli security had done to the Mena House: an eye for an eye, or in this case, a suite!

Our delegation then installed a complete security network between all its members' rooms. The walls of the rooms and corridors, indeed the entire floor, was swept for bugs. It was an onerous and challenging task for Egyptian Intelligence, as well as being somewhat of a confrontation. It certainly was not the first, or the last, confrontation between Egyptian Intelligence's security apparatus and Israeli surveillance teams.

Egyptian Intelligence recommended to us diplomatic members of the Egyptian delegation not to speak about sensitive matters in open spaces outside the hotel buildings. If obliged to sit together in the meeting rooms and conference halls, or discuss the issues among ourselves, we should do so with more than one radio and/or television set turned on at the same time at full volume, which would effectively prevent anyone on the other side of surveillance devices from making out our conversation. We went so far in following these recommendations that we could often be found yelling at the foreign minister in his suite or at each other to make ourselves heard—the devices Intelligence had recommended had effectively drowned us out to the point where we could hardly hear each other speak! We soon found that the best way to converse was outside the hotel, in the gardens or around the pool, in whispers.

Minister of State for Foreign Affairs Boutros Boutros-Ghali prepared Foreign Minister Mohamed Ibrahim Kamel's draft address, which he was to deliver at the airport immediately on arrival, and another for the inaugural meeting of the proceedings of the Political Committee, on the morning of January 17. I read the first speech, as instructed by Ahmed Maher. It made me uncomfortable. I felt it needed strengthening, and that we needed to repeat our positions in the speech itself, namely withdrawal from occupied Arab territories, a just settlement of the Palestinian question, and security for all. With Ahmed Maher's enthusiastic permission, I reworked a great many paragraphs in both draft speeches.

In the speech at Lod Airport, we called for an end to occupation. There could be no peace, we stated, with occupation. We reaffirmed the Palestinian right to self-determination. The speech approved by Mohamed Ibrahim Kamel had been transformed into a fiery address, bursting with daring and giving no quarter, especially as it was being given by the foreign minister of Egypt in the very heart of our opponent's territory!

The Egyptian Boeing 737 took off with all the members of the Egyptian delegation on board, headed of course by Mohamed Ibrahim Kamel, and accompanied by Dr. Esmat Abdel Meguid. Also with the mission was Dr. Boutros Boutros-Ghali, who was asked by President Sadat to take part in this round of talks to assist the minister. All the members of the political working group were on the flight, accompanied by a number of intelligence officers from the Assessment and Information Commission, security personnel, various people from the Ministry of the Interior, communications experts, and others. It was not long until we arrived in Jerusalem, where Mohamed Ibrahim Kamel gave his powerful address.

The Israelis were taken aback by the clear and uncompromising nature of the address. Night had fallen over Lod Airport. The fleet of automobiles bearing the delegation left the airport for Jerusalem, wending through high mountainous regions. I was in a medium-sized vehicle with First Secretary Hussein Hassouna, member of the working group, and the only diplomat who had accompanied Dr. Boutros-Ghali on his visit with President Sadat to Jerusalem in November 1977. We were accompanied by Ely Rubinstein, office director of the Israeli foreign minister, and made small talk about the locations of the battles that had taken place on these narrow mountain passes between the Arabs and Israel: the Jordanian contingent and the Palestinian groups who fought the Haganah and the Irgun, and other paramilitary Israeli groups.

Suddenly, Rubinstein turned to me and said, "And in that direction, you might see the Ramla prison, where we're hosting some of your friends."

I took his meaning, and rose to the implicit challenge. "They're not my friends," I said coolly, "they're my family. We're going to fight for their independence and freedom from Israeli occupation. We'll attain it, too."

Silence reigned for the next half-hour, until we arrived at the hotel.

I must admit here that the arrival in Israel and the drive along the lonely road made me extremely tense. Suddenly, I felt myself getting a nosebleed. I swallowed over and over again, hoping to stop the capillaries from bursting and soaking my shirt or jacket in blood. In a very short while, we were to meet the press. I could see the headlines now: "Egyptian Diplomat Steps from Official Vehicle Dripping with Blood!" I had no handkerchief or anything to stop the bleeding. I spoke to Hussein Hassouna, my traveling companion, about the problem. "Put your head out the window," he said calmly. "The cold air may stop the bleeding."

I did so; Ely Rubinstein had not noticed. The bleeding slowed, even though I felt I might catch pneumonia in very short order. Although the trip was brief, it felt endless, what with the nosebleed and one thing or another, but eventually it ended. We arrived at the hotel. The media—Israeli, Egyptian, and international—was waiting. I put a hand over my nose and hurried into the lobby. Some journalists tried to speak with me and ask me questions, as they did with all the Egyptian delegation members. I managed to slip past them to my room; crisis averted.

A short while later, when the bleeding had stopped entirely thanks to a doctor in our company, I went to Minister Mohamed Ibrahim Kamel's suite. It was opulent and spacious, luxuriously furnished, but the thing that caught my attention was the veritable mountain of fresh and dried fruit on the immensely long table in the minister's dining room. I had never seen anything the size of that thing. The fact is, when the Israelis had been staying at the Mena House, they had ordered great quantities of Egyptian food, enough for an army, though they were extremely few in number. It transpired that this was a way of annoying the hotel staff and straining the hospitality of their Egyptian hosts. We lost no time in repaying the favor with interest: a dinner for eight in the ministerial wing would result in dozens upon dozens of dishes being ordered, far more than any of us could ever eat.

The Israeli Minister of Defense Ezer Weizman arrived to pay his respects to his Egyptian counterpart. Moshe Dayan had left, having met Minister Mohamed Ibrahim Kamel at Lod Airport and seen him all the way to his suite at the Hilton. Weizman spoke some Arabic, in the Egyptian dialect, having served in Her Majesty's Air Force during the Second World War. He showed great pleasure and welcomed the minister warmly. At Ahmed Maher's instruction, I was sitting there to take the minutes of the meeting and make a note of important points raised by the Egyptian foreign minister and any of his visitors. During the small talk between the two foreign ministers, Kamel told Weizman that my father was an Egyptian pilot in the Second World War. Weizman asked my name and my father's. "I knew a great many Egyptian pilots," he said, "during the war, and in the years that followed." He went on to say that he had taken part in a training course alongside a Mohamed Sedki Mahmoud at Andover College in the UK.

"Are you sure you don't mean Gamal Afifi?" I asked. Afifi had mentioned having been with Weizman on the course.

"Yes, yes, that's right. It was Gamal Afifi, not Sedki Mahmoud!" he said. "I was unhappy to hear what became of them after 1967."

I made no reply. He asked me what kind of aircraft my father used to fly. "A Spitfire," I said, "and also a Hurricane, a Halifax, a Lancaster, a Dakota, and a Commando." I mentioned that he had spent his first years flying fighter planes, then moved on to bombers and finally carrier aircraft. "He," I said, meaning my father, "loves to tell his family war stories about the raids they conducted on Israel in '48 and '49."

"It won't happen again," said Weizman. "There will be peace between us."

The minister of defense then resumed his conversation with Egypt's foreign minister, pledging to do his best to achieve peace with Egypt, although he did mention that Israel's central concern was its security and future.

The Political Committee started work on the morning of January 17. Minister Mohamed Ibrahim Kamel delivered a powerful address calling for comprehensive peace, withdrawal from all occupied territories, and the rights of the Palestinian people. The U.S. representative spoke of much the same points that President Carter had mentioned in Aswan on January 4, as well as the points and conception of the agenda that the Americans had presented to the two parties on January 15. This was followed by a statement by Moshe Dayan, which accurately reflected the Israeli stances that were well known at the time. The meeting then adjourned for the committee to move from the mid-sized meeting hall in the basement to the twenty-first floor of the hotel for a tripartite closed conference for the American, Israeli, and Egyptian delegations only.

The three parties spoke once again of their points of view. Discussions revealed the great disparity between the Egyptian and Israeli views on a declaration of principles governing the settlement, which was stipulated in the U.S. agenda both had accepted.

The Israelis put forth their proposal of what the declaration of principles issued by the Political Committee should be:

- The governments of Egypt and Israel insist on continuing their efforts to reach a comprehensive settlement for peace in the region.
- Both governments are prepared to negotiate a peace treaty in order to achieve such a settlement, on the basis of the principles set out in Security Council Resolutions 242 and 338 of 1967 and 1973, respectively.

- Both governments agree that establishing a durable peace requires measures to be taken to guarantee the following:
  1. Israel's withdrawal from lands occupied in 1967.
  2. Ending all states of war and recognizing the sovereignty, integrity, and independence and rights of all states in the region to live in peace within secure and recognized borders, free from any threat of force.
  3. Guaranteeing freedom of navigation through international waterways (meaning, here, the Suez Canal and the Straits of Tiran).
  4. Achieving a just settlement of the refugee problem (please note that this does not refer to Palestinian refugees, but 'refugees' generally, with the goal of forcing us to deal with Israel's claim that there are Jews seeking refuge from Arab countries).
  5. Guaranteeing sovereignty and regional sovereignty via measures including the establishment of demilitarized zones.
- A just settlement for the issue of the Arab Palestinians living in Judea and Samaria, and the Gaza Strip, to be solved via self-rule and self-administration.

It was natural for us in the Egyptian delegation to see this Israeli proposal as unresponsive to our goals or demands. It was completely devoid of any reference to withdrawal from Sinai, the Golan, and the West Bank or mention of the inadmissibility of the acquisition of territory by war. The Israeli proposal also persisted in dealing with the issue of Palestinian refugees as a thing apart from the right to self-determination, which Palestinians and Arabs had specifically requested be addressed.

The working group then proposed the Egyptian draft declaration of principles, as we had prepared it in Cairo, with small modifications added during our stay in Jerusalem, in the light of our dealings with the Israelis:

- The Egyptians and Israelis are prepared to negotiate peace treaties based on the implementation of Security Council Resolutions 242 and 338 in all their parts.
- In order to reach such agreements, the following is required:
  1. Israel's withdrawal from Sinai, the Golan, the West Bank, and Gaza, in compliance with Resolution 242 and the principle of the inadmissibility of the acquisition of territory by war.
  2. Guaranteeing the safety of states' territories and their political independence via measures to be agreed upon and on a mutual basis of reciprocity.

3. Respecting the sovereignty, territorial inviolability, and political independence of all states.
4. A just settlement of the Palestinian problem in all its aspects on the basis of the right to self-determination, via negotiations attended by Egypt, Jordan, Israel, and representatives of the Palestinian people.
5. Terminating all calls to war and establishing peaceful relations among all states in the region via peace treaties based on the UN Charter.

Naturally, the Israelis rejected Egypt's proposal, which made no bones about seeking a fair settlement by means of withdrawal from the lands occupied in 1967, and put the Palestinian problem front and center not as a refugee problem but as an issue of an entire people's right to self-determination and self-rule with complete independence within their own country.

It soon became clear that things were not going to move forward so long as Egypt and Israel remained adamant. Their two positions may appear not so different to the untrained eye or the casual reader; however, trained legal and diplomatic minds would discern immediately the risks and traps embedded in each of the texts. Cyrus Vance came to meet the Egyptian foreign minister to discuss what the US could do in terms of offering initiatives or fresh ideas to overcome the hurdles between the two parties. Minister Mohamed Ibrahim Kamel reaffirmed what he had said to Moshe Dayan at that morning's official meeting. I remember noting at the time that Minister Kamel rejected Israel's call for forming committees to look into the issues and points on the agenda, which would divide the two parties before they could agree fully on the phrasing of the principles governing their negotiations, and thus the political settlement of the dispute.

Minister Kamel, according to the transcript of the meeting that I made at the time, stated that Egypt categorically refused the proposal made by Menachem Begin in Ismailiya and all the positions conveyed by the Israeli military delegation to Cairo on January 11 and 12. With regard to a Palestinian settlement, Egypt, he said, was insistent on the right to self-determination for the Palestinian people. The details of implementing this right, and the stages of execution of any agreement on such a matter, could be studied by Israel with a representative of the Palestinian people, in the presence of Egypt and Jordan, which were the two parties that had control of the West Bank and Gaza before the outbreak of military operations and Israel's attack on Egypt and Jordan in 1967.

Cyrus Vance attempted to broach the subject of Israel's settlements in Sinai. Minister Kamel flatly refused, telling him it was not up for debate.

This, he said, was a military issue to be settled between the Egyptian and Israeli delegates in the Military Committee, which was responsible for arranging the details of Israel's withdrawal from Egyptian lands and vacating the settlements and structures, airfields, ports, and other locations in Sinai to the boundaries between Egypt and Mandatory Palestine. Minister Kamel said that Egypt's understanding of the committees' jobs was that the Military Committee was responsible for all military matters and organizing the relations between the two sides so as to forestall any errors in military action, while the Political Committee's role was to draft an agreement for the negotiations on a political settlement between Egypt and Israel, to be included in a draft peace treaty. Its province was also to negotiate the future of the Palestinian problem in a manner granting the Palestinians the full right to self-determination.

Cyrus Vance listened intently. He was accompanied by his senior assistants, including Alfred Atherton, Harold Saunders, and Hermann Eilts, and other members of the U.S. National Security Council who worked under Zbigniew Brzezinski, such as William Quandt. On the Egyptian side, in addition to Minister Kamel, were Dr. Osama al-Baz, Ahmed Maher, and myself, Ahmed Aboul Gheit. Here I must mention the new situation in the Egyptian delegation's manner of dealing with these negotiations, or I should say consultations and talks. It had become clear that the new foreign minister, Mohamed Ibrahim Kamel, had no desire for a large number of assistants around him. Quietly and gradually, he began to thin the diplomatic working group that had been managing the negotiations over the previous months, specifically from December 1977 until their arrival in Jerusalem. It is my own estimation that Ahmed Maher, whose position greatly expanded in that period, had a decisive role in the process. Minister Kamel was also reluctant to rely on some of the diplomats who had been close to Minister Ismail Fahmy, which trimmed the ranks further. It must be said, though, that Minister Kamel kept up excellent relations with Minister of State for Foreign Affairs Boutros Boutros-Ghali, especially given the traditional tensions between the position of foreign minister, as the ultimate decision-maker for ministerial affairs with the mandate to direct policy, and that of a minister of state for foreign affairs, who might seek a role that is even independent of the foreign minister, which is almost invariably the case when such a system is in place.

Also, Minister Kamel kept up excellent, if wary, relations with Dr. Osama al-Baz. So did Ahmed Maher, thanks to the man's great influence and excellent relationship with all the most senior government officials in Egypt, and his profound knowledge of every Ministry file. I was told by Ahmed Maher and Dr. Osama al-Baz that Dr. Osama had conveyed to Ahmed Maher that members of the political taskforce were afraid of being dismissed, and that some of them were blaming Ahmed Maher. Maher assured them that this was the new minister's style, and that he would not change his methods just because some of them did not like them.

Things stayed as they were in the Ministry: Dr. Osama al-Baz, Ambassador Abdel Raouf El Reedy, Dr. Nabil al-Arabi, and I remained at the reins, doing the work, while the rest of the working group faded into the background, until Minister Mohamed Ibrahim Kamel's resignation in 1978.

Cyrus Vance left the meeting with Mohamed Ibrahim Kamel that evening on January 17 only to meet him again at dinner, to which Menachem Begin, Israel's prime minister, was also invited, with a promise to arrive at a satisfactory phrasing of a declaration of principles that both sides might find acceptable the next day.

18 Israel's Arrogance

T he next crisis to arise at the meeting in Jerusalem, after the failure to agree on a declaration of principles, was an issue raised at dinner by Menachem Begin.

Ambassador Ahmed Maher had asked me to prepare a short speech to be delivered by Minister Mohamed Ibrahim Kamel during the after-dinner toasts between himself and the Israeli prime minister. I prepared something that was the briefest possible, with the essential courtesies, yet balanced and appropriate for the occasion, no more. Ahmed Maher corrected some points of phrasing without changing the thrust of the speech. It was written down on cards, and we went to dinner, attended by what seemed like every Israeli official and decision-maker.

The food was exceptional. The dinner was served at a large number of round tables: we of the Egyptian delegation were not seated together but spread out among the Israeli guests. In addition, there was a long table for the prime minister and the main guests, Mohamed Ibrahim Kamel, Cyrus Vance, and Israel's senior politicians and their wives. Some of the Israelis at my table told me as well as Ahmed Maher, who insisted on my presence with him at all official functions, that the fish we were eating was from Bardawil Lake in Sinai. "We're getting it back," I retorted, but added, to lighten the mood, "and we'll sell it back to you for the market price!"

The dinner progressed with formal calm. In due course, Menachem Begin rose to say a few words of welcome to the Egyptian delegation and his other guests. Suddenly, he launched into an extensive speech, not written on paper but clearly prepared in his mind. He spoke of the sufferings of Jews the world over, their expulsion from Egypt, their torments in the Holocaust at Hitler's hands, the rights of states and communities to repel aggressions perpetrated on peaceful peoples such as Israel, and their rights to keep the spoils of an aggression that had been imposed on them, citing the experiences of European peoples as examples.

I grew progressively uncomfortable as I listened to this long polemic. I looked over at Ahmed Maher, trying to appear calm, but it was hard to hide my disquiet. I did not need to tell him that there were Israelis at our table who spoke Arabic. I tried to glance over at Minister Mohamed Ibrahim Kamel, whose body language from my oblique view of him betrayed tension. The fact is, we had completely failed to prepare for such an eventuality as we were now facing.

I observed the situation, making brief notes of the points covered by Menachem Begin. I also jotted down responses with conceptual and historical bases. We had incontrovertible logic on our side to irrevocably refute his arguments. But Begin's talk ended, and the floor now went to Minister Mohamed Ibrahim Kamel.

Naturally, our foreign minister never took out the notecards with the speech we had so painstakingly prepared. He said that he wanted to thank the Israeli government for their friendly reception and generous hospitality. "However, when I accepted this invitation to dinner, I had hoped to spend a quiet evening in good company with, I must say, very good food. But the prime minister has seen fit to inject issues into his after-dinner speech for which this is hardly the occasion." He went on, "I doubt that this dinner is the appropriate venue to respond to the prime minister. All I shall say is that the principles I laid out in my speech at the opening session of the Political Committee, the same principles the prime minister is rejecting now, are the only basis on which a fair and comprehensive peace can be built." He looked around. "As for my response to what he has said, I will keep it to myself until tomorrow's meeting of the Political Committee, which is the only appropriate venue for it."

The attendees were speechless. The tension was electric. There were no toasts, not by Minister Mohamed Ibrahim Kamel nor anyone else. Menachem Begin, shocked into silence, finally asked Cyrus Vance to speak. The dinner broke up as soon as Vance delivered a few well-chosen words. It was an eventful night in all senses of the word!

For years after that, Minister Mohamed Ibrahim Kamel would tell the story of his experience with Menachem Begin. On his way out of the dinner, Begin placed a hand on his shoulder. "Why so upset, my Egyptian guest? I meant no offense."

Minister Kamel brushed off the offending hand and looked askance at the Israeli. There must have been something in his expression, he recounted, because Begin actually took a step back.

In any case, the Political Committee's efforts ran into a number of thorny issues after only one closed session, issues that took a great deal of effort to overcome. We were in communication with Cairo moment by moment, and also continually exchanged coded telegrams with President Sadat, via the office of Vice President Hosni Mubarak, in which we explained the situation and any difficulties facing the negotiations. Before the ill-fated yet historic incident at dinner, Minister Mohamed Ibrahim Kamel, accompanied by Boutros Boutros-Ghali and Ahmed Maher al-Sayed, who transcribed their meeting, had gone to meet Menachem Begin at his office at the Knesset. Begin had been sharp and critical of all the Egyptian stances and the demands made by the foreign minister, both at Lod Airport on arrival or at the first meeting of the Political Committee in the basement of the Hilton that morning. We apprised President Sadat by telegram. Then came the confrontation at the dinner, whereupon Sadat realized which way the wind was blowing. He urged Minister Mohamed Ibrahim Kamel by telegram to remain calm and not allow himself to be provoked by anything the Israelis did, always offering positive reinforcement and encouragement, reassuring him that he was doing the right thing.

We went en masse—the entire Egyptian delegation, plus Egypt's press contingent—to express our encouragement to the minister in his suite. It was a powerful demonstration of support. That done, I sat with Ahmed Maher in his room next to the minister's suite. I muttered to him that the entire situation was deeply dissatisfying. The minister had been strong and decisive; however, I imagined that we should have responded to all of Begin's points and justifications, especially since the latter was a lover of history and had a profound knowledge of Europe's past. That continent has a record of its countries annexing each other's lands, displacing their populations, and other acts. We could have confronted Israel's logic and justifications with a knockout blow, especially since the dinner had been public, and attended by the international media.

Ahmed Maher looked at me, his eyes full of understanding. "Ahmed," he told me, "Minister Mohamed isn't that kind of person."

We woke the next morning to prepare for the Political Committee meeting. Cyrus Vance was scheduled to leave for DC on urgent business that evening, January 18, after another dinner with the Israelis and the Egyptians. Vance, as I may have said before, was not only a man of wisdom and integrity, he was also deeply committed and a man of his word. I saw him later, working at the second Camp David Summit, in September 1978, and the meeting that preceded it, at Leeds Castle in the UK, not to mention all the consultations I attended with Minister Mohamed Ibrahim Kamel and Ahmed Maher al-Sayed, and he was always quietly serious and committed to his work.

Years later, I saw Vance again, in 1985 and after. This was when I was a member of the Egyptian delegation to the UN in New York. He was in the habit of walking to his office from his apartment near Central Park. Walking from the bus stop that brought me from New Jersey across the Hudson River to Manhattan, I would see him on Fifth Avenue carrying a slim briefcase. My Middle Eastern features made me conspicuous; I always looked over at him and said hello, and he would always greet me back and give me a friendly smile. One day he stopped me. "You're one of the Egyptians we worked with for years in the negotiations, I think?"

"Yes," I said, and told him that I knew him well, from years of negotiations in Jerusalem, Cairo, Alexandria, Leeds Castle, and at the Camp David Summit. "I often sat at table with you."

"I remember now!" he said.

Cyrus Vance was one of America's great diplomats. He resigned from the Carter administration in May 1980 in protest against the failed military operation conducted by the US against Iran during the hostage crisis in the U.S. embassy in Tehran.

But I digress. Cyrus Vance and his assistants came to offer Minister Mohamed Ibrahim Kamel a proposal that sought to reconcile the Egyptian and U.S. views. A new phrasing of the declaration of principles, the U.S. proposal consisted of four specific points:

- The governments of Egypt and Israel insist on continuing their efforts to reach a comprehensive and peaceful settlement for the conflict in the Middle East.
- Within the framework of this settlement, both sides declare that they are prepared to negotiate peace treaties to implement Security Council Resolutions 242 and 338.
- A fair solution to the issues of the West Bank and Gaza will be found, enabling the Arab Palestinians to take part in self-determination, by means of talks attended by Egypt, Jordan, Israel, and representatives of the Arab Palestinians.
- There will be an end to all states of war, the respect for sovereignty and territorial integrity, and the political independence of all states in the region. Peaceful, normal relations will be established through peace treaties.

The U.S. proposal, I must say, was disappointing. The Americans made no mention of withdrawal; worse, it referred to the Palestinians as "Arab Palestinians," Israel's phrasing, with which I imagine the reader is now familiar, in the light of its repetition all that month since December 14, 1977, at the Mena House Conference and up to January 18, 1978.

Mohamed Ibrahim Kamel was frank about the absence of any reference to withdrawal, the ending of Israeli occupation of Arab lands, and what is known as the Palestinian problem and the Palestinian people, not "Arab Palestinians" versus "Jewish Palestinians," as Menachem Begin was attempting to formulate the issue.

The Americans, represented that day by Saunders and Atherton, who were crafting the U.S. vision and leading attempts to bring the two sides closer together, said that we needed to realize that there was another side to the negotiations, the Israeli side, with its own demands and positions. "These are not U.S.–Egypt negotiations, but Israel–Egypt negotiations."

"In that case," we replied, "we have no desire for a declaration of principles that reflects neither our interests, nor our vision or goals."

The Americans then suggested we craft an Egyptian proposal for the Palestinian lands and the issue of Palestine, instead of the one proposed by Begin. We refused to present a comprehensive Egyptian proposal for the Palestinian problem, but we did insist on including the phrase, "a fair settlement of the Palestinian problem in all its aspects." As it happened, developments in the next stage, in May and June 1978, and then in Leeds Castle in July 1978, forced us to offer our own proposal for a Palestinian resolution.

The arguments between the Egyptians and Americans continued for several hours. The meeting then broke up, with plans to resume discussions in the afternoon. I grabbed a quick lunch, having learned from Dr. Esmat Abdel Meguid that he was going to visit al-Aqsa Mosque, and went along.

It was a stunning visit. I entered the mosque; I felt more shaken by this visit than by almost anything that had happened before in my life. The occupation, and its guards, cast a pall over everything. We visited the Mosque of Omar. I stood by the Rock. We took a walk around Old Jerusalem. Our Israeli guides insisted we visit the Western Wall. Dr. Esmat picked up the obligatory yarmulke, but refused to put it on. I watched him through the iron barrier to the courtyard, having preferred not to accompany him myself.

We left there about an hour later, and I went sightseeing with Ahmed Maher al-Sayed in the western quarter of the city, in the company of some Israeli security personnel in civilian clothes. The shops, I noticed, seemed to be doing brisk business. The displays were smart and tasteful, as though I were in a European city transplanted into the Middle East.

The next thing I noted was that a lot of the young men, shopping or walking around, seemed to be carrying automatic weapons. I found it strange and asked our security detail about it. Some of them were about those boys' age. "It's because we need to be vigilant, defend our streets against possible Palestinian attacks. They're motivated. Everyone does their bit."

I must admit I found it an odd phenomenon. There could so easily be an accident—so many accidents—in such a society, armed to the teeth, with or without a reason. I remembered what I had read of the Spartans, of a city always armed and ready for battle.

When we got back to our hotel, Ahmed Maher received the modified U.S. proposal for the principles for a settlement from the Americans, the one Vance had promised to craft and give us after his morning meeting with Kamel. We read it:

- A repetition of the paragraph about the governments of Egypt and Israel insisting on continuing their efforts to reach a comprehensive and peaceful settlement for the region, and that, within the framework of this settlement, both sides declared their readiness to negotiate peace treaties to implement Security Council Resolutions 242 and 338 in all their parts.
- Israel will withdraw from lands occupied in 1967. There will be safe and recognized boundaries for all countries. (This was a new paragraph added by the Americans in light of their meeting with Egypt's foreign minister, which had been absent from the first U.S. proposal.)
- There will be an end to all states of war, the respect for sovereignty and territorial integrity, and the political independence of all states in the region. Peaceful, normal relations will be established between states in accordance with the UN Charter.

It was clear to us after a cursory reading that there was still no response to specific Egyptian demands, either to do with withdrawal, or the Palestinian question, conspicuous by its absence. Bemused by the continued omission, we took the proposal up to Minister Kamel to discuss it with him.

Once upstairs, we were assailed by a barrage of questions from the minister's assistants and security personnel. "The minister's been asking where you were! We're leaving immediately for Cairo on President Sadat's instructions!"

The minister was currently in the delegations' communications center, trying to speak to the president. I went to the minister's suite, while Ahmed Maher went to the communications room to find out more.

Minister Kamel came back into his suite, accompanied by Ahmed Maher. He had been unable to get the president to agree to any postponement of our departure, nor to allow only himself to leave while the rest of the Egyptian delegation remained, as a message that negotiations had not been broken off. Minister Kamel had had a growing conviction, these past few days, that President Sadat's initiative had unlocked a great opportunity for Egypt to succeed, and perhaps the Arabs along with it, in unmasking Israel's stalling and closing off its avenues of evasion. This, he felt, might make the Israelis more inclined to agree to Egypt's and Palestine's demands for withdrawal from Sinai, and accept a fair settlement to the Palestinian–Israeli conflict. The truth, which I find incontrovertible both then and now, is that the initiative did, in fact, unmask the Israeli position, reenergized Egypt's stance, and made it possible to move forward, making progress that culminated nine months later in the Camp David Accords of September 1978.

I gave a lot of thought to the recall order, and spoke to Ahmed Maher about it a great deal. The minister had a firm conviction that Egypt and the Arabs were on the path to starting group negotiations with Israel, by getting back the Geneva Conference of 1977. The Foreign Ministry and the minister were working energetically to plan and execute all the organizational procedures for the Geneva Conference to be held once more. "Can you believe," I asked, "after we took the initiative, visited Jerusalem, got things moving, we're still getting this hard-line haughtiness from Israel?"

"Yes," he simply replied.

"What do you think it would have been like, then, if we hadn't done all that at the Geneva Conference, with all the competition and conflict and disputes about different Arab interests, to say nothing of each country's different leanings?" I added. "President Sadat did well to move independently. Egypt is Egypt, after all."

To return to President Sadat's order for the recall of the Egyptian delegation, Sadat had of course been cognizant of Israel's stubbornness at the Ismailiya Summit on December 25, and that it went all the way to the top. He knew that Israel had bluntly demanded to keep air bases and settlements on Egyptian soil. He was aware of the Israeli view of the nature of a Palestinian settlement, and that the only thing Israel had for the Palestinians was an offer of self-rule for their own citizens, the "Arab Palestinians"(!), which amounted to letting them decide what time to let their businesses open and close, and how to run their cities and villages, as Moshe Dayan told Esmat Abdel Meguid in Ismailiya.

The president also recognized Israel's intransigence, which was clear in its officials' proposals during the Political Committee meetings in Jerusalem, in Minister Mohamed Ibrahim Kamel's meetings with Israeli leaders, and finally in Menachem Begin's after-dinner speech, leaving no doubt that the Israelis remained unconvinced that peace with Egypt would require serious Israeli decisions to withdraw from occupied Egyptian lands, and to propose a sane, serious, and rational vision for a Palestinian–Israeli settlement that was defensible by Egypt and the Arabs. Hence Sadat's decision to withdraw, having realized that a serious Israeli move was not yet in the offing, and that he would need more coordination with the US to apply pressure on Menachem Begin, an appeal to the peaceful tendencies within Israeli society, and international and U.S. pressure, especially from American Jews, to further block Menachem Begin's avenues of evasion and make him feel forced to seek a settlement satisfactory for both parties.

I now return to the meetings conducted by Mohamed Ibrahim Kamel with Menachem Begin, who was, I found, quite curt, indeed belligerent, in all his meetings with the Egyptian minister, who in turn—not unprepared for such incivility—remained calm and collected, refraining from repaying him in kind, perhaps so as not to be accused by the president of giving free rein to his feelings and responding to the gauntlet thrown down by Begin. I spoke to Ahmed Maher of this. "Ahmed," he said in response, "Minister Kamel is a sensible man and will not abort things. It's going to be a long, long road, from all I see and hear."

Cyrus Vance came to the minister's suite late at night on January 18 to express his distress, and President Carter's dismay, at the breaking off of negotiations. He had convinced the Israelis, he said, to accept the modified phrasing for the draft declaration of principles penned by the US, especially the paragraph on withdrawal. He was also, he said, close to a breakthrough in finding a phrasing acceptable to the Israelis on the Palestinian question; he just needed a few more hours.

Minister Mohamed Ibrahim Kamel spoke to him frankly. His opinion, he said, was that the Israeli stances, which were "almost arrogant in nature," had aborted this round of talks. However, what was certain was that there would be future rounds, after more rethinking and planning for the situation.

"I have instructions from President Carter," said Cyrus Vance, "to proceed to Cairo and postpone my return to Washington, in order to take the situation in hand and prevent things from deteriorating." He said he wanted to rebuild a position that allowed for a return to negotiations—a new regrouping and preparation stage.

This new stage Vance spoke of lasted six months. During that time, Egypt intensified its communications with the US, and Washington, in turn, made its own efforts to establish a position conducive to a rapprochement between the Egyptians and Israelis, on the path to the first high-level meeting between the parties in July 1978 at Leeds Castle. Anyone wanting to know more about that period may see the books written by Ministers Mahmoud Riyad, Ismail Fahmy, Mohamed Ibrahim Kamel, and Esmat Abdel Meguid.

19 Attempts to Advance the Negotiations

Sadat's Boeing 737, which the president had placed at the disposal of the Egyptian negotiating team, came in for a landing. It had been used to transport all the members of the Egyptian delegation, their security and intelligence personnel and top-secret equipment and devices, and everything else the huge delegation had packed, in addition to the massive Egyptian press corps accompanying them.

It was 0100 hours when the aircraft took off from Lod Airport en route to Cairo, after about sixty hours in Jerusalem, full of activity, diligent activity, meetings and negotiations. I slumped in my seat, exhausted, and tried to take stock of the situation. Perhaps I could set down my assessment of things in a memorandum for the foreign minister and give it to him later that morning.

But I was too tired. The next thing I knew, I was being shaken awake. We had reached Cairo Airport. Ahmed Maher asked us all to meet him early in his office at the Foreign Ministry in Tahrir Palace, to get our documents in order in preparation for the U.S. secretary of state's arrival the next day, January 20, 1978.

On my arrival at the ministry on January 19, I opened my metal strongbox. This was where I kept all my important documents and notes that might be needed at any moment in the negotiations with Israel or the consultations with the Americans. In these files was everything that had taken place between the Arabs and Israel, between Cairo and Tel Aviv, from 1948 to 1978. Indeed, there were many documents on the background of the conflict that dated back to Theodor Herzl's publication

215

of *The Jewish State* in 1898, through Ottoman rule of Palestine, international Zionist communications with the Ottoman sultan in Istanbul, the Balfour Declaration, and all that had taken place, in sum, on Palestinian soil since the British mandate was decided by the League of Nations at the Versailles Conference in 1919.

The strongbox, as you may imagine, was stuffed to bursting. Over the next nine months, until Camp David on September 5, it was joined by a number of similar strongboxes, containing everything we might conceivably need: international peace treaties, law books, reference books on the history of the region, and a number of papers published by eminent scholars on Palestine and the Arab–Israeli conflict. Today, I often look at my iPad—capable of storing and transporting tens of thousands of documents, to say nothing of the ease of access to thousands of websites for more information—and compare our capacities then with what we have today.

I returned all the files—with help, of course—to their respective closets and filing cabinets. I then started on an evaluation of the general situation we faced after our return from Jerusalem, and the requirements of the upcoming stage of negotiations, or what I thought we would require at any rate.

The diplomatic working group held another meeting to look into the situation. I must repeat that this was an experienced and capable legal team. Ambassador Abdel Raouf El Reedy was a legal mind who had long experience with the UN, in New York more than once, and in Geneva, also more than once. There was Ambassador Nabil al-Arabi, who had a PhD in international law from New York University. They had both debated with legal experts in Israel's delegation during the proceedings of the Political Committee in Jerusalem, and in Cairo as well, at the preparatory meeting at Mena House Hotel. One of these experts was Dr. Barak, who went on to become Israel's public prosecutor, and another was the extreme right-wing legal expert Meir Rosenne.

There was also Amre Moussa, energetic and ambitious as usual, also a law graduate. In fact, the team entrusted with negotiating with Israel was almost entirely composed of legal experts with law degrees from premier universities in the west. Dr. Esmat Abdel Meguid had a PhD from the Sorbonne; First Secretary Hussein Hassouna had a PhD from Oxford; First Secretary Mohamed ElBaradei had a degree from New York University; and Dr. Osama al-Baz had earned his PhD at Harvard. This was a highly qualified team, although, as I have said, it gradually shrank. The Camp David Summit, and before that the negotiating ministers' conference at Leeds Castle, was attended only by Ahmed Maher al-Sayed, Abdel Raouf El Reedy, Nabil al-Arabi, myself, and, of course, the main figure in the negotiations, Dr. Osama al-Baz.

I prepared a general assessment of the situation for Minister Mohamed Ibrahim Kamel, with the permission of Ahmed Maher al-Sayed. It covered the other Arab countries' deep resentment toward President Sadat's initiative, and their inability to understand its intentions or how far it went. I also made it clear that all the communications from different capital cities revealed Jordan's understanding of the initiative and the reasons for it, although Jordan was extremely wary of showing any support for fear of provoking Syria's and the Arabs' wrath outside its borders and of offending the Palestinians living in Jordan on the domestic front. Meanwhile, Saudi Arabia expressed—quietly and in secret—its understanding of and possibly even support for the Egyptian efforts, although publicly it stated that it had reservations and was not assured of the possibility of success. Communications later revealed a Saudi conviction, fueled by Israel's reactions and Begin's offers, that the initiative was on the path to foundering on the rocks of Israeli intransigency.

The Soviets had decided to fight the initiative, which had pushed them out of the equation of Middle East peace efforts. I have written elsewhere about the pressure the Soviets and Syrians brought to bear on then UN Secretary-General Kurt Waldheim to block UN participation in the Jerusalem meetings. At the Mena House, the UN was represented by Finnish General Ensio Siilasvuo and James Jonah from Sierra Leone, assistants to the secretary-general. Waldheim stood firm on Mena House; still, there were mounting pressures on him at the time of Jerusalem. I told Ahmed Maher al-Sayed that it was absolutely essential for Minister Mohamed Ibrahim Kamel to convey his greetings to Waldheim at the first possible opportunity, keep up active and friendly relations with the secretary-general, and otherwise not allow him to fall prey to the pressures of the Soviets or anyone else. In that memorandum, I emphasized that unless the Israelis were genuine and sincere about wanting to return Sinai to Egypt, and unless the situation was similarly clear with regard to a Palestinian settlement and the right to statehood, these demands would be reduced to mere negotiating points and tactical evasive maneuvers. We would find ourselves in deep trouble, I noted, up against a wall of Israeli haughtiness that would take a lot of time and effort to break down.

I then proposed the traditional talking points we always prepared for a foreign minister meeting a counterpart. This was for Minister Kamel's meeting with Cyrus Vance, on his way to Egypt from Jerusalem, en route to Washington. The suggested talking points included a reaffirmation of the Egyptian position, and a reminder that after Sadat's initiative, Egypt had acted with the goal of arriving at a comprehensive settlement of the conflict, both Israel's conflict with its Arab neighbors and the

Palestine–Israel conflict. I then suggested he express his rejection of the Israeli position and their disdain for Egypt's views, and demand that the Americans take a definite stand and impose their view on Israel.

Cyrus Vance arrived in Cairo on January 20 and met with President Sadat and Minister Kamel. He conveyed an invitation to President Sadat from President Carter to visit Washington for consultations on February 4. Vance again presented the U.S. proposal for a declaration of principles, with specific changes. The Americans were still confident in their ability to convince both sides to return to direct negotiations once the US had managed to resolve the dispute about the declaration of principles. I doubt that Vance knew his efforts were for naught: Israel had revealed positions that we were simply unable to accept or live with. The U.S. proposal, mentioned above, contained two references to the Palestinian question in Paragraph 5: one clearly referenced the Egyptian view, while the other took Israel's proposals into account—the proposals that Egypt found unacceptable.

On the same day, we presented Vance with Egypt's responses to his proposals. Egypt insisted on withdrawal from occupied territories, the inadmissibility of the acquisition of territory by war, the indispensability of reaching a settlement for the Palestinians, the right of Palestinians to take part in self-determination, and Palestinian representatives taking part in negotiations with Israel, with the participation of both Egypt and Jordan. It was clear that Egypt had latched onto the phrase Carter uttered in his speech in Aswan on January 4. That phrasing was mentioned by William Quandt, the assistant to U.S. National Security Advisor Brzezinski, in a telephone call from Warsaw to Dr. Ashraf Ghorbal, when Quandt was visiting Poland with President Carter before his visit to Aswan. He told Ghorbal that Carter planned to say this in front of an international audience for the first time, taking a stand vis-à-vis the Arab–Israeli dispute, as a way of dealing with the Palestinian problem.

Vance left after issuing the invitation, which was enthusiastically accepted by Sadat. We in the working group and the Office of the Foreign Minister started to prepare the Egyptian strategy for dealing with this vitally important presidential visit. In our judgment, this stage would require an attempt to seek some flexibility in the Israeli position. We needed to try to shake Israel loose from its almost symbiotic relationship with the Americans, and attempt to convince the U.S. president to use his influence and position to soften the Israeli position, especially as everything we kept hearing from the US indicated that the Jewish community in the United States were exasperated with Menachem Begin's mule-headedness and his insistence on defending the indefensible.

One question kept presenting itself: Did the U.S. president actually want to use his potential influence over Israel, given that it had many supporters in the US? This was what Sadat and Kamel would try to find out on their visit to Washington.

President Carter asked President Sadat to let the Israeli Military Negotiations Committee stay on in Egypt, despite the Egyptian diplomatic delegation having been withdrawn from Jerusalem, and despite the positions taken by Israel in its negotiations—political and military—with Egypt. Sadat agreed. I happen to know that the foreign minister was livid: not two days ago, he had tried to convince Sadat to allow a small working group to remain in Jerusalem so as to retain a thread of connection, however small, but Sadat had refused. Developments, though, proved that Sadat was a fox, patient and far-sighted, always keeping his eyes on the prize. His aim was to keep up the closest-possible relationship with the U.S. president, in the service of his ultimate goals. Naturally, this made him appear at times to offer easy concessions. Still, his motivations were always clear, at least to himself.

One of President Sadat's goals was to secure massive economic support from the west, to make up for Arab economic aid to Egypt being cut off. Sure enough, Egypt began to receive generous aid from the US and other nations, foremost among them Germany and Japan. President Sadat also sought to break the Soviet stranglehold on Egyptian armament supplies, and open Egypt up to western powers. Hence his desire for U.S. fighter aircraft, even ones less advanced than those supplied to Israel and Saudi Arabia, to restore the balance in U.S. relations with the countries in the region. He sought to score a large-scale deal of U.S. F-5 fighters, which, while puny next to their sisters in the American arsenal, were at least a start.

The working group was busy preparing for the visit. Israeli proposals came thick and fast, duly noted and followed up by our ambassadors in various world capitals. A prominent American university professor asked one of our ambassadors about Egypt's decision, specifically the Egyptian minister of the interior's decision, to allow the joint Egyptian–British administration in Sudan to run the area of Halayeb, north of Parallel 22, the line demarcating the Egypt–Sudan border, despite Egypt having sovereignty over this area. The meaning behind her question was perfectly clear: it was an Israeli attempt to probe the issue so as to exploit it in the service of Israel's demand to keep military bases and Israeli settlements in Sinai, although it was completely under Egyptian sovereignty to the borders between Egypt and Mandatory Palestine, the 1922 border, reaffirming Egypt's borders of 1906 with the Ottoman Empire.

Other suggestions were floated. There were all kinds of queries about Gaza, as if Israel saw it as a prize for Egypt and not a burden of responsibility. In addition, there was the danger of further dividing the Palestinian crisis by splitting it into Gaza, under Egyptian administration, and the West Bank, under Israel. Israel kept harping on this issue in public, in official statements issued by the prime minister. UN Security Council Resolution 242 for 1967 did not apply, it said, to the West Bank and Gaza because these lands had fallen into Israel's hands through war. The prime minister elaborated on his views in a proposal to Egypt, dubbed the 'Functional Solution.' He suggested that the Palestinians administrate their own internal issues fully, following a withdrawal of (Israeli) military administration from the West Bank, while the occupation, as described in Yigal Allon's project, continued in a broad swath between Palestinian territory and Jordan's, across the river, which he justified with a claim of potential threats from Iraq against Jordan and Israel.

All of this, as I have said, so provoked many Americans that former Vice-President Hubert Humphrey went so far as to write to Menachem Begin just two days before Humphrey's death of bladder cancer, criticizing the prime minister's actions and calling on Israel to modify its views and attitudes to enable the Israelis to move forward and achieve the peace with the Egyptians that the Middle East so desperately needed.

The Israelis, before Sadat's visit to Washington, had redoubled construction efforts in Yamit, an Israeli settlement on the Red Sea, in Sinai. Egypt kept its temper, ignoring this provocation. In later years, it came out that Menachem Begin had asked Yitzhak Sharon, Moshe Dayan, and Ezer Weizman to meet and discuss the possibility of offering Egypt some flexibility in Israel's demands and positions for a settlement with Egypt. The three generals discussed this issue at a working dinner at Moshe Dayan's home, assisted by a great many maps of Sinai. The articles and books that contained accounts leaked from this meeting stated that Sharon, then minister of agriculture, insisted on the settlements, even asking for a revival and expansion of the building efforts. He did, though, express a willingness to relinquish the Israeli air bases in Sinai in exchange for building replacement bases in the Naqab desert in Sinai, if the US would foot the bill. Ezer Weizman disagreed, calling for the air bases to remain. If given up, he said, they would be extremely costly to replace.

In any case, the generals did not discuss security concerns, which the Israeli side hardly ever failed to bring up in any discussion with Egyptian military personnel. Weizman went on to say the settlements should be dismantled, assuring the others that a single Israeli mechanized infantry division was enough to function as an Israeli colony in the Naqab desert, without the need for settlements.

These studies and articles also mentioned that Menachem Begin and Moshe Dayan ultimately toed the Israeli line on settlements, not only keeping but expanding them. Ditto with air bases, and intensifying their usage. Weizman rejected this. It may be appropriate here to offer a very brief character sketch of Weizman, who managed to convey to Sadat that he was completely convinced of the necessity of peace with Egypt, and therefore the need to make concessions and not make things harder. What is also certain is that Weizman sought to achieve one of Israel's long-term goals, namely a separate peace with Egypt.

Back to the meetings of the Military Committee. From January 31 to February 2, the day before Sadat left for Washington, the committee convened. Ambassador Nabil al-Arabi took part in the Egyptian military delegation, as the delegation's legal counsel. In those three days, three meetings, or extra sessions, were held, over and above those held on January 12. While some progress was made, many of the main issues failed to move forward. The Israelis said they would agree to clear all the air bases in exchange for Egypt's assurance that it would allow them to use a single air base, Maliz or Tamada, and limit the forces using it to one or two fleets, stipulating an additional one of the following:

- The Israelis would only withdraw from this airfield after the rest of the withdrawal from Sinai, outside of the scheduled time frame; or
- The airfield is cleared on schedule, on an extended withdrawal schedule longer than the proposed time frame of three to five years; or
- If a schedule cannot be agreed upon, the alternative is restricting Egyptian sovereignty, that is, limited sovereignty.

The Israelis reemphasized their acceptance of the Egyptian proposal that the early warning stations already established in Sinai be managed by a third party—the US—and noted that the withdrawal would be delayed if the US refused. They then took to negotiating their military presence in Sinai. First they proposed that Sinai be demilitarized in its entirety—which meant that the mechanized infantry division stationed east of the Suez Canal, up to the Sinai passes, would return to the western bank of the canal—in return for the removal of the early warning stations and reduction of the period of Israel's presence in one of the Sinai air bases, by which they meant Ras al-Naqab. The Israelis explained that these proposals did not mean that Egyptian army personnel could not enter Sinai; what it did mean was that Egypt could not station its forces east of the canal.

The Israelis went on making proposals. The Egyptian military representatives, and Dr. Nabil al-Arabi, author of the detailed report later presented to the foreign minister, noted that the Israelis appeared to be calling for a zone in Sinai where the UN flag should be flown until 2001. Their proposals also allowed Israelis to enjoy freedom of movement, of building colonies and settling, and of stationing their forces in Sinai. The Israeli proposals introduced new terminology. "The Arabs of Sinai," they said, could enter this area, with the exception of Egyptian citizens and nationals(!). This finally led the Egyptian military team to conclude that their aim was the establishment of an Israeli zone under the UN flag. This violated Egyptian sovereignty and our ability to defend Sinai and the Suez Canal against any future aggression.

During the same negotiations, Egypt countered with a proposal for complete Israeli withdrawal to international borders, with a UN buffer zone on both sides of the border for a specified period of time, taking into account the Israeli and Egyptian depths so that the Israeli buffer zone would be roughly five kilometers deep. Israel agreed to the buffer zones. The discussion on the depth of each buffer zone persisted for a while, though.

The Military Committee ended its meetings without making any progress, although they did afford an opportunity to find out the details of how the other side thought and planned from the form of their proposed settlement.

It was time to leave for Washington, via Morocco. This was a task that was both difficult and enthralling.

20 Camp David I

The previous chapters covered my observations of the peace efforts, led by President Anwar al-Sadat, and his initiative in going to Jerusalem. They outlined the Egyptian activity that followed, calling for the preparatory conference on December 14, 1977, at the Mena House Hotel in the shadow of the Giza Pyramids; Sadat's summit with Begin that followed in Ismailiya on December 24; the Military and Political Committee meetings with the U.S. secretary of state's participation that failed to produce the required breakthrough; and Sadat receiving an invitation from President Carter to visit Washington on February 3, 1978, to look into how to advance and achieve the goals of the peace initiative.

Egypt's goal, as I mentioned, was to achieve an unprecedented degree of Egyptian–American understanding that could outweigh the Israeli prime minister's stubbornness in refusing to work with the definitely peaceful intentions on the Egyptian side. Sadat's aims never strayed far from that goal. He aimed to get the American Jewish community on his side, and benefit from that community's clout with Israel. Indeed, he hoped to convince American Jewish leaders of this course of action and further convince them to talk some sense into Begin.

As the official responsible for the Palestinian crisis at the foreign minister's office, I took to preparing a great many documents and papers I thought the minister might need to go over at important meetings. I also, at the behest of Ahmed Maher al-Sayed, prepared some briefs that analyzed the situation Egypt faced in its efforts to achieve a breakthrough, as well as what we needed to do to get the US on our side and assist us in pressuring Israel.

We let the minister in on our way of thinking, and briefed him on the opinions of the other departments of the Foreign Ministry. We needed to convey to the US how frustrated we were with Menachem Begin's attitude, actions, and stances, which were pushing the peace initiative to the brink of failure. The unprecedented opportunity to find a peaceful settlement for the Arab–Israeli problem was in grave danger of being wasted.

Egypt's goal at the time was to win over American and international public opinion. President Sadat was scheduled for a great many interviews and speeches, including one before the U.S. National Press Club and other avenues that would afford the president the opportunity to urge the US to see things his way.

It was decided that I should accompany the foreign minister on the difficult mission to the US. Although I preferred to fly commercial, in order to avoid the restrictions that came with flying aboard the presidential aircraft, and also to go directly to Washington with one stopover in a European capital, Ahmed Maher al-Sayed wanted me with him in Morocco, where Sadat was scheduled to stop over on his way to Washington. So I boarded the ancillary services Boeing 737 that accompanied the president's Boeing 707, leaving Cairo about three hours after the first airplane took off.

We arrived in Morocco on February 2. We were staying at the Rabat Sheraton, a first for all of us: Mohamed Ibrahim Kamel, Ahmed Maher al-Sayed, and two members of the office staff, Counselor Mohamed al-Zu'eibi, and me, then first secretary. The first thing I discovered on that short visit was that this hospitable Arab country enjoyed stunning scenery and a profound sense of belonging to its Arab and Islamic roots—the two elements governing everything about Morocco. I visited the Maghreb many times in later years, in the company of every Egyptian foreign minister whom I served as assistant: Kamal Hassan Ali, Esmat Abdel Meguid, and Amre Moussa. I then went as foreign minister myself. During these many visits, although short, I became acquainted with the Moroccan way of life. This deeply Arab society nevertheless enjoys a magnificent diversity, and has managed to preserve its Islamic heritage despite years of harsh French and Spanish colonization.

On the subject of President Sadat's initiative, I traveled with Lieutenant-General Kamal Hassan Ali, deputy prime minister and foreign minister, to Rabat in October 1983 to arrange and prepare for a joint Egyptian–Moroccan effort for Egypt to regain its membership in what was then known as the Organization of the Islamic Conference, which had frozen Egypt's membership after Egypt signed the peace treaty with Israel in 1979. We arrived in Rabat in 1983, on the generous invitation of King Hassan II, who was to head an Islamic summit in Morocco in early 1984. His Majesty wished to coordinate our roles, including what we needed to do in Egypt and what he would take upon himself before the summit to secure an invitation for Egypt to join—an effort that, incidentally, succeeded in due course.

As I was saying, during our stay at a Moroccan guest villa in Rabat, Kamal Hassan Ali told us about his experiences at the start of President Sadat's initiative in 1977, when the Egyptians and Israelis met under Moroccan sponsorship for the first time on Moroccan soil. Kamal Hassan Ali also told this story years later in his book, *Muharibun wa mufawwidun* (Warriors and Negotiators), published in 1986, a year after he left his post as prime minister of Egypt. He wrote that he had been assigned by President Sadat to accompany Hassan al-Tohami on a mission to Morocco in the summer of 1975. They went to Ifrane, Morocco's 'Garden City,' to meet King Hassan II, at one of the palaces in the city.

Kamal Hassan Ali, who was chief of Egyptian Intelligence at that time, told us in 1983, "I went to Cairo Airport and boarded one of the presidential aircraft, with Hassan al-Tohami. On the flight, I expected Hassan al-Tohami to tell me the mission we were traveling for; he didn't. I tried to ask; he deferred answering until we arrived.

"In Ifrane, we were put up at the guest palace facing the royal palace. I preferred not to pester Hassan al-Tohami as to the nature of our mission, and left it to him to decide when I needed to know. Of course, I was eager to find out, and tried to figure it out on my own.

"We went into the palace with the king of Morocco. As we were climbing the palace stairs, the king asked Hassan al-Tohami if he preferred a private meeting—a 'tête-à-tête,' as he called it—or a public meeting. Hassan al-Tohami said he preferred a private meeting.

"We entered a large conference hall in which there were only two people. They looked European, French to be precise. But the face of one of them seemed familiar; if I had not met him, I had at least seen his photograph. We shook hands, then His Majesty guided me outside, leaving Hassan al-Tohami with the two guests.

"No sooner did I leave for the guest palace than a photograph of one of the men leapt to my mind."

In his book, Kamal Hassan Ali recounts his first meeting with Moshe Dayan, the Israeli foreign minister, and Moshe Kamhi, secretary-general of the Israeli Foreign Ministry. He told us this anecdote in its entirety when we were together at that Moroccan guest villa. I could not have imagined at the time that he would speak of it, indeed write it down, in *Muharibun wa mufawwidun* (Warriors and Negotiators). At the time, I thought—still do—that the story held some embarrassment for him, having been dragged from, and to, Cairo without ever being apprised of the nature of his mission.

I was at Kamal Hassan Ali's home while he was writing some of *Muharibun wa mufawwidun* (Warriors and Negotiators) when he was prime minister. I argued that he should cast a modest veil over this incident, which could reflect negatively on his role as a participant in a mission he had no clue about. However, he insisted on setting it down, telling me he wanted to record everything for posterity. He added it was no reflection on him, but on Hassan al-Tohami, who withheld information on what was supposed to be a joint mission for the two of them, as President Sadat revealed to the chief of Egyptian Intelligence on their return to Cairo.

Back to President Sadat's visit to Morocco in February 1978, which was therefore an expression of gratitude from the Egyptian president for the tacit service done him by the king of Morocco, arranging an opportunity for Egypt and Israel to meet twice in July 1977, in preparation for President Sadat's visit to Jerusalem. The visit to Rabat in February 1978 was short, but it paved the way for a great many more, as I mentioned above. I made the acquaintance of the country's magnificent Moorish architecture and enjoyed the famed Moroccan cuisine. I experienced the fabled generosity of Morocco on one notable occasion, when we were invited to a dinner by the Moroccan foreign minister on the evening of February 2. We were seated eight to a table, Egyptians and Moroccans. The banquet began with a large plate of a single dish placed on each table. I wasted no time in tucking in. My Moroccan dinner companions, though, merely tasted the food. I shrugged, and went on steadily eating. Soon enough, the large platter was taken away, and replaced with a second, then a third. There were a total of eight dishes. Naturally, after the third dish, I had had enough; the Moroccans, though, kept on tasting, while I looked on, stomach full! I learned my lesson well. From then on, in every subsequent visit to Morocco, I approached these generous dishes with caution.

We left Rabat for Washington on February 3, and arrived the same afternoon, after a harrowing and dangerous journey. Our airplane had technical difficulties and had to land in the Azores for repairs. The flight out was made unpleasant by the problem, which returned after we left the Azores, forcing us to turn back to the island airport. I was uneasy, as you may imagine. Our eventual return from Washington to Europe was even more fraught. Our Boeing 737 had been scheduled to refuel at

Gander International Airport, Newfoundland, Canada, for the long trip to Munich. We arrived at Gander in the middle of a blizzard. The pilot had terrible trouble landing, and we spent hours in the airport before finally being able to leave for Europe.

When we arrived in DC, we were taken to our quarters at Embassy Row Hotel, close to the Egyptian embassy. Sadat, however, proceeded directly to the Camp David resort, where the American president spent his leisure time. The two presidents spent February 3 and 4 there, sharing ideas about the situation and what they might be able to agree on and get done. All the documents Mohamed Ibrahim Kamel had prepared for President Sadat and their consultations together led to Sadat's conclusion that the Israelis simply would not budge, and that the Egyptians and Israelis would not be able to move forward by themselves. It was not a matter of squeezing the Israelis and blocking their avenues of prevarication, but of the Americans offering proposals to facilitate moving things forward. It may be useful here to read what Minister Mohamed Ibrahim Kamel wrote in his book, *al-Salam al-da'i' fi Camp David* (The Lost Peace of the Camp David Accords), about these negotiations between Presidents Sadat and Carter and their senior aides.

The understanding between the Egyptians and the Americans at the end of these consultations was that the US was prepared to put forth proposals to advance matters; however, to enable the US to play its role Egypt needed to keep up the charade of continuing negotiations with Israel. This would afford Washington the greatest opportunity to keep up contact with both sides, in order to find out where they stood. From this point on, they began to look into whether it was suitable for Egypt to prepare draft counter-proposals to what Israel had proposed in Ismailiya and after, thus enabling Washington to appear responsive to the proposals on both sides by offering its own fresh ideas that would overcome the hurdle.

The assumption was that this understanding was not to be public knowledge, if not actually secret. However, via the powerful Israeli lobby, which had a strong presence in Washington, the understanding could not have remained a secret for long, at least not from Israeli ears in Washington.

Both the Egyptian and American sides had prepared a press release announcing a number of understandings, which included:

Egypt and the US have held talks with a view to assessing the necessary steps for achieving a comprehensive settlement in the Middle East.

President Carter affirms his conviction that the events launched by President Sadat's initiative in visiting Jerusalem have opened the way, after decades of conflict, for the possibility of arriving at a genuine peace, and that nothing should be permitted to stand in the way of this final settlement.

Both parties affirm the importance of continuing negotiations apace, which have been launched in the past few months, and that they are convinced that a peaceful settlement of the conflict has become essential, and must be worked toward.

In his conversations with President Sadat, President Carter has gained a deeper understanding of the concerns felt by the president and the need to advance the peace process without delay.

President Carter affirms to the Egyptian president the U.S. commitment to playing an active part in the search for peace, and to redouble its efforts in the coming weeks to that end. Both also agreed on the importance of providing an atmosphere conducive to achieving tangible progress in the negotiations.

It has been agreed that Assistant Secretary of State Atherton will return to the region to work on achieving said tangible progress.

President Sadat returned from Camp David to Washington on the evening of February 4, and immediately launched into a large-scale flurry of activities to consolidate Egypt's position in influential American circles, which he achieved completely by the end of the visit on February 8. Both presidents met on that day, whereupon a concluding statement on the visit was issued:

- The United States will remain faithful to its historical commitments to the security of Israel and to the right of every state in the area to live in peace within secure and recognized boundaries.
- Helping the parties achieve a negotiated comprehensive settlement in the Middle East remains of highest importance in American policy, and President Carter will spare no effort in seeking ways to advance the peace process.
- A peace settlement must go beyond the mere termination of belligerency. It must provide for the establishment of normal peaceful relations between Israel and its neighbors.
- There can be no just and lasting peace without resolution of the Palestinian problem. The president reaffirmed what he said at his meeting with President Sadat in Aswan on January 4: There must be a solution of the Palestinian problem in all its aspects; it must recognize the legitimate rights of the Palestinian people and enable the Palestinians to participate in the determination of their own future.

- President Carter also reaffirmed the longstanding United States view that Israeli settlements in occupied territory are contrary to international law and an obstacle to peace, and that further settlement activity would be inconsistent with the effort to reach a peace settlement.

It may be useful to compare the phrasing used by U.S. officials today in describing the Israeli practice of building settlements in occupied territory with the phrasing used by Carter—namely, that such settlements are against international law—to recognize how far Israeli policy has succeeded in rolling back the U.S. position on this matter over three decades. At the start, the US adopted strong positions following international law. The rot crept in, and today we have the US saying that settlements are only one of the many things standing in the way of peace, or of a peaceful settlement!

As Egyptians, we were satisfied that the visit was largely a success. It had strengthened Egypt–U.S. ties. The two countries had reached a detailed understanding, based on which the US could, after a period of negotiations with both sides, and after receiving a comprehensive Egyptian proposal for our view of a Palestinian settlement within a few weeks—effectively a counter-proposal to the Israeli one put forth by Menachem Begin in Ismailiya—come up with an integrated proposal and a comprehensive plan for the settlement and its negotiating framework. The joint Egypt-U.S. action relied on the Americans inviting the Israeli prime minister to the US and confronting him with the situation and the need for some flexibility on his part, or risk the Americans coming up with their own proposals regardless of what the Israelis might think.

In the talks, President Sadat stressed the dangers of the continued building of Israeli settlements. The U.S. position was largely sympathetic to international law, a stance that continued during Carter's presidency from 1977 to 1981, but then gradually eroded, as I mentioned above, showing the decline in the U.S. assessment of the situation over the last nearly forty years.

The discussion on Israeli settlements was conducted in January and February 1978. It concerned the presence of nearly fifty thousand Israelis in the occupied West Bank, including around forty thousand in Jerusalem and the surrounding area. Today, the Israeli settlers in the West Bank and Jerusalem number over five hundred thousand. I imagine that the understanding reached in February 1978 greatly influenced the phrasing and concepts of U.S. proposals in the following months, up to the second Camp David meeting in September 1978, which was attended by the Israeli prime minister, Carter, and Sadat. The attentive reader cannot fail to notice that the Americans, as part of their understanding with Egypt in February 1978, set the basis not only for the U.S. role and how Americans would conduct themselves within it, but also for the real foundations and principles that would govern the peace settlement from the U.S. point of view. The Americans spoke of a comprehensive peace, one that went beyond the mere end of armed conflict. They envisioned the exchange of embassies between Israel and its neighbors, foremost among which was, of course, Egypt. Back then, and for quite a while after that, the Americans spoke only of the Palestinians' right to participate in all matters related to the determination of their own future, without mentioning any practical steps or mechanism for how this was to be done.

In addition, President Sadat intuited that he could now convince the US—and after that, the other western powers—of the importance of economic support for Egypt, especially as there were indications that assistance from the oil-producing Arab countries had dried up. This encouraged President Sadat to ask Carter, in the period that followed the Washington visit, for $500 million in immediate aid to Egypt. He also seized the opportunity of his European tour, the week after he left Washington on February 8, to ask all the European countries he visited for financial support for Egypt, which gradually drew a response from them.

I left Washington for Germany that day on the presidential Boeing 737. Minister Mohamed Ibrahim Kamel and Ambassador Ahmed Maher al-Sayed left to accompany President Sadat on his European tour on the 707.

21 Building Political Consensus toward a Settlement

I was on the president's 737 en route to Munich, from which I would go to Bonn, then the capital of West Germany. I was entrusted with delivering the baton of Field Marshall Walther von Brauchitsch, Oberbefehlshaber des Heeres of the Wehrmacht, that is to say, supreme commander of the German army from 1938 to 1941, to its rightful owners. The baton had been smuggled to Egypt from Germany after the fall of the Nazis in 1945. It had ended up in the hands of King Farouk, who kept it until he was deposed in the 1952 revolution. Now that President Sadat had ascended to power and consolidated his relationship with Chancellor Helmut Schmidt, the German chancellor had asked for this baton to be returned to Brauchitsch's family. Sadat saw this as a suitable moment to return the artifact, as we were seeking more German support in our conflict with Israel.

The baton was nestled in a cylindrical box of butter-soft black leather. The length of the flight, I turned over this magnificent artifact in my hands, imagining the hand of the commander wrapped around it as he navigated the German army's difficult years in the Soviet Union. I treasure the memory of my time with that beautiful object whenever I read about the history of Field Marshall Brauchitsch and his role in that terrible war.

When we arrived in Bonn, we were joined by Foreign Minister Mohamed Ibrahim Kamel. Ahmed Maher al-Sayed and I joined him in his meetings with the German leaders, who spoke fulsomely of their appreciation of Egypt's efforts and initiative, although it was clear from their communications with other western parties, primarily the US and the rest of Western Europe, that they believed the negotiations with Israel would be extremely difficult, in light of Israel's continued stubbornness and their insistence on keeping settlements built deep inside Egyptian territory. Our foreign minister repeatedly denounced this practice and stated categorically that it threatened to abort the Egyptian initiative, returning the threat of armed conflict between Egypt and Israel.

At his meeting with Minister Kamel, which I attended, Chancellor Schmidt made the same points that Shimon Peres, head of the Israeli opposition, had made: Israel was prepared to be flexible about their air bases in Sinai, but it was "an impossibility" to clear the settlements. All this had been covered during the Military Committee meetings in late January 1978, during which Israel had been inflexible. Schmidt also, I noticed, said that the Israelis were prepared for an exchange of land between Egypt and Israel, which Foreign Minister Mohamed Ibrahim Kamel had already categorically rejected. Anyone reading this book today and observing what is currently happening between the Palestinians and Israelis will doubtless conclude that Israel's position has not changed: its negotiating style has remained on the path of attempts to keep land, expand where possible, pressure its opponents, and refuse to make any compromises, all the while seeking to frustrate and thwart their opponents in hopes of wearying or exasperating them into submission. Egypt's negotiators, however, proved tenacious, refusing any proposals to exchange land or redraw boundaries.

We stayed in Germany for a few days, while Foreign Minister Mohamed Ibrahim Kamel said his goodbyes to German politicians and officials, and his Arab colleagues, ambassadors, and so on—a formal protocol for goodbyes that was in place until a few years ago. I recall today the minister's personality, and the friendly, informal way he dealt with his employees. The man was aware that he wanted sufficient knowledge and basic information on many subjects—nuclear non-proliferation, Sudan, Somalia, our cases at the UN, and our complicated relations with the Soviet Union—and with admirable humility asked us to prepare a number of briefs for him on these subjects before he left for Washington, so he could be well-informed on the issues that occupied Egypt while he was in his post as Egyptian ambassador to Bonn. We spent a number of nights briefing him. He listened intently, asking questions and checking details. I was pleased that I had the opportunity, while still only a first secretary at the Egyptian Foreign Ministry, to spend hours coaching this modest-spirited, mild-mannered minister on a number of technical issues. I must also mention here that despite his modest manner and decent nature, Minister Mohamed Ibrahim Kamel was a man of profound thought and clearly defined ideas and positions when it came to his country. He had a seemingly limitless capacity for diplomatic maneuvering, coupled with an ability to be direct and forthright if so required.

Foreign Minister Mohamed Ibrahim Kamel returned to Cairo amid the horrific news that the famous writer Yusuf al-Siba'i, then minister of culture, had been assassinated by Palestinian extremists in Cyprus. This was followed by the tragedy in Larnaca Airport.

We began immediately to act on what we had discussed in the US, namely, coming up with ideas and initiatives to allow the US to intervene at a suitable moment with ideas for a settlement on which serious Israel–Egypt negotiations could be built. On February 20, therefore, we presented a modified Egyptian draft declaration of principles on which Egypt and Israel might agree, as a proposed method to govern the negotiations, and thence the settlement:

- Establishing a just and lasting peace requires Israel to withdraw from Sinai, the Golan, the West Bank, and Gaza.
- Achieving a just solution for the Palestinian problem, securing the Palestinian's legitimate rights, including their right to self-determination, through talks attended by Egypt, Jordan, Israel, and representatives of the Palestinian people. A careful reader will notice that this phrasing began to develop at this time and eventually culminated in the Madrid Conference and the launch of talks in 1991, and the emergence of independent delegations of Palestinians capable of negotiating directly and independently.
- Ending all calls for continuation of the state of war, and respecting the sovereignty, territorial integrity, and political independence of all states in the region.

Assistant to the Secretary of State Roy Atherton came to Cairo at the end of February 1978, with instructions from Washington based on understandings between Presidents Sadat and Carter. The visit aimed to move the situation forward, in preparation for an American invitation to the Israeli prime minister to come to the US for more discussions between the US and Israel. The Americans would attempt to limit Begin's avenues of prevarication, forcing him to exhibit the flexibility that had so far been lacking.

Sadat seized the opportunity of the U.S. envoy's visit to give him a message for the Israeli prime minister, the most important elements of which were:

- The president is sending this message with the U.S. envoy, who is making sincere efforts to help the Egyptians and Israelis to a comprehensive settlement based on creating circumstances conducive to a good neighborly relationship.
- President Sadat is concerned that the peace efforts had so far been moving in the wrong direction, contrary to the spirit in which his initiative was meant.
- Instead of focusing on the core of a comprehensive settlement, the discussions are unfortunately stuck in the area of disputing words and phrases. The president suggests that we agree on core issues, primarily the matter of withdrawal, the Palestinian problem and how to settle it, and guaranteeing security for all parties. Unfortunately, Sadat's visit to Jerusalem and the Ismailiya Summit notwithstanding, to say nothing of Egypt's visits to Washington and to Europe, Israel's positions remain the same as prior to Sadat's initiative, without the slightest modification.
- President Sadat remains committed to working toward peace. He is convinced that the Political and Military Committees can return to convening; however, the meetings need to focus more on the positive and less on the negative. Egypt has no desire to impose conditions; however, to achieve an objective and serious leap forward basic guidelines for a comprehensive settlement must be agreed upon.
- The president understands and appreciates Israel's need for security. However, this security should not, and cannot, come at the expense of land or sovereignty.

The message also made it clear that there were individuals in the Arab world and the Soviet Union actively working to sabotage the peace initiative, but that President Sadat and Egypt were standing against them. Terrorist attacks—as we saw with the murder of Yusuf al-Siba'i—would not shake Egypt or force it to back off. Still, the Israeli prime minister must be aware that his actions and attitudes to the initiative had given these dark forces fodder to fight it.

Sadat also emphasized in his message that he had not spoken of burning the settlements on Egyptian soil; all he wanted was that they be vacated and the land returned to Egypt. This was in response to a great furor in Israel and the US, caused by some western news agencies misquoting Sadat in an interview with the Israeli press that he wanted to burn the settlements. Israel had gone up in arms, providing the prime minister with fresh fuel for his fight against Sadat in the international press and the Israeli lobby in the US.

In another paragraph, the president assured Israel that he was still insistent that the main armed forces should not cross the passes deep into Sinai, and mentioned that he had assured Minister of Defense Weizman of this.

Finally, Sadat complained of the Israelis' actions before the start of the Political Committee's work in Jerusalem, specifically their announcement that they would be expanding their building of settlements in the Rafah region of Egypt. This, he said, made it seem that Israel was rejecting any kind of settlement with Egypt. He was still convinced, he said, that Israel did not appear to understand, or did not wish to understand, the goals motivating his initiative in opening the door to Israel. He, Sadat, would move forward in accordance with his own initiative, attempting to achieve peace. He asked Begin a question at the end of the message. Was the prime minister ready for peace? If so, President Sadat was also ready. However, he said, if Israel insisted on clinging to outdated concepts, this would lead to a sterile and vicious cycle inimical to any forward motion.

President Sadat, the foreign minister, and his small and diligent task-force worked hard to implement the understanding they had reached with the Americans in Washington. Egypt was to demonstrate an intent and desire to keep up active communication with Israel, and a commitment to dialogue and negotiations as a means of resolving differences, to give the US a chance to intervene at the right moment, when American society and the international Jewish community realized that Begin's continued stubbornness and resistance to any real change in the Middle East was hurting and not helping. All the indicators we received from Israel at that time, and the results of Begin's and a number of his senior officials' visits to Washington, bespoke a decline in support for his policies, both within Israel and on the level of communications with the US. Indeed, his popular support among the American Jewish community was declining. This had its effect on Israel proper and on the U.S. administration, which often lent the community a listening ear.

The Foreign Ministry pressed tirelessly on to let everyone know that we wanted dialogue and negotiation. On March 6, we gave the Americans a preliminary draft of an Egyptian proposal for a basic settlement for Palestine, whose main elements were:

- Israel is to withdraw from the West Bank, including Jerusalem and the Gaza Strip, which are the lands occupied in 1967.
- Israel's withdrawal from the West Bank should be to the lines of the ceasefire agreement signed in April 1949 between Israel and Jordan,

plus an Israeli withdrawal from Gaza to the lines of the ceasefire
between Israel and Egypt in February 1949.

- An Israeli withdrawal is to include clearing all the settlements built
on land occupied since 1967.

The first Egyptian proposal went on to deal with the legitimate rights
of the Palestinian people. It reaffirmed their right to self-determination
without foreign intervention, and the right of return or compensation
for those refugees forced off their land in 1948, in accordance with UN
General Assembly Resolution 194 of 1948. Finally, it emphasized the
right of those displaced after 1967 to return to the West Bank in accordance with UN Security Council Resolution 237 of 1967.

The Egyptian plan for a Palestinian settlement also put forward a
new idea: giving the UN a role and organically linking the stages of the
settlement. After researching it, the taskforce decided to present the plan
to the Americans. It included a transitional period, or, as it was called at
the time, interim arrangements. The proposal was to establish a short
transition prior to implementing the right to self-determination for the
Palestinian people, freely conducted without intervention from foreign
parties. During this transitional period, the UN would supervise the areas
vacated by the Israelis, with the participation of a representative of the
Palestinian people, a representative from Jordan for the West Bank, and a
representative from Egypt for the Gaza Strip.

The plan stipulated that these provisions would end with a popular
referendum, under UN supervision, with the Palestinian people deciding their own political future. The Egyptian proposal arrived at its logical conclusion on the issue of the right to self-determination: "Egypt
believes that the Palestinian state must have some link with Jordan."
The Egyptian project reveals, early on, that the aim was to establish a
Palestinian state on the full extent of their homeland: the West Bank
and Gaza.

The proposal concluded with a brief reference to the need to agree
on suitable procedures and mutual guarantees of sovereignty, integrity of
territory, and political independence for the states and parties concerned.

The reader may note that this proposal was a faithful summary of
constructive Egyptian thinking, which continued to work toward the goal
of creating a Palestinian state on the full territories of the Palestinian
homeland. The developments in the forty years that followed demonstrated that Egypt stayed true to these ideas—indeed, that its insistence
on them forced all parties, internationally and in the region, to move in
the same direction in later years.

These ideas were the fruit of the taskforce's hard work. I must mention here that they were the brainchild of Counselor Mohamed al-Gawwali, of the Policy Planning Department, under the capable command of Ambassador Abdel Raouf El Reedy. It was al-Gawwali who wrote the first draft of the project, convinced El Reedy of it, and later the taskforce, primarily Osama al-Baz.

Back to President Sadat's message quoted above. Menachem Begin's reply was sent to Egypt with Ambassador Atherton. Dated March 5, 1978, it reflects stubbornness and obstinacy. Begin rejected out of hand any talk of withdrawing from occupied territories, no matter what Resolution 242 said. He then repeated his claims about defensive war, and that war had been thrust upon Israel in 1967. Israel, he said, could not agree to withdraw from the lands that offered it optimal defense capacities.

The Israeli prime minister's reply to Sadat spoke of the right to redraw the boundaries of states and societies in the wake of defensive wars, citing European history. These threadbare ideas were the ideological and legal bedrock of Menachem Begin's thinking—a man from the cold country of Poland, weighted down with the entirety of European history: the tragedy of the failed Treaty of Versailles, followed by the tragedy of the Second World War and Germany's search for revenge for that treaty. This was the source of the prime minister's limited horizons and misjudgments.

Unfortunately, Begin repeated specific elements in his message, including that Israel could never return to the borders of June 4, 1967. This Israeli position has not budged until today. The message went on to affirm that Israel rejected the establishment of a Palestinian state in Judea and Samaria—the West Bank—after the transition, as such a state would represent a grave danger to Israel, one that would not be, he said, ameliorated by the passage of time and eventual stability. Therefore, he said, he could not allow such a state to be born.

Despite Begin's absurdities and his continued inflexibility, President Sadat decided not to break the thread of communication with the Israelis. On March 10, after receiving Begin's message on March 8, he sent a message reiterating his wish for peace, urgently arriving at a just settlement for the Palestinians, and establishing good relations between Israel and its neighbors. Sadat said, however, that all of the excuses cited by Begin were easily refutable: they revealed that Israel did not yet grasp the philosophy driving the Egyptian president's initiative. The prime minister's talk of defensive war did not stand up to historical scrutiny, and was inaccurate. International law, and the international community, Sadat went on to say, rejected the acquisition of territory by war. He called on the Israelis to respect the Palestinian people's legitimate national rights. At the end of the message, Sadat said that what could bring Egypt back to the political and military negotiating table, reenergizing the committees formed in December 1977, was the parties managing, with direct assistance from the US, to agree on clear guidelines for a comprehensive settlement not allowing for demands contrary to international law.

As soon as the message was sent, Israel returned to its usual tactics. It sent a new proposal via the US on March 22 that was new only in name, repeating all its previous points. The Israelis talked about withdrawing from "lands," not "all lands." They spoke of the rights of "Arab Palestinians," not "the Palestinian people." We did not dignify their proposal with a reply, sensing that this was an attempt by Israel to muddy the waters.

Instead, we began talking to the Americans about how we would implement the implicit agreement between Sadat and Carter made during the Egyptian president's visit to Washington in early February. The Americans asked us to give them our ideas, based on which they could propose a comprehensive American project for a settlement between Egypt and Israel, and of the Palestinian problem. In parallel with these U.S. requests, the Americans let slip some general ideas to us: nine points they felt could form the basis of a broader and more comprehensive American proposal. Dr. Ashraf Ghorbal, our ambassador in Washington, came to Cairo bearing these broad concepts in mid-April 1978.

The U.S. ideas, in general, revolved around a settlement for the Palestinian situation based on affording the Palestinians five years of self-rule. The authority would be not Israeli, but an Egyptian, Jordanian, and Israeli triad. An elected committee of Palestinian inhabitants would replace the occupation government. The occupation forces would with-draw to specific locations during the transitional period, and all parties, including Jordan and Israel, would relinquish their calls for sovereignty over the area for the five-year period. Sovereignty would remain sus-pended and unspecified. The negotiations among Egypt, Jordan, and Israel would take place with the participation of the Palestinian council elected by the inhabitants of the West Bank, with the objective of arriving at a final settlement based on clear foundations. These included agree-ing on security procedures and arrangements, Israeli withdrawals that allowed for a redrawing or modification of the boundaries of the 1967 ceasefire, and looking into future links between the territories with Israel and Jordan. The U.S. ideas also stressed the importance of studying the right of Israeli Jews to buy land in the West Bank, the presence of UN or Jordanian forces in the West Bank, development plans for the West Bank and Gaza and a link between them, and the possibility of Egyptian forces in Gaza. Finally, the U.S. thoughts conveyed to us by Dr. Ashraf Ghorbal suggested looking into establishing a mechanism for dealing more comprehensively with the refugee problem.

Back in Cairo, we received these ideas with great reservation, both because they were unclear and because they lacked any reference to a future Palestinian state. Also, we were wary of bringing up the 'refugee problem' without directly calling the refugees Palestinians: this opened the door for the claims of Jews who had left Arab countries. The most worrying element, though, was that the fate of Arab Jerusalem remained shrouded in obscurity.

A scant few days after Ghorbal conveyed these thoughts to us, Atherton paid another visit to Cairo, to officially deliver a paper on what could be considered an American proposal to the parties for discussion and agreement. The official document contained nothing different from what Ambassador Ghorbal had conveyed to us after hearing them in Washington a week prior.

The Israeli position was still stuck, as evidenced by their obduracy in rejecting not only a Palestinian state but also the possibility of one after the five-year interim period under consideration by Egypt, Israel, and Jordan. The Americans, too, in preparing their thoughts, were proceeding with the utmost caution, contrary to how Carter had appeared in his meetings and consultations with Sadat in Washington in February. This forced Foreign Minister Mohamed Ibrahim Kamel to look at other options and suggest them to President Sadat in the hope of providing other avenues that might not necessarily have been his first choice. Since the ministerial council of the Arab League had convened in March 1978, the foreign minister had been searching for alternatives to Arab support, which it had become clear was not forthcoming despite negotiations. I often spoke about this with Ahmed Maher, mentioning my conviction that President Sadat had embarked on a path of no return with the initiative: any turning back would open the door to his enemies in Egypt and the Arab world to attack his position and do serious damage. I did not really believe that President Sadat would accept Minister Kamel's suggestions about reaching a serious understanding with Saudi Arabia, with a view to holding an Arab summit that would welcome Egypt back into the fold, so to speak, of working within a broader Arab framework. The minister not only held but also encouraged us to express such views.

Meanwhile, we were still applying pressure on the Americans to develop their thinking and to expose Israel's intentions vis-à-vis the Palestinian situation at the end of the interim period. We managed to get the US to ask Israel two specific questions about the end of the transitional period: Can Israel be specific about its view of the final status of the lands at the end of the interim period, or is the intention to make a final determination when the time comes? The second question had to do with the mechanism for settling this question.

The Israelis promised to respond to the US' questions, but asked a number of questions in their turn "so as to be able to respond to the US." All the questions concerned President Sadat's attitudes and intentions: Did he intend to negotiate about Palestinian lands if Jordan refused to take part in the negotiations? If the negotiations succeeded, was Egypt prepared to sign peace treaties on the West Bank, Gaza, and Sinai without the Arabs and Palestinians? They also asked how adamant Sadat was about full withdrawal, whether he was amenable to small border adjustments, how accepting he was of the presence of limited Israeli forces in specific areas of a strategic nature, and whether he was prepared to accept the American proposal on the Palestinians and their participation in the determination of their future—the "Aswan wording," as it came to be known—made at the Carter–Sadat summit on January 4.

The Americans began to ask Egypt to make a few modifications in the wording of the ideas they had presented. President Sadat agreed to the possibility of looking into modifications, adding the possibility of Egypt agreeing to oversee the Palestinian administration of Gaza, Jordan overseeing the elected Palestinian council's administration of the West Bank, and the UN alone being mandated to oversee and facilitate the Israeli withdrawal (instead of appointing a representative of the secretary-general to administer these regions).

We sent these modifications to the US in mid-June, whereupon we proceeded to nudge the Americans into developing their ideas, in preparation for presenting them to the parties concerned. We also sent an oral message to the Americans about the issue of the U.S. queries to the Israelis, regarding how they saw the final shape of the situation after the transitional period, and the Israeli questions about the Egyptian stance vis-à-vis the occupied territories. The message from Egypt emphasized that we welcomed the U.S. queries to Israel, as they would reveal Israel's intentions regarding the Palestinians.

Egypt also made clear its response to Dayan's questions to Cyrus Vance about the Egyptian position. "This position depends on Israel's true intentions," the response went, "but there are limits to what Egypt can do for, and the extent to which it can speak for, the Palestinians in their absence, and in the absence of the other Arab parties."

It may start to become clear that all these U.S. and Israeli efforts simultaneously appeared to indicate a clear intent to redraw boundaries and to push Egypt into negotiating for the Palestinians and overseeing the Palestinian administration in Gaza if the transitional period went into effect. Finally, they appeared to be feeling out how prepared Egypt was to reach an agreement with Israel, even in the absence of negotiations or agreements between Syria, Jordan, and Israel. Kissinger had also focused on all of these points in his consultations with Hafiz Ismail in May 1973.

A careful observer of the U.S. attitude and strategy in dealing with the Arab–Israeli settlement—whether the Palestinian problem or Israel's disputes with its other Arab neighbors, foremost among which was Egypt, followed by Jordan and Syria—will easily discern that the U.S. approach had not changed, or even been modified, from Kissinger's time up to the signing of the Camp David Accords in September 1978. I might even add that the US remained faithful to its basic premises until the Oslo Accords in 1993, and the Palestinian Camp David meetings with President Bill Clinton in 2000.

In any case, all this activity and consultation was going on at the same time as Foreign Minister Mohamed Ibrahim Kamel was preparing to visit Saudi Arabia with the objective of opening channels of communication between Egypt and the Arabs that might afford President Sadat more freedom of movement and alternatives. The president gave permission for Kamel to visit Saudi Arabia to feel out where they stood regarding the situation. Ahmed Maher and I accompanied the minister on this thirty-six-hour visit. It became clear that the Saudis were taking a hard line and still disapproved of Sadat's actions. Although Minister Kamel felt at the end of the visit that he had opened new avenues for Sadat with Saudi Arabia and the Arabs, I remained unconvinced. I was certain that President Sadat would not back down from his initiative now, or declare it a failure and break off negotiations, for any strategic goal, unless one of two things happened: Israel changed its tune on a settlement with Egypt or the Palestinians, or the US offered some novel idea to close the rift between Egypt and Israel with regard to a Palestinian settlement.

Although all three parties had proposed establishing Palestinian self-rule in Gaza and the West Bank for a transitional five-year period, Egypt was the only one to insist that the period should end with the dawn of an independent Palestinian state, or one linked in some manner with Jordan. Israel kept on prevaricating, refusing to commit to any change in the Palestinians' status at the end of the five-year period that remained at the core of the negotiations.

22 Leeds Castle

The foreign minister left for New York in late May 1978 to take part in the UN General Assembly session on disarmament. Personally, I was deeply disappointed at not being part of the delegation accompanying the minister on this visit, not, I admit, because of any special interest in the subject or the resolutions the session might produce, but mainly out of a desire to return to New York, which I had not seen since I left in October 1977, after years as a member of the Egyptian delegation to the UN. I always firmly believed that my membership in any Egyptian delegation to the UN General Assembly's various sessions over the years was a learning experience, strengthening my chance to shine in the Foreign Ministry and making me one of that small elite of Egyptian diplomats down the generations who had the opportunity to serve their country in the highest positions and missions abroad, including Ismail Fahmy, Mohamed Riyad, Ahmed al-Messiri, Abdullah El-Erian, Mohamed Hassan al-Zayyat, Esmat Abdel Meguid, Abdel Raouf El Reedy, Mohamed Shaker, Abdel-Halim Badawi, Nabil al-Arabi, Amre Moussa, and many more who served long and repeatedly in New York.

In any case, I followed Minister Kamel's communications and meetings from my post in Cairo. He met with Cyrus Vance on the sidelines of the session in New York. They were still discussing the possible implementation of the Sadat–Carter scenario of the first Camp David meetings in the first week of February. On this specific point, Mohamed Ibrahim Kamel writes in *al-Salam al-da'i' fi Camp David* (The Lost Peace of the Camp David Accords):

Vance said they were still awaiting Israel's response to the two questions posed by the US on the future of the West Bank and Gaza. Vance
added that he did not expect a positive response, but if there was one,
it would be possible to launch another round of direct talks between
Egypt and Israel. However, if the response was negative, he would then
present the Egyptian project to Israel, after which the US would step
in with its own proposals and thoughts on the matter. I agreed, saying
that it was not enough for the US to find the responses positive; Egypt,
too, had to approve them. We would not accept a return to direct talks
with Israel without actual positive responses, not mere sleight-of-hand
in phrasing with the intent of making it appear as though Israel was
softening while the reverse was true.

In Cairo, we followed the situation in Israel, and the domestic dialogue taking place around answering the US' questions. Our goal in all
our meetings with the Americans throughout June 1978 was to urge them
to make their suggestions as specific as possible, thus forcing Israel to
acknowledge the Palestinian people's right to independence and right
to their lands in the West Bank and Gaza. Accordingly, the Americans
offered Vance's idea, which he had discussed with Minister Kamel in New
York, of a new round of talks to be held in London in the last week of
June. On Ahmed Maher's instructions, I wrote a draft brief for President
Sadat, giving an overview of the situation and its developments, with a
focus on the relations between Egypt's proposals and the upcoming U.S.
proposal. I discussed how these proposals related to the US' questions
to Israel and the latter's delay and failure to answer, and, finally, the US'
suggestion of holding a meeting in London for the three ministers to
discuss the situation.

My assessment was that the Americans felt the pressure of a possible
U.S.–Israeli confrontation if the US offered a proposal not in accordance
with Israel's interests. This was their motivation for calling the three-way
meeting, so that each party could have a chance to air, once more, its
positions and goals, after which the U.S. proposal could be made, each
party having been heard and its views taken into account and the situation having been evaluated from all angles. I was concerned about the
Americans' attitude and their adoption of a great many of the elements
in Israel's basic thinking, embodied in the US' lack of reference to the
final destination of the transitional period of Palestinian self-rule. This
motivated the recommendation of Ahmed Maher and myself to Minister
Kamel that Egypt agree to the three-way meeting in London and, impor-
tantly, remind the Americans of their promise that their next proposal for

an interim Palestinian settlement would have a firm link to the framework for a permanent and final settlement. This proposal, therefore, needed to be closer to Egypt's position than Israel's.

After reading the brief, Minister Kamel insisted on adding another element, namely that he recommended not holding the tripartite meeting if the Israelis' response to the Americans—due to be announced in a few days—was negative. I felt this to be unnecessarily obdurate, and was skeptical about affording such importance to Israel's attitude. The goal was to achieve a sympathetic and suitable American attitude toward our position, and therefore accommodating the American request stood to place us in a favorable light. To his credit, Minister Kamel presented our brief to President Sadat. As we were waiting for his feedback, the Israeli response to the Americans' questions arrived. The Israelis agreed to look into a future relationship with the Palestinians at the end of the five-year transitional period. This response was a prime example of Israeli evasiveness, concealing any sense of Israel's conception of the final status of the West Bank and Gaza. It also made clear that any agreement on the settlement's final form would require negotiations attended by representatives of those living in Palestinian lands.

The response was deeply disappointing to Egypt and to the US. Still, I was sure at the time that Israel could never offer a positive response to these strategic and crucial questions from the US. In spite of the oddness of the response—which had become something of an after-dinner story for Minister Kamel—President Sadat agreed to go forward with the London meeting, over the minister's protests. He did, though, make it clear to Minister Kamel and to the Americans that this was the *only* meeting he would attend, after which the scenario Egypt and the US had agreed upon was to be implemented.

The British decided to hold the meeting at Leeds Castle in South London on July 18 and 19, 1978. I started preparing the documents and working briefs for our foreign minister. On this specific point, it must be said that the working group of consultants on whom Minister Kamel depended for assistance worked like a well-oiled machine under Dr. Osama al-Baz. The latter wore two hats: the first, his duties at the vice president's office, and, the second, his job as permanent undersecretary at the Foreign Ministry. This gave him great influence to get things done his way. If he was in agreement with Minister Kamel on something, they moved as one; if the reverse was the case, he used his influence to carry out what he and Sadat had agreed upon, on the pretext that he was only following presidential instructions. In spite of this, there was never once any conflict between Kamel and al-Baz.

In parallel, although I was working with Ahmed Maher in the consultants' group, we had free rein, thanks to our affiliation with Minister Kamel. We made proposals and suggestions without having to first obtain the working group's approval. Also, we were responsible for the wording of the minister's talking points and official positions. This gave the two of us a great deal of influence.

The Egyptian delegation accompanied Minister Kamel to the VIP hall of Cairo Airport early on July 17, to board the second presidential aircraft—the very same Boeing 737 that had put our lives at such risk on the way home from Washington in February, making an emergency landing at Gander Airport in a blizzard that terrified both passengers and crew. The delegation consisted of the foreign minister, Osama al-Baz, Abdel Raouf El Reedy, Ahmed Maher al-Sayed, Nabil al-Arabi, Hamdi Nada, the press spokesman for the delegation, and finally, First Secretary Ahmed Aboul Gheit, from the minister's office. We were accompanied by a great many ancillary and administrative personnel, code and telex operators, an English-language typist, and a good number of Intelligence personnel, from the Department of Information and Assessment and the National Security Agency. There were also a number of secret service personnel accompanied by technical staff, to make sure that our quarters in Leeds Castle were free of bugs.

After takeoff, Ahmed Maher al-Sayed asked me to brief the minister on the draft proposal he would present to the media on arrival at Heathrow, as well as some briefs on the content and agenda of the meeting, to discuss the two proposals for a Palestinian settlement brought by Israel and Egypt. I did this, and eventually we landed at noon, London time.

The runway at Heathrow Airport had become a fortification: there were armored vehicles and police cars all around the runway, driving alongside the aircraft until we arrived at a secluded part of the airport. We disembarked, only to find more iron-clad British security. There were members of the army, and even some light tanks, Scorpions if memory serves. Minister Kamel delivered the statement we had prepared, responding to a number of questions on the goals of the meeting, his expectations for it, and his assessment of Israel's credibility and desire for peace. We then boarded two helicopters, U.S.-made Chinooks. This was my first time on an aircraft of this type. We flew quite low, which gave me a spectacular view of the ravishing English countryside, especially as it was a clear day.

The minister's helicopter landed first, followed by the one bearing the other members of the delegation. We met the Egyptian team that had arrived several days earlier, and they gave us our delegate identity cards and acquainted us with the list of British instructions. Everything was meticulously organized.

Leeds Castle was like something out of a Hollywood movie about the Knights of the Round Table. It was surrounded by a moat and had a working drawbridge. Inside the castle, there was a dizzying array of medieval weapons displayed on the walls; there were suits of armor, lances, and halberds. I was very impressed.

We went to our rooms. The room I shared with Secretary Ahmed Hamdi Nada was tiny but elegantly furnished in Old English style. All the original furnishings and walls of the castle had been restored just a few weeks earlier, making it a true gem. An anecdote that may be amusing is that when we retired for the night on July 17, we did not notice a small teakettle in the room, which allowed us to make tea whenever we pleased. We also failed to notice that the castle staff had set the timer to make tea at 0530 hours.

I had never seen such a device before in my life. At 0530 hours the next day, I woke in a panic at a shrieking, whistling device in the corner of the room, bubbling and spewing hot steam. Still, after my rude awakening, I was able to enjoy a lovely British cup of tea and biscuits.

The evening of my arrival—July 17—I went to the minister's reception room with Ahmed Maher to prepare for the dinner we had been invited to by Cyrus Vance in the castle's dining room. Our host came to the minister's room for a brief consultation, accompanied by Eilts, the U.S. ambassador to Egypt, and the Secretary of State's assistant, Atherton. Vance offered his idea of a possible schedule and agenda for the next day, July 18 (the day of the Tea Awakening), and suggested that each party, Egypt and Israel, could present their ideas and proposals, allowing the US, at a later date, to set out its own ideas for a Palestinian settlement. Vance then gave Minister Kamel a shock: he said that at the conclusion of the meetings, he planned to announce that he was pleased with the progress achieved at the tripartite meeting, and that the parties had agreed to a second meeting, attended, in addition to the foreign ministers, by the defense ministers of Egypt and Israel.

Kamel categorically, and rather firmly, rejected a future meeting, as per Sadat's orders. He did try to maneuver by saying that he had no choice but to wait and hear the Israeli point of view before taking a stance regarding the U.S. proposal. We would, said the minister, say our piece and explain our views in detail to the Israelis and Americans. Still, he expected nothing new from Israel and Foreign Minister Moshe Dayan, not on a Palestinian settlement nor on an agreement to empower Palestinians to take their fate into their own hands and enjoy the right to self-determination.

After this meeting, we attended a brief reception held by the British, then went to dinner in a magnificent hall that gave me the impression of being at a medieval banquet. Moshe Dayan was accompanied by his two assistants, Ely Rubinstein and Meir Rosenne, the legal counsel for the Israeli Foreign Ministry. Finally, there was Aharon Barak, who was appointed attorney-general of Israel after the Camp David Summit in 1978. Dayan was accompanied by his second wife. Vance also had his wife with him. This helped ease any tensions and make the dinner far more informal than it might otherwise have been, and we stayed away from serious subjects. Still, Dayan launched into a monologue about his hopes that the states and societies of the Middle East could accept and recognize Israel once there was a comprehensive peace. I suddenly found myself asking the Israeli minister a specific question—I was seated quite close to him. "Would our attitude to Israel have been different, do you think—at least Egypt's—if Israel had warned Cairo that Britain and France were preparing for the Tripartite Aggression on Cairo in October 1956?"

I was referring to a personal conviction I had that if the Israelis had warned us, Israel would have stood to gain a great deal: it would have proved to its Arab neighbors that it was actually part of the Middle East. Dayan was silent for a time. Finally, he said that the circumstances surrounding Egypt and Israel at the time had prevented it. Israel, he added, was then seeking to align its future with the western world. It is a phrase that gives the lie—in my estimation—to any request for Israel's membership in the Middle East.

On the morning of July 18, and all day long, the three delegations met in a Leeds Castle meeting room. Ahmed Maher had me take the minutes. Just as we expected, Vance summarized the goals of the meeting, which was the first encounter of its kind between Egypt's and Israel's foreign ministers since the Egyptian minister left Tel Aviv in January 1978 and the talks stalled.

Vance asked the Israelis to present their thoughts, which they had previously shared at the Ismailiya Summit. Dayan began to lay out their ideas of how to enable the Palestinians to rule their own affairs via the election of a Palestinian council, and for the transitional five-year period, after which all parties would go back for more discussion and negotiation on the elements of a settlement.

Minister Kamel then took the floor. He categorically rejected the Israeli proposal: it did not, he said, express the Palestinian hopes of self-determination. Dr. Osama al-Baz followed up with an explanation of the draft Egyptian proposal, saying that Egypt's goal was to secure Palestinian participation in talks with Israel, and insisted on a clear conception of the nature of the settlement from its inception, at the start of the interim period, which Egypt agreed should be five years. The transitional period should end, he said, with the establishment of a Palestinian state with some links to Jordan, to be agreed upon. Dr. al-Baz also insisted that this state would maintain good neighborly relations with Israel.

Dr. al-Baz then launched into a dialogue with Dayan and his assistants about many elements of the Egyptian proposal and what they aimed to achieve. The argument lasted a while, and it was clear that the Israeli side was still stalling and being evasive to refrain from acknowledging the Palestinian right to self-determination and any link between the inhabitants and the land. Egypt rejected this, insisting on Palestinians' right to their state, and stating that it was unacceptable to break the link between a land and its people, asking them to enjoy self-rule while deprived of sovereignty.

Throughout that day, al-Baz, the presidential spokesman, demonstrated a flawless and articulate command of English, profound legal knowledge, and a comprehensive understanding of the situation in the Middle East and the hopes of the Palestinians. Under pressure from Egypt, the Israelis attempted evasion, asking to look into another subject: Israeli–Egyptian relations and the ideas about security arrangements that President Sadat had brought up in discussions with Ezer Weizman a few days before the Leeds Castle meeting. The Egyptian delegation replied calmly that this was not under discussion, as it was not on the agenda.

The morning meeting over, the three parties had a working lunch together. Dayan spoke to Minister Kamel about Egypt's relations with Israel, in the presence of Cyrus Vance, for about twenty minutes before lunch. He discussed proposed security measures related to Egypt's agreement to demilitarized zones on both the Egyptian and Israeli sides and establishing early-warning stations on the borders, managed by a third party. This would not have been the first time such an idea was carried out: Kissinger had previously implemented it between the two parties in the Second Disengagement Agreement in Sinai, in May 1975.

The Egyptian response included a number of additional possibilities, one of which was establishing areas of partially demilitarized zones in both quantity and type—another idea implemented by both parties in the Second Disengagement—and stationing international peacekeeping forces on the borders. Finally, Egypt recognized the Straits of Tiran as an international waterway, with the right of passage ensured for all.

Dayan appeared unconvinced by some of the Egyptian ideas, especially the suggestion of UN peacekeeping forces on the borders, citing these forces' failure to prevent war from breaking out between the two parties in May 1976. Despite this, he was interested in obtaining specific explanations from Minister Kamel on the Straits of Tiran. Minister Kamel, however, avoided going into too much detail about this idea. With his customary cunning, Dayan changed the subject back to Israel being prepared to acknowledge Egypt's sovereignty over Sinai, although an exchange of territory between the two parties was something to be looked into, he said, and security measures needed to be stepped up for both countries, especially in the vital region of the port of Eilat.

Minister Kamel refused—again—any exchange of territories. Dayan then repeated that Israel was prepared to acknowledge Egyptian sovereignty over Sinai while keeping Israeli settlements and air bases in the peninsula, with guarantees in place to allow Israeli access. Kamel replied that this was not on the table.

After the short lunch break, the parties returned to the meeting. The argument continued between the two sides around the requirements for implementing Resolution 242. Egypt insisted on full withdrawal from all territories, while Israel still prevaricated by referencing the text of the resolution, which said that Israel should withdraw from "territories occupied" and not "the territories occupied" in the recent conflict. The argument dragged on, without the two parties reaching an understanding.

They broke up for dinner—this time, each party separately—and to assess the situation and the results of that day's meetings. I was fed up, if I may say, with the Israeli attitude, although I had not yet lost hope. I had been pretty sure that Israel would reject any and all suggestions allowing a Palestinian state to emerge.

A final meeting was held on the morning of July 19 to discuss some ideas regarding Jerusalem. Egypt was insistent that the Palestinians—or Arab countries—have control over East Jerusalem. President Sadat's view was that Jerusalem should not be partitioned, but remain a unified city managed by a Supreme Council. This, too, was not resolved.

The meeting ended with Cyrus Vance's announcement that now that each party had shared its positions and views, the two days could be said to have resulted in useful discussions. Vance did not speak about a future meeting—an idea that the Israelis had been promoting and demanding, especially General Weizman, who was eager to be included in the negotiations because of his rivalry with Dayan.

Weizman's personality played an important role in all the peace efforts, from the launch of Sadat's initiative in November 1977 to every element of the May 1982 peace agreement. Weizman worked hard to win President Sadat's trust and give him the impression that he was motivated by an understanding for the need for a balance of interests between both parties. The truth, however, was that despite his ingenuity and jokey, informal manner, he was one of the strongest adherents to the Israeli government's party line on the West Bank territories. He displayed some flexibility in the Gaza department; in the years that followed, he repeatedly offered Egypt the chance to administrate or control that territory. We steadfastly refused, then and now.

We left Leeds Castle for London by automobile, in preparation for our return to Cairo. We did, though, spend two days in the capital city, during which the foreign minister met David Owen, the British foreign secretary, who received us in his office at the House of Commons.

Owen's contributions, I felt, were wishy-washy and showed a distinct lack of interest in the whole affair. When he did speak, however, he said he understood how hard it was for Israel to agree to clear the settlements. This was an unpleasant surprise, and Minister Kamel was quick to respond. But I must express my criticisms, at this point, of how the Arabs have been dealing—or rather, not dealing—with the building of settlements in the West Bank for decades now. I recall reading a telegram sent by the Egyptian ambassador to Morocco, in which he quoted an address delivered to a group of Arab leaders by Prince Hassan bin Talal, the brother of King Hussein of Jordan, on a visit to Morocco. The Jordanian prince said during his visit, on January 25, 1978, that Jordan estimated the number of Jewish settlers in the West Bank at about ten thousand. However, in and around Jerusalem, they numbered about forty thousand. Any comparison of today with yesterday is no doubt painful to us all.

Owen's position was a shock to us, by any standard; however, it was not the first or last time he took Israel's side. When Owen paid a visit to Cairo in 2010, on the invitation of our most famous journalist, Mohamed Hassanein Heikal, I noted that he stuck to the Israeli view of the October War and its military outcomes: he suggested that Israel had won the war, or at least had been on the verge of inflicting a crushing defeat. I beg to differ. The early chapters of this book describe the reason why.

On our return to London on the afternoon of July 19, we received a sudden telephone call from Cairo. It was the daily newspaper *al-Ahram*, asking what we had to say about the item it planned to publish the next day, regarding how both sides agree to meet again for more negotiations. We were flabbergasted. Minister Kamel hit the roof. Ahmed Maher was told to root out the source of these lies. We finally found out that Hamdi Fouad, *al-Ahram*'s diplomatic correspondent, who was with us on the trip, had sent a telegram to Cairo with this news, which the US had "leaked" in order to corner us. Hamdi Fouad received a severe dressing-down from the minister. The Leeds Castle meeting was over. We returned to Cairo to conduct a full assessment of the talks, our next steps, and where we would go from there.

On the flight, I rewrote the minutes of the meeting. They came to forty pages of foolscap.

23 The Road to Camp David

President Sadat's Boeing 707 took off at 1200 hours on Tuesday, September 5, 1978, from Paris to Washington. The president was due to take part in the summit meeting called by President Carter for the Egyptian president and the Israeli prime minister.

We had arrived in Paris with the president, on the afternoon of Monday, September 4, where we spent a night at the famous Grillon Hotel, which had been the site of a great many historical events, especially during the World War, the Versailles Conference, and Woodward Wilson's meetings with Clemenceau and Lloyd George.

The official delegation accompanying the president comprised the foreign minister, Minister of State for Foreign Affairs Boutros Boutros-Ghali, Hassan al-Tohami, who was a close friend of President Sadat's since they had served together in the army and been comrades in the 23 July Revolution, Head of the Presidential Cabinet Hassan Kamel, Permanent Undersecretary at the Foreign Ministry Dr. Osama al-Baz, Office Director of the Foreign Minister Ahmed Maher al-Sayed, and myself. Ambassadors Abdel Raouf El Reedy and Nabil al-Arabi had left Cairo for Washington a few days earlier on commercial flights.

It may be noted that the ministry taskforce was even more limited now than it had been in July 1978: only Osama al-Baz, Abdel Raouf El Reedy, Nabil al-Arabi, Ahmed Maher, and myself. Amre Moussa had left the group a few months earlier: the fierce competition between him and Ahmed Maher al-Sayed had led Minister Kamel to dispense with his services rather than have sparks constantly flying between these two competing forces. I recall an attempt made at the time to move Amre Moussa to San Francisco as Egyptian consul general for the West Coast; he was resistant to the idea, though, despite the temptations. He asked my opinion. I said he should say no, resist, and stand firm: I was confident that life is not unfair, and that all his efforts and hard work would be rewarded in future.

The President's aircraft included sleeping quarters and a sitting room. There was another sitting room with armchairs for the official ministerial delegations, and finally a group of ordinary seats at the rear of the plane for the ancillary technical team and the editors-in-chief of Egyptian newspapers. I noted that there was quite a large area of the aircraft without any seating at all, which allowed us to stretch out and have a nap. This made the bigwigs and important ministers quite jealous, eventually joining us in a bid to share our comfy space!

Strangely enough, *Time* and *Newsweek*'s Cairo correspondents were also with us on the flight: they had asked President Sadat for interviews, and he had decided to give them on the plane. I recall that these journalists, William Schmidt and Wilton Wynn, went systematically round every member of the delegation to get their views and expectations of the upcoming summit. I believe they conveyed a positive estimation to official U.S. quarters of the Egyptian view of the possible outcomes of the summit. Experience showed, however, that President Sadat often did things that surprised even his senior aides; being ignorant of his real intentions and attitudes often rendered them unwitting liars in their statements to the press. The American journalists also discussed the situation in Iran, then in the grip of tensions and demonstrations that indicated an uncertain future. Both the reporters agreed with us that Iran was heading—according to many U.S. sources—for a sea change within ten years, culminating in the shah's son ascending to the Peacock Throne. What is interesting here is that change did not wait for ten years—it came about within three months of the clashes in Iran's cities, toppling the old state and allowing the Islamic Republic to emerge under a theocratic leadership, while liberal forces were crushed.

In the years that followed, I often met Schmidt, the veteran *Newsweek* journalist, and reminded him of what he had said and predicted about Iran. He appeared quite ashamed of his own failure, and others', to read into the situation the first stirrings of a revolution. I always tried to comfort him, saying that one of the attributes of revolutions throughout history is that they tend to break out without clear pre-indications.

The period after our return to Cairo from Leeds Castle (from July 22 to August 3, 1978) was characterized by a great deal of movements and skirmishes between the negotiating parties. Tension reigned in Egyptian–Israeli relations. As I have mentioned above, the US kept pushing for a second Egyptian–Israeli–American meeting, attended by all three countries' foreign ministers and ministers of defense, for more studies on advancing the peace efforts. Both President Sadat and Foreign Minister Kamel resisted this American demand: they were now sure that Israel would not change or modify any aspect of the positions Moshe Dayan had explained to Minister Kamel in Great Britain. These positions frustrated President Sadat, as they showed clearly that despite his initiative in visiting Jerusalem, Israel's designs on Sinai, the West Bank, and Gaza had remained unchanged.

Minister Kamel began to convey to us—Ahmed Maher and myself—his impressions of what President Sadat was thinking, to help us assess the situation and assist us in preparing our briefs for the minister, briefs from him to the president, and draft communications for him to send to the US and other parties. I recall the foreign minister saying that the president had visited Austria in mid-July 1978 to take part in international socialist meetings, and said that in his estimation, the Egyptian initiative was proceeding on schedule. It would, he said, end with our achieving our objectives. On the contrary, though, this European visit caused a severe glitch in Egypt–Israel relations. What happened was that in Austria President Sadat had met Israeli Defense Minister Weizman at the latter's request, and Shimon Peres, head of the Israeli opposition, who was taking part in the same international socialist meetings. During the meetings, Weizman made two proposals to the Israelis: the first was calling for Israel to relinquish Arish and Gabal Moussa, in the center of Sinai, which meant in reality the implementation of the withdrawal in stages to the line of Arish/Ras Mohamed. The second was a number of points suggested by the president related to security arrangements in Sinai between the Israeli and Egyptian parties in the future, after an agreement or peace treaty had been reached. These were points that Moshe Dayan had tried hard to get Minister Kamel to discuss in Leeds, to no avail. In any event, the suggestion that Israel relinquish Arish was duly conveyed to the Israeli Cabinet for study and examination, then rejected loudly and arrogantly: "Nothing in return for nothing," said Menachem Begin of their decision and response, adding that nothing came for free. Some of the Israeli press even said that he was not in the habit of leaving tips!

As you may imagine, Sadat was hardly pleased. This incident strained Egypt–Israel relations, which finally led to the president's decision to refuse to accept a written communication that Menachem Begin tried to send him containing his response to the Egyptian proposal at the Vienna meeting, after which Egypt went on to request the departure of the Israeli military mission, which had remained in Egypt at the Gianaclis Airfield northwest of the country since the talks between the Political and Military Committees had failed in January 1978.

Israeli press sources at the time criticized the Israeli prime minister's performance. Some Israelis reported that he had thought when Sadat visited Jerusalem in November 1977 of reaching out in response by implementing a new and additional Israeli withdrawal from Sinai, conveying a strong gesture of goodwill to Egypt. However, the psychological and moral climate that prevailed in Israel at the time had meant the idea was stillborn.

In this climate, Minister Mohamed Ibrahim Kamel embarked on an attempt to consolidate the Egyptian position. He proposed that President Sadat contact Jordan to arrange an urgent visit for the foreign minister to inform the Jordanians of the results of Leeds Castle, and attempt to intuit Jordan's intention, or lack thereof, to take part in Egypt's talks with Israel. At that time, the talks' main focus was on the future of the West Bank and Gaza, and all the proposals on the table gave Jordan an important role. Moshe Dayan, as the reader may remember, had asked in his counter-queries to the Americans' questions in 1978 what the Egyptians would do if Jordan refused to take part in the negotiations, revealing Israel's keen interest in Egypt's intentions and whether it meant to shoulder Jordan's responsibilities if the latter bowed out of the talks. The Americans were also interested in our answer: the reader may recall that some of these questions were asked in Hafiz Ismail's consultations with Kissinger in May 1973, five years before Leeds Castle.

I accompanied Minister Kamel on my first-ever visit to Amman. I was charmed by the Jordanian capital, which grew over the years into a highly organized and well-run metropolis, reflecting the discipline and sophisticated administration in Jordanian society.

Minister Kamel met King Hussein of Jordan, the Jordanian prime minister, and the Jordanian foreign minister and head of the royal cabinet, and acquainted them all with the Egyptian view of the situation, the developments in the talks with Israel, and the outcomes of Leeds Castle, from briefs I had prepared and Ahmed Maher had approved. Minister Kamel, although he gained a great deal of confidence in the peace talks and a great many other subjects within his purview, was greatly reliant—like many ministers in other countries—on the briefs prepared by his assistants.

The visit was a qualified success in Minister Kamel's view. The Jordanians had listened attentively to the Egyptians' proposals, and gave flattering responses; however, King Hussein clearly had no intention of abandoning his traditional caution, nor of linking his country with an

Egyptian action whose outcomes were not yet clear, and might even have serious repercussions for Egypt—how much worse, then, might it be for Jordan, whose population at the time was made up of a large percentage of Palestinians?

On the flight back from Amman to Cairo, the seven-person Mystère aircraft bobbed and weaved—I offered up a prayer of thanks when we were back on solid ground! This plane, along with its three sister aircraft, was used by President Sadat and high-ranking state officials, such as the ministers of defense and foreign affairs and the prime minister, on short-haul foreign visits, or when President Sadat needed them in a hurry at one of the many places he stayed around the country: Aswan, Ismailiya, Alexandria, and so on. I often traveled abroad on these planes when accompanying Egyptian foreign ministers: with Kamal Hassan Ali to Iraq, Jordan, and Sudan, Esmat Abdel Meguid to Jordan and Syria, and Amre Moussa to Israel, Syria, and Saudi Arabia. Years later, when I became foreign minister, I was forced to use these same aircraft, maintained and repaired with superhuman effort by the Egyptian air force. Come 2005, this aircraft was approaching its thirtieth birthday! I held my breath whenever it took off on a mission to a neighboring country or somewhere in the Middle East, or with Major-General Omar Suleiman, chief of Egyptian Intelligence, on our many missions together.

Back in the US, the office of the secretary of state sent Ambassador Atherton to the region toward the end of July 1978, in part to inform both Jordan and Saudi Arabia of the American view of the situation, and also to visit Egypt and Israel to explore what were and how they assessed the results of the Leeds Castle meeting, and look into possible future steps and actions. Atherton met the Egyptian foreign minister on the afternoon of July 29 in Cairo, accompanied by his senior aides. I took down the minutes of the meeting, the tone of which was rather acute, at least on Minister Kamel's part. He blamed the Americans for failing, so far, to offer their proposals for a settlement in accordance with the understandings of the first Camp David in February 1978. He also objected to the U.S. call for a new tripartite meeting on the pretext of affording the US a chance to present their own thoughts on the matter afterward. Egypt, Kamel said, had had its fill of this Israeli stalling, as evidenced by Leeds Castle, and the US' failure to take a stand with Israel, which was now standing up to the Americans and outright refusing the U.S. point of view.

Atherton then went to meet President Sadat in Alexandria on July 30. The meeting was also attended by Ahmed Maher, Minister Kamel, and Dr. Osama al-Baz. President Sadat was firm and unequivocal. I believe it may be important to offer a detailed account of this meeting, by dint of its importance, and also because it reveals how Sadat had come to envisage the situation at this stage. Sadat's ideological framework reveals a great deal of his views regarding any settlement with Israel, at least insofar as Egypt was concerned.

Atherton began the meeting by telling Sadat that he was giving him a message from President Carter. The U.S. president wanted to convince Egypt to hold an additional tripartite meeting for the ministers of defense and foreign affairs. Atherton added that he had discussed it with Foreign Minister Ibrahim Kamel, and that the U.S. goal was to seek a settlement for the Palestinian problem via agreeing on basics at the start of negotiations, that is, the principles governing such a settlement: it needed to be understood and settled from the start of the transitional period that any final settlement should be based on Resolution 242, which included a need for Israel to withdraw. This proposed method differed from the thinking of the Israelis, who sought to leave this matter open, without any prior commitment. The United States, Atherton added, was currently listening to a variety of ideas from many sources so as to select the ones on which to focus. These sources included Begin's local-governance project; the nine points presented to Egypt in April 1978; and finally, Egypt's proposal for Israeli withdrawal, including security guarantees. The U.S. representative said that the points they were contemplating debating with us regarding the West Bank and Gaza were in no way a replacement for a declaration of principles, but an addendum to same; the US was moving in this direction after it had become clear that basic issues pertaining to a comprehensive settlement and detailed aspects related to the West Bank must be tackled simultaneously. All of these ideas would be complementary to Carter's Aswan wording, which would be featured in the draft declaration of principles.

In response to a direct question by President Sadat, Atherton went on to speak of the domestic situation within Israel. There were, he said, a great many divisions within the government, and criticism within his own party of the manner in which they had dealt with President Sadat's ideas: this, however, in no way indicated that Begin was weaker. On the contrary, he retained his well-established position and power, enjoying a majority evidenced by the voting in the final sessions, when a vote of confidence in the government was taken. Atherton was obliged to tell Sadat that when he, Atherton, had met Begin, the meeting had been attended by Yigal Yadin, Weizman, and Dayan, and that he had presented the U.S. proposals to them on modifying Israel's thinking and its stance on the West Bank and Gaza. He, Atherton, had been astonished when Begin had lent him a careful ear, not responding with a barrage of counter-arguments as he had done in every previous session, when he had stood his ground and rejected out of hand any opinion that differed from his own. He appeared to be more contemplative these days. Some of those close to him were saying that he was more inclined to be flexible these days, which was borne out by the fact that he was prepared to develop the Israeli response to the Americans' question as to the future, or post-interim, fate of the West Bank and Gaza. Dayan and Vance had looked into ways and means for reformulating the issue of sovereignty over the West Bank and Gaza. Although this was hardly sufficient, it was certainly a great leap forward for Israel. Atherton was delighted when Begin expressed his readiness to look into the issue of sovereignty, feeling that this paved the way for resolving this point. This was the first time, in the U.S. view, that Begin had taken a stance that could be interpreted as allowing for any acceptance of the possibility of Arab sovereignty over the West Bank and Gaza at the end of the line.

In order to correctly assess the situation, we here in Egypt, as of this writing, in 2011, need to be aware that this was what the US was conveying to the Egyptians in late July 1978. In any case, Atherton went on to explain his view that there was a need for a new meeting between the parties concerned, to further consolidate in everyone's view that no forward motion would be achieved without decisive U.S. intervention.

Foreign Minister Mohamed Ibrahim Kamel took the floor. He had, he said, conducted extensive consultations with Atherton. The main points of contention between Egypt and the US were those that American thinking had become ossified, so far. We had been astonished, he said, that the U.S. proposals were a replica of Begin's, and that the only commitment required of Israel during the transition was to attend negotiations around some points, including withdrawal. Ibrahim said he had spoken to Atherton of two possible approaches for the US. A) Washington accepted that their ideas constituted a compromise, and invited Egypt and Israel to sit at the negotiating table on that basis—meaning that the parties would then negotiate a new compromise with the U.S. starting point. In this case, the U.S. compromise (given the Israeli methods of negotiation) needed to be 100 percent compliant with the Egyptian one. B) The US offered a new proposal for a settlement to be accepted as is, not up for debate.

Minister Kamel requested of Ambassador Atherton that the US seriously reconsider the wording offered by Egypt for a Palestinian settlement, to guarantee Jordan's participation, since Jordan's absence rendered all these efforts to reach a Palestinian settlement moot.

President Sadat then took the floor. There was, he said, an important point in President Carter's message, namely that he put a great deal of stock in a third round of tripartite negotiations; however, when studying this suggestion, we needed to closely examine our very recent past, namely Israel's continued stalling in order to conceal their main goal, namely annexation of lands and expansion. This had come to the surface at Leeds Castle, where Israel's goals had become plain: they wanted land, and land alone. To convince Israel to abandon their designs, we offered them the six security arrangements the president had spoken of with Weizman.

President Sadat went on to say that he had gone far enough. He had even offered his agreement to a military alliance between the US and Israel in return for abandoning its regional designs on more land. Now, he affirmed that he would not sit down to negotiate with the Israelis without a clear admission that the lands invaded in 1967 were not subject to compromise or debate in any shape or form. "I am prepared," he said, "to give Israel anything under the sun, other than land and sovereignty." He would even, he said, give them water to irrigate an area of the Naqab in exchange for each settlement they relinquished in the West Bank, just so long as it was understood that Israel would remain within its borders and not expand. "I would be open to the possibility of a peaceable settlement by means of which Israel gets whatever it needs to guarantee its security. I will do what it takes to normalize relations and secure open borders. I will do anything to keep Egypt from relinquishing a centimeter of its land or sovereignty."

At the time, I asked both Mohamed Ibrahim Kamel and Dr. Osama al-Baz about Sadat's real intentions on the issue of water. Their responses were identical: "It's a gambit. He's selling them a bill of goods; it isn't practicable, and he can't commit or agree to such a thing in practice."

The president concluded with a request to Atherton to tell President Carter where he stood, and ask the US to offer its own vision, as it had promised. The main thing was that this U.S. proposal not be a reiteration of Israel's own vision, nor based on wishy-washy deferrals in the name of compromise, or we would be forced to reject it; we wished to avoid rejecting U.S. proposals whenever possible. Israel, the president said, was acting like a spoiled child that insists on getting what it wants regardless of the consequences: this wasn't even good for Israel, he said, if it really did want peace. One day they would realize that they had lost their last hope for peace, in perhaps two thousand years. "I am confident," he said, "of our eventual victory, no matter what happens; I repeat, if the people of Israel want to live with us in the region as our neighbors, then we say, 'Yes.' But if they dream of becoming the region's superpower, that is when we say, 'No.' That will never happen."

The president spoke for some time of what he believed was America's best course. It would be best to avoid getting mired down in details, concentrating instead on the broader framework for a settlement; after this, the US could ask the parties concerned to sit down together and work out how to set out the general principles to be implemented, instead of wasting time on fruitless discussions. "All that is required of you is to say: No land by force. No illegal settlements. The parties need to sit together to plan security arrangements and good neighborly relations. But to launch into discussions of details before agreeing on the basics—that will definitely open the door for them to use this against us, and you as well."

What Sadat said to Atherton and U.S. Ambassador to Egypt Hermann Eilts evidenced that Sadat had outlined a strategy for the coming period, which required the US to come up with a clear general framework for the elements of a settlement, followed by negotiations between the parties on how to implement each of the items in this framework. The two American officials followed up on what Sadat said by asking questions, clarifying some points, and making their own. "If we come up with proposals without holding sufficient talks," Eilts said, "we will be opening ourselves to the charge of trying to impose a solution, which is a delicate matter. This is why we believe it is necessary to hold another meeting between the parties concerned to create the impression that we are trying to push them toward an agreement." He added, "Please let me ask the following. Assuming that the USA issued an official statement, as President Sadat is suggesting, of the general framework for a settlement—would Egypt then be prepared to attend such a meeting?"

This last question was evidence that the U.S. side had not yet grasped what President Sadat was trying to achieve. In any event, the president responded to Eilts, "Let me say this. You, like us, were waiting for Israel to come up with something new. They have; but it's the reverse of what is required. Israel's position in Leeds was absolutely negative; so was that of the Knesset, including the letter I refused to accept. I have said before that we are now at the climax of this operation. I tell you frankly: If the Israelis feel that they can say all this with no shame, no one will be able to stop them. In your proposals to them, I hardly think it practical to get mired down in details. All that is required of you is to say: In accordance with international ethics, the UN Charter, and Security Council Resolution 242, there must be a balance. The land occupied in 1967 must be outside the scope of negotiations. The parties must then sit down to discuss two issues: peace and security. The United Nations will sit down with them to assist them in agreeing on these two points.

"I say to you today: If President Carter truly wants things to move forward, then anything that appears impossible today will become possible once we have peace, security, and normalization of relations. If he so wishes,

Carter can keep my demands suspended indefinitely on the grounds of security requirements. My advice to my friend Carter is not to be mired in the details of a verbose proposal, but stick to the principles on which there can be no disagreement."

Finally, at the end of this important meeting with the president, Atherton said, "Mr. President. We have always operated on the assumption that new positive elements will come from us, not Israel. However, you have said that you consider our efforts to have reached a pivotal point. I don't see how we can now continue with implementing the strategy we agreed upon."

The meeting concluded. We did not have to wait long for the U.S. response in the form of an announcement that Cyrus Vance would be visiting the Middle East in a few days.

Vance arrived in Israel on August 5, and Egypt on August 7. He met with Minister Kamel, accompanied by their two assistants, in one of the rooms of the Palestine Hotel in Alexandria, where both delegations were staying (although I personally preferred to stay at my father's cabin in the nearby beach resort of Ma'mura). I noticed that the Americans made no mention of the ongoing peace process or the negotiations at Leeds Castle or elsewhere: Vance and his assistants confined their speech to the developments in Iran and what was then known as the 'crescent of crisis'—the belt extending from Pakistan and the Indian Peninsula in the east to Iran in the west, passing through Afghanistan, where the unrest was on the verge of plunging the country into an unprecedented historical crisis, which finally came to pass on December 1979, and persists today.

Despite the Americans' reluctance to speak of the settlement efforts—Egypt's main area of interest—Minister Kamel nevertheless spoke on a number of points we had prepared for him. These included a comprehensive overview of the situation since President Sadat's initiative in visiting Jerusalem: it covered the Israelis' continued stubbornness on the issues both of the present and future of Palestinian lands in the West Bank and Gaza, Israel's insistence on keeping up a military presence plus settlements in Sinai after the—nominal, in that case—Israeli withdrawal from the peninsula to the Egypt–Mandatory Palestine borders.

On the evening of August 7, Cyrus Vance met President Sadat privately. We learned that morning from Minister Kamel that President Carter had invited the leaders of Egypt and Israel to meet with him at Camp David to look into a settlement and achieve a breakthrough in the stalled negotiations. Although some news agencies had jumped the gun at Vance's arrival in Alexandria, announcing that President Carter might issue such an invitation, I was a little concerned at the fact that it had actually materialized. My fears took full rein.

I spoke a great deal of this with Minister Kamel at the time. The leap forward to a summit conference, no less, with insufficient preparation, and a lack of U.S. firmness with Israel, threatened to scupper the summit. This would have serious, not to say dangerous, consequences for Egypt and the US, not to mention Israel. The US might find itself obliged, during the summit, to push forward half-baked ideas or wishy-washy compromises that threatened Egypt and our objective for peace. My memos to the minister flew thick and fast, analyzing where the various parties stood and their capacities for negotiation: all my conclusions were pessimistic in the extreme. There was no way around it; I feared the consequences of such a summit.

Meanwhile, our Foreign Ministry working group was busily conducting its own studies and assessments of the situation, preparing for possibilities. The situation was unclear, and we were unsure of what the US wished to achieve; this cast a pall over the assessments that Ahmed Maher and I sent to the minister. Our thoughts and assessments were informed by the same conclusions reached by Dr. Osama al-Baz's taskforce.

We monitored the situation closely for any American indications of intent, or of the Camp David agenda. Our experienced Egyptian Ambassador to the US Ashraf Ghorbal sent us, for example, on August 23, 1978, a summary of a talk he had had with William Quandt, who was responsible for the Middle East file at the U.S. National Security Council. He quoted Quandt as saying, "The US appreciates, and shares, Egypt's concepts of security and peace. America is closer to Egypt's view on this. However, there is an Israeli question that Moshe Dayan has asked repeatedly of late: 'What happens if Camp David succeeds in announcing a framework for a solution? What is the next step? What guarantees are there that Jordan will take part in the negotiations afterward? Also, if Jordan refuses to take part, what will Egypt do?' What Dayan wants," Quandt clarified, "is—assuming an agreement is reached at Camp David—to know where Egypt will stand if the other Arab countries should refuse to enter into negotiations afterward. Will Egypt then be free to go ahead with the portion related to its own land and interests?"

Dr. Ghorbal responded by warning Quandt that Israel might be attempting to create the impression of the meeting ending with a unilateral agreement or separate peace between Egypt and Israel. Both the Israeli and U.S. media had been singing this tune for a while recently. Quandt said they had already told the Israelis that such thinking was not

welcome in Egypt, nor was it Washington's focus. The two countries—
Egypt and the US—were focused on a larger concept of fairness. The US'
attitude to a Palestinian settlement, he said, would be free of surprises. It
was important to emerge with a clear and specific framework for peace,
allowing for no conflicting interpretations. As soon as a statement was
issued specifying this framework, Washington would enter into the stage
of making the necessary communications with Jordan and Palestine to
convince them to participate.

In preparation for the Camp David Summit, Ambassador Ahmed
Maher al-Sayed called me into his office on the evening of Sunday,
September 3, immediately after he returned from Ismailiya, where he had
been accompanying Minister Kamel to a meeting of the main members
of the delegation with President Sadat. We had been asked to prepare a
draft general framework for settlement that could be sent to the president
that same night.

Quickly, we did as we were asked, although I had no idea why Minister
Kamel had asked for this document, especially as all the thoughts and
briefs sent to the president by the Foreign Ministry had recommended
an agreement on a declaration of the principles for a settlement, not this
detailed framework of the concepts and issues governing a settlement. In
any case, we fulfilled the tall order and sent it to the president's office. We
received no reply.

The morning of Monday, September 4, we took off from Abu Sueir
Air Base near Ismailiya. President Sadat and First Lady Jehan al-Sadat
took off as well; the first lady disembarked in Paris, though, leaving the
president to go on alone. I recall a large marquee erected at the air base.
Hundreds of people, ordinary citizens and Egyptian political parties, had
gathered to see the president off on this important trip and show that
there was popular support for his actions and the objectives of his mission.

24 Camp David II

resident Sadat's Boeing 707 landed on Tuesday afternoon, September 5, 1978, at Edwards Air Base near Washington, DC. This was the main air base used by the U.S. president and his senior aides in their travels, as well as the reception point for foreign VIPs visiting DC. President Sadat then boarded a presidential helicopter, while the rest of us boarded a Chinook, and we headed directly to the Camp David resort. The U.S. president and the first lady, we noticed, were there to greet Sadat upon arrival.

American security was extremely tight. Identification was mandatory; we were required to display our identity cards at all times. The press was not admitted. Exit from the resort required written permission from the Americans. Upon our arrival, we were given orientation brochures that contained information and maps of the layout and hidden nooks and crannies of the resort, the paths and various buildings, and of course each delegation's living quarters.

Camp David is located north of Washington, in a mountainous area of Maryland. There are immense, majestic trees as far as the eye can see, giving the impression of a wooded area. President Sadat was lodged in a modest bungalow, dubbed Dogwood, while the Egyptian delegation was in another bungalow, Maple. Mohamed Ibrahim Kamel and Boutros Boutros-Ghali shared one room, and Hassan Kamel, head of the Cabinet, and Ashraf Ghorbal shared another. We of the taskforce were in a third bungalow, called Hawthorn. Ahmed Maher, Nabil al-Arabi, and I shared a room, and Dr. Osama al-Baz and Abdel Raouf El Reedy were in another room.

265

The resort was crisscrossed by tiny asphalt paths, only wide enough for pedestrians, bicycles, or golf carts. The Americans provided each of the members of the delegation with a bicycle to allow us to move quickly between the buildings and the main cafeteria.

On the flight, Dr. Osama al-Baz had given Ahmed Maher al-Sayed the draft Egyptian settlement framework, which he had prepared and run by President Sadat when the two of them were in Abu Sueir a few days before Camp David. Osama al-Baz's influence on President Sadat and Vice President Hosni Mubarak was often a source of concern, not to say worry, for Ahmed Maher. He was unsure how this influence would affect the minister, although Minister Kamel himself remained unconcerned. Thus, we of the minister's office were somewhat surprised at Osama al-Baz's presence in Ismailiya in the days before the trip. I realized the reason when Ahmed Maher showed me the draft framework for a working agenda that Egypt was to propose at the summit. I also realized the background to Maher asking us for another draft framework to send to the Presidency, after which our documents disappeared. Clearly, the president had gone with the one prepared by al-Baz. To be fair, that document reflected everything our team had been preparing, only with the elegant phrasing that was to become Osama al-Baz's trademark.

Over the months prior to Camp David, Egypt had released two main documents. The first was at Leeds Castle and dealt with the Palestinian settlement and the idea of the transitional period, namely the requirement to define its nature and ultimate end. The second was the framework for peace. The latter document, in a powerful preamble, spoke of the parties' desire to achieve peace, end the dispute, and establish good neighborly relations, as well as the parties' preparedness to sign peace treaties based on a complete implementation of UN Security Council Resolutions 242 and 338 in all their parts. The path to this, the preamble stated, necessitated Israel's fulfillment of its withdrawal from occupied territories in accordance with the inadmissibility of the acquisition of territory by war and the completion of withdrawals from Sinai, the Golan, and the West Bank to ceasefire lines. The document stipulated the removal of Israeli settlements in the occupied territories in tandem with establishing security arrangements, based on the points proposed by Sadat to Weizman in Vienna. The document also stipulated that the parties both accept the binding jurisdiction of the International Court of Justice in case of any and all disputes, and the inadmissibility of either the threat or actual use of force. The document went on to explain Egypt's view of how the transitional period could be managed in the occupied Palestinian territories. It then said that the parties should establish normal relations, such as those between states in peacetime, including complete recognition, the end of the Arab embargo, and guarantees of navigation in the Suez Canal in accordance of the Convention of Constantinople of 1888.

I was reading the second document over Ahmed Maher al-Sayed's shoulder when Minister Mohamed Ibrahim Kamel came to the rear of the plane, carrying a copy of the same document, given to him by President Sadat. The three of us were seeing it for the first time. El Reedy and al-Arabi had no knowledge of it as yet, having gone directly to Washington.

The three of us agreed that this Egyptian document was a suitable basis for preliminary negotiations. Minister Kamel said that President Sadat had assured him of his intention to submit the paper at his first meeting with Carter and Begin. If the Israeli rejected it outright, Sadat planned to leave Camp David for Washington to launch a media and political firestorm aimed at exposing Israel's insistence on not budging, after which he would go back home.

I must say I found his intentions odd. Was the president truly convinced he could withdraw just like that? It could not be that simple. Minister Kamel was meanwhile urging the president not to submit the Egyptian proposal at the start, but to wait until the U.S. and Israeli intentions became clear. It seemed a waste, and abortive, to lay the proposal on the table right at the start of negotiations. The minister also shook his head at Sadat's vow to leave Camp David the minute Begin's rejection of his proposal should become clear. As matters would have it, I had no doubts whatsoever about what Minister Kamel was conveying to us about Sadat's negotiating style and the veracity of his intentions. Still, I was not really convinced that this approach was doable in practice, as it inevitably entailed a clash with our American hosts, which Sadat had always sought to avoid. Indeed, he had worked tirelessly in the past months, not to say years, to build stable and strong relations between the US and Egypt, with Egypt as a powerful and influential regional power that America would do well to make friends with—the reverse, of course, being true, by dint of the US' power and influence worldwide.

The three parties, it is important to note, were at Camp David to achieve a comprehensive settlement for the dispute, divided—at least in the case of Egypt and Israel—by distinctly different views. Israel refused to withdraw from the Sinai air bases and to clear the settlements, despite its acknowledgment of Egypt's full sovereignty over Sinai and the international boundary between Egypt and Mandatory Palestine. Israel also believed it had a right to the West Bank, and therefore was reluctant to make concessions that could lead to the emergence of a Palestinian state there. Meanwhile, the goal of the Egyptian negotiators was to retrieve the lands on two fronts, being prepared to make concessions in both locations.

In *al-Salam al-da'i' fi Camp David* (The Lost Peace of the Camp David Accords), Mohamed Ibrahim Kamel tells the story of the twelve days in the Camp David negotiations. He tells how Sadat submitted the Egyptian proposal to both Begin and Carter on the afternoon of Wednesday, September 6, and asked them both to look into it and give their feedback. Mohamed Ibrahim Kamel says that Cyrus Vance conveyed some preliminary observations to him on September 7, which were significant, revealing the true course on which the US and Israel were embarking in their scheme to facilitate a settlement leading to Camp David's success. Vance said, with regard to the item regarding the clearing of Israeli settlements in the occupied territories on a clear schedule agreed upon within a specific time frame, that "the American view is that the position is clear on the settlements in Sinai, and that they are in agreement with us that they must be dismantled. However, dismantling the settlements in the West Bank and Gaza is a huge problem, and Israel cannot agree to this since it poses a threat to its security." U.S. Vice President Walter Mondale, who was present at the talks between Kamel and Vance, suggested a five-year freeze on settlements, coupled with negotiations between Jordan, Israel, and a representative of the Palestinians to discuss the future of the settlements. Minister Kamel agreed to a freeze in settlements in principle. Observing the Palestinian–Israeli negotiations in recent years, and the efforts of successive U.S. administrations since Bush the elder, through Clinton and Bush the younger to Barack Obama, it is easy to see that negotiations concerning the issues of settlement-building are alive and well, as is the eternal call for a freeze on settlements, and agreeing to the elements of such a freeze, in a perpetual Greek tragedy.

The Tripartite Summit was held on September 7. It was a heated encounter. Menachem Begin rejected the Egyptian proposal, with regard both to ending the Israeli presence in Sinai and to withdrawing from the air bases there. He proposed some ideas that would keep the settlers on Egyptian soil. Sadat roundly rejected them. Tension reigned. Still, the evening concluded with the three teams attending a formal dinner at President Carter's invitation, at which the Marines entertained and impressed us with a stunning military parade.

Carter invited Sadat to meet with him that night, with only three members of each delegation present, to guarantee secrecy and efficacy. Sadat was accompanied by Hassan Fahmy, Mohamed Ibrahim Kamel, and Boutros Boutros-Ghali. On the American side, Carter was accompanied by Vice President Mondale—who cared primarily that the president's popularity not be affected by any negative outcome of Camp David—and Cyrus Vance and National Security Advisor Zbigniew Brzezinski.

In the next few paragraphs, I will rely on Mohamed Ibrahim Kamel's account of this meeting, held at 2300 hours on September 7. President Carter said he wished to speak first about Sinai, then move on to the West Bank and Gaza. The main issue in Sinai, he said, was that of the Israeli settlements and air bases established there. Israel and Egypt were clearly in conflict on this issue. The Israeli prime minister already felt he had made great concessions in Sinai, as evidenced by his proposal in Ismailiya.

Mondale then asked what would happen if a solution was found for the issue of settlements. Would there be a way to resolve the other issues?

Cyrus Vance then took over. There was no legal or ethical basis, he said, for the settlements to remain in Sinai. As for the air bases in the peninsula, he said, this was a military issue to be discussed by military representatives. Vance was adamant—and here is why I am relying on Minister Kamel's book in my account of this meeting—that the situation in Sinai and the Golan was completely different from that in the West Bank and Gaza. There was an Egyptian government with the right to sovereignty over Sinai; there was a Syrian government capable of controlling the Golan. The situation in the West Bank and Gaza was completely different, as there was no clear political power possessing sovereignty over these areas.

Brzezinski proposed converting some of the settlements in Sinai into training camps for the U.S. military. This had been proposed by Cyrus Vance and summarily rejected by Minister Kamel during the talks at Leeds Castle.

President Sadat then clarified his position, namely, not giving up any land or sovereignty in the Sinai Peninsula. Carter followed up with his plan to submit the U.S. proposal, which they had spent months preparing, for the West Bank and Gaza. Carter's wording and comments revealed that he was basing our long-awaited U.S. solution on the Israeli proposal Begin submitted in Ismailiya on December 24.

Minister Ibrahim Kamel spoke up, voicing criticism of the use of the Israeli proposal as a basis for the U.S. approach. He suggested that the Egyptian suggestions, from Leeds Castle or Camp David, instead be used as the basis for negotiations. Among other things, he explained, this would win the approval of a large number of Arab countries for whatever agreements, if any, were reached. The US could also draw inspiration, he said, from what U.S. elder statesmen had been telling us for months. At this point, Hassan al-Tohami started to kick Minister Kamel under the table, trying to get him to calm his ire toward Carter and the rest of the U.S. delegation. "Quit that!" Minister Kamel snapped at him under his breath.

In any event, the meeting ended with Kamel and Boutros-Ghali extremely worried about what the Americans were planning and what fresh cards they had up their sleeves. We waited for a response from the US, which was notably slow to arrive in the days that followed, until September 11, six days after the start of the Camp David Summit. All that time, I wondered about the reasons behind the US' delay in presenting us with documents and proposals, and instead holding meeting after meeting between Egypt and the US, either headed by Vance and Kamel or by al-Baz, Saunders, and Atherton. These meetings all focused on each party's attitude and their views on the developments in the region, starting from western Asia and the Indian peninsula, through Afghanistan and Iran, to the Horn of Africa, plus the developments in Somalia and Ethiopia. According to Cyrus Vance, the US wanted to help Egypt carry the burden of the crisis in the Middle East, which it currently bore alone, thus allowing Egypt to use its full influence and fulfill its role in dealing with the region's pressing issues.

It was with some suspicion and trepidation that we heard this line of reasoning: none of those present would be able to agree to Egypt joining Iran and Turkey, known for their pro-western policies, in being the region's policeman, responsible for defending the interests of the US and the west. In my estimation, the Americans were deferring the moment of submitting their proposed Palestinian settlement to make it appear a direct result of their discussions and consultations with both parties over the six days, especially as the U.S. administration had failed to effect the second meeting they insisted on between the Egyptian and Israeli foreign and defense ministers because Egypt had categorically refused. It was also my view that the U.S. administration feared that any misstep would anger the pro-Israel lobby domestically, which in turn might affect the upcoming elections in the US, due in less than a year.

On Sunday, September 10, the delegations went to Pennsylvania, which borders Virginia and Maryland, to visit the site of the Battle of Gettysburg, often said to be the turning-point in the American Civil War and the beginning of the end for the Confederates. I had read a great deal on this subject; still, I found it odd that our guide, who gave us an account of the battle and its results, started with the third day of the battle and then went backward chronologically to the second and then the first. Still, the tour was effective: by the end of the lecture, which lasted over two hours, I had a full understanding not only of the battle and how it had been managed but also of the personalities of the main commanders and of the battle's results and repercussions.

That evening, after our return from Gettysburg, Atherton and Saunders came to notify us that they would be unable to submit the U.S.

proposal before running it by Israel. It transpired that Israel had produced a document signed by Kissinger in the 1970s stipulating that the US would not present any surprise written proposals on the Middle East without showing them to Israel in advance, before any of the other parties. Naturally, we were not pleased; however, we waited.

On Monday morning, the Americans finally showed us their proposed settlement plan. The U.S. document was titled "A Framework for Peace in the Middle East, Agreed at Camp David." The proposal included a preamble that closely resembled the one proposed by Egypt on September 6, with specific references such as the inadmissibility of the acquisition of territory by war and that peace required the establishment of normal relations between nations, including agreement on security arrangements. After the lengthy preamble, the document was divided into two parts, the first concerning Israel and Egypt and the second concerning the West Bank and Gaza. The first portion was missing a great many details, specifically regarding Israeli withdrawal and the clearing of settlements and air bases, but it did refer to Egyptians having full sovereignty up to the internationally recognized border between Egypt and Mandatory Palestine and to establishing peace between the two countries. In the second portion, it became clear that the US desired Egypt and Israel to negotiate any future Palestinian settlement in all its aspects, and that the target solution should admit the legitimate rights of all Palestinians and enable them to participate in determining their own future.

The U.S. proposal adopted the concept of a five-year transitional period and enabling the inhabitants' full self-rule. The idea was for Egypt to bear the responsibility for the negotiations if Jordan refused to participate.

The Egyptian working group met to discuss the U.S. proposal. While still in the meeting, I also jotted down some observations for Minister Mohamed Ibrahim Kamel to present to the president.

Ultimately, we ended up drafting an Egyptian document with modifications to the U.S. one. Over the next few days, the American proposal underwent a number of gradual changes, especially between September 11 and 14, at the behest of both the Egyptians and the Israelis. The Americans presented one modified draft after another to the two parties. Some of these were disappointing to Egypt, others to Israel.

My notes to Minister Kamel covered a number of points. I was disappointed in the wording of the American document. Some of the points concerning the interim period were marred by granting Israel supremacy in the West Bank and Gaza, which would make Israel a source of political authority in addition to Egypt and Jordan. The practical management of the region was in the hands of a committee over which Israel had veto power.

References to 'security' in the document referred, in practice, to one party's security only: Israel. I noted that Egypt's and Jordan's roles remained unclear, but that the document appeared to envision their role in the transition as confined to making sure the Palestinians submitted to Israel. Even when there was mention of a Jordanian role, this was limited to allowing Jordanians into the local police force.

My criticisms of the U.S. proposal referenced the Americans' vision for the end of the transition: in contrast to the Aswan statement, no reference was made to the legitimate rights of the Palestinians. Indeed, the term 'a people' did not appear once. In addition, it seemed that the interim period might well go on indefinitely, in the absence of any text mandating Israel's withdrawal from the West Bank and Gaza at any point.

The text on Jerusalem also lacked any reference to returning Arab Jerusalem to the Arabs or Israeli withdrawal from the city. Even reference to the refugee problem was marred by the US pushing the concept of Jewish refugees as somehow equivalent in this context to Palestinian refugees.

This brief, which I presented to Minister Kamel, pointed out the main shortcomings in the U.S. draft.

The argument between the Egyptians and Americans continued, while tensions rose between Egypt and Israel. I often saw Menachem Begin yelling at Moshe Dayan and Ezer Weizman as he strode down the narrow, winding asphalt paths, "This is unacceptable!"

We on the Egyptian side were not immune to the tensions, either. Minister Kamel's responses and comments on Hassan al-Tohami's and Boutros Boutros-Ghali's meetings with the Israelis were equally scathing, and there were more strolls down the winding paths of the resort both for relaxation and rethinking, not to mention avoiding the bugs that might be planted in the meeting halls and bungalows.

The Egyptian negotiators, we felt, were in grave danger. We were constantly beset by the fear of things breaking down, and the repercussions if the US blamed Egypt for the failure and how this would reflect on the future of Egypt–U.S. relations. Meanwhile, the foreign minister and his team were at risk of abandoning the basic tenets of the Arab position for fear of losing the goodwill of our neighboring Arab countries. Consequently, Ahmed Maher and I kept urging the minister to keep up the pressure on the US. It was essential that they be alerted to the importance of improving their proposal. It was also important for us to prepare ourselves for the possibility that this summit might fail, and thus make a list of all the points that demonstrated that the responsibility for the failure did not lie with us. This included preparing a massive political and media campaign supporting President Sadat, both at home and abroad—the same idea we had before Camp David.

During one of our strolls—perhaps on Wednesday, September 13—Ahmed Maher and I glimpsed President Carter in jeans, cycling down one of the other paths. He stopped to chat with Minister Kamel. The American president was attempting to reassure the Egyptian foreign minister that what he was trying to achieve was a comprehensive settlement that afforded Palestinians their rights within a specified time frame. He said he planned to invite Prince Fahd bin Salman and Prince Sa'ud al-Faisal of Saudi Arabia to Washington immediately on the heels of the summit for their approval. He was aware, he noted, that King Hussein of Jordan was currently sitting on the fence, unwilling to take any risks. Carter said that he nevertheless planned to invite that worthy to the US and convince him of the importance of taking part in the upcoming negotiations with Israel regarding the future of the West Bank and Gaza.

In my estimation, President Carter was very confident—perhaps overconfident—in his ability to convince these Arab parties to accept the agreement and give their blessing. Carter explained that he wanted to avoid burdening President Sadat with the task of arriving at a settlement for Jerusalem, which was why he was exempting Jerusalem from any draft framework or agreement being planned for Camp David.

Minister Kamel took issue with Carter's premises. Neither Prince Fahd bin Salman nor King Hussein would take part in any effort without being sure of a result, or based on a fair agreement guaranteeing the Palestinians their rights. In Kamel's view, the one currently on the table failed to achieve justice for the Palestinians. If Carter truly wanted an Arab–Israeli breakthrough, he needed to make a few modifications to the draft framework, or include ideas taken out by the Israelis.

I hurried away to make my notes on everything that was said in this chance meeting between Kamel and Carter, in which the U.S. president expressed many of his convictions, as well as his intentions vis-à-vis Saudi Arabia and Jordan, whose leaders, he had boundless confidence, he could inveigle into participating in the American effort after Camp David. These notes I presented to Minister Kamel after lunch. He hurried to discuss them with Sadat in the president's quarters.

In the brief period from September 11 to 14, we met often, by choice and by chance, with the U.S. team, to discuss things and try to influence them. On one of these days, Ahmed Maher and I were having breakfast at the resort cafeteria, where all the delegations met to chat and discuss significant points. Zbigniew Brzezinski came in and joined us at our table.

Brzezinski began to speak in elegant English with a heavy Polish accent. We all wore a blue sweater, which I possess to this day, bearing the U.S. president's logo, which we had been given on arrival. "You should not be afraid of the U.S. proposal about the West Bank," he said, "and full self-rule for the Palestinians." He continued, "Some of the points in the draft are still unclear, but what is certain is that the proposed five-year transition will allow the Palestinians to manage their own affairs completely. Also, the presence of an effective Palestinian police force, and an administration with capabilities, will lead to influential new mechanisms and dynamics." He went on to say self-rule would have a snowball effect. He seemed to mean that once the emerging Palestinian authorities played their role to good effect, this would lead to Palestine imposing its demands on Israel, which, apparently, would have no choice but to accept.

We listened intently. Not only did Brzezinski appear completely convinced of what he was saying, he was also a more convincing personage than all the U.S. officials we had spoken with. For years, even after leaving his post at the White House, Brzezinski continued to voice this conviction. However, the delay in implementing the framework agreement on the Palestinian conflict meant that his idea could not be put to the test at the time. Still, it must be said that the years following the Oslo Accords in August 1993 suggested some progress in Israeli thinking, although it still did not meet Arab and Palestinian requirements.

As I mentioned, the cafeteria was where people naturally met and chatted, and the site of fuel for interesting anecdotes. One of these, which I thought quite embarrassing for our side, was Hassan al-Tohami's loud boast that he could stop his own heart from beating for a few minutes. Israeli and American doctors gathered around him, trying to find out what was going on, or perhaps merely if he really was *non compos mentis.*

The situation became more sensitive starting on September 14, as the Israelis insisted that they would make no concessions, in any way, shape, or form, on a Palestinian settlement or full withdrawal from Sinai. The Israeli defense minister conversed frequently with President Sadat, accompanied by his main assistant, General Tamir. I got to know Tamir quite well in later years, when I worked with Lieutenant-General Kamal Hassan Ali during his tenure as foreign minister. Weizman requested that President Sadat meet with Moshe Dayan. The president, Weizman said, might be able to convince him to go along with Egypt's demands, thus allowing him to influence Menachem Begin. Carter chimed in on the same note. President Sadat met Dayan at 1500 hours on the afternoon of September 14. I think it important at this juncture to set down the minutes taken by Dr. Osama al-Baz, dictated by President Sadat after the meeting, as I consider them to be extremely significant.

The meeting was held at 3 pm on Thursday, September 14, at the request of Ezer Weizman, as follows:

> Sadat: I want the truth, Dayan. It's not right to waste our time and President Carter's. What's going on, exactly?
>
> Dayan: Your Excellency the President. I know you like honesty and hate beating around the bush. There are difficulties that make it impossible for any Israeli government to take action, regardless of who is the head of that government. Neither Begin, Weizman, nor I can do anything. The decision is in the hands of the Knesset and the Israeli people. The difficulty is that neither the Knesset nor the people will agree to leave the settlements in Sinai. This is because of the psychological make-up of our people: all Begin can do is play on that chord in our people.
>
> As to the West Bank, things are different. It is easy to reach a solution. We can also agree to fly an Arab or Islamic flag in Jerusalem.
>
> However, there can be no solution to the settlements in Sinai until the Israeli people change their way of thinking; this will take four to five years. It appears that what is available in these circumstances, and given these considerations, is one of the following solutions:
>
> - We sign the framework agreement here in Camp David, then enter into negotiations for three months only to confront the impossibility of reaching an agreement, or signing a peace treaty, because no decision can be made on Sinai at this stage;
> - We admit that we are unable to reach a solution, and abandon the whole thing; or
> - We make a list of the points where we agree, and where we disagree. In that case, we find that the real disagreement boils down to Sinai. On the West Bank and Jerusalem, we can reach an agreement.
>
> Consequently, the more prudent alternative is to reach an interim solution on both fronts: withdrawal from Sinai to the Arish/Ras Mohamed line, with Israel keeping a belt roughly 10 kilometers wide to protect our interests from the Red Sea to Sharm al-Sheikh. The settlements and the air bases are within this belt, except for Arish Air Base. It was my idea to establish Yamit, and the 'safety belt' to protect our interests, in response to the threats made by the late President Nasser. I think, Your Excellency, that the situation has changed, after all that has happened, it's true; however, the Israeli people have not changed. It is very hard to convince the Israelis: anything offered to us,

however reasonable, must be run by the Knesset, who will never agree to relinquish this belt.

Sadat: This means that the Egyptian initiative has changed nothing in Israel.

Dayan: What I'm trying to say is that Begin isn't the problem. He isn't empowered to sign anything here. And he isn't going to. All he can say is, "I'll take this back to the Knesset." And if that happens, nothing will happen, because the Knesset won't agree to anything. And the Knesset holds this line because the Israelis are a domineering people: there isn't an Israeli leader who would dare to make a decision counter to the will of the people. This goes for the Labor Party, too, whatever they may say or show about being prepared to go further than Begin in finding a solution.

Sadat: Strange. But I appreciate your honesty. It's better to know how things stand, without beating around the bush. I want to be clear with you, too:

There will be no giving up any part of the Sinai Peninsula.

The settlements cannot be allowed to remain.

You cannot be permitted to keep the air bases.

When you're ready for peace, you're welcome to call us.

The Egyptian people have changed their outlook completely since the initiative. But it's clear that your people haven't.

Dayan: They still need some time. What I wanted to convey to Your Excellency is, don't be too hard on Begin. He is not the obstacle to peace.

Sadat: Why come to Camp David then, and waste everyone's time, and tie up the schedule of the president of the United States of America for ten days? Do you know he sat yesterday for fourteen hours straight with a member of the Egyptian delegation and another of the Israeli team, discussing every detail with them word for word?

Dayan: True. But couldn't we look into the third option I mentioned? An interim solution for the Palestinian problem and for Jerusalem, and a solution in Sinai where we withdraw to Arish/Ras Mohamed, and leave the 10-kilometer strip to a third stage? As I said before, the issue of the settlements and air bases can only be resolved after four to five years.

Sadat: You know full well that this is unacceptable. I won't even look into it. You have my decision.

No more disengagement of forces.

No half-measures.

No unilateral solutions.

No interim solutions.

We're talking about a comprehensive peace, man, not about this kind of trivial details! If you aren't ready to absorb the magnitude of these concepts, it's a shame. But that's your problem, not mine. In any event, I appreciate your honesty.

Osama al-Baz apprised Minister Kamel of the situation, and told the rest of our team about what had transpired between President Sadat and Foreign Minister Dayan. There was a deep sense that we had reached the sticking place: the responsibility for the success or failure of the conference now lay squarely on America's shoulders. If the US could not make Israel change its tune, the summit would break down, with all the consequences of failure.

I spent a sleepless night. The next morning, we discovered that President Sadat had put in a request to leave for Washington that same day: September 15. The members of the delegation went to pack. Each of us put our suitcase outside his bungalow door, to allow the U.S. presidential staff to collect them for sending on to our hotels in the U.S. capital.

That morning, I went to Minister Kamel's bungalow. The minister had gone to meet the president at his request, to make a plan for the next few days to manage our sudden exit from Camp David. I started to speak with Minister Boutros Boutros-Ghali, who immediately asked me to take a walk with him.

Once outside the bungalow, I asked Minister Boutros-Ghali for his assessment of the situation. Did he think President Sadat genuinely intended to pull out and go home?

"I'm positive it's a gambit," said Boutros-Ghali. "He's trying to raise the ceiling of Egypt's demands and pressure the Americans to carry them out. They've got to take a serious stand with the Israelis, especially now that they've come right out with their unsavory intentions." He was referring to what Moshe Dayan had said to Sadat the previous day.

I agreed with Dr. Boutros-Ghali immediately. "That's why I didn't pack my clothes or briefcase!" I had left my briefcase in the operations room of the Egyptian delegation under the supervision of President Sadat's men, who were there twenty-four/seven.

No sooner did the Americans get wind of Sadat's step than Cyrus Vance visited him in his quarters, asking him to reconsider. Sadat stood by his decision. He complained bitterly about Israel's positions as explained by Dayan. Vance left Sadat and headed straight to President Carter. A few moments later, we saw Carter jogging over to Sadat's bungalow. At this point, it was about 1100 hours. They spent nearly forty minutes together.

Later, we learned that he had convinced the president to stay for a day or two more, with promises to do his very best to meet Egypt's needs.

Mohamed Ibrahim Kamel and Dr. Osama al-Baz indicated that President Sadat told them that Carter was shocked at his decision and said that it would lead to him losing the next election. In fact, American sources writing in the years after Camp David revealed that Carter told Sadat that if he left he was not to expect any support from Carter in future. Furthermore, he said that the failure of Camp David would lead to tensions between Egypt and Israel that no American efforts could alleviate, possibly even leading to a new war.

My own analysis of the situation is that Sadat, having witnessed first-hand the difficulties inherent in the Israelis' inflexible position, sought to obtain full U.S. support for his request that America carry out its specific plans for Sinai, namely that it be completely cleared and given over to Egypt. This is why Dr. Osama al-Baz continued with his consultations and negotiations on the wording of the peace framework. From September 13, President Carter had suggested that each party nominate a member to take part in wording sessions, mentioned in the American draft framework. Carter would spend long hours in seclusion with Dr. Osama al-Baz and the Israeli representative, Attorney General Aharon Barak. Osama al-Baz would then go back to get President Sadat's approval on specific wording. He also continued to rely on El Reedy and al-Arabi's experience and expertise; they, along with al-Baz, were the legal mind of the Egyptian delegation.

It must be said here that many American officials conveyed to us Carter's astonishment that al-Baz was spending long hours in extended sessions with himself and Barak, sometimes up to ten hours, hardly eating anything except, for example, a glass of milk and an apple.

Sure enough, on September 15 and 16, a final agreement was reached on a framework for peace and the formulation of the settlement.

The agreement in essence stated that the Israeli delegation, immediately upon returning to Israel, within fifteen days, would submit the matter of a full Israeli withdrawal from Sinai and clearing the settlements to the Knesset for a vote. President Sadat would accept this way out in exchange for the proposed peace framework on Sinai, the West Bank, and Gaza, given the Knesset voted in favor.

I thought long and hard about this. How, I asked myself, had the Americans managed to convince the Israelis to withdraw from Sinai and clear the settlements and air bases that Moshe Dayan had assured President Sadat just one day ago, as we have seen, Israel could not withdraw from?

I began to go over a number of situations with the Americans that I had witnessed, and things U.S. officials had said: Quandt's conversations with Ashraf Ghorbal; Cyrus Vance's statements to Mohamed Ibrahim Kamel that clearing the Sinai settlements was a requirement, after which some agreement could be reached regarding the air bases; and Carter and Weizman's joint insistence that Sadat meet with Dayan.

I arrived at the conclusion that the US and Israel had known from the start that Israel would not be able to maintain a military presence or settlements on Egyptian soil, on any pretext and in any form. They had wanted to get Sadat's agreement on the framework for the West Bank and Gaza. This was why Dayan had met with Sadat: to frustrate him and goad him into escalation, whereupon Carter was to come and tell him that he would get Israel out of Sinai. It is my firm conviction today, as it was then, that Carter told Sadat to give him just two days and he would get it done.

We left Washington with Minister Mohamed Ibrahim Kamel on September 18, for Paris, and thence to Cairo. On the flight back to Cairo, I told the minister my thoughts, and that I had mentioned my theory to Ahmed Maher, who agreed with me. Maher stayed behind in Paris: his sister, who lived there, had died a few days before. Minister Kamel said that what happened in Camp David meant that this kind of evasiveness on the part of the Americans and Israelis was not unlikely, in his view.

In the months that followed the signing of the Camp David Accords in the White House on September 17, a great many articles were written in the *New York Times* by two Israeli writers on a number of the points and elements of the Camp David Summit and the events that led to them. The articles, which analyzed Israel's performance at the talks, stated that General Weizman, because of his continual meetings with President Sadat over a number of months, had concluded that the Egyptian president, despite his repeated insistence on an integrated and comprehensive agreement for a settlement that linked withdrawal from Sinai to a move toward solving the Palestinian problem, would ultimately accept a partial solution that gave Egypt its rights and deferred the Palestinian issue for the interim period. All President Sadat wanted, the writers said, was to get a "fig leaf" to cover him with other Arab countries. This was what the Israelis—and possibly the Americans as well—read into the thinking and attitudes of President Sadat. I immediately submitted these articles, important at the time, to Minister Mohamed Ibrahim Kamel.

Returning to the negotiations before the agreement was signed, Osama al-Baz continued holding intensive talks with President Carter and Barak. He frequently clashed with the U.S. president when Carter would claim that Sadat had given his agreement to this or that article, whereupon al-Baz would argue that he spoke for the president.

The hours dragged heavily on September 15 and 16, full of concern and apprehension. On Saturday, I visited Minister Kamel's bungalow upon hearing from Boutros Boutros-Ghali, whom I had met in the cafeteria for breakfast, that Minister Kamel did not want to get out of bed. I went to convince him to come for breakfast, but he would have none of it. Finally, I went to the cafeteria and brought him something to eat, including some fruit and a hot drink. He was still lying in bed, clearly exhausted and discouraged.

Mohamed Ibrahim Kamel left the whole matter of the talks with the Americans and the Israelis in the hands of Dr. Osama al-Baz, who was speaking to both sides in the name of Egypt and President Sadat. I might even say that the foreign minister, having failed to convince President Sadat not to go ahead with signing the Camp David framework—about which he had serious reservations—had withdrawn completely. I found this extremely disturbing.

"I've been following everything you've been doing very closely," I said, handing him his breakfast. But, I went on to say, his current course of action could have only one logical ending: he would hand in his resignation or wait for it to come from the president.

My words appeared to shock the minister. "Of course I know what happens next!" he retorted with some asperity. I had no idea back then that Mohamed Ibrahim Kamel had already informed the president of his intention to resign. Ahmed Maher, who knew what the minister was thinking and was aware of his exchange with Sadat, had not told me.

Saturday went by. The agreement and peace framework began to take shape. President Sadat insisted that the framework for peace on the West Bank and in Gaza come first in the document, followed by the segment on Sinai and Egypt, to emphasize that Egypt prioritized Palestinian interests over its own. My opinion, then as now, was that this failed to produce Sadat's hoped-for effect.

There was also an understanding that the city of Jerusalem would be excluded from the terms of the agreement. Each party would set down its views on the city's status and submit them to the US, which would undertake to convey the messages to the other party. The messages included one to Carter from Sadat on full withdrawal from Sinai in accordance with the peace framework, noting that Egypt was not bound by the framework unless Israel withdrew from Sinai in accordance with the agreed-upon process of securing the Knesset's approval. Another message announced that Egypt was prepared to bear the Arab side's responsibilities, that is to say, to negotiate with Israel for the Palestinian territories in Gaza and the West Bank after consulting with Jordan.

Nabil al-Arabi, the legal counsel for the Foreign Ministry, came to Minister Kamel that evening. Ahmed Maher and myself were with him, along with Dr. Boutros-Ghali, and he was loudly declaiming his objections to these messages, which, he said, were not binding on any of the parties concerned. The minister of state for foreign affairs responded that he had conveyed this to the president, but that Sadat had refused to back down. Nabil al-Arabi asked Minister Kamel to allow him to visit President Sadat in order to submit his own vision. It was well known in our circles that al-Arabi was a close relative of First Lady Jehan al-Sadat. This allowed him the president's ear when it was most needed. Since al-Arabi was also a relation by marriage of Mohamed Hassanein Heikal's, the years during which Heikal worked with the president placed al-Arabi in a privileged position. However, when Sadat was in conflict with Heikal, some tension inevitably crept into his relationship with al-Arabi. Be that as it may, Nabil al-Arabi went to visit President Sadat.

Forty minutes later, al-Arabi returned, so pale that he was almost yellow. He began to tell us about his meeting with Sadat. After meeting the Israeli prime minister, Sadat was sitting on the verandah of the bungalow with the Presidential Guard. He asked al-Arabi what he wanted, then took him into the reception room of the bungalow. Dr. al-Arabi told us that he spoke at length about his view that the messages going back and forth had no legal status. The president appeared to be listening attentively. When al-Arabi finished, the president said, "I have listened, as you can see, very carefully to everything you've said. Your opinions have gone in this ear and out the other. You Foreign Office diplomats know nothing of politics, or of your country's interests. Your talk is all very well on paper, but it's all theory. I might as well be talking to a bunch of philosophers—or plumbers!

"You have no idea, have you, that your children and grandchildren could live for years in the shadow of an occupied Egypt. My first responsibility is to Egypt. As a statesman, I must do everything in my power to free my land and its territories from being mortgaged or held for ransom as they are now. And I'm going to do it. None of your ill-advised words or half-baked opinions will sway me."

Al-Arabi went on to tell us how Sadat had raged at Heikal, who, he claimed, was scheming against him. He threatened to punish him and gave al-Arabi a warning to deliver to Heikal.

Once the summit was over, we drove to Madison Hotel in Washington. The president went straight to the White House to sign the agreement. Minister Kamel was absent, as was the entire Foreign Ministry working group, including Osama al-Baz, who had no appetite for the official protocol-laden occasions that accompanied the signing of the peace frameworks. We watched on television as the ceremony unfolded in the White House to great media fanfare. Minister Kamel asked me to summon Dr. Osama al-Baz to discuss some of the peace frameworks. I went to his room, which was next to the minister's, to find him sitting in bed in nothing but his shorts, writing out some of the statements to be delivered by President Sadat at occasions in the coming days in DC. We spoke briefly. I asked him his opinion of the agreement, he alone having handled the negotiations concerning a lot of its wording and content.

Dr. al-Baz responded with a single word, in English: "Bad." He went on to say that the agreement would cause unprecedented complications in Egyptian–Arab relations. The Palestinian settlement would fail out of the gate. In the next phase of the process, Egypt needed, he said, to focus on negotiating a peace treaty with Israel. According to the agreement, we had three months in which to do this. Finally, he said that Egypt's interests imposed this new situation on us.

For years, al-Baz's response never left my mind. I thought it very spontaneous at the time, although tinged with fear at the time that Israel's deliberate stalling and evasion might scupper the Palestinian settlement. Dr. al-Baz said to me before meeting with Mohamed Ibrahim Kamel, "You must prepare to do your part in this next stage. It'll be difficult." I said nothing.

Mohamed Kamel refused to remain in Washington with the president, who was scheduled to spend a few more days in the U.S. capital city before leaving for Morocco to prepare his next move. We left in a hurry for Paris. We were met at the airport by Ambassador Mohamed Hafiz Ismail, who had been assigned to the French capital in 1976. Hafiz Ismail appeared eager to hear Kamel's assessment of the situation, and of Camp David, although I noticed he seemed unenthused about the agreement. He did not argue with Minister Kamel's conclusions.

We eventually landed at Cairo Airport. I disembarked laden with bagfuls of documents and briefs—copies of the Camp David agreement, messages that had been exchanged, the minutes of all the meetings, and records of the activities of the presidential delegation during the summit—and headed directly for the Ministry of Foreign Affairs, then still in Tahrir Square. I left everything in the care of the secretaries in the minister's office, and went home to my place in Heliopolis. I told my wife I was quite ready to leave for Alexandria the next day for a few days at the beach. I had already obtained permission for a vacation from Ahmed Maher. I had also told Minister Boutros Boutros-Ghali, in charge of the Foreign Ministry now that Minister Kamel's resignation was officially in effect, that I was spending a few days in the Agami resort, west of Alexandria.

As soon as Dr. Boutros-Ghali returned, in the president's company, the wheels of diplomatic information began to turn again. Telegrams went out to Egyptian embassies all over the world, containing the gist of the agreement, our views on it, and what it achieved; invitations were issued to foreign ambassadors in Cairo for meetings to give them the necessary information; there were interviews with the media to bring them up to date on the issues; messages were sent to foreign ministers abroad, including one to the secretary-general of the United Nations; there were talking points explaining the situation for the Ministerial Cabinet; and other diplomatic procedures.

Boutros-Ghali requested that I meet him at his home the evening he returned from Morocco. It is worth noting again that Ahmed Maher remained in Paris. Also, Boutros-Ghali could not presume to task Osama al-Baz with such a mission (to report to ambassadors on the decisions reached during their trip), especially as al-Baz had launched into a round of visits to Cairo's elite sporting and social clubs upon his return, giving talks explaining the situation, defending the agreement, and explaining its benefits. Someone had told Boutros-Ghali that I was not in Cairo, whereupon he lost his temper. Some had even—a practice frowned upon in our Foreign Ministry, and in the Foreign Offices of a lot of countries—put it about that I had resigned from my post, and that Ahmed Maher al-Sayed had also stayed on in Paris after handing in his resignation. The goal, of course, was to smash our strong team and replace it with another.

Meanwhile, Nabil al-Arabi had proceeded with all haste from Washington to New York to work with Dr. Esmat Abdel Meguid, Egypt's representative to the United Nations. The capable Ambassador Abdel Raouf El Reedy had returned to Cairo and thence gone to Islamabad to serve as Egypt's ambassador to Pakistan. This meant that I was the only one with access to the Camp David documents, although I am certain that Dr. Osama al-Baz was in possession of the original copy of them all.

The Foreign Ministry telephoned the Agami police with an urgent message for me to return immediately. However, the police department failed to locate me. I returned to Cairo a week later to find Dr. Boutros-Ghali ranting and raving. At that time, I was a mere first secretary in a ministry without a minister—an unenviable position.

I entered my office directly via the main door, without going through the secretary's office, which I had always done when Mohamed Ibrahim Kamel was minister. This is what I did with Boutros Boutros-Ghali, especially in later years when Lieutenant-General Kamal Hassan Ali was deputy cabinet minister and foreign minister, from 1982 to 1984, and then with Dr. Esmat Abdel Meguid when I rejoined his office from 1989 to 1991 and Amre Moussa was foreign minister.

In any case, I responded quite frankly to Dr. Boutros-Ghali, assuring him that I had informed him of my intention to take time off and obtained his approval at the time. He finally remembered that I had spoken with him and apologized for the trouble he had caused me. This gained my respect.

Dr. Boutros-Ghali, and Dr. al-Baz, had received verbal instructions from President Sadat not to depend in future on "those boys in the diplomatic corps who messed up Ibrahim Kamel's mind." This was another reason for the rumors that flew around that this group was about to be dismissed from the Foreign Ministry, or at least be relieved of the Middle East file. However, Boutros-Ghali and al-Baz defended us in the taskforce with a strength and enthusiasm that blunted the force of the president's criticism.

On my return to Cairo, I found myself mobbed by friends and acquaintances who wanted to know what I thought of the agreement. "I don't have any definite conclusions right now," I kept replying, and, "I can't really know what's going to happen next with any clarity," adding that time would tell whether President Sadat had been right to take this course. I must admit that as the days and weeks went by, however, I began to realize that President Sadat had done what was best for Egypt at that stage.

"I shall liberate Egyptian territory," Sadat said to Nabil al-Arabi, "which is my primary responsibility to my people. A few years later, you'll have to decide for yourselves what to do."

His view of matters then was correct, there can be no doubt. He agreed to an Egyptian–Israeli agreement that returned Sinai in its entirety to Egypt, free and clear of any Israeli military or civilian presence. Some said that parts of Sinai were covered by rules and regulations of armament or by restrictions on Egyptian armed forces. Sadat calmly responded, "The main thing to me is that our armed forces, from where they are stationed in Sinai, are capable of defending the Suez Canal and its cities at any moment." He added that the number of troops allowed by the agreement enabled the defense of the area from the canal to the eastern Sinai passes. Also, the Egyptian army had never maintained more than one infantry division, plus the requisite arms, in Sinai at any one time, so this was not imposed by the agreement.

As to the framework for peace regarding the West Bank and Gaza, no one can deny that the circumstances at the time would not have allowed for anything more than what the Egyptians managed to get out of the negotiations. This is evidenced by the fact that the Oslo Accords signed in

1993 between Palestine and Israel represented a more developed version of the concepts outlined at Camp David. True, the Oslo agreement went far beyond Camp David, which gave the Palestinians a real chance to move forward in their struggle to reclaim their right to a Palestinian state, but we should not forget that this took place in a context very different from the circumstances governing Camp David in 1978. This was my conclusion a few weeks after Camp David, and it has not changed. Sadat did a good thing for Egypt in ending Israeli occupation of Egyptian soil, and ultimately paid for this heroic act with his life.

At the same time as outrage erupted in the Arab world at the signing of the Camp David agreement, we prepared to send a large Egyptian diplomatic delegation to negotiate the peace treaty that would lead to Israel's withdrawal from Sinai, and to formulate Egypt's relationship with Israel afresh. Minister of Defense Kamal Hassan Ali was appointed to lead the delegation. Dr. Boutros Boutros-Ghali was a member of the delegation, for the sake of continuity with the previous team, so that those with the best knowledge and experience of the situation could continue to shoulder the responsibility for the task. I remember thinking at the time that appointing Kamal Hassan Ali reflected President Sadat's desire to convey a message to everyone in Egypt and abroad that the Egyptian armed forces supported the upcoming peace treaty, so much so that they were negotiating for it, in the person of the Egyptian minister of defense himself. Some put it about that he was only appointed to this task because he was being groomed for the post of foreign minister, to which he was appointed in 1980, as his rheumatoid arthritis was becoming too crippling to allow him to continue on as defense minister. These rumors are baseless as he was still agile and spry at the time of this mission.

The powerful taskforce that had worked with Minister Mohamed Ibrahim Kamel since December 1977 had by now disbanded. The only remaining member was Dr. Osama al-Baz, who headed once more for Washington to assist Kamal Hassan Ali and oversee the Egyptian position in the negotiations with Israel. Amre Moussa joined a new taskforce assembled by Dr. al-Baz. Ahmed Maher told me that al-Baz wanted to take me to Washington. I said that I would prefer to stay with Ahmed Maher in Cairo, especially as I suspected him to be under threat: a great many people were seeking to eliminate him from the Ministry. Indeed, it was being bandied about—I never did verify the veracity of the claim—that President Sadat had asked Dr. Boutros-Ghali to arrange for the transfer of Ahmed Maher al-Sayed, and again Amre Moussa, to a position outside the Foreign Ministry. They survived this threat, however, climbing the diplomatic ladder to the top and both eventually attaining the position of Egypt's foreign minister.

The members of the diplomatic taskforce that had accompanied Minister Mohamed Ibrahim Kamel were a strong group indeed: Dr. Esmat Abdel Meguid, who became foreign minister in 1984; Amre Moussa, foreign minister from 1991 to 2001; Ahmed Maher al-Sayed, foreign minister from 2001 to 2004; Ahmed Aboul Gheit, foreign minister from 2004 to 2011; and, finally, Nabil al-Arabi, who also attained this highest of positions. I must not forget to mention the rumor that Dr. Osama al-Baz had been offered the position of foreign minister after Mohamed Kamel's resignation, but that he preferred to remain free of the burdens and responsibilities that came with such a weighty position.

In any event, the new Egyptian delegation left for Washington on October 10, 1978, to start negotiating the peace treaty with Israel. I remained in Cairo with Ahmed Maher at the ministry without a minister. It had been decided that Dr. Boutros Boutros-Ghali, the minister of state for foreign affairs, would perform the ministerial duties and manage Egyptian diplomacy until such a time as a new minister was appointed. Boutros-Ghali had a great deal in common with Ahmed Maher: they were both French-educated, were from old Egyptian aristocratic families, and had a lot of respect for each other's abilities. Boutros-Ghali decided to keep Ahmed Maher in his post of office director for the foreign minister. Despite having his own office staff as minister of state, Ghali began increasingly to rely on Maher in ministerial and administrative matters, and finally in the peace process and the negotiations with Israel. This kept me working on the Middle East file, which included the peace process.

The Egyptian delegation telegraphed all the latest developments in the Washington negotiations to Cairo via the foreign minister's office, which allowed Ahmed Maher and me to keep abreast of things as they happened. Indeed, we were asked to prepare regular briefs to keep the Presidency, the Cabinet, and other state bodies informed of developments in the negotiations. We were also the conduit for the president's orders to the delegation, and sent them the information they needed to carry out their mission.

The peace treaty negotiated by the Egyptian delegation began with a preamble affirming the link between this treaty and a comprehensive settlement for the Middle East conflict. Nine main points followed:

1. Ending the state of war and establishing peace.
2. Borders remain inviolate.
3. Future relations.
4. Security arrangements.
5. Freedom of maritime navigation and air traffic.

6. Commitments are interrelated.
7. Dispute resolution.
8. Reparations.
9. Concluding clauses.

The negotiations started on October 11. The Egyptian and Israeli delegations agreed as soon as they arrived in Washington that the basis for negotiations should be an American paper submitted to Egypt and Israel, reflecting both parties' positions. Each party would make comments on this paper and introduce the required modifications. Although Egypt had already prepared a draft resolution in response to the by-now-traditional Israeli draft, it was found that discussing the American document as a baseline would provide equal opportunity for both parties to submit desired modifications and suggestions. It was also agreed that the work should proceed with the Americans meeting each party in turn and receiving their modifications and comments. They would make a note of this feedback for a future draft to be discussed in a meeting among all three parties. It was also agreed in a later meeting to form a legal team to word the agreement and to discuss the parties' proposals.

The negotiations progressed. The U.S. proposal was developed, and developed again, until it had gone through eight drafts. Once again, anyone examining the sheer effort of the Egyptian negotiating team and its veritable legal and diplomatic battle with its Israeli counterpart can only offer up sincere appreciation to all these diplomats and legal minds who achieved such a result for Egypt in wording a peace treaty that protects Egypt's interests with the greatest possible clarity.

25 The Egyptian and Palestinian Paths

With the signing of the Egypt–Israel peace treaty on March 26, 1979, the implementation phase began. Naturally, this was accompanied by the start of Egypt's obligations in the Camp David framework, relating to the Palestinian part of the settlement. We did not imagine at the time that this settlement would go down a different road and be deferred so long. It stalled completely for ten years, from 1981 until the end of the Second Gulf War, in March 1991. Since then it has moved forward at a snail's pace, but only in fits and starts. In the pages to come, I will attempt to give an overview of these years and stages, which I had the opportunity to play a part in from 1989 until my appointment as foreign minister in July 2004. The story starts with preparing for the Madrid Summit, and launching the peace process with Palestinian participation for the first time ever, goes to the Oslo Accords in 1999, which established a Palestinian authority on Palestinian soil, and finally goes to the important Security Council resolution calling for an independent Palestinian state alongside Israel, with peace and security for both.

From the start of the implementation of the Egypt–Israel peace treaty, Egyptian negotiators, I still say, were always careful to link the settlement between Egypt and Israel to the settlement between Palestine and Israel, as a package deal, or at least to appear to in order to protect Egypt's position in the Arab world. Egypt's moves on both fronts were always interrelated. One of the important initial moves of the Egyptian team sent to Washington on October 11, 1978, to negotiate a peace treaty between Egypt and Israel was submitting a memorandum to the US on

October 13, which outlined confidence-building measures to be implemented in the Palestinian occupied territories. Egypt asserted that these measures needed to be implemented immediately in the West Bank and Gaza in order to create a new, positive atmosphere, in which people's humanity was valued and which would lead, it was hoped, to a lessening of tensions. Among these measures, the foremost were a freeze on settlements in the West Bank and Gaza during the interim period; for Israel to be open to any Palestinian negotiating group that accepted Security Council Resolution 242; and disallowing Israeli settlers from voting in the election of a Palestinian authority, while allowing Arabs living in East Jerusalem to take part in this vote.

The Egyptian memorandum called upon the Israelis to implement a laundry list of procedures: lifting the ban on political assembly; doing away with all restrictions on movement for the inhabitants of the West Bank and Gaza; an end to military maneuvers in the West Bank and Gaza; pardoning Palestinian prisoners; reuniting Palestinian families by allowing the return of those displaced since 1967; agreeing to UN or international observers supervising the elections of a Palestinian authority; implementing the immediate withdrawal of some of their forces from parts of the West Bank and Gaza; and starting to redistribute the Israeli forces remaining in the West Bank and Gaza during the transition.

Throughout the Egypt–Israel peace treaty negotiations, which lasted from October 12, 1978, to March 26, 1979, the Egyptian negotiators also held firm on a number of basic positions engineered to protect the rights of Palestinians and conclusively to dismiss the myth that Egypt had thrown Palestinian concerns to the wind while trying to lift Israeli occupation from our lands. This became clear in a number of messages sent by Dr. Mustafa Khalil, the prime minister of Egypt, who simultaneously served as foreign minister, to U.S. Secretary of State Cyrus Vance, in which Egypt refused the concepts and procedures Israel touted or implemented in the West Bank and Gaza. One of these messages, dated February 23, 1979, rejected the continuation of settlement-building in the West Bank and Gaza, calling it "null and void" and "devoid of validity and legitimacy."

The Egyptians worked to achieve full coordination with the US to confirm the package deal of Egypt and Palestine in the Camp David agreement. The schedule for the implementation of the Egypt–Israel treaty also took the course of the Palestinian settlement into account. The Egyptian president and the Israeli prime minister sent a letter to the U.S. president on March 26, the day of the signing of the treaty, stating,

Desirous of achieving a comprehensive peace settlement in the framework of Camp David, Egypt and Israel will commence implementing
the texts related to the West Bank and Gaza; they have agreed to start
negotiations one month after exchanging the documents ratifying the
peace treaty. The Hashemite Kingdom of Jordan has been invited to
take part in the negotiations, and the Egyptian and Jordanian delegations may include Palestinians from the West Bank and Gaza, or
Palestinians from other regions subject to joint approval. The goal of
these negotiations will be to agree, prior to the elections, on arrangements for establishing the elected self-rule authority, and the specifics
of its competencies and responsibilities. In the event that Jordan elects
not to take part in the negotiations, they will then proceed between
Egypt and Israel. Both governments agree to continual negotiations in
a spirit of goodwill so as to complete these negotiations as soon as possible. They also agree that the goal of the negotiations is establishing
the self-rule authority in the West Bank and Gaza.

Egypt and Israel set themselves a goal: to get the negotiations done
within a year, so that the elections could be held as soon as possible after all
the parties reached an agreement. The self-rule authority would be established and start work a month after being elected. This would signal the
start of the five-year transition period, at which point the Israeli military
government and civilian administration would withdraw, to be replaced
with the self-rule authority, as specified in "A Framework for Peace in the
Middle East." At this point, the Israeli armed forces would withdraw and
the remaining Israeli forces would be stationed at specific security points.
    Having agreed on the treaty implementation schedule, on May 25
Egypt reaffirmed, via Minister of Defense Lieutenant-General Kamal
Hassan Ali, at the opening session of the self-rule talks, a number of specific concepts and elements:

- First:
  We are not here to decide the future of the Palestinian people;
  the Palestinians are the only ones who can make such a decision.
  Self-determination is their God-given right. Our duties do not go
  beyond specifying the powers and responsibilities of the authority
  for full self-rule, as well as its election procedures. This is the letter
  and the spirit of the Camp David agreement, and related texts. Our
  joint responsibility consists in the need to agree on the necessary
  steps for the transfer of authority from the Israeli military government to the Palestinian government.

- Second:
  The inadmissibility of the acquisition of territory by war must be respected as set out in Resolution 242, and implemented with regard to the West Bank, including Arab Jerusalem and the Gaza Strip, up to the territories annexed in 1967. Arab Jerusalem will thus become living proof of the possibility of co-existence and cooperation among all the peoples of the region.
- Third:
  Resolution 242 must be respected in all its parts as related to a full solution to the Palestinian problem, as stipulated in the framework.
- Fourth:
  The Geneva Convention Relative to the Protection of Civilian Persons in Time of War applies to occupied Arab territories in their entirety.
- Fifth:
  Respect for human rights and basic freedoms for the Palestinian people in the West Bank and Gaza must be maintained fully and with integrity.

These were the points that governed the Egyptian announcements, or talking points, in negotiations with Israel over the years, indeed decades, of resisting occupation. Egypt's stance was uniformly loyal to the Palestinian position. This is borne out by the actions of the Palestinian leadership after the signing of the Oslo Accords, and their adherence to the positions Egypt had taken before. Egypt never failed the Palestinians.

But what is truly sad is that a review of the negotiations in those years from 1979 to 1982, and until today, quite easily yields the discovery that all of us in the international community, and in Arab and Islamic states, have been caught in a vicious cycle of demands and assertions of legality and justice, while Israel blithely pursues its interests in flagrant violation of international law and legitimacy. Israel continues to build settlements; people are thrown out and displaced and deported; the will of Israel is imposed on Palestinians, who must submit by force; and Palestinians' right to an independent state with sovereignty over the West Bank and Gaza is systematically denied. I may add that the Palestinians' actions and rivalries, in addition to divisions between Arabs and conflicting viewpoints, have played a role in weakening the Arab and Palestinian positions in this extended struggle.

The link between the Egyptian and Palestinian paths was clear and specific during the negotiations, at least as evidenced by the dates in the planned timeline. The agreement was signed on March 26. The start of negotiations for self-rule was scheduled for May 25, and the first stage of Israel's withdrawal from Sinai was set to begin on May 26, two months after the signing of the treaty for withdrawal from Arish. Israel's withdrawal from the northern part of the coast of the Gulf of Suez was scheduled for July 25, three months after the exchange of the documents ratifying the treaty, followed by its withdrawal from the southern part of the central sector of Sinai on September 25. The Israeli withdrawals from Sinai continued on schedule, six in total. They were completed in April 1982, with the Israelis' full withdrawal within their own borders.

In practice, there was remarkably precise adherence, by both parties, to the agreed-upon timeline. This was evident in all its parts: terminating the state of war, establishing diplomatic relations, sending diplomatic missions, and so on. In parallel with all these procedural steps, the parties—Egypt, Israel, and the US—were negotiating among themselves on implementing the Palestinian part of the Camp David agreement. Technical meetings were held on the ministerial—and indeed the presidential—level. Ideas and proposals were submitted, and the parties argued on and on, until Egypt and the US realized at the end of 1982 that Israel would remain unresponsive to Egypt's views on the full self-rule portion of a settlement for Palestine. The Egyptian and Palestinian settlements parted ways. This, however, did not stop Egypt from continuing to defend Palestinians' rights during the darkest hour of Egypt–Palestine relations, starting in 1978 and continuing throughout the decade that followed.

I stayed on with Ahmed Maher al-Sayed in the Foreign Ministry in 1978 and 1979. We kept a close eye on all these developments, while serving our new foreign minister, Dr. Mustafa Khalil. He was appointed on February 22, 1979. For some time previously, the job had been held by Boutros Boutros-Ghali, who was acting minister, though he was never afforded the actual title. This close association lasted until I was posted to the Egyptian embassy in Moscow.

Those were hard times for Egyptian–Soviet relations. The Soviet Union was strongly opposed to both the Egypt–Israel peace treaty and the Palestinian self-rule negotiations, mainly because the US had denied it a role in the process. The peace treaty afforded the United Nations a role in the form of sending its peacekeeping forces to monitor the implementation of the treaty on the ground on the Egyptian side. A great deal of information trickled into Egypt to the effect that the Soviet Union would veto any UN role in monitoring the implementation. The US accordingly began to build a multinational peacekeeping force in the form of individuals and units sourced from friendly nations, to be sent to Sinai to monitor the implementation of various elements of the treaty.

I remember writing a brief for Dr. Boutros Boutros-Ghali before I left for Moscow, in which I suggested Egypt be aggressive at the Security Council. We should, I said, publicly propose an international peace-keeping force to be established by the Security Council, giving many strong justifications. The goal, I said, would be to embarrass the veto-armed Soviets and put them in a defensive position. By using the veto to abort an Egyptian–U.S. initiative for a peacekeeping force, they would appear to pose a threat to international peace and security in opposing a peace treaty between two formerly warring nations. In my estimation, the Soviets would not permit this request before the Security Council: it would to be a seal of approval for a treaty they had so vehemently opposed as a threat to their interests.

In any event, Dr. Boutros Boutros-Ghali read my brief, which Ahmed Maher described to him as "a guided missile," but said he would prefer not to deliberately arouse the ire of the Soviets, or to completely embarrass them. Who knew—we might need them in future under other circumstances.

I spent three years in Moscow, from August 1979 to July 1982. Upon my return, the peace treaty was complete, all of its steps having been taken at the appointed time. However, the self-rule negotiations had foundered on the rocks of Israel's stubbornness, eventually coming to a complete standstill in late 1982.

Those years in Moscow, as I mentioned above, were hard. The Soviets never stopped, at any point during that time, making trouble for Egypt and the US, and generally doing their best to hamper the peace efforts.

The Afghanistan issue was very much a part of the Middle East equation. It was an area of competition for the US and the Soviet Union in Western Asia. Unfortunately, Egypt involved itself in confronting the Soviets on Afghan soil. I believe the Egyptians were motivated by a desire to show themselves to be on the side of the US and the western powers in their confrontation with the Soviets, seeking to strengthen their ties with the west and to garner not only U.S. military aid but also intensified efforts to smooth the path to a Palestinian settlement and a solution to the Arab–Israeli conflict. During this period, Egypt also led the way with regard to the Ethiopia–Somalia conflict in the Horn of Africa, standing with Somali President Siad Barre in the Ogaden region.

Egypt was clearly gradually allying itself—at least until President Sadat's death in 1981—with the interests and goals of the west. Carter's words to Mohamed Ibrahim Kamel at Camp David, namely that he wanted to help Egypt end the Middle East crisis and free itself to play a greater role in confronting Soviet movements in, and designs on, the region, might well explain Sadat's actions at the time. "Help us solve the Arab–Israeli conflict," our actions seemed to say, "and you'll find us by your side in neighboring regions."

My years in Moscow were full of challenges. Despite my best efforts to completely understand Soviet foreign policy and its main orientations, or to evaluate its economic and military capacities in relation to the US, I could not have imagined that this other bloc of the post-Second World War world would fall apart not a decade after I left Moscow. Never would I have dreamed of seeing Mikhail Gorbachev, in the final months of his premiership, and his foreign minister, Boris Pankin, docilely following the US' lead at the Madrid Summit of 1991. Today, I say that the Madrid Summit would never have been held if it had not been for the decline of Soviet influence on all the powers that stood against Camp David.

In the years after my return from Moscow, I worked with Lieutenant-General Kamal Hassan Ali, deputy cabinet minister and minister of foreign affairs. This was a period of Egyptian diplomacy attempting to rise above the difficulties with its fellow Arab countries and the Communist bloc that started with Sadat's visit to Jerusalem. They were the hardest years in the history of Egypt's diplomatic corps, because of the Arab boycott of Egypt and the Soviets' belligerency, but they were also the years that offered the sharpest challenges and the greatest thrill of diplomatic victory and achievement: first Camp David, then the peace treaty, and finally the negotiations for Palestinian self-rule. The Camp David framework was the subject of accusation after accusation, and many people objected to the peace treaty and to Egypt's participation in the self-rule negotiations.

I always felt that time, and only time, would tell the truth of whether the Camp David agreement hurt or helped Egypt. Today, as I write this, I say that Egypt liberated its territories and ended an occupation that weighed heavily on us, after which it unleashed its energies in the direction of growth and development, fulfilling a great many of the demands of the Egyptian people, crushed and drained from years of military confrontation with Israel. The collapse of the Soviet Union in December 1991 was the final confirmation that Egypt had escaped by the skin of its teeth and emerged unscathed onto the horizon of peace—not a moment too soon. In the absence of the counterbalance provided by the Soviet Union, neither the Egyptians nor the Arabs would have managed to impose any settlement on Israel by threat of war.

A great deal has been said in criticism of the Camp David framework. Some have complained that the exchange of messages was not binding, weakening Egypt's position. This was a mere technical legal observation, thankfully ignored by the far-sighted and canny Sadat. Others have declared that Egypt sacrificed Palestinian interests to regain Sinai. The truth is that the gradual settlement concept in the Camp David Accords—despite the Palestinians' rejection of it in September 1978—was the building block upon which the Palestinians' partial success at the Oslo Accords was based, affording them a better opportunity to establish a Palestinian state. Oslo was based on the fundamental concept of Camp David: establishing an interim period of Palestinian self-rule while forming a Palestinian security force with the strength and capacity to achieve security and stability in the occupied territories. As I write this, I must say that history has largely cleared Camp David of any Palestinian and Syrian failure to get back their occupied lands, and of hampering the emergence of an independent Palestinian state. The blame for the current state of the peace process can be laid at the door of Israeli stubbornness and U.S. indecisiveness and pandering to Israel's positions due to the pro-Israel lobby within the US, in addition to the growing rifts between the Palestinians after the death of Yasser Arafat.

To be fair to Camp David, it remains to say, the Palestinians and Arabs agreed to attend the Madrid peace conference knowing full well that the Americans' method, of which they had notified all parties concerned, was to launch peace talks between the Palestinians and Israelis with a view to an interim or transitional agreement, and then to start negotiations during the third year of that agreement to formulate a final settlement for Palestine. This is the Camp David philosophy.

In mid-1985, I left for New York to take on my duties with the permanent Egyptian delegation to the United Nations, where I remained until July 1, 1989. I was then entrusted once again with responsibility for the Middle East/Palestine file before the UN Security Council and the General Assembly. This stage was also beset by difficulties for the Egyptian delegation, due to the Arab boycott of Egypt. The Arab diplomats at the United Nations viewed us with wariness, not to say suspicion. This did not prevent them, however, from picking our brains and asking for help in preparing for Arab action in support of the Palestinian intifada in the General Assembly and before the Security Council. They also asked for our support for the PLO's significant move in mid-December 1988 of declaring their rejection of terror and the end of their attempts to destroy Israel, in order to gain broad international recognition for the declaration of a Palestinian state, in accordance with the decision of the Palestinian National Council in Algiers.

26 The Madrid Conference

I arrived in Cairo from New York in mid-July 1989, at the end of my four-year stint in the service of Egypt's delegation to the UN. I joined the team of Foreign Minister Esmat Abdel Meguid, in charge of the Palestinian problem and the Middle East crisis. I immediately noticed that the US was preparing a new effort to move what was known as the 'peace process' forward, especially with the Palestinian National Council's decision in Algiers in mid-December 1988 and a new Republican administration in the White House in January 1989. There had been a great many developments on the international scene. As things turned out, there were more to come—changes unprecedented since the Second World War, namely the breakup of the Soviet bloc and the weakening of the body politic of the Soviet Union. This gave George H.W. Bush's America a great opportunity to carry out policies and implement principles the mere possibility of which would have been hard to imagine in the past.

The Palestinian intifada was having a profound effect on the way the world, and the US, viewed Israel's policies in the occupied territories. These developments forced Israel and the US to take action. Israel did its best to promote the notion that it was working hard to achieve, and genuinely desired, peace with the Palestinians. The US appeared in the role of a serious worker enabling an active and credible peace process.

In early 1988, under President Ronald Reagan, the US began to promote specific concepts to energize the peace process in response to the pressures of the Palestinian intifada, aimed at empowering the

Palestinians to take the reins of their own affairs and prepare for negotiations on the form of the final situation in the occupied territories.
In its last year in the White House, the Reagan administration issued
a document affirming that the US was prepared to commit to working
with the parties to achieve peace on all fronts, on the basis of Security
Council Resolution 242. It also affirmed the proposed method for a
Palestinian settlement, based on the fast-track implementation of a transitional period for the occupied Palestinian territories, coupled with
negotiations concerning the final situation in these territories. The US,
it said, would work with the parties to hold an international conference
to achieve these ends.

Another U.S. document that analyzed each party's position and suggested strategies for securing their cooperation with the U.S. approach
ended up being leaked to the parties themselves. The document stated
explicitly that Israel, especially Prime Minister Yitzhak Shamir, was wary
of the US' intentions: the Israeli prime minister was suspicious that the
US might attempt to make Israel withdraw to the 1967 borders. As for
Jordan, the U.S. analysis was based on that country's desire to secure
direct negotiations, allowing King Hussein to join in. Jordan, said the
document, also wanted assurances that Washington was not about to
take the Likud's part in the upcoming settlement. Finally, it spoke of the
Jordanians' fear that the peace process would stop after the agreement on
a transitional period, which would last indefinitely, effectively making it a
final solution. In its assessment of the Jordanian view, the document concluded that if a strong link were forged between the transitional period
and the final solution, Jordan would accept a more symbolic conference,
encouraging Shamir not to object.

The Reagan administration offered an overview of the kind of help
the US could provide. To get the parties to the negotiating table, it said,
the US would be prepared to produce a specific description of its own
view of what these transitional arrangements should be for the occupied
territories, and of the final form the settlement should take. America
knew beforehand, the document said, that its own view and vision would
be criticized by both parties; however, there was hope that its position
might be a starting point for the negotiations.

The U.S. document went on to specify that the interim arrangements
would depend on what understandings had been reached so far in the self-
rule negotiations, meaning the Egypt–Israel negotiations on Palestinian
self-rule. A final settlement would be based on President Reagan's initiative (any form of Jordanian-Palestinian link, while discouraging the
formation of an independent Palestinian state). The document concluded

with a timeline leading to the start of the transitional period in February 1989, and the simultaneous launch of the negotiations on the final stage.

It may be noted that these American suggestions—except for the agreement to hold a peace conference—were an extension of the views held by the US since Camp David, or during the full self-rule negotiations, which had lasted from 1979 to 1982.

The concepts floated by the Reagan administration were inherited by the Bush administration in 1989, which then ran with them. This culminated in the Madrid Conference, despite opposition from Israel. The Israeli prime minister attempted to forestall Bush's moves, along with those of proactive Secretary of State James Baker, with an initiative that, however, only regurgitated the same old Israeli positions and ideas clothed in new verbiage. Still, Israel was talking for the first time ever about U.S.-led international efforts to resolve the issue of Arab refugees, and about a temporary settlement with the aim of establishing an elected Palestinian authority in the occupied territories to manage the region and negotiate the form of the final settlement. All of this found its first expression at Camp David.

Immediately upon my arrival home from New York in mid-1989, I took it upon myself to read all the papers and documents submitted by the parties in previous years, to update my knowledge on what had occurred and have the tools to deal with what was coming in the future, from Israel, the US, or Egypt. At the forefront of the ideas that dominated the situation were the U.S. secretary of state's statements to the American–Israeli Public Affairs Committee, on May 22, 1989, which summarized the Bush administration's vision, and was launched four months after the Bush administration took office and one month after the Israeli prime minister's initiative mentioned above.

The statements indicated a need to protect American national interests, first and foremost by settling the Palestinian problem. This idea cropped up repeatedly over the twenty years that followed, to the present day. Secretary of State Baker went on to mention the favorable—although incomplete—changes in the Soviet Union, concluding by discussing the global push for democracy and liberty in the context of accelerating and profound technological developments unprecedented in the history of humanity. He noted that it was only right that the states and peoples of the Middle East should be able to enjoy all these developments. Baker then offered five points summing up the U.S. position:

- The goal of the peace process is to arrive at a comprehensive settlement through direct negotiations based on Security Council Resolutions 242 and 338.

- The negotiation process will move forward on two concomitant paths: negotiations between Israel and the Arab states, and between Israel and the Palestinians.
- The negotiations between the Israelis and Palestinians will take place in stages, first with talks concerning a transitional period and then with talks on the final situation in the occupied Palestinian territories.
- The Palestinians will be represented by leaders from the occupied territories who are accepting of the suggested path.
- A conference will be held under the sponsorship of the US and the Soviet Union, opening the door to contact between the parties and launching direct negotiations between them.

Baker announced his support for the Shamir initiative, and asked for a Palestine–Israel dialogue to be held to feel out their positions and prepare for the launch of serious talks. The secretary of state then spoke of the need to change the status quo, which required both parties to be responsive to the US' ideas, especially the concept of direct dialogue, which had by then become an American demand. The US worked enthusiastically and tirelessly to prepare for such a dialogue in the year that followed.

Things began to move forward thanks to the two proposals, American and Israeli. Egypt was responsive to both, although it had already prepared an official outline of its views in ten points that it formally announced over the months that followed, all the way to the end of 1989. I coordinated my work with that of Dr. Esmat Abdel Meguid. I was convinced of the importance of safeguarding Egypt's vision and performance by notifying the United Nations, with great transparency, of a set of principles and views specific to Egypt. This would help guard against any Arab party accusing Egypt of speaking for the Palestinians or of going against the Arab party line, especially as Egypt had only just regained full membership in the Arab League.

Egypt's vision, sent in an official document to the UN in November 1989, included the following elements:

- The Palestinian intifada is the genuine mover of this serious and ongoing effort for progress in the peace process in the region.
- The PLO's initiative and the National Palestinian Council's decision in December 1988 to recognize Israel, relinquish violence, and enter into negotiations to resolve the conflict infused a new and positive attitude into the peace process that promises positive developments, especially as these decisions were received with general approbation by the General Assembly at its historic assembly in December 1988.

- Egypt considers Israel's proposals, presented by Shamir and approved by the Israeli Cabinet, an encouraging sign that Israel understands how critical the situation has become.
- Egypt believes it must contribute to the current process. We have submitted ten points to sharpen the focus and bring things on the right track. Egypt also proposes that the Palestinian–Israeli talks mentioned by Secretary of State Baker in Cairo be held, to agree on the election process in the occupied Palestinian territories. These talks are by no means meant to replace an international peace conference, which will be held at a later date, and should not stand in the way of other roles or contributions to the peace process, within the UN, or directly between the concerned parties.
- The role of Egypt in these efforts is ancillary and participatory. We do not consider ourselves a stand-in for the Palestinian side, not in decisions regarding the talks or in choosing the Palestinians to participate in them. That said, the Egyptian view is that Palestinians from within and outside the occupied territories should take part in the dialogue, and that the delegation should be formed by the legitimate Palestinian leadership.
- Due to the delicate stage of these efforts, it is essential, in Egypt's view, not to offer any assurances in secret to either side that might obstruct the peace process.
- The ten Egyptian points presented to the United Nations, of which all the parties have been made aware, focus on holding elections in the Palestinian territories and the details of these elections in all their elements.

In the months after Shamir and Baker announced their ideas, our main concern in Cairo was to hold consultations with the Palestinians on one side, and with the US on the other, in order to prepare for the Israeli–Palestinian dialogue to be held in Cairo. The communications between the Egyptians and the Palestinians came thick and fast. Egypt conveyed and defended Palestine's attitudes to the Americans, urging the US to initiate direct dialogue with the Palestinians. The Palestinians gradually grew more responsive to the Americans' proposals, although they remained adamant on a few points and made several requests for clarification and explanations of certain U.S. proposals.

The Palestinians made it clear that the PLO had the right to select the Palestinians, from within and outside Palestine, who would make up the delegation that would engage in dialogue with Israel. They also requested that each party have the right to speak about whatever positions and visions it saw fit. These dialogues, they said, would represent a step toward an effective international conference. Egypt agreed to these requests, which accompanied the first time Palestinians agreed to sit down for direct talks with Israel. Dr. Esmat Abdel Meguid entrusted me with conveying the PLO's position to the Americans.

The US responded to us with alacrity, saying that Egypt could not replace the Palestinians. Egypt was to consult with the Palestinians on all aspects of the proposed dialogue, including the make-up of the delegation. The US, the Americans said, appreciated that the members of the Palestinian delegation would enjoy the support of the main influential forces in Palestinian society. The issue was that the US insisted that the PLO not publicly reveal its role in selecting the members of the delegation. The Americans explained that they could not allow for Israel to appear as though it were selecting, or vetoing, the members of the Palestinian delegation, but that Israel would definitely not sit at the negotiating table with someone it had no desire to sit with. Still, as soon as the Palestinians accepted Baker's five points, all issues related to selecting the delegation could be settled in a manner acceptable to Palestine and Israel. It was understood that as long as the dialogue focused on the elections in the West Bank and Gaza, the delegation should mostly be made up of inhabitants of those areas. The US concluded by mentioning the international peace conference, affirming that it needed to be adequately prepared for at the appropriate time, but that the current situation did not require an international conference or international supervision.

I conveyed the U.S. response, which arrived by way of the U.S. embassy, to Dr. Esmat. The U.S. embassy remained the contact in all these efforts. The foreign minister entrusted me with conveying the US' response to the Palestinians. I duly informed Said Kamal, the Palestinian representative to Cairo. Kamal, since the early 1970s, had been a prominent figure in Cairo, and the main contact between the PLO and both Egypt's Foreign Ministry and Egyptian Intelligence. This was not my first time communicating with Said Kamal; on instructions from Dr. Mustafa Khalil and Dr. Boutros-Ghali, Ahmed Maher al-Sayed and I used to inform Said Kamal of all the developments in the 1979 negotiations among Egypt, Israel, and the US regarding full Palestinian self-rule for him to convey to Yasser Arafat. Those negotiations ended in 1982 with no real result except a good foundation for efforts post-Madrid.

In any case, with these developments, the US gained enough confidence to launch an additional idea in October 1989: a call for a tripartite meeting among the foreign ministers of Egypt, Israel, and the US to prepare for talks between Israel and Palestine. Just as we received the

US' invitation to this tripartite meeting, we received feedback from the Palestinians criticizing the US' response to the PLO's questions. The Palestinians asked Dr. Esmat Abdel Meguid, the foreign minister, to convey their criticisms to the Americans. They mainly took issue with the US failing to mention the PLO as the party in charge of, and speaking for, their side in the upcoming Israeli–Palestinian talks. Any reference to the main and effective political parties in the Palestinian movement that ignored the PLO was a deliberate snub to that organization.

In Egypt, we found the Palestinian position awkward, in that it might hold up the U.S. efforts to advance the process. We therefore advised the Palestinians not to submit any brief critical of the U.S. position and undertook instead to convey their outrage verbally to the Americans in person.

I was tasked with this by Dr. Esmat Abdel Meguid. I telephoned the U.S. ambassador to Egypt, Frank G. Wisner, to convey the message. Meanwhile, the foreign minister worked to reassure the Palestinians that Egypt would not abandon the PLO or minimize its role. On the contrary, he assured them, we would promote and strengthen the Palestine–U.S. dialogue launched after December 1988, taking into account the positive developments in the situation. He emphasized the importance of a positive response to Secretary Baker's five-point proposal to kick-start the Palestinian–Israeli dialogue, break the deadlock, and get peace efforts moving again—a step Egypt viewed as vital. After a string of meetings with the Palestinians, we managed to convince them to allow us to tell the Americans that the PLO was prepared to deal with the U.S. proposal, on condition that its views be conveyed to the US and taken into account.

The preparations for the tripartite meeting were underway, with the aim of preparing for the next talks, this time between Palestine and Israel. I remember suggesting to the foreign minister that we address the logistical requirements of the dialogue, including meeting places and lodgings, the shape of the negotiating table, the possibility of using flags or signs, the open agenda (at the PLO's behest), and, finally, the international dimension and the Soviet Union's participation.

The Americans suggested that the talks be held in Cairo. We had no objections; indeed, we were quite enthused, as it would put Cairo back on the map as the Arab capital working hardest to move things forward and find a solution. The US met with more Israeli stalling, which the Americans chose to take as agreement to participate in this first public dialogue between the two parties. The next steps, the US decided, would focus on the composition of the delegations, especially the Palestinian one, and on the agenda. In their estimation, the formation of the Palestinian delegation might be a thorny issue, ultimately posing a threat to the talks, but they appreciated that creative solutions could provide a way out. The Americans asked the Soviets to help them persuade the PLO to demonstrate the flexibility required to form the delegation, especially as the PLO insisted that its role be made public, to reinforce its authority over the entire nationalist movement for Palestine.

At the start of December 1989, I submitted a number of ideas to Dr. Esmat Abdel Meguid that could be presented to the Americans at the proposed tripartite meeting in Washington. He agreed to them, and we sent them to our distinguished ambassador to DC, Abdel Raouf El Reedy, along with his assignment to prepare for the meeting with the Americans. He was also made aware of the broad outlines of his consultations with the US: he was to tell Washington that Egypt was working to obtain the names of proposed candidates for the talks—quietly—from the Palestinian leadership and that, in our view, it was important that the delegation be composed of Palestinian citizens from the West Bank and Gaza, plus one or more members from East Jerusalem. We suggested that the inclusion of two or more Palestinian figures in exile from Palestinian lands should also be looked into, for a total in the region of twelve delegates. The instructions issued to Ambassador El Reedy also suggested that the agenda for the Palestine–Israel discussions cover both the broader issues and the finer points of elections in the occupied territories, plus the ten points written by Egypt, which dealt mainly with the issue of elections. Finally, we proposed that the meeting be attended by the countries that supported membership in the Security Council to monitor the dialogue; if this proved too hard, U.S. and Soviet participation would have to suffice.

The Egypt–U.S. consultations, and the Egypt–Palestine consultations, intensified. The developments in 1989, Shamir and Baker's proposals, and Egypt's responses to them revealed that relations between Egypt and Palestine had returned to normal after a ten-year rift. Egypt delved into the formation of the Palestinian delegation; the Americans, as per our agreement, felt it important to agree on guidelines or criteria for member selection via a long list followed by a short list. Meanwhile, the Palestinians felt it was their prerogative to submit a specific list of the delegates they wanted, free from meddling, as long as the delegates met certain previously agreed-upon qualifications.

In our communications with the US, we emphasized the importance of the US not seeking to erode or weaken the leadership role of the PLO in the dialogues and the first round of negotiations, until such a time as the PLO was able to appear publicly in the negotiations. We also emphasized the importance of the US obtaining assurances from Israel that it would negotiate with the Palestinians in good faith. In late December 1989, by way of encouraging the Americans and the Palestinians to conduct more direct talks in preparation for this massive step, we suggested holding a U.S.–Egypt–Palestine meeting in parallel to the Egypt–Israel–U.S. talks.

To reassure the PLO, which feared that the Israelis and Americans might attempt to block its role in leading the negotiations, I suggested to the foreign minister, in a brief dated January 3, 1990, that the names of the Palestinian delegates be announced in a statement by the leadership of the Palestinian intifada, worded in such a manner as to show unequivocally that these delegates had their mandate from the PLO. This could be followed by some or all of the Palestinian delegates meeting Yasser Arafat in Tunisia, or in Cairo, an appropriate amount of time before the official meeting in Cairo, and looking into encouraging the Palestinian ambassador to Cairo to meet the Palestinian delegation at Cairo Airport. These measures were calculated to protect the PLO's mandate and focus on the specifics of its role, especially as we had also suggested that the Palestinian monitor at the UN notify the secretary-general in writing of this development.

The PLO, responding to the US' views, had asked Egypt to submit a Palestinian document to the US on January 16, 1990, that presented its delegate selection criteria. It said that the delegates must be citizens of the occupied territories, including Arab Jerusalem, as well as Palestinians from abroad, all politically active. The participation of the main PLO figures would be deferred at this stage. The PLO memorandum also asked that the strong link between the transitional period and the final Palestinian settlement be emphasized, and that the US reaffirm the assurances mentioned in President Bush's statements of April 1989 and in Secretary Baker's statements of May 1989.

In December 1989 and January 1990, it appeared that the Americans hoped to achieve a quick victory by reaching an agreement on all the aspects of a Palestine–Israel dialogue so as to get everything done by February 3—the date Baker was scheduled to visit Moscow. This would allow the US to score one over the Soviets during Baker's visit. In light of the US' interests, we attempted to secure its assistance with pressuring international financial institutions, especially the International Monetary Fund, whose managing director, Michel Camdessus, appeared unenthusiastic about helping Egypt just when it needed international financial support. We strove to establish a link between our helping to influence the Palestinian attitude and the US' assistance with international monetary institutions.

It was decided that Dr. Esmat Abdel Meguid would leave for Washington on January 16. I accompanied him on this important visit.

The foreign minister met President Bush, Secretary Baker, and Brent Scowcroft, the national security advisor. I noted the warm welcome that President Bush gave to Dr. Esmat; they had been colleagues at the United Nations, each having been the leader of his country's delegation in 1978. Bush insisted on taking the foreign minister to meet First Lady Barbara Bush in the president's living quarters at the White House. At the end of this visit, upon my return to Cairo and at the minister's instruction, I prepared a brief in his name to submit to President Hosni Mubarak. An overview of its main points may be useful here, as it largely reveals the nature of the stage we were at, the maneuvers of the parties concerned, and the parties' efforts to move the Israel–Palestine negotiations forward.

The Situation on January 22, 1990
A Brief
On our Impressions of Secretary Baker's Position on the Peace Initiative

First:
1. I noted immediately upon my arrival in Washington on January 16 that just as Secretary Baker is clearly and deeply invested in the matter of supporting Egypt with the IMF, he expects the same alacrity from us on the issue of the tripartite meeting in Washington and the preparations for the Palestine–Israel dialogue. It did not escape our notice that Baker broached the subject of the IMF talks at the first meeting immediately following our arrival, and was careful to express strong indications that the US would support Egypt in this regard. He then followed up with a request, at our second meeting in the hotel the day of our arrival, that we assist him in holding the Egypt–U.S.–Israel meeting in Washington before he leaves for Moscow on February 3. He affirmed that he has no wish to arrive there without having achieved a measure of success on the Middle East.
2. At the second meeting with Baker on the evening of January 16, I submitted the Egyptian–Palestinian working paper to him, the contents of which were agreed upon with Yasser Arafat on January 14. It specified selection criteria for Palestinian delegates, the method of announcing the delegation's formation, and the safeguards and assurances requested by the Palestinians from the US in response to the US' assurances to Israel. Baker promised to study the contents of the paper.
3. The consultations between the Egyptian and American delegations resulted in the following:

a. The U.S. side is prepared, generally speaking, to accept the proposed criteria. They also expressed interest in possibly deleting the reference to respected PLO officials not taking part in the dialogue at the present time.

b. The US also has no objection to the possibility of permitting certain forms of Soviet participation in the Cairo talks; Moscow should be called upon to exchange diplomatic representation with Israel in return for this participation.

4. I also noticed that the US, finding the preparatory stage of the dialogue complex and fraught with issues, foremost among which are the composition of the Palestinian delegation and setting the agenda, prefers to focus more on the matter of how to go about forming the Palestinian delegation, and the names of its members. However, I made a point of mentioning the ten-point Egyptian plan and that it is essential to include it in some form in the dialogue agenda.

5. Baker told me that they are currently preparing a draft message to us containing the assurances and guarantees they can offer at present, in the light of the positions the US has taken publicly vis-à-vis the Palestinian problem. He planned, he told me, to submit to us a draft message on Saturday, January 20, for our feedback, before sending it to us officially. The Americans have not yet sent us a copy of their official message to Israel, since the latter intends to demand some modifications and additions, and it remains unclear how prepared the Americans are to accept.

The Draft U.S. Message:

6. The Americans have already sent us their draft message. I have noted that it does not deviate in general from what we know of the American attitude to the Palestinian problem, while it does attempt to avoid any conflict with Israel that might be caused by this message. Its most important elements are:

a. U.S. policy affirms that the objective of the peace efforts is to arrive at a comprehensive settlement by means of direct negotiations based on Resolutions 242 and 338.

b. For any negotiations on the final settlement to succeed, they must include the concept of land for peace.

c. Security, recognizing Israel, for all the states in the region.

d. Securing the legitimate political rights of the Palestinian people.

e. An international peace conference with sufficient preparations, held at the appropriate time, might help facilitate negotiations.

f. Conceding the importance of an interim period interlocked with the final situation of the negotiations; similarly, conceding that

the Palestinian–Israeli dialogue, and the elections, represent an
initial, practical step in the efforts leading to negotiations.

g. The US insists that no party may decide the results of the negotiations in advance. Neither party may take independent action
with the goal of settling issues that can only be solved via negotiations. (This indicates that the US disapproves of any Israeli
annexation, permanent occupation, or control of the West Bank
and Gaza, and, similarly, of the establishment of an independent
Palestinian state.)

h. The US disapproves of Israeli settlement building and has no
plans to support it.

i. To safeguard the peace process, the Palestinians *must* participate. There can be no just or lasting peace without taking into
account the political demands and needs of the Palestinians.

j. The US has held a dialogue with the PLO with the goal of
encouraging the organization to adopt practical, pragmatic
positions in support of the peace process. So long as America
can see that the PLO is fulfilling its commitments, U.S.–PLO
dialogue will continue. If the PLO is prepared to adopt a practical method of achieving peace, the U.S.–Palestine dialogue will
be productive.

k. The US is not working to choose who will speak for the
Palestinians in this process, nor is it seeking to weaken
Palestinian interests. On the contrary, the U.S. efforts aim
to initiate a political negotiation process that includes direct
Palestinian participation and presents a method for realizing
Palestinians' political rights.

7. The U.S. message also included a reference to each party having
the right to bring any position to the negotiating table following
the start of negotiations. Israel may defend its right to annex Arab
territories; the Palestinians may defend their call for independence.
The US will not support either demand while the negotiations are
in session.

8. Although the message repeats the general U.S. positions, which are
well known, it makes no mention of Palestinian refugees or of East
Jerusalem. These are two points that the Americans doubtless wish
to avoid at present, so as not to complicate the situation. However, it
is my view that Paragraph 8 above is phrased in a manner that may
be unsatisfactory to the Palestinians and may well complicate their
response. Consequently, I am considering asking the Americans
to delete the reference. We are also considering extremely limited

modifications and additions, which may help strengthen the message. My aim, naturally, is to avoid focusing on the message to the exclusion of the main subject at hand, namely the Palestinian–Israeli dialogue.

9. I held a third meeting with Baker on Tuesday, January 19. In the first half, we discussed the matter of negotiations with the IMF and the economic reform program; in the second, Baker reaffirmed his eagerness for the third meeting to be held in Washington at the first opportunity, before he left for the Soviet Union. Although a desire on the part of each of the powers to achieve political gains ahead of the other is quite natural, in matters of summit meetings or foreign secretary meetings—evident in Baker's eagerness to get the Palestinians' agreement to the five-point program before the Malta summit on December 2, 1989—I realized precisely what was motivating Baker this time. When I met the UN secretary-general in New York on January 20, he notified me that Shevardnadze and Gorbachev had expressed their convictions that the U.S. efforts to push the dialogue forward had failed. The Middle East, they said, would top the agenda at the Moscow talks on February 6 and 7. Dennis Ross, director of planning at the U.S. secretary of state's office, hinted that both sides, the US and the Soviet Union, might agree on a joint statement on the Middle East.

10. Baker submitted to me in strictest confidence a list of seven Palestinian names, saying he felt they were suitable candidates for the Palestinian delegation, and asked my opinion. Naturally, I felt this to be a sensitive matter that required secrecy and circumspection, and must be discussed with Mr. Yasser Arafat in person.

Second:
1. In light of the above, I propose the following plan of action:
   a. We use our sources to find out the substance of the Palestinian figures the Americans are considering. That said, I strongly suspect that they have already been looked into with Israel during Yitzhak Rabin's visit to Washington. Rabin contacted our ambassador to Tel Aviv with a list of excluded Palestinian personages, and another of Palestinians from East Jerusalem he felt to be suitable candidates for the delegation.
   b. We secure—with the U.S. ambassador to Egypt—the Americans' approval of the selection criteria.
   c. We work with the Americans, and quickly, to make the necessary changes in their message to us, also finding out when they

plan to submit it to the two parties, that is to say, Egypt and Israel.

d. We find out the U.S. reaction—via the U.S. embassy—to the suggested method of announcing the Palestinian delegates.

2. We meet Arafat, soon, to notify him of, and discuss, the following:

   a. The high esteem for Arafat and his recent announcements that we noted in Baker's and Scowcroft's attitude, and their view that his efforts must be supported.

   b. Informing him of the U.S. approval, in general, of the four criteria.

   c. Showing him privately the names that Baker feels meet the criteria, as examples he can use in the process of selecting delegates, and asking him to present his eventual selection unofficially. (This requires that we conclude as soon as possible the process of vetting the people on the list and checking any intelligence we have about them.)

   d. Informing him—by way of encouragement—that we mentioned quietly in passing that a meeting, or more, might be held between our ambassador to Tunisia and Balawi, Palestine's ambassador to Tunisia, and Pelletreau, the U.S. ambassador to Tunisia. We should add our conviction that it can be done if we manage to avoid a media circus and if it is done unofficially.

   e. Affirming that we must keep our eyes on the prize: the start of a Palestinian–Israeli dialogue, with all its effects on attitudes toward efforts to reach a settlement.

   f. Agreeing with Arafat on moving to hold the Washington meeting, his first step being to concentrate on selecting the delegates and announcing the composition of the delegation, while the agenda setting may come later, during talks between the parties in capital cities.

   g. Warning Arafat against falling into a Soviet trap encouraging him to lose momentum until after the Moscow meeting with claims that the Soviets will be able to secure concessions from the Americans for him and the PLO.

3. We continue indirect consultations with the Americans on the composition of the Palestinian delegation. Once this is agreed upon in general terms, and a number of names—unofficial and non-binding—is added by Arafat, the meeting can be scheduled and a narrow agenda approved. The US can then issue a press release referring to advances in the situation (without offering details) and stating that the parties will remain in consultation to agree on pending matters.

Utilizing the media, in a clearly defined media campaign, is essential to preventing over-optimism or any expectations of great results, or later impressions that the meeting was a failure.

This was the state of activity and communication at this stage: there was constant rivalry and maneuvering between the Soviets and the US. The Soviets spread the word that the US' efforts had failed. The Americans sought to win a point against the Soviets before Baker's departure for Moscow, as I mentioned. For my part, I prepared an overview of the situation upon my return from Washington. I also wrote an extra brief for Dr. Abdel Meguid. I have decided to quote it in full here, as it quite clearly reveals all the elements of the situation at the time.

January 21, 1990
Brief for the Eyes of His Excellency the Deputy

First:
1. Communications in Washington in general reveal a consensus between Egypt and the US, linking Egypt's position on peace with U.S. support of Egypt's applications to international [financial] institutions. Guaranteeing continued U.S. support for Egypt's proposals to the IMF will require not only Egypt's continued efforts to implement strong economic reform, but also that we remain responsive to the US' efforts to hold a tripartite meeting in Washington. It is virtually a certainty that Egypt can utilize this U.S. requirement in the service of our suit to the IMF.
2. Baker's wish to hold the tripartite meeting in Washington before February 3 reveals the extent of the US' eagerness not only for dialogue but also to have something to show at the Baker/Shevardnadze meeting in Moscow that will put a stop to any Soviet plans and emphasize the lopsided balance between the two states with regard to the Middle East. There are a number of indications of this:
   a. Gorbachev's statement to the UN secretary-general that he is "concerned" about the situation in the Middle East, and Shevardnadze's statement that, the U.S. attempts having "failed," the Middle East would top their agenda of talking points with the Americans.
   b. Tarasov, the Soviet representative to the Middle East, arriving in Washington on January 25, and Dennis Ross mentioning that they may manage to produce a draft joint statement with the

Soviets on the current peace efforts. Such a statement would be largely constrained by the success or failure of the Americans in moving things forward before the planned Moscow meeting. It remains to be seen if this statement will carry any weight or is just a restatement of both states' wish for peace in the region, and whether it will be limited to a mere desire for Palestinian–Israeli dialogue or go beyond this to seeking a general framework for a settlement.

3. Our general impression so far is that the US is prepared to allow the Soviets a role—within limits, of course—in return for their commitment to encouraging and supporting the U.S. role, and at the same time benefiting from it (Dennis Ross has said that the Soviet Union is in dire need of some foreign policy success in its current circumstances). Given the above, Abu Ammar [Yasser Arafat] must be alerted of the conflicting and/or convergent Soviet–U.S. interests, specifically that the Soviets may attempt to hinder progress until after the Moscow meeting on February 6–7. The risk to Palestine's interests is loss of momentum, which could cripple the entire process, negatively impacting on Arafat's chosen strategy (and naturally, Egypt's interests in the form of U.S. assistance on the IMF front).

4. In my estimation, the responses to U.S. assurances to the Arabs, and to Israel, are not the main issue, but should be viewed in proportion, namely, as maneuvers by both sides vis-à-vis the US, or each other, with no real significance.

Second:

1. During the Washington consultations, the US clearly considered the make-up of the Palestinian delegation to be a matter of great importance. The agenda, in contrast, was relegated to the background. In an interview, Dennis Ross said that the tripartite meeting in Washington might issue a statement on the progress achieved in preparing for dialogue, and that the remaining issues would be dealt with at a later date. Our estimation is that the U.S. efforts will be confined to forming the delegation at this stage, moving fast until the end of this month. If the required progress is made, they will then move on to setting the agenda and other matters at a later stage, culminating in the dialogue in Cairo.

2. In Egypt, there are questions being asked and decisions being made. This raises a number of questions:

   a. Are the names under consideration by the US the same ones that Rabin hinted to our ambassador in Tel Aviv were with him, and that he wanted to discuss with us? How far does U.S.–Israeli coordination go in this matter? It may be hard to ascertain this, since there must be no discussion of the matter with the Israelis in any shape or form, and the Americans should only be consulted.

b. Will Egypt agree to go to Washington to take part in a semi-successful—or semi-failed—meeting, with all the unflattering media furor surrounding it? If attending a tripartite meeting is vital to Egypt at this stage, both for its communications with the IMF and to placate the Americans, we can set the scene for the media coverage by emphasizing that this meeting has extremely limited goals. However, the danger in this tactic is that a second tripartite meeting may be required (another Camp David, in other words). If we go that route, we will need to confine the follow-up consultations to communications between the capital cities, or with a U.S. team visiting the region after the Moscow meetings to continue preparations for a dialogue. Doubtless, this will keep Egypt front and center with the Americans, thus serving our need for U.S. support with the IMF.

Third:

1. The situation thus requires that we formulate an Egyptian plan of action for the coming period as regards
   a. Vetting the names suggested by the Americans in secret, without fuss.
   b. Notifying the US of Egypt's feedback on Baker's draft letter to us (after commissioning an analytical study of the project).
   c. Checking the US' reaction, via the embassy, to the proposed means of announcing the Palestinian delegation. If the US is in favor, which is not unlikely, it is important to conduct a detailed study of the procedural mechanism for the announcement. However, it is doubtful that Israel will accept the plan in the Egyptian paper.

2. Regarding the Palestinians, it is important that Yasser Arafat come to Cairo at the earliest possible opportunity to agree on specifics so that the tripartite meeting may be held in Washington before Friday, February 2. The following is a proposed framework for presenting the situation to Arafat:
   a. Notifying him of U.S. approval of the four criteria.
   b. Informing him privately of the names put forward by Baker as conforming to the four criteria, to assist him in compiling his

own list of delegates. Requesting that he present us with this list unofficially. (If we were to do the reverse and merely accept Arafat's nominations while keeping the names on Baker's list to ourselves, this might complicate matters later, as we would almost certainly be required to share the list with him at a later stage. Arafat's nominations would naturally be known to his team, making any change or modification potentially embarrassing to him. However, if he has advance knowledge of the names suggested by the US, it will allow him to maneuver a few of them onto the Palestinian list without awkwardness.)

    c. Agreeing on a main list and a reserve list, leaving more room for negotiation.

    d. Setting limited goals for the Washington conference with Arafat, confined to selecting the delegates and the mechanism for announcement. The agenda will be set later via consultations between the parties concerned, in their respective capital cities.

3. Continued (informal) consultations with the US on the composition of the Palestinian delegation. If a broad agreement is reached on this, the tripartite meeting may then go ahead, complete with a draft agenda accompanied by a U.S. press release stating that there have been "advances" in the situation without supplying specifics, saying only that the parties concerned will remain in consultation to finalize any deferred issues.

4. The issue of Baker's draft message remains. It may be worth considering the merits of deleting the paragraph on opposing an independent Palestinian state, or retaining it while explicitly rejecting references to annexation.

5. It may also be worth considering—despite the difficulties—submitting an alternate draft. Another recourse would be to prepare a document indicating that there are one or two points missing from the U.S. response and proposing references to them. In either case, the following is advised:

    a. Personally notifying Arafat of the contents of the proposed letter to us.

    b. Also letting Arafat know of the high esteem for him evidenced in Baker's and Scowcroft's dialogues with His Excellency the deputy minister, and their conviction that his efforts must be supported.

    c. Emphasizing that we must keep our eyes on the prize: launching a Palestinian–Israeli dialogue, with all its effects on everyone's attitudes to the efforts to reach a settlement.

d. Informing him—by way of encouragement—that we mentioned quietly in passing that one meeting or more might be held between our ambassador and Balawi, Palestine's ambassador to Tunisia, and Pelletreau, the U.S. ambassador to Tunisia. We should mention our conviction that it can be done if we manage to avoid a media circus and if it is done unofficially.

e. Consulting with Arafat on the position to be taken regarding Soviet participation. Despite our support for the Soviets having a role, we must be aware that this would mean not only their participation in the dialogue but also exchanging diplomatic representation between Israel and the Soviet Union, which may not be the most suitable matter to expedite at this opening stage of the dialogue.

Since we were closely coordinating our efforts with the Palestinians, we felt it was important to invite the Palestinian leadership, represented by Yasser Arafat, and get his detailed take on the developments in the situation and the possibility of starting a Palestinian–Israeli dialogue. We also needed to bring him up to date on the results of our foreign minister's visit to Washington and what U.S. leaders thought of the arrangements for launching the dialogue. Finally, it was important to share with Arafat all the details of Israel's positions, as revealed in Egyptian–Israeli communications at the time.

Esmat Abdel Meguid received Arafat on January 27 and 28. Well briefed by his team, the minister revealed all the developments to Arafat and covered the required talking points. Abdel Meguid then broached the main issue that needed resolution with Arafat, namely the status of delegates, rejected or otherwise, in returning to the occupied territories. This was the first thing Yitzhak Rabin requested from Washington; his second was the issue of selected delegates from East Jerusalem having two mailing addresses. The foreign minister asked Arafat for a list of PLO members he thought would make suitable Palestinian delegates, and finally warned him to guard against any leaks of information or arrangements, emphasizing that these would not help but hinder the process, even if it seemed otherwise, and play right into the hands of those who wished to hamper the peace process. On January 24, the Kuwaiti newspaper *Al-Anba'* had published the full text of the Palestinians' queries on November 27, 1989, and the US' response the following day—this is what provoked Abdel Meguid to issue such a warning.

The consultations between the Egyptians and the Palestinians concluded with an agreement that Egypt should inform the US of the PLO's acceptance of the universally agreed-upon selection criteria for the delegates, limited to the Palestinian personages accepted by high officials in the US and Israel, with the understanding that the Palestinians would either refrain from selecting anyone else or confine themselves to people with similar characteristics. The Americans were also warned against announcing any of these candidates to the Palestinians or publicly circulating their names in any form. Finally, Arafat agreed with Minister Abdel Meguid that Egypt would emphasize to the State Department that the PLO would form the Palestinian delegation according to the agreed-upon criteria, and then inform Egypt of the names of the delegates.

The foreign minister met U.S. Ambassador to Egypt Frank G. Wisner and notified him of the results of the Egyptian–Palestinian consultations, as he had previously agreed with Arafat. Dr. Abdel Meguid informed the ambassador that Arafat had told him privately that he had no objections to the Palestinian delegates from East Jerusalem having two addresses, one in the city and one elsewhere. In other words, Arafat found it expedient for any Palestinians prevented from entering the occupied territories to return to that region if selected as delegates.

In Egypt, we were doing all we could to enable the Palestinians to enter into the dialogue, which we felt would be a major development that would bolster the Palestinians' position and their demands in the international arena. It would also put Israel in the predicament of having to reopen this file and discuss every element of the settlement under pressure from Egypt, the US, and the world.

Meanwhile, Shamir was stalling. Moshe Arens, the Israeli foreign minister, began to obstruct the process, raising questions and making trouble for the Egypt–U.S. effort. Weeks, then months, passed with no breakthrough in launching the talks. What is certain, however, is that our effort was not wasted: the groundwork was laid for Palestinian participation when the time came for a comprehensive peace process.

The U.S. secretary of state met with President Mubarak while they were both visiting Moscow. Dr. Abdel Meguid informed me of the topics they covered during their meeting, as I accompanied him on the tour, which started with Moscow, went on to Pyongyang, and finished in Peking, returning by way of Great Britain. Secretary Baker, the minister informed me, had told the Egyptian president that he laid the current situation—the stalling of the peace process, the delays, and the unresponsiveness—squarely at Israel's door. He also clarified his view that it was important to reveal to the world Shamir's resistance to moving things forward. Secretary Baker was considering, he said, an agreement with Egypt and other unnamed Arab countries to promote a joint Egyptian–American position on the need for a Palestinian–Israeli dialogue, and for Israel to accept the "land for peace" position. Significant in Baker's statement was the mention of "land for peace," a phrase first used in the Jordanian–Palestinian agreement of February 11, 1985.

The secretary of state went on to say that if this joint position were announced, and agreed upon by Israel, it would then be incumbent on the Arabs to recognize Israel and act accordingly—in other words, to take steps to revoke the 1975 UN General Assembly resolution on Zionism being "a form of racism and racial discrimination," and to declare their readiness to cancel the Arab boycott of Israel and take steps to establish peace between Israel and the Arabs. Finally, Secretary Baker noted that, while he was aware of the difficulty inherent in this position and these ideas, his goal was to expose Shamir's resistance to the peace process.

I was concerned by what the minister had shared. I viewed it as a bare-faced bid by the US to get things out of the Arabs that the US or Israel had never got before, in exchange for a step that, by this time, constituted a mere matter of procedure, namely agreeing to a dialogue with the Palestinians. I was confident that our ultimate goal was not the start of negotiations—nor should it be—but a guarantee of seriousness in these talks and that they would lead to credible negotiations. In this, Baker was no different from his predecessors, nor yet his successors: they wasted no opportunity to work toward Israel's interests, something I have always observed.

Nothing changed. In fact, the situation suddenly deteriorated when a Palestinian organization led by Abu Abbas, or Mohamed Zaidan, the man behind the *Achille Lauro* hijacking, attacked Israel on May 30, and the US stopped negotiations with the PLO. The dialogue between the US and the Palestinians had begun after the PLO conference in Algeria, at which the organization had renounced violence as a means to solving the Palestinian problem. Consequently, our foreign minister left once again for Washington for meetings with the Americans. On June 24, I prepared a number of points to guide the discussions. It may be relevant to quote them in full, as they provide an accurate view of the issues and what the Middle East was undergoing at the time.

First:
1. The situation in the Middle East has deteriorated worryingly in the past few months, after a period of dedicated hard work in which Egypt and the US worked together to make progress on peace. We were all hopeful that with the resources available, we could move toward peace, especially after the momentous step taken by the Palestinians in November/December 1988, and the concomitant start of Palestinian–U.S. dialogue.

2. The elements of this deterioration from the point of view of Egypt, and, largely, the Arab world as well, are as follows: The Israeli position may be said to be crippled, evidencing no ability whatsoever for positive progress in the direction of actively accepting Secretary Baker's plan, after which the Israeli government appears to have adopted an extremist and hard-line position. The Arabs are concerned about:

   a. Israel's continued escalation of its repressive tactics vis-à-vis the intifada, and the sense that the US has been blocking an international action against this via the Security Council for months.

   b. Jewish immigration from the Soviet Union has skyrocketed. Shamir's statement on "greater Israel" has had its repercussions on the Arab view of the situation. It has raised deep concerns for Jordan, a key party, and other Arab countries as well, that Israel has no desire for peace but rather is leaning toward offering an "alternative homeland."

   c. The media campaign of mutual mud-slinging between Iraq and the western powers complicated a great many issues in these difficult months.

   d. A distinctly hard-line position has been taking shape in the US, reflected in the Congress' attitude to Jerusalem and the administration's position on the resolution on Zionism being racism. However, we must not ignore President Bush's, and Secretary Baker's, positive contributions.

3. Despite these difficulties, President Mubarak's meeting with Baker in Moscow was a good opportunity to evaluate positions and agree on action immediately following the formation of the Israeli Cabinet. However, tensions rose again, because the U.S. administration granted Israel loan guarantees of $400 million to expedite immigrants' transition to Israeli citizens, with no guarantees that these new settlers would not be housed in the occupied territories; because the US sent a memorandum to Arab League Secretary-General Shazli al-Qalibi making demands regarding the Arab summit; and, last but not least, because in the Security Council the US vetoed sending an international committee to study the situation in the occupied territories and look into ways to protect the Palestinian people.

4. A raid was attempted on the Israeli coast on May 30, the last day of the Arab summit—a summit in which Egypt made great efforts to secure a sense of balance and objectivity among the Arabs on many of the items on the table, such as peaceable approaches to a settlement, Jewish immigration, and so on.

5. Now that the U.S.–Palestinian dialogue is on hold, we find ourselves in an unenviable position. The peace process has stalled. It is
   certain that it stalled before May 30, and the direct reason—in our
   opinion—is the actions of the government of Israel. On this we can
   agree, as may be seen from your statements and our positions. There
   can be no doubt that the stalling of the peace process bears grave
   dangers and gives hardliners and extremists on both sides opportunities to achieve their own unsavory ends. Some are saying that the
   peace process will remain stalled for many months; the US will be
   busy, both with the upcoming elections starting in November 1990
   and with reorganizing the situation in Europe, including relations
   with the Soviet Union and its role on the global stage. Although this
   has merit, we however feel that we have a vital duty to work actively
   toward salvaging the situation in the Middle East, stopping the rot,
   and reactivating the peace process.

6. Egypt's view is that certain requirements must be met if the Middle
   East is to move toward peace. At the forefront of these are:

   a. The Palestine–U.S. dialogue needs to be reactivated as soon as
      possible. The US must be informed of the main elements of the
      Palestinian message:

      i. An investigation committee [into the attack] is currently
         preparing a report for the Palestinian National Council.

      ii. The Palestinian leadership had no prior knowledge of the
          Abu Abbas attack.

      iii. The Palestinian leadership condemns all military opera-
           tions whose goal is to terrorize civilians.
           (It is important that Egypt and the US agree on U.S.–
           Palestinian parallel steps that can be implemented to pave
           the way for a U.S. announcement that it will resume dia-
           logue with the PLO.)

   b. The US must intensify its efforts to convince the new gov-
      ernment in Israel to move in the direction of peace or risk a
      domestic crisis, which might result in improvements in the new
      year.

   c. The US needs to be more responsive to the international
      community on a number of important issues related to the
      Palestinian problem, including:

      i. Taking a decisive stand against the continued building of
         settlements.

      ii. Looking into available means to protect the Palestinian
          citizens of the occupied territories from Israel's actions.

    d. It is important to reassure Jordan with regard to Israel's inten-
tions, while curbing any possible action against other Arab parties, especially Iraq.

7. We must reassure the US that the Middle East, unlike Shamir's government, is fully prepared to move toward a peaceful settlement, and
that the PLO, Jordan, and Syria are clearly predisposed to peace.

8. It is important to obtain a reading of how the US views the situation
and proposes to move in future, as well as a clear idea of the time
frame the US is considering.

Second:

1. It may also be appropriate to listen to the U.S. assessment of the
situations in Iran, India, Pakistan, Kashmir, and Afghanistan.

2. It may also be appropriate to listen to the U.S. assessment of
Gorbachev's position, the internal situation within the Soviet Union
and the Middle East, and, finally, where they stand on German
unification.

President Bush met with Egypt's foreign minister, Dr. Esmat Abdel
Meguid, on June 26. I took part in the meeting, along with Dr. Osama
al-Baz and Ambassador Abdel Raouf El Reedy. The conversation started
by focusing on Abu Abbas' attack of May 30 and its effects on the situation,
particularly in terms of stalling the Palestine–U.S. dialogue. Esmat Abdel
Meguid stated that suspending the dialogue negatively impacted the peace
efforts. Bush's response was that he had fully considered the effects on the
moderate Arabs when he suspended the talks. Dr. Abdel Meguid reminded
him of Egypt's hopes for American, and indeed Palestinian, steps to restore
this dialogue, especially as it had taken so much time and effort to achieve
and resulted in a major step forward for the PLO and Yasser Arafat in
November 1988, namely accepting General Assembly Resolution 242.

Our foreign minister emphasized the importance of a forward-look-
ing effort to retrieve the momentum toward peace. President Bush asked
what guarantees the PLO could offer to confirm its repudiation of terror-
ism and its rejection of Abu Abbas' actions. Dr. Abdel Meguid responded
that this was Egypt's first priority. Why, asked Bush, had Abu Abbas not
been punished? Osama al-Baz replied that any penalties would be the
purview of the Palestinian National Council, scheduled to convene in
October 1990. Bush responded that he was prepared to look into the
possibility of resuming dialogue with the PLO.

There was also extended talk on the subject of Iraq and the Iraqi president's penchant for issuing blustering threats against Israel and the west.

President Bush said he had brought up the issue with King Hussein, who had appeared concerned about the possible consequences of this situation. According to Osama al-Baz, the king's concerns stemmed from fears of a possible Israeli attempt to topple the Jordanian regime and propose an "alternative Palestinian homeland" in Jordan.

We returned to Cairo with no guarantee of regaining momentum for the peace process. The Middle East was approaching its greatest storm yet.

27

The Invasion of Kuwait, the Destruction of Iraq, and the Road to Madrid

The situation in the Middle East and the Arab world saw a sudden downturn when on July 14, 1990, the president of Iraq accused Kuwait of violating petroleum-pricing policies in a way that would affect the price of oil and therefore impact Iraq's vital interests. Kuwait, he said, was stealing Iraqi petroleum from the Rumaila oil well on the border between the two countries.

On July 24, the Egyptian president made a lightning tour of Iraq, Saudi Arabia, and Kuwait in an attempt to keep the situation under control. Although the Iraqi president gave assurances that he had no intention of attacking Kuwait or attempting to seize the massive Rumaila oil well, he had altogether different intentions. The Iraqi mobilization near Kuwait's border continued to grow, and at roughly 0230 hours on August 2, I was awoken by a phone call from Kuwait. It was the deputy minister at the Kuwaiti Foreign Ministry, Ambassador Sulayman Majid al-Shahin. "I'm trying to put through a telephone call to Dr. Osama al-Baz to tell him about critical developments," he said, referring to the increasing Iraqi mobilization and the start of heavy fire on the Kuwaiti border checkpoints.

"It'll be hard to get through to him right now; he doesn't answer his phone at night," I said. The truth of the matter was that it was outright annoying to try to get through to Dr. Osama al-Baz on the phone with a message from the minister or anything urgent. Pretty much all of Egypt's higher echelons had suffered from this for years.

I promised Sulayman Majid al-Shahin that I would find Dr. al-Baz and deliver the message, and also inform the foreign minister of this development as soon as I could get through to him. I tried to put through the call, but failed to reach him. Finally, I decided to go back to bed for whatever sleep I could salvage.

At 0400 hours, still on August 2, my telephone rang again with a long-distance call. It was Kuwait again. Sulayman Majid al-Shahin was frantic. The Iraqi army, he said, had moved into Kuwait.

"Calm down," I said. "It might be a maneuver by the Iraqis to try and intimidate Kuwait." This was especially plausible in light of the fact that consultations between the two countries were scheduled to start in Jeddah that same day.

"They're downstairs." Calmly, he continued, "Iraqi tanks and armored vehicles are outside the Kuwaiti Foreign Ministry as we speak. I've got to get out of the building in a few minutes at most." He added that he had managed to get through to Dr. Esmat Abdel Meguid a few moments ago, although he still wanted to give Osama al-Baz specifics to convey to the president.

I called Dr. Abdel Meguid. He answered his phone and said he wanted to hold an immediate meeting of the ministers of the Arab League, who, as luck would have it, were all in Cairo to take part in a ministerial conference of the Organization for the Islamic Conference.

Egyptian diplomacy went to work like a well-oiled machine. I telephoned the director of protocol to prepare a large hall at the Intercontinental Hotel for the meeting, scheduled for 1000 hours on August 2. I also called the conference director to ensure his participation and coordination with the Protocol Department to get everything ready. Finally, I woke Ambassador Ehab Wahba, head of the Arab Department at the Foreign Ministry, with a request to get a team ready by 0700 hours to study all the political and legal aspects of the matter and suggest positions for Egypt to take and options to offer the foreign minister. After consulting with Dr. Abdel Meguid, I also asked for a draft Egyptian statement to be prepared for delivery at the Arab meeting, and another draft Egyptian statement of our position and views on this critical development.

The Arab meeting began on schedule after reaching the required quorum. The Iraqi representative took part. The discussions that followed shocked us Egyptians: we found the Palestinian delegation, headed by Farouk al-Qaddumi, seeking justifications for the Iraqi action, as did Yemen, Jordan, and Sudan, all of whom felt we "needed to understand the Iraqi position"!

A deep rift emerged between the Arab states. Egypt and Syria stood by the Gulf Cooperation Council. To analyze the situation for a moment, I must admit to being baffled by the position taken by Sudan, which should have steered clear of supporting Iraq. However, it was clear that self-interest remained the most powerful motivator. The Sudanese, Palestinians, and Jordanians, being closest to Egypt, would have, I thought, shared or at least comprehended our views; that this did not occur can only be imputed to a misreading of the situation.

The meeting of August 2 concluded without the Arab states adopting a unified position. I realized then, when I read the Charter of the League of Arab States, the insufficiencies in that document compared to the UN Charter, with regard to the decision-making process and the extent to which it allowed for action to be taken.

On the morning of August 3, the third ministerial meeting was held. No decisions were made; no vision was achieved. The Iraqi representative asked us to wait for the arrival of Saadoun Hammadi, the minister of state for foreign affairs. The conversation became far more heated when the Iraqi minister eventually arrived. "This is a warning from Iraq: Do not stand against us or our policies," he said. "The wealth of Kuwait must benefit poorer Arabs."

Saadoun Hammadi asked for a meeting with Minister Abdel Meguid. They had a private audience in the afternoon, during the fourth session of meetings, on one of the hotel balconies. I was there, taking the minutes. "Iraq is offering Egypt a grand prize," Hammadi began, "a sizable share of Kuwait's resources." He went on to say, "Iraq hereby declares the annexation of Kuwait to its territories. If any Arab party tries to stop us, we'll cut their hand off."

This made matters tense, to put it mildly. Dr. Abdel Meguid ended the meeting, saying, "We reject the Iraqi position. We will stand against it and condemn it." He concluded, "I'm very much afraid that this will end in Iraq's hand being cut off—or broken."

The foreign minister then called President Mubarak on the telephone. The president had been meeting with King Hussein to try and find a way out of the crisis. By now, it was clear that things were on a collision course. Abdel Meguid proposed a draft resolution to the president, condemning the Iraqi action and supporting the UN's rejection and condemnation of Iraq's activities.

When we returned to the conference hall, we put the draft resolution we had prepared to the vote. The resolution passed by majority vote, with objections from the PLO, Jordanian, and Sudanese delegations. The rift in the Arab world was confirmed.

In the above, I attempted to show the effects of Iraq's invasion of Kuwait on the Arab stance, and pinpoint how it affected the PLO in particular in its relations with Egypt, Syria, and Saudi Arabia. The PLO stance negatively affected its standing and the developments that followed, especially the results of the Arab summit of August 9 and 10 in Cairo, which led to a deeper divide in the Arab world. The PLO lost a great deal of its influence. The peace process ground to a halt pending an end to this Arab issue, which deeply impacted the situation in the Arab world for many years. When President Mubarak chaired the Arab summit sessions, Yasser Arafat's conduct can only be described as confrontational: he heckled Mubarak, the Syrian president, and the Saudis, and the rest of the Gulf Cooperation Council members into the bargain.

As the situation in Kuwait developed, communications were broken off between Egypt and Palestine. The PLO, we felt, was losing heavily in terms of deteriorating relations with the west and its fellow Arab nations. There was nothing we could do but wait for the crisis to be resolved, with all its ramifications.

War broke out between Iraq and the international coalition forces. Eventually, Iraq sustained a military defeat and Kuwait was liberated. With the restoration of Kuwait's legitimacy and the end of the Iraqi aggression, many began to call for the US to return to sincere efforts to move forward with the Middle East peace process. The momentum was slow in 1989 and 1990, and it fell completely in the seven months of the Kuwait crisis. Many began to press for the peace process, especially as Iraq had managed to link the matter of finding a settlement for Palestine with a resolution of the crisis in Kuwait. During the war, Iraq launched missiles at Israel from January 17 to February 24, 1991.

It was decided that the U.S. president would deliver an important statement on March 6 before a joint session of Congress, part of which would be dedicated to the situation in the Middle East. Many U.S. sources told us of the importance of listening very closely to everything the president said to the House and Senate. The U.S. ambassador to Damascus even called to alert me to the upcoming statement, and stressed the importance of showing it to Dr. Abdel Meguid as soon as we had a copy. We were in Damascus at the time, at the signing of what came to be known as the Damascus Declaration, a joint declaration by Egypt, Syria, and the countries of the Gulf Cooperation Council. In Cairo, we duly received a copy of President Bush's statement the morning of March 8, 1991.

The minute I saw it, I could tell that it reflected what seemed like a serious will to galvanize the stagnant situation in the region and relaunch the efforts that had stalled many months before. Bush said, "Our commitment to peace in the Middle East does not end with the liberation of Kuwait." He went on to speak of "four key challenges to be met." These were as follows:

First, we must work together to create shared security arrangements in the region. Our friends and allies in the Middle East recognize that they will bear the bulk of the responsibility for regional security. But we want them to know that just as we stood with them to repel aggression, so now America stands ready to work with them to secure the peace. . . .

Second, we must act to control the proliferation of weapons of mass destruction and the missiles used to deliver them. . . .

Third, we must work to create new opportunities for peace and stability in the Middle East. . . . We've learned in the modern age geography cannot guarantee security, and security does not come from military power alone. . . . In the conflict just concluded, Israel and many of the Arab states have for the first time found themselves confronting the same aggressor. . . . We must do all that we can to close the gap between Israel and the Arab States—and between Israelis and Palestinians. . . . A comprehensive peace must be grounded in United Nations Security Council Resolutions 242 and 338 and the principle of territory for peace. This principle must be elaborated to provide for Israel's security and recognition and at the same time for legitimate Palestinian political rights. . . . The time has come to put an end to Arab–Israeli conflict.

Fourth, we must foster economic development for the sake of peace and progress. . . . Now, the challenge is to reach higher, to foster economic freedom and prosperity for all the people of the region.

The US had begun to regain the attitudes that drove its enthusiasm for a Palestinian–Israeli dialogue a year or two earlier. We now followed the U.S. approach closely, to find out what the Americans planned to do to make Bush's vision a reality.

Alongside these developments, the Egyptian diplomatic leadership was undergoing something of a shake-up. Dr. Esmat Abdel Meguid was called to the Arab League to serve as the new secretary-general, replacing Shazli al-Qalibi, whose tenure was at an end. This also heralded an end to the League's absence from its permanent headquarters in Cairo. Dr. Esmat Abdel Meguid asked me to come with him to the Arab League. I remember telling him at the time that I wanted to serve the Egyptian flag and no other. I thanked him profusely, despite his clear disappointment and perhaps annoyance.

"What will you do?" he asked.

"I'll wait for the incoming foreign minister," I said, "and work with him."

"What if the new minister doesn't want your services?" Dr. Abdel Meguid asked me.

With a confidence that bordered on arrogance, I said, "I have confidence in my own abilities. Anyone who doesn't want to make use of me would be losing my years of experience and expertise in the field. After all, I know all the details and everything that's in the files."

My hunch proved correct. Amre Moussa was appointed foreign minister on May 15. He called me on the telephone from New York on May 13, where he was serving as permanent representative to the UN, and asked me to meet him at the airport "to start work together."

I had met Amre Moussa at the airport not a month before. He had been called to Cairo by the president in late April. At Amre Moussa's request, I had picked him up there, after which I had invited him to my home. We had a long conversation that extended over two days, before and after his meetings with the president, attended in part by Ahmed Maher al-Sayed, whose relationship with Amre Moussa was improving. For the twenty years that followed, this was the succession of foreign ministers of Egypt: Amre Moussa, Ahmed Maher al-Sayed, and finally Ahmed Aboul Gheit. Sometimes I wonder at life.

Egyptian–Palestinian relations had largely stalled after Palestine supported the Iraqi invasion of Kuwait. Yasser Arafat had stopped coming to Cairo. We were back to square one, all those years after President Sadat's initiative in visiting Jerusalem, the Camp David agreement, and Egypt's peace treaty with Israel.

With the resurgence in U.S. interest and the appointment of a new foreign minister, the Palestinians began to make discreet overtures toward Cairo. The Palestinian leadership was presenting Mahmoud Abbas, known as Abu Mazen, as the principal Palestinian personage who had rejected the Iraqi strategy and opposed Yasser Arafat's enthusiastic alliance with Iraq. Abu Mazen came to Cairo after the Kuwait crisis ended, as he had many times throughout 1989 and 1990.

In his meeting with the new Egyptian foreign minister, at which Dr. Osama al-Baz was also present, Abu Mazen said that Yasser Arafat was fully aware of his own predicament, isolated and rejected, and that a return to Egypt and a meeting with President Mubarak might salvage his situation. "I'm not telling you this merely out of regard or respect for Arafat," Abu Mazen added, "but as a political matter whose dimensions are quite clear. Arafat may well go to Syria. That would mean that Syria has forgiven his stance on the Gulf conflict. For Syria to resume relations with the PLO—no matter how good friends Syria and Egypt are—Egypt must also accept him into the fold."

In his continued attempts to motivate Cairo to accept Arafat, he said that Arafat might also go to Jordan to bolster his position. "However, the president of Egypt is something else entirely."

Osama al-Baz took it upon himself to respond to Abu Mazen. "Arafat has flown in the face of everything the Egyptian leadership is trying to achieve." In the end, however, he offered a lukewarm statement, echoing all of our sentiments at the time, that he would put it to President Mubarak.

The consultations between Abu Mazen and Amre Moussa on June 5 covered all the elements of the Middle East conflict. They discussed the current situation and the Syrian view of the step taken by the US. Abu Mazen said that President Hafez al-Assad was now convinced that the US was serious in its efforts for peace; however, the road was bound to be long, and the Syrian president did not want to see Lebanon taking part in the efforts. They also touched on a possible international conference that might launch the peace process. The reader may recall that the matter of an international peace conference had been raised a year before Bush's statement of renewed interest in reviving the peace process in March 1991. This brought the discussion to possible candidates for the Palestinian delegation: would it be an independent delegation, a joint one with Jordan, or an Arab delegation that brought all the parties together?

Abu Mazen's responses revealed that the Palestinians lacked understanding of Syria's position, even though a large Palestinian delegation had just been in Damascus before he arrived in Cairo. The Syrians, it seemed, were lukewarm about a tight-knit five-state group of Arab 'ring states,' and distinctly unwelcoming of any Palestinian–Jordanian collaboration. Abu Mazen hinted that Syria was pursuing its own interests and position, nothing else.

Abu Mazen's visit also made it clear that the Palestinians had resumed in-depth direct dialogue with the U.S. administration. Interestingly, the US had consulted the Soviets on so many of the preparations that then-Foreign Minister Alexander Bessmertnykh had become the Palestinians' only window into developments in the situation. Throughout 1989 and 1990, the Palestinians went over all the main points and elements toward which they were working in an attempt to convey them afresh to all parties concerned. They emphasized that they would be glad to attend a peace conference based on the position President Bush had expressed, with a Palestinian delegation from Palestinians within and outside the occupied territories. While they would prefer a uniquely Palestinian delegation, they were not, they said, closing the door to any other options, in order to help move things forward. This included a Palestinian–Jordanian delegation or an Arab delegation bringing everyone together—a proposition strongly rejected by Syria.

In all their communications, the Palestinians expressed a strong desire for a halt to Israeli settlement-building immediately at the start of the peace conference: a demand the Palestinians have been continually making over the past twenty years, with no result or any response from Israel. The Palestinians insisted on linking the stages of a solution and not being fooled by the Israelis into implementing the transitional self-rule period and then seeing the peace process grind to a halt—a fear that was not unjustified, as revealed by Israel's actions since the signing of the Oslo Accords in 1993.

Secretary Baker's visits to the region resumed with their former frequency, as they were before the war in Iraq. The Americans laid out their views and plans to the parties in the region, the Soviets, and the European Community. Egyptian–Palestinian communications intensified, with Abu Mazen making several visits to Cairo in June and July 1991. Meanwhile, Baker continued to communicate with Palestinians in the occupied territories and in the diaspora, while not going so far as to resume official dialogue with the PLO.

Foreign Minister Amre Moussa warned the Palestinians to act prudently so as to corner Israel, which would allow the US to take a stand against Israel in the form of their housing loans if Israel remained adamant about rejecting the dawning peace efforts shared by all concerned. In his meeting with Abu Mazen on July 21, attended by PLO officials Hakam Balawi and Said Kamal, the Egyptian foreign minister emphasized the need for the PLO to announce the formation of a joint Palestinian–Jordanian delegation that would take part in the peace conference, and to issue a statement in support of an end to the Arab boycott of Israel, provided Israel ceased building settlements.

At the height of these discussions between the Egyptians and the Palestinians—which were accompanied by the verbal consultations and assurances that Secretary Baker was offering to the Arab parties concerned, especially Syria and Palestine, encouraging them to attend a conference and agree to the peace process—the Israeli foreign minister dropped a media bombshell, revealing Israel's intentions perhaps to explode the situation or at least to weaken the US' assurances to the Arabs. David Levy announced ten points of understanding between Israel and Secretary Baker as regards the peace conference, which Israel expected Washington to stand firmly behind. These had, he said, been agreed upon during the talks held when Baker was in the region. The ten points were to the following effect:

1. A bilateral inclination to allow Israel to negotiate concurrently with several Arab governments and with Palestinians living under Israeli occupation.
2. The talks will be held with no prior conditions.
3. The peace process is not designed to establish a Palestinian state.
4. The PLO will not be a partner in the peace process nor have any part in it.
5. Negotiations on the Palestinian issue will be in stages as specified in the Camp David agreement.
6. Palestinian negotiators must accept the bilateral wording and the method of advancing in stages outlined in the Camp David agreement. They must have the desire to live in peace with Israel.
7. Israel is under no obligation to agree to the request worded as "territory for peace" as a precondition for holding direct talks.
8. The peace conference will be non-binding. It will not have the power to issue resolutions. Its only goal will be direct negotiations between the parties.
9. Bilateral Arab–Israeli working groups will be formed to submit regional development projects for eventual international funding.
10. The Soviet Union and the European Union must accept these points of understanding if they are to be allowed to attend the conference.

Palestinians reacted to this with escalation. It became clear that the crux of the whole matter was the issue of how the Palestinians would be represented at the conference, especially in light of the differences surrounding the participation of Palestinians in East Jerusalem and living abroad. The Palestinian statements became more strongly worded and hardline as a result of the PLO's fears of being excluded from the peace efforts and losing its position on the political scene.

On August 7, the foreign minister of Egypt met with Abu Mazen once more. Osama al-Baz and I were also present. The minister said that things were moving fast. A definite date had been proposed for the long-awaited peace conference, which made it necessary to take a final and definite stand on the Palestinian–Jordanian delegation, as well as for the PLO to accept the role it had been asked to play in the preliminary stages of the conference. In an attempt to convince and reassure the PLO officials, the minister added that both the US and Israel acknowledged the role of the PLO and that it was a mistake for the Palestinians to assume that the PLO had been sidelined. He noted, however, that the situation on the ground and this critical stage of the peace process—preparing and holding the international conference—required the PLO to remain in the shadows for a while.

In his comments and responses to Egypt's foreign minister, Abu Mazen explained that the PLO absolutely insisted on clear and unequivocal assurances from the US, and that East Jerusalem must be represented in the Palestinian–Jordanian delegation. Osama al-Baz warned the Palestinians against slipping into any kind of confrontation with the US. Abu Mazen said that there was time—it was October 1991—for a limited degree of confrontation in the service of his people's interests. Mahmoud Abbas then returned to the issue of a possible visit to Cairo by Yasser Arafat, saying that while the final say concerning conference participation and the form it would take was Arafat's, he would not make a decision until he was confident that Egypt supported him and stood behind his positions. In other words, it became clear from the conversation that Arafat was predicating the PLO's peace efforts not only on his visit to Egypt but also on receiving Egypt's support. This would enable him to quell his critics within the PLO and convince them that this was the correct course for the PLO to take.

Amre Moussa summarized the situation at the end of the meeting in five main points:

1. There is no objection in principle to a joint Palestinian–Jordanian delegation.
2. There are no objections to compiling a list of the Palestinian leaders within the occupied territories who might join the delegation.
3. A mechanism must be found for the participation of delegates from East Jerusalem. Egypt's suggestion is using two addresses.
4. The inclusion of members from Jerusalem, once the issue of the Palestinian delegation is settled, does not indicate that Jerusalem will feature on the agenda in the preliminary stages of the conference.
5. U.S. assurances are required for the Palestinians, commensurate with any possible U.S. assurances to Israel, or indeed to what the Israeli foreign minister announced on July 21.

At the start of October, the month of the international conference and the start of direct negotiations between the Arabs and Israel, Amre Moussa decided to visit Damascus to meet President Assad to see about the possibility of coordination and cooperation between Syria and Egypt. I accompanied him on this important visit. He was received by President Assad on October 7.

Assad requested an immediate five-state summit for the Arab ring states to prepare for the negotiations and reassure our respective peoples that there was full coordination among the Arabs, in contrast to what Abu Mazen had said earlier. Amre Moussa's response was that there would be many stages to the conference, which would allow plenty of time for the requested summit to be held. In addition, there was no call for a summit at the first stage of negotiations; it would be quite sufficient to hold meetings at the ministerial level, specifically the Foreign Ministries of the relevant countries. This ended up being the course of action taken.

President Assad said it was important to defer multilateral negotiations until such time as the course of the bilateral negotiations became clear, which would allow us to be sure of the Israelis' intentions. If things did move forward, and Israel proved serious about the bilateral talks with each Arab country, multilateral talks could be considered. It was clear that Assad was pessimistic about the Israeli position and suspicious of Shamir's intentions toward the Arabs.

President Mubarak decided to take a step that would reflect Cairo's intention to reconcile with Arafat. The Egyptian president and Mahmoud Abbas met in Cairo on October 10. The Palestinian representative to Cairo, Said Kamal, telephoned me that evening to convey some of the Palestinians' thoughts to Foreign Minister Amre Moussa. Kamal sought to reaffirm a point that came up in Abu Mazen's conversation with the president: that Arafat intended to stay in Amman for a while during the conference proceedings in order to jointly oversee the delegation and avoid any conflicting instructions or statements. The ambassador added that King Hussein, having studied the situation and received the input and recommendations of the Jordanian Secret Service, had agreed to allow Arafat to stay, on condition that he not engage in any political activity during his time in Jordan, unlike what occurred between June 1967 and September 1973.

Said Kamal re-read a Jordanian document discussed by Abu Mazen and President Mubarak that morning. This document had already been discussed by the Jordanians and the Palestinians, and, according to Said Kamal, it stipulated that the delegation would be Jordanian-led, while the Palestinians wanted there to be two leaders, saying that Jerusalem could only be represented if the Jordanian delegation included someone originally from that city, currently living in Jordan. The Palestinians proposed including a Palestinian in the joint Israeli–Jordanian preparation committee when it eventually convened. The document also stated:

1. No flags of any party to be placed on the negotiating tables.
2. Palestinian delegates to be announced either via West Bank and Gaza newspapers, or via the intifada leadership's statements.
3. Official speaker for the joint Palestinian–Jordanian delegation to be Palestinian, with a Jordanian deputy.
4. Forming a high commission composed of King Hussein of Jordan and Yasser Arafat, and a political committee made up of Abu Mazen and Taher al-Masri, and a third technical committee made up of Shayth and Toubaz, two of Prince Hassan bin Talal's assistants.
5. The goal of negotiations is complete withdrawal, followed by interim arrangements for a period to be set during the negotiations, followed by a final solution consisting of a federal union between Jordan and Palestine.
6. An end to Israeli settlement-building at the start of the conference.

With the start of the second week of October, communications intensified among all parties. Secretary Baker visited the region no fewer than eight times, while Yasser Arafat took to maneuvering to achieve his goals. The prevailing thought among us was that Arafat truly believed that his refusal to attend the conference would make it impossible for the parties concerned to participate in this international effort; however, we in Cairo, most of us at least, felt that Arafat could not afford to waste this opportunity. His participation was a foregone conclusion; all he was doing was playing for political gains.

We agreed to play along to help him achieve his aims, not sharing, of course, what we thought. The Americans started upping the pressure on the Palestinians. Baker met a Palestinian delegation from the West Bank and Gaza in Washington on October 10 and demanded that they head for Amman as soon as the meeting was over to announce the Palestinian–Jordanian delegation. He threatened that if there was any delay he would cancel his upcoming tour of the region—his eighth. Secretary Baker also made it clear that he expected to receive the list of delegates before October 15, with a preponderance of delegates from the occupied territories and none from Jerusalem. The US, he said, would not go beyond Camp David in the matter of Palestinian self-determination. As for resumption of dialogue with the PLO, this was not, he said, on the table right now. Finally, Secretary Baker notified them that the US was not currently in favor of any international or multinational, or even American, presence in the West Bank and Gaza.

Developments made it clear that Amre Moussa and Osama al-Baz's hunches had been correct: their fears that the PLO would slide into a conflict with the US were about to come true. Abu Mazen's words, "we do not fear conflict," had made things between the US and Palestine so bad that they threatened the conference itself.

The Palestinians went directly from Washington to Amman, and Secretary Baker came to the region in mid-October. Still, Arafat informed President Mubarak, via Said Kamal, on October 14, that he had no intention of presenting the list of Palestinian delegates until the matter of Jerusalem's representation had been resolved. His demand was to add Hanan Ashrawi and Faisal al-Husseini to the Palestinian list, or the latter to the Jordanian list. There was a lot of pressure, he said, on the Palestinian decision, and this needed to be taken into account.

Secretary Baker arrived in Cairo on the afternoon of October 13, immediately meeting Foreign Minister Amre Moussa. I was at the meeting. They discussed, again, the issue of Palestinian representation and the U.S. demand for the list of Palestinian delegates to show to Israeli Prime Minister Shamir. The U.S. attitude revealed a great deal of wariness, if not fear, about upsetting Israel. This became especially clear when the issue was Palestinians speaking at the conference or the method of delivering their invitations.

I discussed this with Dennis Ross, Baker's consultant. The Americans' behavior, I said, was not weakening the Palestinians but revealing the U.S. administration's weakness, which made me—and others—doubt that the Americans really had any ability to apply any pressure on Israel when push came to shove.

I had a positive working relationship with Dennis Ross. Over Baker's visits to Cairo from October 1989 until I left to take up my position as Egypt's ambassador to Rome at the end of the summer of 1992, I always arranged to drive him to his hotel from the airport, while Egypt's foreign minister took Secretary Baker. The thirty minutes between the flight landing and arrival at the hotel—which is how long it took in Cairo traffic at the time—gave me ample opportunity to speak with Ross about how the Americans were thinking, the thoughts and objectives behind their visits, and his impressions of Israel on his visits there. In Cairo, we always insisted that the U.S. ambassador visit us at the end of his tours of the region, to give us his overview of the situation.

When the reception was over, before the official consultations with the Americans began, I hurried to our foreign minister to discuss what I had heard from Ross and compare notes so as to analyze the situation properly.

The delegation included many respected diplomats, such as Edward Djerejian, who also served as U.S. ambassador to Jordan and Syria.

I developed a good relationship with him and Françoise, his Armenian–French wife, during our tenure together in Moscow from 1979 to 1982. I always felt that he genuinely cared about the Arabs and had a sincere wish to help us within the limits of his position and responsibilities. His closeness to Secretary Baker doubtless contributed to our ability to communicate directly with the secretary of state, bypassing those of Baker's assistants we did not trust.

Also in attendance was Richard Haass, assistant to National Security Advisor Brent Scowcroft. As of this writing, Haass is the president of the U.S. Council on Foreign Relations. He always struck me as an honest and truthful gentleman.

Last but not least there was Aaron Miller, who often disagreed with Dennis Ross, despite being his policy planning deputy, taking stances that reflected a clear understanding of, not to say sympathy for, the Arab view—which ultimately led to him leaving the U.S. State Department.

October 1991 was fast drawing to a close. The Americans were upping the pressure on the weakest Arab link, namely the Palestinians, who for their part complained constantly about the way the Americans dealt with—or indeed threatened—them. We were in continual contact with the Americans via long-distance telephone calls between Cairo and Washington. These often began at 0600 hours Eastern Standard Time, when I called them from Cairo on their home numbers in DC to discuss the issues in telegrams that had arrived from our embassy in Washington that same morning or the evening before.

The complaints were not, it must be said, one-way. The Americans, too, constantly expressed their displeasure at the Palestinians' positions and their penchant for backing out of things to which they had previously indicated agreement. We were continually intervening to bring the two together. It was our firm conviction that holding an international conference and the start of negotiations between the Arabs and Palestinians, in one camp, and the Israelis, in the other, would ultimately benefit the Palestinians and the Arab side, replacing the stalemate that currently characterized the conflict. Consequently, we were always conveying ideas, presenting proposals, and making efforts to move intractable positions, while never losing sight of the basic principles for a settlement agreed upon by the Arabs.

When the invitations were issued by the US and the Soviet Union, the US informed everyone of the messages, pledges, and written assurances the Americans had issued to all the parties—a lot of them contradictory. As for Israel, Secretary Baker wrote to the Israeli prime minister on October 18 that:

- These guarantees offered by the US represent the US' intentions and understanding of the conference and negotiations. The US has offered no guarantees to either side without the other's knowledge.
- We promise you that our commitment to Israel's security remains unchanged. So does our commitment to preserving Israel's advantage in the region.
- Israel has the right to secure borders agreed upon in direct negotiations accepted by its neighbors.
- Peace means the signing of peace treaties and establishing full diplomatic relations between Israel and its Arab neighbors.
- The US does not support the establishment of an independent Palestinian state. Nor does it support the continued control or annexation of lands occupied by Israel.
- The US does not support linking different sets of negotiations to achieve a comprehensive settlement.
- The Israel–Palestine negotiations will be conducted in stages. At the start, the objective will be to negotiate an interim five-year settlement for self-rule. These talks on the interim period will end within one year. Starting with the third year of the interim period, negotiations will start on a final settlement.
- The US, in keeping with President Ford's promise to Israeli Prime Minister Yitzhak Rabin on September 1, 1975, supports safeguarding Israel's security from any attack from the Golan Heights in any comprehensive settlement with Syria or any peace treaty with the Syrians. The US has not yet reached a final position on the matter of borders. When it is obliged to do so, it will take very much into account Israel's position that any peaceful settlement with Syria must be based on Israel remaining in the Golan Heights. The US is prepared to offer guarantees of the security arrangements on the borders eventually agreed upon between Israel and Syria, in accordance with U.S. law.

In parallel with this message to Israel, the Americans sent the Syrians a message of reassurances, or guarantees, dated the same day, October 18:

- Syria's agreement to take part in this conference called by the US is an important step on the way to a comprehensive settlement of the Arab–Israeli conflict on the basis of UN Security Council Resolutions 242 and 338.
- This message specifies the US guarantees of its intentions and concepts related to this conference and the negotiations between the parties concerned.

- These assurances to the parties must not clash with the policies of the US, nor can they be in conflict or at variance with the principles on which the conference is based.
- Any settlement in the Middle East must achieve security and recognition for everyone—including Israel—and the legitimate political rights of Palestinians.
- The final settlement will be reached via credible negotiations. Resolution 242 and the principle of 'territory for peace' applies to all fronts, including the Golan Heights. Throughout the negotiations, the US will continue to refuse to acknowledge, or accept, the unilateral Israeli declaration that Israeli law, or its extension, applies to the Golan. Similarly, the US will continue to oppose Israel's settlement-building activity in the lands occupied since 1967.
- The U.S. secretary of state repeats the proposal submitted by President Bush to President Hafez al-Assad on May 31, 1991, stating that the US is prepared to offer guarantees of the borders mutually agreed upon by Syria and Israel, taking the U.S. constitutional process into account.

The US affirmations to Israel and Syria included a vague reference to the US securing the borders agreed upon by both parties. In the months that followed, we learned what it meant. Djerejian, by now U.S. ambassador to Syria, informed me that the US had been prepared to agree to send units from its Airborne 101st Division as a buffer between Syria and Israel as soon as the two nations reached a peace agreement. This was later confirmed in 1994–95, up to the killing of Yitzhak Rabin during the fast-paced Syrian–Israeli settlement negotiations. These promising talks ground to a halt with Rabin's murder and the ascendancy of the Likud under Benjamin Netanyahu.

The last U.S. message of assurance was addressed to the Palestinians, who had been the first to call for one, fearing that the traditional U.S. commitment to Israel first might negatively affect their interests or limit the US' ability to deal with Israel. The Arab–Israeli negotiations over the years, indeed decades, have revealed the extent to which Israel has managed to tie America's hands when it comes to the free exercise of diplomatic efforts related to any matter to which Israel is a party. We may remember the commitment made by Kissinger to Israel in 1975, that the US would not submit any proposals on a peace process in the Middle East without prior notice to and approval from Israel, which of course means that it nipped in the bud anything that runs even remotely counter to Israel's interests.

The message to the Palestinians, also officially submitted to them on October 18—although we obtained access to a number of preliminary drafts, as had the Palestinians—stated:

- It has always been the US' conviction that Palestinian participation in this effort is essential to its success. The US wishes to inform all parties that it has offered no guarantees to either side without the other's knowledge.
- The US is convinced of the necessity of ending the Israeli occupation via serious negotiations and the Palestinians obtaining their rights to take the reins of their own affairs, politically and economically, and in every aspect of their life and future.
- The Palestinians alone have the right to form their negotiating team. These delegates will be inhabitants of the occupied territories amenable to the concept of negotiations and of a solution in stages. Being aware of the importance of East Jerusalem to Palestinians, the US wishes to affirm that any decisions taken by the Palestinians on forming the delegation at this stage of negotiations will not impact on the rights and demands of Palestinians regarding the east of the city, which must not be divided again. Hence, the US does not recognize the annexation process of East Jerusalem implemented by Israel. The U.S. position acknowledges the right of Palestinians in East Jerusalem to take part in the elections for the self-rule authorities. Palestinians in East Jerusalem and others outside the occupied territories will all have the right to participate in the final negotiations when they commence in the third year of the transition.
- The U.S. affirmation message covers the goals of the negotiations and the interim settlement, or settlement in stages, plus the two negotiation routes, that is, bilateral and multilateral.

This message, with all the complexities inherent in its commitments, and its loose phrasing in some areas and precision in others, represents the U.S. technique for managing the fears and apprehensions of the parties involved. Our experience with negotiations in the years that followed revealed to us, as it will to the attentive observer, that many of these assurances were not met—not least because the parties concerned failed to insist on follow-through or neglected to demand them afterward. However, what is abundantly clear is that the United States was eager to include a plethora of other nations in its vigorous efforts to make the negotiations a reality, and was happy to encourage them to attend. Foremost among these nations was the Soviet Union, then on the brink of dissolution, which in fact limited its efficacy due to circumstances on the ground and the deterioration of its ability to exert its previous influence. Also included was the soon-to-be-united Europe, which had expressed a desire for a seat at the negotiating table. While the European Community had no real political influence at the time, the US was counting on it to foot part of the bill for costs incurred through any future comprehensive settlement, as has been extensively covered in the literature on this period. The United States' assembling of this large group of nations was part of a comprehensive strategy to get the parties concerned into the conference hall and finally sitting at the negotiating table for the first time in the long and checkered history of the Middle East conflict.

28 Peace Talks Begin along All Paths

U.S. Secretary of State James Baker and Soviet Foreign Minister Boris Pankin finally agreed during their visit to Israel on October 18, 1991, to issue the invitations to the peace conference scheduled for October 30 in Madrid. A number of cities and world capitals made a bid to host the conference; the US decided that holding it in Madrid would best serve the conference, thanks to Spain's decades-long balanced position on the conflict.

The invitation, submitted at each capital city, included a number of points that had already featured in the letters of assurances received by each party. It explained the objective of the conference: "To assist the parties to achieve a just, lasting, and comprehensive peace settlement, through direct negotiations along two tracks, between Israel and the Arab states, and between Israel and the Palestinians." It went on to present the process and schedule in some detail:

> Direct bilateral negotiations will begin four days after the opening of the conference. Those parties who wish to attend multilateral negotiations will convene two weeks after the opening of the conference to organize those negotiations. The co-sponsors believe that those negotiations should focus on region-wide issues of water, refugee issues, environment, economic development, and other subjects of mutual interest.

The invitation also stated that the co-sponsors had invited Israel, Syria, Lebanon, Jordan, and a number of Palestinians who would "attend as part of a joint Jordanian–Palestinian delegation." It went on to specify that "the European Community will be a participant in the conference, alongside the United States and the Soviet Union, and will be represented by its Presidency"—the Netherlands at that time. It also stated that,

> The Gulf Cooperation Council will be invited to send its secretary-general to the conference as an observer, and GCC member states will be invited to participate in organizing the negotiations on multilateral issues. The United Nations will be invited to send an observer, representing the secretary-general.
>
> The conference will have no power to impose solutions on the parties or veto agreements reached by them. It will have no authority to make decisions for the parties and no ability to vote on issues of results. The conference can reconvene only with the consent of all the parties.
>
> With respect to negotiations between Israel and Palestinians who are part of the joint Jordanian–Palestinian delegation, negotiations will be conducted in phases, beginning with talks on interim self-government arrangements. These talks will be conducted with the objective of reaching agreement within one year. Once agreed, the interim self-government arrangements will last for a period of five years; beginning in the third year of the period of interim self-government arrangements, negotiations will take place on permanent status.

It was judged at the time that the invitation to the conference, and the proceedings, were very much to Israel's liking. The invitation addressed a great many of Israel's concerns. Israel had shied away from any conference that seemed empowered to impose any vision or settlement. Still, the prevailing opinion in Cairo was that holding a conference might still pave the way for a real movement toward a serious peace process, if the parties concerned acted in good faith to achieve the "real peace" mentioned at the very start of the invitation, which stated that "the United States and the Soviet Union believe that an historic opportunity exists to advance the prospects for genuine peace throughout the region . . . based on United Nations Security Council Resolutions 242 and 338. The objective of this process is real peace."

Once the invitations had gone out, the Soviet Union announced, during a visit to Israel by Soviet Foreign Minister Boris Pankin, the resumption of diplomatic relations between Israel and the Soviet Union. This was Israel's first success of the conference.

Meanwhile, back in Cairo, along with our copy of the invitation, we received a request from the US, which had also been sent to

Jordan and Syria, to send a representative of the foreign minister to Washington for pre-conference consultations, to evaluate ideas and encourage suggestions, in hopes of achieving the greatest-possible success. Minister Amre Moussa entrusted me with this task.

I arrived in DC on October 25. The following day, the consultations began. The Americans were represented by Assistant Secretary of State Edward Djerejian and Director of Policy Planning Dennis Ross, as well as Ross' deputy Aaron Miller and William J. Burns from Near Eastern Affairs. Although the invitation to the conference dealt with a great many subjects related to his specialization, how exactly these would be managed remained a mystery. This was my objective in DC: find out what the Americans weren't telling.

The reason it was my task to get to the bottom of the US' way of thinking and the road map it was preparing is that I knew the Americans were extremely detail-oriented and careful: they would not leave a loophole without calculating everything it might lead to and what damage it could do.

The meeting started. The goal of talking to us, and to others, Djerejian said, which would continue in Madrid, was to find out how to deal with the bilateral negotiations on all their different fronts and ensure their success. The opening statements of each delegation were thus of great importance: it was essential that they evince a spirit of peace and flexibility. This was especially the case for Syria, which the Americans suspected was still uncomfortable and suspicious of the US' intentions. The US felt it important that each party take steps to build confidence. It believed that Israel might well offer to facilitate some procedures, and expected the Palestinians to follow suit. Dennis Ross said that, while they admitted that the Palestinians might well have legitimate points, it was important to avoid raising any issues that might complicate the negotiations before their commencement. What, he asked, did the Palestinians have to offer the Israelis in exchange for steps the latter might take to mitigate the severity of border procedures in crossing to Jordan, and other steps that might make life easier for the ordinary Palestinian citizen?

"I don't imagine the Palestinians have anything to offer," I responded. I went on to explain that, being under occupation, all they had was resistance.

The consultations went on to the Syria–Israel negotiations. This was a special case, said Ross, as it would be the first time the parties had talked to one another directly. The US' experience with Syria had demonstrated that the Syrian response time frame was always delayed. The Americans were studying how to come into the negotiations, and whether it would not be better to focus on studying the agenda or to look into the philosophical framework for a settlement, meaning to study politics, security, and other related issues, plus advance toward an agreement on general principles for a solution, finally requesting that each party offer its own proposals, to be developed with the addition of U.S. proposals.

I responded that since Syria was a high priority for the US, the Americans could take some general steps that would be encouraging to President Assad. One of these, for example, could be facilitating Syria's Czech deal for two hundred T-72 tanks, which Prague wanted to get rid of. Another could be Syria receiving economic impetus from countries in contact with the US, such as Japan.

The Americans responded that it was hard, for a number of reasons, to look into the matter of weapons for Syria. However, they could look into some aid and economic measures, or other steps, during the multilateral negotiations, if Syria ultimately decided to participate in them.

I asked the Americans to speak to the Israeli prime minister. His speech, it was only fair, should have the same spirit and leanings they mentioned with regard to the Arab delegations. I also emphasized that they should not let the extremist elements within Israel take any steps—to build settlements or otherwise—that could obstruct the conference proceedings. Both Ross and Djerejian told me that they had already broached this issue with Israel. They were now asking Egypt to raise it with Israel directly.

I telegraphed the foreign minister from Washington, apprising him of the situation. He was preparing to leave for Madrid. In my report, I told him that the meeting had revealed the US' respect for Egypt's role, especially in modifying the Syrian stance. The Americans hoped for Egypt to continue to support them in positively influencing Syria's positions and persuading Damascus to show the flexibility they required. They also hoped we would keep encouraging the Palestinians to take positive, balanced positions vis-à-vis any steps taken by Israel in the area of confidence-building, especially as they had noticed that the Israeli delegation included two officials responsible for the West Bank and Gaza. They considered this to indicate that Israel was willing to take positive steps toward building trust. I said in my report, however, that the Americans—although I had asked point-blank—did not share with me a comprehensive vision of how things would happen in the bilateral talks, or of Egypt's direct role in them.

My report also mentioned that the Americans spoke positively of the Soviets' role. The Soviet Union, they said, was prepared to respond to any steps taken by the US. I did not add my own analysis or evaluation of this point, but I felt the Soviets' approach was only natural given cir-cumstances in the Soviet Union at the time, meaning the failed coup to overthrow Gorbachev on August 20 and the Soviet Union being on the brink of collapse—which occurred by the end of that year.

I left the U.S. capital on the evening of October 27 with the general impression that the Americans did not, in fact, have a specific plan for how the negotiations would proceed. They were feeling their way, adopt-ing a 'wait and see' approach, and hoping that trial and error would reveal the best way forward.

Before noon on October 28, I arrived at the Ritz Hotel in Madrid, only to find that a great many of the Egyptian delegates had beaten me there. Foreign Minister Amre Moussa was due to arrive that evening. As his office director in Cairo, I headed up the diplomatic and tech-nical team that accompanied him. Once in Madrid, I began to assign tasks and divide up the workload among the members of the delega-tion, the members of my own office, other departments in the Foreign Ministry, and members of the Egyptian security apparatus, as was the custom at that time. The delegation also included many Egyptian aca-demics who specialized in matters we felt would become appropriate in due course.

The Arab delegations and other participants poured in. We launched into a series of separate meetings with each delegation, assessing their positions and intentions. The Palestinian delegation handed a copy of a message from popular Palestinian politician Faisal al-Husseini to the U.S. and Soviet consuls in Jerusalem on October 27:

> Having received a letter of assurances and an invitation, the
> Palestinians hereby declare that their position is this: to participate
> in the conference, while adhering fully to their political position, to
> Palestinian political programs, to their right to raise any issue they wish
> to have looked into, to the interconnectedness of the stages of the set-
> tlement, and to the cessation of settlement activity with the commence-
> ment of the conference.

The message added that the Palestinians were comfortable with the position of the co-sponsors on the interim period, and their support for the quick and orderly transfer of power from the Israeli authorities to the Palestinian people. This would allow the Palestinians to be masters of their own political and economic decisions, which included control of water, land, population, and citizenship, in addition to the legislative and judicial branches of government.

Faisal al-Husseini's message stated, "We understand that your position is that a confederation [of Jordan and Palestine] constitutes a not unlikely result of these talks. We will not relinquish our right to an independent state."

He then arrived at a pivotal point regarding the PLO:

> The fact that the PLO has agreed not to be a direct and prominent participant in these talks at the present time does not impact in any shape or form on its status as the sole legitimate representative of the Palestinian people wherever they may be, and the single body authorized to, and capable of, negotiating and entering into agreements in the name of the Palestinian people. We therefore expect its full participation in the process at a future stage, and the full resumption of talks between the US and the PLO as soon as this becomes feasible.

The Palestinian announcement struck a palpable hit against the Israeli inclination to sideline the PLO. It did, however, anger the Americans. We told them, "Don't expect the PLO to renounce its role." It was hard for the US to do anything except bluster and threaten at that point: it was a fait accompli, as everyone was already in Madrid. Indeed, to emphasize that it was the PLO that selected the Palestinian delegates, a number of the delegates left Madrid on October 29 to meet with Yasser Arafat in Algiers and returned at dawn on October 30 to attend their sessions. The message was clear to all and sundry.

It was time for the conference. We all left the hotel for the Royal Palace in Madrid on the morning of Wednesday, October 30, in a number of minibuses. The Royal Palace was a stupendous sight. I was awestruck by its magnificence, splendor, and scale, but not surprised. This was Spain, after all, of the Spanish Empire, credited with discovering the western hemisphere in the fifteenth century, which had spread across the Atlantic and Pacific Oceans.

A moving moment for me was when the Spanish diplomat accompanying our delegation took us on a tour of the palace gardens. He led us round the southern garden and brought us to an ancient Andalusian stone gate inscribed with some verses of the Qur'an. "This is one of the gates to the old Islamic palace," he said, "and the furthest point reached by the Islamic forces in the Iberian Peninsula."

Although he was as polite and flattering as could be, I was provoked by his reference to western Christianity's eventual overthrow of Islam in Andalusia. Feigning casualness, I said, "The Turkish Muslims were changing the religious and political landscape at roughly the same time on the eastern side of the European continent."

It was clear that this conference—and this U.S.–Soviet-sponsored summit—was being held under the clear and obvious control of the United States, despite Soviet President Gorbachev's attempts to appear a full partner equal in influence and power to U.S. President Bush. The US was the major player here. The results of the Cold War were clear; it was also clear who had won.

The Americans, who could see that this was a real opportunity to achieve peace between the Arabs and Israel, set out their vision in President Bush's speech. He said that the objective was to effect peace through direct negotiations between the two parties, and that the way forward lay in compromise and mutual give-and-take. Peace must be achieved, Bush said, through the parties to the conflict themselves—not imposed by an external power—and through a practical mechanism for advancement.

Meanwhile, the Soviet Union's goal was to maintain the balance with the US and a fading Soviet Empire, although there was no hiding the decline in its role and influence. Gorbachev mentioned in his speech on peace and stability in the Middle East that the region was "saturated" with arms, especially nuclear technology, and other weapons of mass destruction. There can be no doubt that the US heard him clearly, understanding the Soviet hints that "since you are not giving us a role, we will play a positive one in controlling the arms race in the region." Students of the period will recall that this was a preoccupation of the U.S. government, having achieved decisive victory during that era.

For the European Community, Hans van den Broek emphasized his commitment to strengthening the peace efforts, and called upon the Arabs to end their economic boycott of Israel in exchange for an Israeli freeze on settlements in the occupied territories—advice Egypt's foreign minister had offered the Palestinians, which had been rejected, in June 1991.

The first day of the conference ended without clash or crisis, but we had to wait for the second day to hear what the Israeli prime minister had to say.

In a speech that followed the Jordanian statement, the Palestinian representative, Dr. Haidar Abdel Shafi, called for the formation of a Palestinian state after the interim period. He made it clear that the Palestinians' acceptance of an interim period in the occupied territories by no means indicated that it should become permanent. He called for international protection for the Palestinian people during the transition. Significantly, Dr. Abdel Shafi mentioned the PLO by name, in the historical context that it had launched its own peace initiative in 1988 on the basis of Security Council Resolutions 242 and 338. Jerusalem, he announced, was the capital of the future Palestinian state, and Israel's annexation of it was unlawful. He also quoted Yasser Arafat directly, from his address to the UN General Assembly in 1974: "Do not let the olive branch fall from my hand."

I was witness to that historic address when it was first given. Arafat repeated that statement many times, as a sign of goodwill and as a warning.

Now came the turn of the Israeli prime minister. His tone and the content of his speech put everybody's back up, filled the room with tension, and led to the second session, on the second day, degenerating into pandemonium.

The Israeli prime minister spoke at length and in detail on the history and justifications for the establishment of the state of Israel. He insisted that Israel was not created by the United Nations, but was a revolt against foreign imperialist rule. He also affirmed one of the most important tenets of Zionist thinking, namely that Israel brought together Jews from all over the world.

He then accused the Arab governments of exploiting the Cold War in their struggle against Israel, mobilizing military, political, and economic support from the Communist bloc against it. The Arabs, he said, had turned a local, regional conflict into an international powder keg, which flooded the Middle East with arms.

Shamir claimed that the Madrid Conference, the fruit of continued American efforts, was built upon the Camp David-based Israeli peace project Shamir submitted in 1989. He then asserted that the Madrid Conference was no "conference" at all, since—he said—as per the U.S. initiative, the objective of this encounter was to conduct direct negotiations between Israel and each of its neighbors, followed by multilateral talks on regional issues. Nonetheless, Israel, he said, had agreed to attend this "celebratory event" prior to starting the bilateral talks.

He demanded a condemnation of the PLO Charter, which calls for the destruction of Israel, and the statements of the Tehran conference. He urged the Arab states to enable their Jewish citizens to leave if they wished to do so.

The Israeli prime minister avoided any reference in any form to Security Council Resolutions 242 and 338 and the 'territory for peace' principle. He said that he was aware that Israel would receive regional requests from his partners in the negotiations. Such regional requests were unrelated to the nature of the Arab–Israeli conflict, which, he said, predated Israel's control over Judea, Samaria, Gaza, and the Golan.

Shamir also played the familiar Israeli tune of four million Israelis only controlling 28,000 square kilometers, whereas the hundred and seventy million Arabs had control of 14 million square kilometers. (Note that the area he mentioned includes the occupied territories.)

Lebanese Foreign Minister Farès Boueiz spoke next, followed by Syrian Foreign Minister Farouk al-Sharaa. Al-Sharaa emphasized that the conference was no "celebratory event" as one of the members wished, meaning Israel, but a major international event with the goal of real peace and not immediate gains for one party or another. He accused Israel of a great many inhumane and unlawful practices over the decades, then indirectly criticized (which we found odd) the Egypt–Israel peace treaty. He blamed the 1979 treaty for "enabling" Israel to announce the annexation of Jerusalem in 1980 and the Golan in 1981.

The Israeli prime minister then decided to escalate. In his response to Farouk al-Sharaa, he launched an attack on Syria. The country, he said, was hardly a paragon of liberty, abrogating the rights of its Jewish citizens. He added that Syria embraced terrorist groups in its own territories, and was occupying Lebanese land.

A number of Arab leaders responded to Shamir: Jordanian Foreign Minister Kamel Abu Jaber, Haidar Abdel Shafi, Farès Boueiz, and Farouk al-Sharaa. The situation quickly deteriorated into an exchange of accusations, in a repeat of what I had witnessed over the years, quite frequently I might add, since the start of my tenure with the Egyptian delegation to the UN in 1974, and to this day.

The Egyptian position as explained by Foreign Minister Amre Moussa was exemplary in that it coupled a decisive position vis-à-vis Israel with support for the Arabs. He said that Egypt, being a full partner and equal in the quest for peace, would leave no stone unturned, no path untrodden, no route unexplored, to fulfill its responsibilities to its Arab and Palestinian brethren. The minister also warned Israel that there would be no wriggling out of Resolutions 242 and 338, and that the settlement-building must be stopped.

The Egyptian statement had taken a while to prepare in Cairo; Amre Moussa had read it over and over again, making changes and modifications. When I left Cairo for Washington, he was still mulling over the main points—so much so that the final version, and the official English translation, were only completed at dawn on October 31. This meant great difficulties for and threats to the delegation members, mainly First Secretary Abd al-Rahman Salah, a delegation member, and the foreign minister's office, whose responsibility it was to prepare the address for distribution and publication, including a copy for the Egyptian minister. Just before the session during which Amre Moussa was to speak, he and I took a stroll around the palace interior. On a massive square veranda dozens of meters long, we discussed the importance of this historic moment—the Egyptian foreign minister, after more than twelve years of a peace treaty between his country and Israel, standing with his Arab nation, now that his views, the views of his country, and the views of his president, Sadat, had proved right, namely the call for negotiations as a way of achieving one's ends, although we were both wary of the Israelis' intentions. They should not, we felt, be allowed to fool the world at large, but needed always to be called out and cornered into disclosing their true intentions. I assured the minister of my conviction that his speech, and the tone in which it would be delivered, would raise him to heights hitherto unscaled in the history of Egyptian diplomacy—and I was right.

When the stormy session was over, I said, "You have withstood the test of battle and emerged unscathed. You were magnificent."

Our meeting with Yitzhak Shamir was at hand. He had requested a meeting with the Egyptian foreign minister. We met on Thursday, October 31, in a crowded hotel room. Shamir was accompanied by Deputy Foreign Minister Benjamin Netanyahu, Office Director of the Israeli Prime Minister Elyakim Rubinstein, and a number of senior officials. In addition to myself, the Egyptian side was represented by Director of International Organizations Reda Shehata and Nabil Fahmy, a member of the minister's office staff, plus of course Amre Moussa. Moussa explained Egypt's position and our vision, and that he expected us to conduct our business in a spirit of gravity and sincerity.

Shamir gave the most hard-line answer it was possible to give. He would go no further, he said, than Palestinian self-government; he would not go into the "unknown," or agree to the establishment of a Palestinian state that could, indeed would, one day threaten the security of Israel. He would negotiate and negotiate, he said, and draw out the negotiations for ten years, without making a single concession or giving the Palestinians a thing.

We found this brutally honest Israeli position provocative, to say the least. Amre Moussa argued, but Shamir was adamant. For long years since that day in October 1991, during my tenure as the Egyptian representative to the United Nations from 1999 to 2004, and before that, when I was Egypt's ambassador to Italy from 1992 to 1996, I told many people about Shamir's position, which I think Netanyahu, twice prime minister of Israel (1996 to 1999 and 2009 to date), does not plan to abandon. It would take extreme pressure from every international power to make him do so, which I cannot see happening at this stage.

Some might ask, "Why did you enter into a peace process when you were well aware that Israel was not sincere?" The answer is that there were no alternatives. Negotiation, and never giving up on the basics, was the method by which we could up the pressure, corner Israel, mobilize support, achieve Arab consensus on the main issues, and enable the Palestinians to come together for a shared effort, all of which might, in the fullness of time, impose the Arab will upon Israel.

We took it to Secretary Baker, and all his assistants. We told him that we fully intended to predicate progress on the multilateral front on the progress of the bilateral negotiation. If the bilateral talks, especially with the Palestinians, resulted in nothing concrete that reflected any serious Israeli intent, we would take positions that would abort any progress on the multilateral front—supposedly the real prize for Israel.

The US offered many justifications: that Israel must be encouraged to advance on the path to peace by working together with the Israelis regionally; that we should open doors to the Israelis, not close them, until such time as we were aware of their intentions. These U.S. and European opinions were unconvincing, to say the least. We decided to await the results of the next Israeli elections, which, we hoped, might change Israel's position.

We spent several more days in Madrid, following the Arab delegations and Israel as they prepared for bilateral talks for the first time ever. We received a dinner invitation from Prince Bandar ibn Sultan, the Saudi ambassador in Washington and the head of the Saudi delegation to the conference, in the Spanish countryside outside Madrid, for Saturday, November 2. The two delegations, Egyptian and Saudi, headed out of Madrid in minibuses to a restaurant renowned for its kebabs. I must say, I enjoyed a veritable feast that remained the subject of my conversation with Prince Bandar for many years to come.

Prince Bandar was not often to be seen in the corridors of the conference. In addition, his seat in the Hall of Columns was behind a massive column that blocked him from seeing, or being seen, during the proceedings. For years to come, he would complain about this seat, which I would have thought very comfortable for him. In any case, Bandar offered Amre Moussa a ride to Cairo in one of his private planes. A Boeing 707 arrived from Paris, equipped with a number of personal cubicles. I left for Cairo with Amre Moussa, while the rest of the Egyptian delegation returned a few days after the conference by commercial flight.

At cruising altitude, Minister Moussa and I compared notes on the proceedings and accomplishments of the conference. In our estimation, much would depend on how the Americans acted and their commitment to advancing a settlement, refusing to accept Shamir's and the Likud's stalling, and convincing the Israeli community and the American Jewish community that this leadership clique did not serve the true future interests of Israel. We also concluded that the Soviet Union's role had diminished, and would remain so for years, pending the revival of the Soviet economy and its situation as a whole. Never in our wildest dreams could we have imagined that the Soviet Union, that sprawling empire with the nuclear capacity to wipe out the US several times over, would evaporate within sixty days of our conversation. As to the role of the European Community, they were proceeding with their standard caution, at the pace of their weakest links—in other words, the countries most inclined to make concessions to Israeli interests—taking positions calculated not to anger the Americans, but remaining a few steps ahead of them nonetheless, motivating the US to catch up later when the time was right.

The foreign minister felt it was important to move fast to advance a Palestinian settlement and the rest of the bilateral Arab–Israeli settlements, while expressing sincere goodwill with regard to the multilateral negotiations. It was also important, however, that the multilateral negotiations not outpace the bilateral ones. Therefore, we had to keep a tight rein on the situation: there must not be a major qualitative change in the region's relations with Israel until it offered proofs of its sincere intent for peace and cooperation with all the Arab countries whose territories it occupied, including Palestine, in the bilateral negotiations.

The minister asked me to reacquaint the Palestinians with all the documents and papers on the self-government negotiations from 1979 to 1982, and offer them a session with the Egyptian delegations who had negotiated on their behalf during the Arab boycott of Egypt, to pass on their accumulated experiences in negotiating with the Israelis, who always had highly qualified and well-equipped teams. I spoke with the minister about the need to prepare a great many documents to assist the Arab delegations in the multilateral negotiations, enabling Egypt to play our traditional role in leading the Arab effort in this area, especially in such a high-profile international effort.

As soon as we got back to Cairo, a number of Egyptian working groups from the Foreign Ministry and other Egyptian state bodies, with experts from various ministries and government agencies, began to prepare the documents to be presented to the committees on the multilateral path. They covered regional security, limiting armaments, regional economic collaboration, water, the environment, and refugee issues. Once more we began to work closely with the Americans to find out their intended plans for regional collaboration in all its aspects.

The days that followed the Madrid Conference were filled with preliminary meetings between the Israeli and Arab delegations, both Palestinian–Jordanian and Syrian. The meetings were held in the US, and we received regular reports of progress or lack of it. We followed them closely, offering advice to those who would accept it. On another front, the Americans and Russians had begun preparations for the multi-lateral path, at the Moscow Conference, which was planned for February 28 and 29, 1992.

Once again we headed for the conference, amid great international enthusiasm for the normalization of relations between Israel and the rest of the Middle Eastern region. Syria and Lebanon were absent, as President Assad was opposed to facilitating Israeli relations with the rest of the region as long as the Israelis did not demonstrate any positive intent to withdraw from the occupied territories or respond to Palestinian demands. The Moscow meetings were held at the House of the Unions, in the famous Pillar Hall.

The group was addressed by Boris Yeltsin, the president of the Russian Federation, the legitimate heir to the Soviet Union. Although the meeting was held on Russian soil, it was clear that the true host and the actual agent behind every position and development was the U.S. sec-retary of state and his team. Russian Foreign Minister Andrei Kozyrev, who had inherited the position of foreign minister from such greats as Maxim Litvinov, Vyacheslav Molotov, Andrei Gromyko, and Eduard Shevardnadze, was a mere guest, ineffectual and virtually invisible. I still believe that this period of Russian diplomacy, in my estimation and that of many of my friends in the Russian diplomatic corps, was one of the hardest for them professionally.

The Americans quickly launched the various paths. The meetings, two rounds of talks, were held from May to the end of October, covering all the paths previously agreed upon, as listed above. We had prepared a great many documents and studies, with the participation of many special-ized Egyptian agencies, to formulate Egypt's positions and visions. They had worked with an enthusiasm and zeal that often amazed me, as did the dedication of our delegations to the multilateral talks and the fact that our assessments so often proved correct. Shamir's words to Moussa, that Israel would stall for ten years or more, engaging in 'negotiations' without conceding anything, were a constant alarm in the back of our minds.

Finally, at the end of October, I left my place at Amre Moussa's side to take up the duties of Egypt's ambassador to Italy and the Food and Agriculture Organization in Rome. I kept a close eye on developments; I had a hunch I might once more be called upon to serve my country's interests, and those of the Arab nation.

29 Oslo, Camp David, and Resolution 1515

I arrived at my job in Rome in October 1992. Alongside my new responsibilities, I closely monitored developments in the bilateral and multilateral negotiations, which were being held in a number of capital cities in the US and Europe. The Palestine–Israel bilateral negotiations were proceeding apace in Washington, full of enthusiasm. It emerged, after the Left came to power in Israel in 1993, that there had been a sea change in the Israeli position, whereby Israel agreed to enter into direct and parallel secret talks with the PLO. The world was stunned when the two sides reached an interim, or transitional, settlement in Oslo in August 1993, which was signed in September of that year at the White House, at an official ceremony attended by Yasser Arafat, Israeli Prime Minister Yitzhak Rabin, and U.S. President Bill Clinton.

The agreement was not very different in principle from the US and Israeli vision of the interim settlement, or even the Egyptian vision. We had agreed to it in principle, but rejected the linking of the interim settlement with the final settlement so as to avoid an indefinite transitional period, a final status masquerading as a temporary stage. Egypt had worked to develop this vision since the Leeds Castle talks in July 1978, in Camp David in September 1978, and then in the full self-government negotiations in which the Egyptian negotiating teams fought a pitched diplomatic battle with Israel between 1979 and 1982 after the talks stalled upon Israel's withdrawal from Sinai.

The Oslo Accords, as I have said, were not very far from the letter and spirit of Camp David, which the Palestinians rejected in 1978.

355

While the Oslo agreement was definitely a more detailed document as regards a Palestinian settlement, it was not so different from Camp David's main idea: a five-year transition, a budding Palestinian authority on the ground, and negotiations starting in the third year of the transition with a view to a final settlement. When I read this new document in September 1993, I compared it to the Camp David document of September 1978. I must admit that the new document included a great many new gains for the Palestinians, such as the right to a port in Gaza, roads linking Gaza to the West Bank, the two being considered a single land unit, and other details granting Palestinians clear benefits leading to mechanisms and dynamics that would "snowball," as Zbigniew Brzezinski told me and Ahmed Maher at breakfast at Camp David in 1978. It also included the right to hoist a flag, enact legislation, mint currency, and all the elements of a fledgling national authority, which matured quickly as the agreement was implemented. Soon enough there were elections. Arafat and his team returned. Things were going well, until Rabin's assassination in 1995.

With the implementation of Oslo, matters progressed between Jordan and Israel. The two sides reached a peace agreement in 1994. Tensions in the Middle East appeared to be receding. Some even recalled Bush's speech in Madrid, namely his statement that there was no enmity more ferocious than that between France and Germany in 1945 but that these two countries were now allies. The same seemed to be happening, or about to happen, in the Middle East.

The Israeli prime minister was welcomed in Muscat, Oman, and walked down the red carpet. He was given a guard of honor in Morocco. The first Middle East economic cooperation conference was held in Casablanca, and the second in Amman, Jordan. We were approaching the third conference in Cairo in September 1996. Everyone was optimistic; only Syria stood apart, still finding the situation strange. Amre Moussa cautioned against rushing forward impulsively without any guarantees that Shamir's policy would not reassert itself in Israel once more.

The information that reached me in Rome, from my Egyptian, European, American, and regional sources, was that Syria and Israel were making progress in their negotiations to get the Golan back for Syria. The Americans were encouraging both parties to make more progress. The US spoke once more of U.S. safeguards and bringing American troops to the borders. Dr. Osama al-Baz often came to Rome during this period. We spoke at length about the situation. I learned from him at the time that the Syrian president was feeling especially disgruntled and belligerent with Yasser Arafat, who had signed the Oslo Accords and moved blithely forward—in Assad's view—with no regard for Syria or Syrian interests. President Assad insisted on Syria reclaiming the waterline on Lake Tiberias, also known as the Sea of Galilee, in any settlement with Israel—in other words, the June 4, 1967, borders. The Israelis, displaying blatant disregard for the fact that this was Arab land, said that the land had been theirs before Syria "invaded" it in 1948, and that what they could accept was the Syria–Mandatory Palestine border of 1923, a border several hundred yards *into* Syria and away from the lakeshore. President Assad was quoted as saying, "I used to bathe in the lake before June 5, 1967," and that he wanted to do the same after the hoped-for agreement. He would not, he said, use the waters of the lake in any circumstances.

Israel refused. The negotiations ground to a halt, and remained so for several years. Toward the end of the 1990s, the Americans made another attempt to advance the talks. There were summit meetings between Clinton and Assad in Geneva, and then between the foreign ministers of Syria and Israel in Pennsylvania in 1999, with no results.

From 2004 to 2011, I witnessed President Mubarak telling his guests that Rabin had come to him in Cairo one fine morning in 1995, complaining that President Assad had reneged on his promise to agree to an Israeli embassy in Damascus once the two sides had hammered out an agreement on the withdrawal from the Golan. Mubarak attempted to help smooth things out, despite the Syrians' secrecy and refusal to tell Egypt—or indeed anyone—anything.

Rabin's assassination in October 1995, however, was the final nail in the coffin of this process, as indeed it was for the Palestinian advancement, with the return of the Likud to power in June 1996 and the rise of Netanyahu, Shamir's prize pupil, to the post of prime minister. Netanyahu proceeded to implement the Likud's strategy as outlined to Minister Moussa by Shamir in Madrid: "We will drag the negotiations out for ten years, and they'll get nothing."

I returned to Cairo in late August 1996, my work in Italy done. I was appointed assistant to Foreign Minister Amre Moussa for Ministerial Office Affairs. Once more I found myself in the thick of settlement efforts, which were gradually being eroded by Netanyahu's first government refusing to implement many items in the Oslo Accords, especially the required withdrawals from Palestinian lands in the West Bank. This period from mid-1996 until the Likud lost the elections in mid-1999 was a difficult one for Egypt–Israeli relations. Israel claimed that Egypt was holding up the multilateral negotiations. Egypt felt that the Israeli government's actions had effectively put an end to any chances for regional cooperation. The committees stopped convening; the multilateral path was no more.

Egypt kept up its efforts to make Oslo a success, however. Osama al-Baz went to Israel several times to urge Netanyahu to take action and fulfill his part of Oslo, to no avail. The prime minister created obstacle after obstacle. I accompanied Minister Amre Moussa to Israel in an attempt to overcome them, but again the effort failed.

Meanwhile, I had been appointed permanent representative for Egypt to the United Nations in December 1998—every young Egyptian diplomat's dream—and the time to leave for New York was fast approaching. This post is not only an acknowledgment of one's efficiency and abilities by the Egyptian Foreign Ministry, but also a step on the way to the position of Egyptian foreign minister, the illustrious position sought by every serious diplomat in Egypt.

In May 1999, I left for New York. Now, I followed the situation from afar, albeit very closely. It helped that Dennis Ross' Washington-based team, who were still working on the Middle East file, remained in close contact with me. The Israeli Left came to power once more in July 1999. There were excited whispers that Ehud Barak might become prime minister of Israel. Barak had met with us during Amre Moussa's visit to Israel in April 1999. In the VIP reception hall at Lod Airport, before we left that evening, he had promised to move speedily with Arafat to fulfill all the elements of the Oslo Accords, and to enter into talks about the West Bank and Gaza with an open mind. He was, he said, aware of the requirements of the situation and of the Palestinians' needs. This led me to hope that upon winning the elections, he would seek a breakthrough in his relations with Arafat and in advancing the Palestinian settlement. I followed the movements between Israel and Palestine, and the U.S. interventions. We, the Egyptian representatives to the UN, decided to respond to the Palestinians' request and not push aggressively against Israel; in other words, to hold off on the strong draft resolutions against Israel that we proposed annually at the General Assembly regular or resumed sessions until their intentions became clear.

Hope returned to the Israeli–Palestinian negotiations. Under pressure from Israel, and at the insistence of the Israeli prime minister, the Americans agreed to another summit at Camp David in July 2000. The Israelis and Palestinians would take part, with the stated goal of reaching a final settlement to end the conflict in one fell swoop.

The summit was held, but failed to deliver. Arafat found it impossible to agree to the insufficient Israeli offers. There were heated arguments about who was right or wrong. I discussed this issue at length with Amre Moussa in several conversations in late July and early August 2000, then again in December of the same year and January 2001. "The Palestinians should have shown a bit more flexibility," I said, "especially as this was an opportunity for an unprecedented settlement." Moussa, though, was unmoved. Arafat, he said, was afraid of being judged by history. My advice was for the Palestinians to initial the document they had negotiated with the Israelis after the July 2000 Camp David Summit. This document, dubbed the Clinton Parameters (the Clinton Taba frameworks in the Arab world), brought them much closer to a final settlement. However, they failed to seize the opportunity. The situation was rapidly becoming more complex, with the outbreak of the second intifada following a provocative visit by opposition leader Ariel Sharon to al-Haram al-Sharif (known in the west as the Temple Mount).

My conversations with President Mahmoud Abbas in the years that followed the death of Yasser Arafat in 2004, when I was Egypt's foreign minister, revealed that Abu Mazen had agreed with my line of thinking at the time. I recall that Moussa was uncomfortable with the pragmatism and flexibility shown by Abu Mazen in his evaluations of American and Israeli proposals: Mahmoud Abbas always attempted to press these proposals into the service of his country's interests. I recall a heated argument between Abbas and Moussa in 1998, in the minister's hotel wing at the Plaza Athenée Hotel in New York. Minister Moussa was vociferously objecting to a number of positions adopted by the PLO at the time to advance matters with Israel. Amre Moussa was firmly convinced that Israel only wanted peace on its own terms, which Egypt would not allow the Palestinians to accept. Abu Mazen, then Arafat's advisor, felt that Palestinians were in an unenviable position, and if they did not move fast they would be gradually stripped of what land they had left, eventually suffering utter defeat. This argument between Moussa and Abbas lasted for years, throughout Moussa's tenure as secretary-general of the Arab League.

The parties never did initial the Clinton Parameters, a document that emerged thanks to the Taba negotiations between the Israelis and the Palestinians in late 2000. A new, Republican, administration came to the White House, with no desire to make any moves now that Clinton had failed. The Likud clawed their way back to power in Israel. There can be no doubt that the Palestinian intifada pushed Israeli voters to the right, removing the Left from power and bringing back the right-wing Likud. Once more, the settlement efforts had run aground, in what has been called "the history of missed opportunities."

Many times during my tenure as foreign minister, from 2004 to 2011, I heard President Mubarak speak of Clinton's annoyance at the failure of the Camp David Summit. Clinton did not appreciate why Egypt had not spoken to Arafat, or attempted to mollify him, during the course of the conference. Mubarak told us that he had seized the opportunity of Clinton's short visit to Cairo on an African tour to explain to him the importance of Arab Jerusalem to Arab Muslims and Christians. No one, he said, could take a position that threatened the rights of Arabs living in the east of that sacred city. Mubarak criticized the Americans demanding that Egypt intervene without being fully apprised of the situation and developments in the Camp David negotiations. The disagreement between the US and Egypt was settled, though, before Clinton left the White House.

The negotiations were already stalled when George W. Bush came to power in January 2001. The Palestinian intifada continued. Instead of negotiations, there were clashes, killings, and destruction of Palestine's resources at the hands of both the Israeli Left and the Likud Right. Tensions rose once again at the United Nations. The Arab countries, supported by the non-aligned powers, adopted their annual group of draft resolutions against Israel's actions. As Egypt's permanent representative to the UN, I took part in all these efforts, collaborating closely with Palestine's representative, Dr. Nasser al-Qudwa.

This was a period of international efforts to bring the situation under control. Influential international powers—the US, the Russian Federation, and the European Union—formed what came to be dubbed the Quartet on the Middle East, which also included UN Secretary-General Kofi Annan. The Quartet worked to ease the tensions and create a roadmap for different stages of ending the conflict.

By now, the concept of establishing a Palestinian state was increasingly gaining international recognition. It began to appear in the political literature of many parties. The Arab Group at the United Nations proposed a draft resolution in 2002 on the need to acknowledge two states, one Palestinian and the other Israeli, living side by side in peace and security. The group began to apply pressure at the Security Council to secure U.S. approval for such a resolution, including such a reference. We conducted shrewd negotiations; I worked closely with the Palestinian representative, and we maneuvered with all parties concerned until we arrived at a text that, we felt, achieved most of our objectives.

We were close to seeing whether we could get an agreement to put it to the vote. We had no prior knowledge, or guarantees, whether the US would allow it through.

The draft resolution went into the inner sanctum. I waited outside in the hallway of the Security Council with Dr. Nasser al-Qudwa, who later became foreign minister of Palestine. Except for us, the vast hall was completely deserted. Suddenly, a senior assistant to the U.S. ambassador stormed over. "I warn you!" he said. "You're going to lose all your successes if you persist in this escalation. My advice to you is to go in now and cast your vote."

He sounded belligerent, but I could sense his honesty. This was a man I had known since 1985; he had been consultant to the U.S. delegation on Middle Eastern Affairs during my first tenure at the United Nations. He said nothing about how the US had voted, but naturally he meant that the US had decided at this time, and at this stage, to allow the draft resolution through to the Council.

The resolution passed by a vote of fourteen in favor to none against, with one abstention. The reference to two states in a Security Council resolution was the first healthy development in international positions on this issue.

The following year, in May 2003 to be precise, the Quartet issued a roadmap for a Palestinian settlement. The secretary-general of the United Nations sent a letter on May 7 of that year to the president of the Security Council, referring to Security Council Resolution 1397, adopted in March 2002, appended to which was the road map that governed the path of the settlement for many years to come. I am proud to have had a role in drafting that resolution.

Under pressure from Russia and the Arabs, the Security Council adopted a new resolution supporting the international trend toward establishing a Palestinian state next to Israel, in accordance with Resolution 1515, in November 2003. UN Secretary-General Kofi Annan had a great deal of appreciation and respect for Egypt's positions and its role in handling the situation in the Middle East for decades. Consequently, he was always in close contact with me during my tenure in New York, exchanging opinions and advice. I was as frank and direct with him as possible. I recall that when the Quartet issued its first statement on being formed, at a meeting of its leaders in Madrid in 2002, Annan called me from the Spanish capital to tell me how optimistic he was about what had happened and that he hoped I could meet him upon his return to New York to share opinions and look into how Egypt could best consolidate this effort. This was repeated when the Quartet produced the road map for a settlement; Annan assiduously sought our opinions and evaluations. He was clearly glad when there were any advances at the UN that could help the Palestinians. He was especially glad at Resolutions 1397 and 1515.

Despite these important resolutions, the fact is that the actual process was at a complete standstill. President George W. Bush was adamant about not taking any initiative for fear of failing, as had occurred with the previous administration. I often remembered the day I saw Yasser Arafat, the leader of the PLO, addressing the UN Security Council in October 1974, demanding recognition of the legitimate national rights of the Palestinian people and the right to self-determination, and the decades-long struggle that followed—confrontation accompanied by stalling and evasiveness and Israeli intransigency.

In July 2004, I received instructions to return to Cairo to take the weight of Egypt's Foreign Ministry upon my shoulders. I remained foreign minister for nearly seven years.

On the flight, I recalled the long hard years in New York, working toward a Palestinian solution, and hoping to expand the peace to Syria and Lebanon. The Middle East could have been a region of peace, stability, and development.

In my book on my years as foreign minister, I included a chapter on the Palestinian settlement and Egypt's attempts to convince the US to take action during G.W. Bush's administration and that of his successor, President Barack Obama. As I documented in that book, those efforts did not bear the fruit I hoped. Once again, Israel simply refused to budge; it remained inflexible for decades of attempts at negotiation. The successive U.S. administrations were not strong enough to risk angering Israel. As I write this, I feel that Israel is still hungry for more Palestinian land, actively threatening the two-state solution on the land that, historically, has been Palestine. This will have repercussions, adding ever more conflict and complexity to the struggle in the Middle East. There can be no stability or contribution to human civilization while this conflict lasts; as things currently stand, it will continue for years, and where it ends, nobody knows.

30 Conclusion

Having offered my testimony on war and peace, directly or indirectly witnessed, allow me to conclude with a number of observations I find significant.

First, the war with Israel began prior to its declaration of statehood in 1948, not in 1973, the starting point of this book. Peace with that state, despite the treaty signed in 1979, is not yet a reality. A great many rights of the Arab people remain crushed in Israel's fist.

Egypt took upon itself the responsibility and the mission of facing Israel militarily from May 15, 1948, to the end of the battle in 1973. Arab leadership lay in Egypt's hands, as it was then the largest Arab state with the greatest abilities and resources, demographically, militarily, and economically. Egypt, and the Arabs with it, suffered a number of defeats at the hands of an army with European methods and training, supported by all the vast resources and capabilities of diverse western powers: the Soviet Union and its Communist bloc, the United States, and all of America's European allies. It took a Herculean effort from Egypt to stand up to Israel; we accomplished the mission in the battle of 1973.

Second, my testimony to the events I have witnessed, the documents I have read, and the meetings and activities I have taken part in, during which I submitted working papers and initiatives, are first and foremost a product of my work with the Egyptian national security advisor to President Sadat before, during, and after the war of 1973; the meetings and negotiations that preceded and followed the war, when I was part of working groups under the leadership of Egypt's foreign ministers; my work as an ambassador and permanent representative of Egypt at the United Nations; and finally my tenure as foreign minister of Egypt.

I have offered documents for your perusal. I have described interactions and events, and demonstrated how Egyptian, regional, and international decision-makers developed and changed their thinking, just as I observed it, with the greatest possible impartiality and objectivity—or so it seems to me. You may be the judge. I have covered up no mistakes; I have defended no shortcomings or errors of judgment, if any occurred here or there. I leave it to you, and to those who will come after us, to find out more and learn from Egypt's political and military history in this saga, with its many stages of war and negotiations toward peace.

Third, you may notice that I offer my conclusions at every stage, in war and in peace, toward the end of every chapter, or so I have attempted. Hence, I will not repeat these conclusions in this final note. In a previous chapter, I make clear Egypt's objectives in engaging in a massive military operation: to correct the imbalance of power between Egypt and Israel, and to enter into negotiations to end the Israeli occupation of Sinai. The negotiations first required, indeed were predicated on, this large-scale military effort. In my estimation, it was carried out as well as it possibly could have been, given the circumstances.

I have offered a great many of my opinions. The future holds dozens of theses in support of or opposition to Egypt's actions and the new reality they bore, whether the battles were managed successfully, and whether there was as much coordination as there could have been with our Arab brethren and Soviet friends (not to mention our partner in battle, Syria).

I have witnessed an Egypt embroiled in armed conflict, girding its loins and sending a million of its sons to war. I have seen its army's military prowess regained, after nearly a hundred and forty years without notable military capacity or a significant role in the region. These years also revealed a strong and capable Egyptian diplomatic corps, which defended Egypt's interests time and time again. All this took from the sad evening of June 9, 1967, to the signing of the peace treaty between Egypt and Israel on March 26, 1979, and the start of its implementation over three years, until April 26, 1982. This period was followed by an extended diplomatic battle to reclaim the rest of the rights due to the Arabs and Palestine, which lasted decades and continues to this day.

Fourth, the wars and conflicts with Israel were a principal incentive to Egypt to work toward consolidating and intensifying its role in the region and, indeed, on the world stage over the long decades of confrontation. The Egyptian role in the region expanded, as it did in the international arena. Naturally, Egypt benefited from the Cold War between the two superpowers throughout the years of the confrontation between the Soviet Union's Communist bloc and the US with its allies in Western Europe, in NATO, and in other organizations. Throughout those years, the west was mainly focused on how to protect and secure Israel, adding to its power and influence in Middle Eastern politics. Egypt's position vis-à-vis Israel therefore attracted international attention, especially as the confrontation developed at a time when the international situation was undergoing a sea change. Foremost among these changes was the end of colonialism and the appearance of new international powers in the Third World.

Then came the Egypt–Israel peace treaty. It calmed fears of a new conflict erupting between the Arabs and Israel. The west even tried to encourage Egypt to broaden its horizons beyond the focus on the Arab–Israeli conflict, and to press its resources into the service of broad-based western strategic interests in other regions, exploiting the fact that Egypt traditionally had a presence in some areas of Africa, or in the larger Middle East by dint of being an Islamic country. I refer to the moment in Chapter Twenty-Four at Camp David, when U.S. Secretary of State Cyrus Vance said, "We want to help Egypt lift the burden of the Middle East, and allow it to play its full role and influence in tackling the pressing issues in the region." The Americans, in my estimation, were preparing Egypt for a role in the region with the shah of Iran and NATO-affiliated Turkey, as if we had come full circle to the western policies of the early 1950s. The Egyptian Foreign Ministry—and, I would add, the Egyptian mentality that always harbors a slight distrust of western governments' intentions—viewed this with some suspicion. The shah of Iran fell at the end of 1979. Egypt was gaining importance in the west's view, with estimations that its role might become greater still. We might all recall the American writings about the "Crescent of Crisis," the situations in Iran, Afghanistan, Pakistan, and other Islamic countries. Egypt's role might have changed inasmuch as it was no longer an enemy to Israel or leading the Arabs into battle against it, but it was still significant in confronting the Soviets and the powers that sided with them, and in the non-aligned movement.

Sadat left the stage suddenly. There was after a new, more cautious president of Egypt. Mubarak was no longer prepared to go along with the west's vision for Egypt's status and role. The importance of Egypt was on the wane. It was no longer a feared possible opponent of Israel. It had regained its lands in Sinai, a paramount Egyptian goal, and had no desire to play along with western and U.S. interests in hotbeds of tension or in borderline regions between the Soviet Union and the western world. Was it prudent to convert our relationship with the US to a quasi-strategic one?

Was the Egypt–Israel peace treaty, with its mutual checks and balances, up to the Arabs' expectations? Did it contribute to the furthering of the Palestinian cause? It is my conviction today that these, like many other questions, will remain unanswered.

The west often fancied that Egypt's value lay in its ability to wage war on Israel, and thus attempted to limit Egypt's power. Some in the region, indeed in Egypt itself, believed—with a great deal of truth—that relinquishing war and confrontation was an abandonment of Egypt's role. The western powers arranged a new role for Egypt. It refused, while keeping alive its vital relationships with the US and the west, in order to achieve important interests in the region, and for Egypt itself, in the areas of economic growth and development. The Soviet Union then left the scene, affirming that Egypt's reading of the international arena had been correct, as borne out by developments in the 1980s and 1990s.

The west's assessment of Egypt's regional role must not be taken to mean that Egypt gave up its importance in exchange for land in Sinai. The Egyptian state and its diligent diplomatic corps acted with strength and to great effect, after healing the years-long rift with the other Arab nations, to defend the Palestinians' hope for a nation of their own. Egypt also expanded its circle, restoring relations with the Soviet Union and later Russia, China, and other emerging world powers and securing Egypt's international interests.

Fifth, in the early chapters of this book I revealed Egypt's situation as the 1973 war approached. It was so embarrassing as to be untenable: a weak economy, the first stirrings of sectarian strife, rage in the streets urging for war, and well-prepared and trained armed forces with no qualms about sacrificing themselves but faced with a superiorly armed enemy, positioned in our territories, with the ability to strike deep inside Egypt. All this came at a time when the international decision-makers were based in Washington and Moscow, and both warned Cairo unequivocally against military action, saying it might have unknown consequences in terms of a broader conflict.

President Sadat—in what I believe was the greatest strategic decision of his life—asserted that war was inevitable. Afterward, he saw that friendship with the US and the west was the way out for Egypt. Therefore, he ignored the repercussions of a change of allegiances, and of the peace treaty, on the so-called role of Egypt in the region. He also seems to have believed, as may be seen from his performance in the post-war years, that peace would bring hoped-for prosperity for Egypt and improve the standard of living of the Egyptian people. Still, there were a great many obstacles in Egypt's path in terms of investing in the outcomes of peace. Egypt never managed to overcome the pressures, which were many, and outside the scope of this book. However, they must be briefly covered, if Egypt's predicament from 1973 to this day is to be explained. First and foremost, naturally, is the paucity of Egypt's resources and the constant growth in population. There are the difficulties in eradicating illiteracy, and the lack of a system of education capable of saving Egypt from its crippling conditions. These are all continuing challenges no less important, and no less critical, than the situation when Egypt made war to achieve peace.

Sixth, on June 5, 1967, I was twenty-five years old, a fledgling diplomat. I left my post as foreign minister on March 6, 2011, at sixty-eight. There are about forty-three years between those two dates, during which Egypt fought to liberate its land—the first priority—and to reclaim the rights of the Palestinian people and enable them to acquire their homeland, their state, in the West Bank and Gaza—the higher Arab goal espoused by Egypt.

Egypt used all the resources at its disposal, including war and diplomacy, to achieve this higher goal of reclaiming land and honor. With its defeat in 1967, Egypt lost everything it held dear. Unfortunately, for decades to come, Egyptian society will not manage to seek answers or learn the lessons of this bitter defeat. It should have been studied when it was still possible, and evaluated seriously and honestly. Responsibility should have been placed on the relevant shoulders, and names named. It is not right that this chapter in our history should be closed just like that—all of us in Egypt should be able to learn lessons from what happened, in victory as in defeat.

Today, now that Sinai is liberated, no different from the rest of the soil of our homeland, all of Egypt's children are called upon to safeguard this sacred earth and not allow it to be despoiled in any way. This is why we have always needed courageous opinions, insight, prudence, responsibility, and the strength to block any gamble—or gambler—from dragging Egypt once more into such tragic circumstances as we witnessed that dark night in June 1967. It must not be repeated.

Egypt is aware that the Arab–Israeli struggle is not over. Reclaiming the Palestinian people's rights to their land, and making Israel withdraw from the occupied territories in the Golan, will remain a principal Egyptian concern in the Middle East. Occupation is a threat to stability and a constant dark cloud of pressure at a time when the world is working toward unprecedented breakthroughs in development, prosperity, and peace.

I cannot, however, suppress my hope. Egypt may yet succeed, in the fullness of time, in overcoming its difficulties, achieving economic growth and social development, and moving toward a future that will confer upon it a status in the Middle East worthy of its name.

INDEX

Abbas, Mahmoud *see* Abu Mazen
Abd al-Moneim Palace 21, 83
Abdel Meguid, Esmat 167, 176, 183,
    209; and Begin 175; Iraqi invasion of
    Kuwait 324–25, 327; Ismailiya Summit
    177–79; Mena House Conference 108,
    168–70, 173–74; and Dayan 180; talks
    with George H.W. Bush 305–306, 320;
    talks with Arafat 315–16
Abdullah, Abd al-Fattah 23–24, 59
Abu Mazen 328–35, 359
Al-Ahram newspaper 104, 251
air force: Egyptian 4–10, 27, 41, 125, 160;
    Israeli 27, 58, 61; Royal (UK) 6
Algeria 41, 43
Ali, Kamal Hassan 171, 176, 225–26, 285
Annan, Kofi 361
Arab oil embargo 41, 113, 123
al-Arabi, Nabil 221–22, 281, 283, 283; *see
    also* Camp David
Arafat, Yasser 306, 309, 320; Camp David
    358, 359–60; consultations with Egypt
    310, 312–16; Madrid Conference 334,
    335, 346; Oslo Accords 356–57; recon-
    ciliation with Egypt 328–29, 332, 333;
    speech at the UN 348, 362; *see also* Abu
    Mazen; Baker, James; al-Baz, Osama;
    Palestinian Liberation Organization
    (PLO)
Assad, Hafez 60–61, 329; *see also* Syria
Atherton, Alfred Leroy 49, 209, 223, 239;
    meeting with Begin 258–59; meeting

with Sadat 257–62

Bab al-Mandeb: closure and siege of 84,
    100, 101, 112, 113, 123, 131, 161
Badawi, Ahmed 126
Baker, James: and Arafat 309, 314, 335;
    Israel–Palestine peace process 311,
    312, 316–17, 318, 330–31; Madrid
    Conference 309, 314, 334, 335, 341–
    42; position on the Peace Initiative
    306–307; proposal for Palestinian–
    Israeli dialogue 299–301, 302, 303,
    304, 309; and Shamir 299, 317, 336–
    37; visits to Cairo 335–36; West Bank
    and Gaza 334
Barak, Ehud 358
Bar-Lev line 28, 66
al-Baz, Osama 2, 245, 285, 286; Camp
    David 277, 278, 279, 280, 281–82, 283,
    284; Iraqi invasion of Kuwait 323–24;
    Leeds Castle 248–49; meeting with
    Abu Mazen 329, 331–32, 334–35;
    meeting with George H.W. Bush
    320–21; and Netanyahu 358; and Sadat
    260, 266; Syria 356–57
Begin, Menachem 258–59; arrogance
    205–207, 218; 255; Camp David 220–
    21, 267, 268, 272, 275, 276; Ismailiya
    Summit 189, 193, 201; and Kamel
    206–207, 209, 212; Mena House
    Conference 175, 178, 179; and Sadat
    233–35, 237